BULLET TRAIN

Kotaro Isaka

BULLET
TRAIN

Translated from the Japanese
by Sam Malissa

Harvill *Secker*

LONDON

1 3 5 7 9 10 8 6 4 2

Harvill Secker, an imprint of Vintage, is part of the Penguin Random House group of companies whose addresses can be found at global.penguinrandomhouse.com

Penguin
Random House
UK

Copyright © Kotaro Isaka / CTB Inc.
English translation rights arranged through CTB Inc.
English translation copyright © Sam Malissa 2021

First published by Harvill Secker in 2021

First published in Japan with the title *Maria Bītoru* by Kadokawa in 2010

A CIP catalogue record for this book is available from the British Library

penguin.co.uk/vintage

ISBN 9781787302587 (hardback)
ISBN 9781787302594 (trade paperback)

Typeset in 11/16pt Scala by Jouve (UK), Milton Keynes
Printed and bound in Great Britain by Clays Ltd, Elcograf S.p.A.

The authorised representative in the EEA is Penguin Random House Ireland, Morrison Chambers, 32 Nassau Street, Dublin D02 YH68

Penguin Random House is committed to a sustainable future for our business, our readers and our planet. This book is made from Forest Stewardship Council® certified paper.

BULLET TRAIN

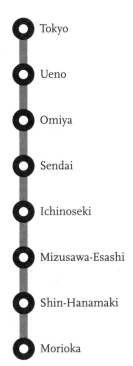

Tokyo

Ueno

Omiya

Sendai

Ichinoseki

Mizusawa-Esashi

Shin-Hanamaki

Morioka

KIMURA

TOKYO STATION IS PACKED. It's been a while since Yuichi Kimura was here last, so he isn't sure if it's always this crowded. He'd believe it if someone told him there was a special event going on. The throngs of people coming and going press in on him, reminding him of the TV show he and Wataru had watched together, the one about penguins, all jammed in tight together. *At least the penguins have an excuse,* thinks Kimura. *It's freezing where they live.*

He waits for an opening in the stream of people, cuts between the souvenir shops and kiosks, quickening his pace. Up a short flight of stairs to the turnstile for the Shinkansen high-speed bullet train. As he passes through the automated ticketing gate he tenses, wondering if it will somehow detect the handgun in his coat pocket, slam shut while security swarms around him, but nothing happens. He slows and looks up at the monitor, checking the platform for his train, the Hayate. There's a uniformed police officer standing guard, but the cop doesn't seem to be paying him any attention.

A kid with a backpack brushes by, looks to be eight or nine years old.

Kimura thinks of Wataru, and his chest tightens. He pictures his beautiful boy, lying unconscious and unresponsive in a hospital bed. Kimura's mother had wailed out loud when she saw him. 'Look at him, he looks like he's just sleeping, like nothing even happened to him. He might even be hearing everything we're saying. It's too much.' The thought of it makes Kimura feel scraped out from the inside.

Bastard will pay. If someone can push a six-year-old boy off the roof of a department store and still be walking around, breathing easy, then something in the world is broken. Kimura's chest clenches again, not from sadness but from rage. He stalks towards the escalator, clutching a paper bag. *I quit drinking. I can walk a straight line. My hands are steady.*

The Hayate is already on the track, waiting for its turn to depart. He hustles to the train and boards the third car. According to the info he got from his former associates, his target is on the three-seater side of the fifth row in car seven. He's going to enter from the next car and sneak up from behind. Nice and easy from behind, sharp and alert, one step and then another.

He enters the gangway. A recess with a sink is on the left, and he pauses in front of the mirror. Pulls the curtain shut on the small vanity area. Then looks at his reflection. Hair unkempt, beads of gunk in the corners of his eyes. Whiskers sticking out at odd angles, even the downy fuzz on his face seems coarse. Ragged and raw. It isn't easy to see himself this way. He washes his hands, rubbing them under the water until the automatic stream cuts off. Fingers trembling. *It's not the booze, just nerves,* he tells himself.

He hasn't fired his gun since Wataru was born. He only even touched it when he was packing his things for the move. Now he's glad he didn't throw it out. A gun comes in handy when you want to put a little fear into some punk: when you need to show some asshole that they are way out of line.

The face in the mirror twists. Cracks split the glass, the surface bulges and warps, the face curls into a sneer. 'What's done is done,' it says. 'You gonna be able to pull the trigger? You're just a drunk, couldn't even protect your boy.'

'I gave up drinking.'

'Your boy's in the hospital.'

'I'm gonna get the bastard.'

'But are you gonna be able to forgive him?'

The bubble of emotion in his head is no longer making sense, and it bursts.

He reaches into the pocket of his black tracksuit jacket and draws out the gun, then pulls a narrow cylinder from the paper bag. He fits it to the muzzle, twists it into place. It won't completely eliminate noise from the shot, but on a little .22 like this one it'll muffle it down to a tiny *thunk*, lighter than a pellet from a toy gun.

He looks in the mirror once more, nods, then puts the gun in the paper bag and steps away from the sink.

A female car attendant is prepping the snack trolley and he almost barrels into her. He's about to snap 'Move it', but his eyes fall on the cans of beer in the cart and he backs off.

'Remember, one sip and it's all over.' His father's words flash through his mind. 'Alcoholism never really goes away. One sip and you're right back where you started.'

He enters car number four and starts up the aisle. A man seated just inside the car on his left bumps Kimura as he passes. The gun is safely tucked away in the bag, but it's longer than usual due to the silencer, and it catches on the man's leg. Kimura hastily hugs the bag towards himself.

His nerves spike and he feels a violent surge. He whips towards the man – nice-guy face, glasses with black frames – who bobs his head meekly and apologises. Kimura clicks his tongue and turns away, about to move on, when the nice guy pipes up. 'Hey, your bag is torn.' Kimura pauses and looks. It's true, there's a hole ripped in the bag, but nothing sticking out that could be obviously identified as a gun.

'Mind your own business,' he growls as he steps away.

He exits car four, and moves quickly through cars five and six.

One time Wataru had asked, 'How come on the Shinkansen car one is at the back?' *Poor Wataru.*

Kimura's mother had answered, 'Whichever car is closest to Tokyo is car number one.'

'Why, Daddy?'

'The closest car to Tokyo is car one, the next is car two. So when we take the train to where Daddy grew up, car one is in the back, but when we go back to Tokyo car number one is up front.'

'When the Shinkansen's heading to Tokyo they say it's going up, and trains heading away from Tokyo are going down,' Kimura's father had added. 'It's always about Tokyo.'

'Granny and Grandpa, you always come up to us!'

'Well, we want to see you, that's why. We come all the way up the hill, heave-ho!'

'But you don't do it, the Shinkansen does!'

Kimura's father had looked at him then. 'Wataru's adorable. Hard to believe he's yours.'

'I get that all the time. Who's the dad.'

His parents ignored his sulky remark, chattering away happily. 'The good stuff must have skipped a generation!'

He enters car seven. On the left side of the aisle are rows of two seats and on the right side are rows of three, all facing forward, backs of the seats to him. He puts his hand in the bag, closes it around the gun, then takes a step in, once, twice, counting the rows.

There are more empty seats than he had expected, just a sprinkling of passengers here and there. In the fifth row, by the window, he sees the back of a teenager's head. The kid stretches out, white-collared shirt under a blazer. Clean cut, like an honours student. He turns to stare out the window, dreamily watching other Shinkansen pull into the station.

Kimura draws closer. One row away he's seized with a moment's hesitation – *Am I really gonna hurt this kid? He looks so innocent?* Narrow shoulders, delicate frame. Looking for all the world like a schoolboy quietly

4

excited about a solo trip on the Shinkansen. The knot of aggression and determination inside Kimura loosens ever so slightly.

Then sparks burst in front of him.

At first he thinks the train's electrical system is malfunctioning. But it's his own nervous system, gone haywire for a split second, first sparks and then blackness. The teenager by the window had whirled round and pressed something into Kimura's thigh, like an oversized TV remote. By the time Kimura realises it's the same sort of home-made stun gun those schoolkids had used before, he's paralysed, every hair on his body bristling.

Next thing he knows he's opening his eyes, seated by the window. Hands bound in front of him. Ankles too, wrapped in bands of sturdy fabric and duct tape. He can bend his arms and legs, but his body isn't going anywhere.

'You really are stupid, Mr Kimura. I can't believe you'd be so predictable. You're like a robot following its programming. I knew you'd come for me here, and I know exactly what you came to do.' The kid is sitting right next to him, talking brightly. Something about the double-folded eyelids and the well-proportioned nose looks almost feminine.

This kid had pushed Kimura's son off the roof of a department store, laughing while he did it. He might only be a teenager but he speaks with the self-assurance of someone who's lived several lives. 'I'm still surprised that everything went so smoothly. Life really is too easy. Not for you though, sorry to say. And after you gave up your precious booze, and got yourself all worked up for this!'

FRUIT

'HOW'S THAT CUT DOING?' TANGERINE, in the aisle seat, asks Lemon, next to the window.

They're in car three, row ten, the three-seater. Lemon is staring out the window, muttering. 'Why'd they have to get rid of the 500 series? The blue ones. I loved them.' As if finally hearing the question, he knits his brow, 'What cut?' His long hair sticks out like a lion's mane, though it's hard to tell if he styles it that way or if it's just bedhead. Lemon's complete lack of interest in work, or in anything really, shows in his eyes and his curled upper lip. Tangerine wonders vaguely if his partner's looks dictated his personality or the other way round.

'From when you got slashed yesterday.' He points. 'The cut on your cheek?'

'When did I get slashed?'

'Saving this rich kid.'

Now Tangerine points at the guy sitting in the middle seat. A younger guy, early twenties, long hair, wedged in between them. He keeps staring back and forth from Lemon to Tangerine. He's looking a lot better than when they rescued him the night before. They had found him tied up, worked over, shaking uncontrollably. But it hasn't even been a full day and he seems pretty much back to normal. *Probably nothing going on inside,* thinks Tangerine. Often the case with people who don't read fiction. Hollow inside, monochrome, so they can switch gears no problem. They swallow something and forget about it as soon as it goes down their throat. Constitutionally incapable of empathy. These are the people who most need to read, but in most cases it's already too late.

Tangerine checks his watch. 9 a.m., so, nine hours since they rescued the kid. He was being held in a building in the Fujisawa Kongocho part of town, in a room three floors underground, this rich kid, Yoshio Minegishi's only son, and Tangerine and Lemon busted him out.

'I'd never do something so stupid as get slashed. Gimme a break.' Lemon and Tangerine are the same height, around five ten, and both have the same rangy build. People often assume they're brothers, twins even. Twin killers for hire. Whenever anyone refers to them as brothers, Tangerine feels a deep frustration. It's unbelievable to him anyone could lump him in with someone so careless and simplistic. It probably doesn't bother Lemon, though. Tangerine can't stand Lemon's sloppy ways. One of their associates once said that Tangerine is easy to deal with but Lemon is a pain. Just like the fruit – no one wants to eat a lemon. Tangerine had agreed wholeheartedly.

'Then what's that cut on your cheek from? You've got a red line from here to here. I heard it happen. That punk came at you with a blade and you screamed.'

'I'd never scream because of that. If I did scream, it was because the guy went down so fast and I was disappointed. Like, oh my God, is he really such a wuss, you know? Anyway, this thing on my face isn't from a blade. It's just a rash. I've got allergies.'

'Never seen a rash look so much like a slash.'

'Are you the creator of rashes?'

'Am I the what?' Tangerine looks dubious.

'Did you create the rashes and allergic reactions in this world? No?

Then maybe you're a health critic, and you're denying my twenty-eight year history with allergies? What exactly do you know about rashes?'

It's always like this. Lemon gets all puffed up and starts casting wild aspersions, spouting off at random. If Tangerine doesn't either accept the blame or stop listening altogether, Lemon will keep it up indefinitely. But they hear a small sound between them, coming from the kid, Little Minegishi. He's making uncertain noises. 'Uh. Um.'

'What?' asks Tangerine.

'What?' asks Lemon.

'Um, what, uh, what were your names again?'

When they had found him the night before, he was tied to a chair and wrung out like a limp rag. Tangerine and Lemon woke him up and carried him out, and he just kept saying I'm sorry, I'm sorry, he couldn't get anything else out. Tangerine realises that the kid probably has no idea what's going on.

'I'm Dolce, he's Gabbana,' he says off-handedly.

'No,' says Lemon with a nod, 'I'm Donald, he's Douglas.'

'What?' But even as Tangerine asks, he knows that these are characters from *Thomas and Friends*. No matter what the subject is, Lemon always manages to steer the conversation to *Thomas*. A long-running TV show for kids, filmed with model trains – Lemon loves it. Whenever he needs an allegory chances are he'll pull it from an episode of *Thomas and Friends*. Like everything he ever learned about life and happiness came from that show.

'I know I've told you this before, Tangerine. Donald and Douglas are twin black locomotives. They speak very properly. Well, well, if it isn't our good friend Henry – like that. Talking like that makes a good impression. I'm sure you agree.'

'Can't say I do.'

Lemon sticks his hand in his jacket pocket, rummages around, pulls out a glossy sheet about the size of an address book. He points at it. 'Look, this is Donald.' There are a bunch of trains on it, *Thomas and Friends* stickers. One of them is black. 'No matter how many times I tell you, you always forget the names. It's like you're not even trying.'

'I'm not.'

'You're no fun. Look, I'll give this to you so you can remember their names. Starting from here, this is Thomas, here's Oliver, see, they're all lined up for you. Even the Diesel.' Lemon starts rattling off names one by one. Tangerine shoves the sheet of stickers back at him.

'So, uh, what are your names?' asks Little Minegishi.

'Hemingway and Faulkner,' says Tangerine.

'Bill and Ben are twins too, and so are Harry and Burt,' puts in Lemon.

'We are *not* twins.'

'Okay, Donald and Douglas, sirs,' says Little Minegishi earnestly. 'Did my dad hire you to save me?'

Lemon begins digging around in his ear, looking disinterested. 'Yeah, I guess that's right. Although if I'm being honest, we kind of had to take the job. Too dangerous to say no to your dad.'

Tangerine agrees. 'Your father is a frightening individual.'

'Do you think he's scary too? Or maybe he goes easy on you cos you're his boy.' Lemon pokes the rich kid, only very lightly, but the kid jumps.

'Uh, ah, no, I don't think he's that scary.'

Tangerine smiles acidly. He's starting to settle in. That particular train seat smell. 'You know about the things your father did when he was in Tokyo? There's all kinds of crazy stories. Like the one about when he was loan sharking and a girl was five minutes late on her payment and he chopped off her arm, you heard that one? Not her finger, you know, her arm. And we're not talking about five hours, she was only late five minutes. And then he takes her arm –' And here he cuts himself off, feeling like the well-lit world of the Shinkansen isn't the place for gory details.

'Yeah, I've heard that one,' mutters the rich kid, sounding uninterested. 'And then he put it in a microwave, right?' Like he's talking about the time his dad tried some new recipe.

'Okay, okay, how about the one –' Lemon leans forward and pokes the kid again – 'where Minegishi had a guy who wouldn't pay up, and he got the guy's son, and he stood father and son in front of each other and gave them both box cutters and –'

'I've heard that one too.'

'You heard about that?' Tangerine is nonplussed.

'But really, your father's smart. He keeps it simple. If someone's giving him a problem, get rid of them, he says, and if something's complicated, he just says forget about it.' Lemon watches through the window as another train pulls out of the station. 'A little while back there was a guy in Tokyo named Terahara. Made a ton of money, and made a mess doing it.'

'Yeah, his organisation was called Maiden. I know. I've heard about him.'

The kid's starting to feel comfortable, giving off a whiff of entitlement. Tangerine doesn't like it. He could get into a story about a spoiled kid if it was in a novel, but in real life he isn't interested. All it does is aggravate him.

'So, Maiden fell apart six, maybe seven years ago,' continues Lemon. 'Terahara and his kid both died, and the operation was split up. In the aftermath, your father must have known that things were gonna get ugly, so he just picked up and left town, up north to Morioka. Like I said, smart.'

'Um. Thank you.'

'What are you thanking me for? I'm not praising your dad here.' Lemon keeps his eye on the white body of the departing train as it fades into the distance, apparently sad to see it go.

'No, I mean thank you for rescuing me. I thought I was a goner. They tied me up, there must have been thirty of them. They had me underground and everything. And I had this feeling that even if my dad paid the ransom they'd kill me anyway. They seemed to really hate my dad. I was like, this is it for me, for sure.'

The rich kid seems to be getting more and more talkative, and Tangerine makes a sour face. 'You're pretty sharp. First, basically everyone hates your dad. Not just your friends from last night. I'd say you're more likely to meet someone who's, I don't know, immortal than find someone who doesn't hate your dad. Second, like you said, they would have killed you the moment they got the money, no doubt about it. When you thought you were a goner, you were right.'

Minegishi had contacted Tangerine and Lemon from Morioka and tasked them with bringing the ransom money to the captors and rescuing his son. Sounded simple enough, but nothing is ever simple.

'Your pop was very specific,' Lemon grumbled as he counted off on his fingers. 'Save my son. Bring back the ransom money. Kill everyone involved. Like he thinks he's gonna get everything his heart desires.'

Minegishi had prioritised the list. Most important was bringing back his son, then the money, then killing all the perpetrators.

'But, Donald, you did all of it. You did great.' The rich kid's eyes are sparkling.

'Wait, Lemon, where's the suitcase?' Tangerine is suddenly worried. Lemon was supposed to be carrying the suitcase with the ransom money in it. It didn't feel quite big enough for more than a few days away but it was a decent-sized model with a sturdy handle. At the moment, it's not on the luggage rack or under the seat or anywhere in sight.

'Tangerine, you noticed!' Lemon leans back and props his legs up on the seat in front of him, smiling broadly. Then he starts to fish around in his pocket. 'Here, check this out.'

'The suitcase doesn't fit in your pocket.'

Lemon laughs, though no one else does. 'Yeah, all I've got in my pocket is this little piece of paper.' He produces something the size of a business card and waves it in the air.

'What's that?' The rich kid leans in for a closer look.

'It's an entry for a giveaway from the supermarket we stopped at on the way here. They run it once a month. Check it out – first prize is a paid ticket for a holiday! And they must have messed up because there's no expiry date, so if you win you can go whenever you want!'

'Can I have it?'

'No way. I'm not gonna give it to you. What do you need travel tickets for? Your dad can pay for your holidays. You've got dad tickets.'

'Lemon, forget about the giveaway, tell me where the hell the suitcase is.' There's an edge in Tangerine's voice. A nasty premonition flickers through him.

Lemon looks over at him serenely. 'You don't know much about trains so I'll break it down for you. On current models of the Shinkansen there's storage space in the gangways between the cars for large luggage. Big suitcases, ski equipment, that kind of thing.'

Tangerine is at a momentary loss for words. To relieve the pressure of the blood boiling in his head he reflexively elbows the rich kid in the arm. The kid yelps, then whines in protest, but Tangerine ignores him. 'Lemon, didn't your parents teach you to keep a close eye on your belongings?' He does his best to keep his voice even.

Lemon is obviously offended. 'What does that even mean?' he sputters. 'Do you see anywhere I could have put the suitcase? There are three people sitting here, how exactly was I supposed to fit the suitcase?' Gobs of spit rain down on the rich kid. 'I had to store it *somewhere*!'

'Could have used the overhead rack.'

'You weren't carrying it so you don't know, but that thing's heavy!'

'I did carry it for a bit, and it isn't that heavy.'

'And don't you think that if anyone noticed a couple of shady-looking dudes like us with a suitcase they'd figure Oh there must be something valuable inside, and then the jig would be up. I'm trying to be careful here!'

'The jig would not be up.'

'It would. And anyway, Tangerine, you know that both my parents died in an accident when I was in kindergarten. They didn't teach me much of anything. I guess if they taught me one thing it was not to keep suitcases nearby.'

'You're so full of shit.'

The mobile phone in Tangerine's pocket vibrates, making his skin buzz. He takes out the phone, checks the caller ID and grimaces. 'It's your father,' he says to the rich kid. As he stands and heads towards the gangway, the Shinkansen starts to pull away.

The automatic door opens and Tangerine accepts the call as he steps into the gangway. He puts the phone up to his ear and hears Minegishi. 'Well?' The voice is quiet but penetrating. Tangerine draws up next to the window and follows the passing city scene with his eyes.

'The train just left.'

'Is my son safe?'

'If he weren't, I wouldn't be on the train.'

Then Minegishi asks if they have the money, and what happened to the kidnappers. The noise of the train running gets louder and it becomes harder to hear. Tangerine makes his report.

'Once you've brought my son back to me, your work is done.'

You're just up there relaxing in your villa, how much do you really care about your boy?

Tangerine bites his tongue.

The line goes dead. Tangerine turns to go back but stops short: Lemon is standing right in front of him. It's a strange feeling, facing someone exactly his height, like looking into a mirror. But the person he sees is more careless, more badly behaved than he is, giving Tangerine the peculiar sensation that his own negative traits have taken human form and are staring back at him.

Lemon's natural jumpiness is on full display. 'Tangerine, this is bad.'

'Bad? What's bad. Blame me for your problems.'

'It's your problem too.'

'What happened?'

'You said that I should put the suitcase with the money on the overhead rack, right?'

'I did.'

'Well, it started to worry me too, so I went to get it. To the storage space in the gangway, on the other side of our car.'

'Good thinking. And?'

'It's gone.'

The two of them fly through car number three to the gangway on the other side. The storage space is next to the bathrooms and sink area. Two racks, one large suitcase on the top. Not the one with Minegishi's money inside. Next to them is a small empty shelf that looks like a payphone used to live there.

'You put it here?' Tangerine points at the empty rack below the large suitcase.

'Yeah.'

'And where'd it go?'

'The toilet?'

'The suitcase?'

'Yeah.' It's not clear whether Lemon's playing or serious as he steps over to the men's room door and yanks it open. But when he shouts, 'Where are you? Where'd you piss off to? Come back!' his voice sounds frantic.

Maybe someone took it by mistake, thinks Tangerine, but he knows that's not true. His heart rate rises. The fact that he's shaken up shakes him up.

'Hey, Tangerine, what three words describe our situation right now?' A twitchy muscle in Lemon's face keeps firing.

Just then the snack trolley enters the gangway. The young attendant stops to see if they'd like anything but they don't want her to hear their conversation and they wave her on.

Tangerine waits until she and the cart disappear through the door. 'Three words? "We are screwed"?'

'We are *fucked.*'

Tangerine suggests that they return to their seats to calm down and think. He starts off and Lemon follows. 'But hey, I'm not done. Any other three-word combinations?' It may be that he's confused, or that he's just simple-minded, but there's not a shred of gravity in his voice.

Tangerine pretends not to hear him and enters car three, makes his way down the aisle. The train isn't crowded, only maybe forty per cent full on a weekday morning. Tangerine doesn't know how many people are usually on the Shinkansen, but this feels quiet.

Since they're walking towards the back of the train, the passengers are facing them. People with arms folded, people with eyes closed, people reading the newspaper, business people. Tangerine scans the overhead racks and the footrests. Looking for a mid-size black suitcase.

Little Minegishi is still in his seat, halfway down the car. He has the seat leaned back and his eyes closed, his mouth gaping, his body lolling towards the window. He must be tired after all – two days ago he was kidnapped, held and tortured, then busted out in the middle of the night and hustled to the train without a wink of sleep.

But none of these thoughts cross Tangerine's mind. Instead his heart goes full jackhammer. *And now this.* He flounders for a moment but reins himself in, swiftly sits next to the kid and feels his neck.

Lemon steps closer.

'Sleeping in a time of crisis, young master?'

'Lemon, our crisis just got worse.'

'How?'

'The young master's dead.'

'No way.' Several seconds pass before Lemon adds, 'We are *royally* fucked.' Then he counts on his fingers and mutters, 'Guess that's four words.'

NANAO

NANAO CAN'T ESCAPE THIS THOUGHT: if it happened once it can happen again, and if it happened twice it can happen three times, and if three times then four, so we might as well say that if something happens once it'll keep happening forever. Like a domino effect. Five years ago, on his first job, things got way hairier than he expected, and he had mused to himself, *If this happened once, it could happen again.* There must have been some kind of binding power in his idle thought, because his second job was a disaster too, and his third. Always a total mess.

'You're overthinking it,' Maria had said on multiple occasions. Nanao gets his jobs from Maria. She describes herself as basically just an agent, but Nanao doesn't think that's all there is to Maria. Words floated through his mind like epigrams, *I prepare the food and you eat of it, You command and I obey.* Once he asked, 'Maria, why don't you do any jobs?'

'I've got a job.'

'I mean a *job*. You know, like in the field. That kind of job.'

Nanao tried to put it in terms of a genius football player standing on the sidelines shouting orders to their amateurish teammates stumbling around on the field, chewing them out for their blunders. 'And you're the genius football player, which makes me the amateur. Wouldn't things go smoother if the genius got in the game? Less stress for everyone, and better results.'

'Come on. I'm a woman.'

'Yeah, but you're really good at kenpo. I've seen you take out three men at once. And I'm sure you're more reliable than I am.'

'That's not what I mean. I'm a woman, what if my face gets messed up?'

'What year are you from? Ever heard of gender equality?'

'This conversation is sexual harassment.'

He couldn't get anywhere with her on the subject, and Nanao had given up. It seemed there would be no altering the situation: Maria calling the shots and Nanao following orders, the genius coach and the amateur player.

Maria said the same thing about this job that she said about all of them: 'Simple. You'll be in and out, easy-peasy.' Nanao had heard these promises before, but he almost couldn't bring himself to protest.

'I'm guessing something'll go wrong.'

'So pessimistic. You're like a hermit crab who won't leave its shell because it's worried about earthquakes.'

'Is that what hermit crabs worry about?'

'If they weren't worried about earthquakes, they wouldn't have portable houses, would they?'

'Maybe they just don't want to pay property taxes.'

She ignored his desperate attempt at a punchline. 'Listen, the kind of job we do is basically all rough stuff, dangerous work, so it shouldn't surprise you if there's some trouble every time. You could say that trouble is our job.'

'Not *some* trouble,' Nanao said emphatically. 'It's never just *some* trouble.' He wanted to be one hundred per cent clear on this point. 'I've never only just had *some* trouble. Take that job in the hotel, when I was supposed to get photos of that politician having an affair. You said that one would be simple, in and out.'

'It was simple – all you had to do was get some photos.'

'Sure, simple, as long as there isn't a mass shooting in the hotel.'

A man in a suit had suddenly opened fire in the lobby, spraying bullets all around. He was later identified as a prominent bureaucrat who had been suffering from depression, leading him to kill several guests and end up in a stand-off with police. It had no connection whatsoever to Nanao's job, just a total coincidence.

'But you did great. How many people did you end up saving? And you broke the shooter's neck!'

'It was him or me. And then what about that job where I was supposed to go to a fast-food restaurant and try the new thing on the menu and make a big showy deal about how it's so delicious, it's an explosion of taste, I was supposed to say?'

'You're saying it wasn't delicious?'

'It *was* delicious. But then there really *was* an explosion in the restaurant!'

A recently fired employee had set off the bomb. Although there weren't many casualties from the blast, the interior quickly filled with smoke and flames, and Nanao had done everything he could to get the customers outside. But a famous criminal happened to have been in the restaurant at the same time, and an expert marksman contract killer was targeting him from outside with a high-powered rifle, plunging the scene into even more chaos.

'But you handled that too – you found out where the sniper was hiding and beat him to a pulp. Another one of your great successes!'

'You told me that job would be simple too.'

'Well, what's hard about eating a hamburger?'

'And it was the same with that last job. Hide some money in a restaurant toilet, that's all, you said. But my socks got soaked and I almost ended up eating a hamburger drowning in mustard. There's no such thing as a simple job. It's dangerous to be so optimistic. Anyway, you still haven't told me anything about this job you want me to do now.'

'I did tell you. Steal someone's suitcase and get off the train. That's it.'

'You didn't tell me where the bag is, or whose it is. You just want me to get on the Shinkansen and you'll contact me with more details later? Doesn't sound to me like it's going to be so simple. And you want me to get off the train with the bag at Ueno? That's only a couple minutes after it leaves Tokyo. I won't have enough time.'

'Think of it this way. The more complicated a job is, the more you need to know ahead of time. Special considerations, trial runs, contingency plans. On the other hand, not getting any details beforehand means the job'll be simple. Like what if you had a job that was breathe in and out three times? Would you need details beforehand?'

'That's some sideways logic. No thanks. No way this job'll be simple like you say. There's no such thing as a simple job.'

'Sure there is. There are plenty of simple jobs.'

'Name one.'

'Mine. Being the go-between is the easiest thing in the world.'

'Well, that's just great for you.'

Nanao stands waiting on the platform. His phone vibrates and he brings it up to his ear, just as a station announcement comes in over the loudspeaker: 'The Morioka-bound Hayate–Komachi train will arrive momentarily on track 20.' The male voice reverberates across the platform, making it difficult for Nanao to hear what Maria is saying.

'Hey, are you listening? Can you hear me?'

'The train's coming.'

The announcement causes a buzz of movement on the platform. Nanao feels like he's suddenly enveloped in an invisible membrane, blocking off the sounds around him. The autumn wind blows crisply. Wisps of cloud dot the sky, making the clear blue seem to shine.

'I'll get in touch with you as soon as the info on the suitcase comes in, which I guess will be just after the train leaves.'

'Will you call or message?'

'I'll call. Keep your phone handy. You can do that, right?'

The slender beak of the Shinkansen glides into view, leading the white length of the train into the station. It slows to a stop at the platform. Doors open, passengers exit. The platform overflows with people, filling up empty spaces like flowing water covering dry land. The orderly lines of people waiting to board are scattered. Waves of humans pour down the stairs. Everyone left on the platform re-forms their lines, no one speaking, no one looking at anyone else. There is no signal, everyone just falls into place automatically. *So bizarre*, thinks Nanao. *And I'm doing it too.*

They can't board just yet though – the doors remain closed, presumably for the cleaning staff to give the train a once-over. He lingers on the phone with Maria for a few more seconds before hanging up.

'I wanted to go in the green car!' A voice nearby. He turns to see a woman with heavy make-up and a short man holding a paper bag. The man is moon-faced and bearded. He looks like a kid's toy version of a pirate. The woman wears a sleeveless green dress, showing off her powerful-looking arms. Her skirt is ultra-short. Nanao turns away from the exposed thighs, feeling more uncomfortable than he should, fingering his black-framed glasses.

'Green car's too expensive.' The man scratches his head, then shows the tickets to the woman. 'But look, we're in car two, row two. Two-two, like February the second. Your birthday!'

'That is *not* my birthday. I wore this green dress cos I thought we were sitting in the green car!' The well-built woman wails her displeasure and punches the man in the shoulder, causing him to drop the bag and spill the contents on the ground. A red jacket comes tumbling out, a black dress, a little garment avalanche. Mixed in is something black and furry-looking, like a small animal, which makes Nanao start. He gets goosebumps at the sudden appearance of the unidentified creature. The man scoops it up irritably. Nanao realises it's a hairpiece. More like a full wig. Upon closer inspection the woman in the green dress is not a woman, but a man in make-up. Adam's apple, broad shoulders. Micro-skirt and the bare thighs. 'Hey, buddy, ogle me a little more, why dontcha?'

Nanao flinches, realising the voice is being directed at him.

'Yeah, buddy,' the bearded man with the toy face says as he takes a step closer, still bent over, 'get a good look. You want these clothes? I'll sell 'em to you, ten thousand yen. Well? Show me the cash.' He keeps shovelling them back into the bag.

I wouldn't buy that stuff for a hundred yen, Nanao wants to say, but he knows that will just get him further involved. He sighs. *It's happening already.*

The man presses. 'Come on, chop-chop, I'm sure you've got the money.' Sounds like he's shaking down a schoolkid. 'Nice black frames, brain. You a brain?' Nanao does an about-face and walks away.

Stay focused on the job.

His task is simple. Get the suitcase, get off at the next stop. *No problem. Nothing's going to go wrong, no surprises.* He had been yelled at by a cross-dresser and a man with a beard, and that would be it as far as bumps in the road. He tells himself this like performing a ritual, like he's banishing bad energy from the path ahead.

A loudspeaker voice thanks the people for waiting. It's a pre-recorded message, but it seems to soothe the stress of standing around. At least it soothes Nanao, even though he hadn't been waiting for all that long. He hears a train attendant call out that the doors will open, and then they do, just like magic.

He checks his seat number. Car number four, row one, seat D. He remembers what Maria had said when she handed him the ticket: 'The Hayate is all reserved seats – did you know that? I made sure to reserve yours early since you'll need to get off quickly. I figured an aisle seat would be easiest.'

'What's in the suitcase, anyway?'

'I don't know, but I'm sure it's nothing that important.'

'Oh you're sure? You really expect me to believe that you don't know what's in it?'

'I'm telling you, I don't. You wanted me to ask and piss off the client?'

'What if it's something contraband?'

'Contraband, like what?'

'Like a dead body, or a stash of money, or illegal drugs, or a swarm of insects?'

'A swarm of insects would be scary.'

'The other three would be worse. Is the bag hot?'

'I couldn't rightly say.'

'It's hot, isn't it?' Nanao was starting to lose his temper.

'However bad what's in the suitcase is, all you have to do is carry it. No problem.'

'That doesn't make any sense. Okay, fine, how about you carry it?'

'No way. Too risky.'

Nanao eases into his seat at the end of car number four. A fair number of seats are empty. He waits for the train to depart, keeping his phone in his hand and his eyes on his phone. Nothing yet from Maria. They'll arrive at Ueno Station just minutes after pulling away from Tokyo Station. He'll have very little time to steal the bag. This concerns him.

The automatic door whispers open and someone enters the car. Just as this is happening Nanao tries to adjust his crossed legs and bumps his knee into the paper bag in the hands of the man who enters. The man glares. He looks decidedly unwholesome – stubble uneven, face pallid, eyes sunken. Nanao quickly apologises. 'Sorry about that!' Strictly speaking it was the man who had bumped into him, and should have been the one to apologise, but Nanao doesn't mind. He wants to avoid any friction. He'll make as many apologies as he has to to avoid friction. The man angrily starts to move on but Nanao notices a hole torn in the paper bag, probably from when it hit his leg. 'Hey, your bag is torn.'

'Mind your own business.' The man shuffles off.

Nanao takes off the lightweight leather waist pack he wears to check his ticket once more. The pack is stuffed with items – pen and notepad, metal wire, a lighter, pills, a compass and a powerful horseshoe magnet, a roll of heavy-duty tape. There are three digital wristwatches with alarms. He's found alarms to be useful in all sorts of situations. Maria makes fun of him, calls him a walking Swiss Army knife, but it's all just stuff he had in the kitchen or bought at a convenience store. Except for the steroid paste and blood-clotting cream, in case he gets burnt or cut.

A man who gets no love from Lady Luck has no choice but to be prepared. That's why Nanao always brings his bag of tricks.

He fishes the Shinkansen ticket out of where it was stuffed in the waist pack. The printing on the ticket makes him do a double take: it's a ticket from Tokyo all the way to Morioka. *Why Morioka?* Just as he thinks this, his phone rings. He answers immediately and hears Maria's voice. 'Okay, here you go. It's between cars three and four. There's a luggage storage space, and a black suitcase there. Some kind of sticker near the handle. The person the bag belongs to is in car three, so once you get the bag head in the other direction and get off as soon as you can.'

'Got it.' He pauses for a moment. 'I just noticed something though. I'm supposed to get off at Ueno, but for some reason my ticket goes to Morioka.'

'No reason in particular. For a job like this it just made good sense to get you a ticket till the end of the line. Just in case anything happens.'

Nanao gets a little louder. 'So you *do* think something's going to happen.'

'It's just in case. Don't get all worked up about it. Try smiling. What's that old saying, a smile is a door for good fortune?'

'I'd look pretty weird sitting here smiling all by myself.' He hangs up. The train starts moving.

Nanao stands and heads to the door behind him.

Five minutes till Ueno. Cutting it close. Luckily, he finds the luggage storage immediately and locates the black bag with no problem. It's mid-sized, fitted with wheels. Sticker by the handle. It's hard-sided, though he can't tell what material it's made from. He pulls it off the rack as quietly as he can. *Simple job,* Maria had said in her honeyed voice. Simple so far. He checks the time. Four minutes until arrival at Ueno Station. *Come on, come on.* Nanao returns to car four with the suitcase, taking regular, even steps. No one seems to be paying him any attention.

He passes through car four, then car five, steps into the gangway between five and six.

Then he stops and exhales with relief. He was worried that there might be something blocking the door, some kids dozing in front of it or doing their make-up, just taking up space, and when they caught Nanao looking at them they'd say What's your problem or fling some other abuse at him and get in his face, or there might be some couple having a lovers' spat and they would turn to him and demand to know whose side he's on, suck him into their nonsense, whatever it was, he was certain there would be something to trip him up.

But no one is by the door, so he feels relieved. All there is left to do is pull into Ueno and get off the train. Exit the station and call Maria. He can already hear her poking fun at him, *See how simple that was,* she'll say, and though he doesn't love being teased, he'll take that over serious trouble any day.

The outside goes suddenly dark as the train begins to slope underground, signalling the imminent arrival at Ueno's subterranean platform. Nanao squeezes the suitcase handle and checks his watch, though he has no reason to.

He catches his reflection in the window on the door. Even he has to admit, he looks like the sort of guy who has no good luck, no good fortune, no good mojo whatsoever. Ex-girlfriends had complained to him – Since we started dating, I keep losing my wallet; I always seem to be messing things up when I'm with you; My skin just keeps getting worse. He had protested that none of that could possibly be his fault, but somehow he knew it probably was. Like his bad luck had rubbed off on them.

The high-pitched hum of the train on the tracks starts to ease off. The doors will be opening on the left. The view outside brightens, and suddenly the station appears, like stumbling on a futuristic city inside a cave. People here and there on the platform, already receding. Stairwells and benches and digital displays disappear to the left.

Nanao stares at the glass, making sure no one is coming up from behind. If the bag's owner or anyone were to challenge him, things could get complicated. The train starts to drop speed. It makes him think of the one time he played roulette in a casino. The way the wheel slowed seemed to lend great significance to each slot the ball might come to rest. He gets the same impression as the Shinkansen pulls in, like it's choosing where to stop, which car in front of which passenger, lazily shedding speed, oh who to pick who to pick. And then, it stops.

A man stands on the other side of Nanao's door. Smallish, wearing a flat cap that makes him look like a private eye from a kids' story. The door doesn't open right away. There's a long moment, like holding your breath underwater.

Nanao and the man are now standing opposite each other, with the window between them. Nanao frowns. *I know a guy with the same gloomy face, same stupid detective hat.* The man he's thinking of is in the same line of work, back-alley stuff, dangerous business. He's got some run-of-the-mill name, but he talks big, always making outrageous claims about his exploits or badmouthing everyone else. People call him the Wolf. Not because he's heroic and solitary like a lone wolf. More like he's the bullshit wolf that the boy keeps crying about. But he doesn't seem to mind the derisive name, proudly declaring that it was given to him by Mr Terahara. Terahara was busy steering the whole underworld and it seems hard to believe he would waste time coming up with a nickname, but the Wolf at least says it went down that way.

The Wolf has a lot of tall tales. Like one he once told Nanao when they happened to be in the same bar. 'You know that guy, the suicide guy, who knocks off politicians and bureaucrats and makes it look like a suicide? Calls himself the Whale or the Orca or something, big guy? People are saying they don't see him around no more. Know why? Cos I did him.'

'What do you mean, "I did him"?'

'It was a job, you know. I killed the Whale.'

The suicide specialist who went by the Whale had in fact suddenly gone missing, and people in the business were talking about it. Some said the killer was one of them, others said he was in a horrible accident, some even said the Whale's body had been acquired at a high price by a politician with a grudge who hung the corpse up in his house as decoration. But whatever the truth, one thing was clear: for a big job like that, no one would ever hire the Wolf, who only worked as bag man or to rough up girls or civilians.

Nanao had always done the best he could to avoid dealing with the Wolf. The more he looked at the guy the more he wanted to punch him in the face, which he knew would only cause trouble. And he was right to be concerned about his ability to control himself, because one time Nanao actually had attacked the Wolf.

He was walking down a backstreet in the bar district when he chanced upon the Wolf, who was about to beat up three kids who couldn't have been older than ten.

'What do you think you're doing?' Nanao asked.

'These little kids were making fun of me. I'm gonna give them some medicine.' And then he balled up his fist and hit one of the petrified kids across the face. Blood surged into Nanao's head. He knocked the Wolf down and kicked him in the back of the skull.

Maria heard about the incident and made sure to get her jabs in. 'Protecting the children, you're a real sweetheart.'

'It's not because I'm nice.' It was something to do with the image of a frightened kid, defenceless, begging for someone to save them. 'When kids are in trouble, I can't help myself.'

'Oh, you mean your trauma? So on-trend.'

'That's not fair, it's more complicated than a buzzword.'

'The trauma boom is over,' she said with some disdain.

He tried to explain that it wasn't a boom. Even though the term trauma had become a cliché and suddenly everyone's traumatised by something, people still had to cope with the pain of their past.

'Anyway,' she added, 'the Wolf, he's always dealt with kids and animals, things weaker than him. Really, he's the worst. As soon as he thinks he's in any danger he starts mouthing off about Terahara, "I've got Terahara's protection, I'll tell Mr Terahara." '

'Terahara's dead.'

'I heard that when Terahara died, the Wolf cried so much he got dehydrated. What a moron. So, in the end, you gave him the medicine.'

Being kicked in the head by Nanao hurt the Wolf's pride as much as his body. He fumed, eyes bleary, promising that Nanao would be sorry next time they met, and then ran off. That was the last time they had seen one another.

The Shinkansen doors open. Nanao is about to get off, suitcase in hand. He's now face-to-face with the man in the flat cap, who looks exactly like the Wolf, an unbelievable likeness really, and then the man points at him, 'Hey, *you*,' and he realises that of course it is the Wolf and none other.

Nanao hastily tries to get off but the Wolf's face is a mask of grim determination as he barrels forward, forcing his way onto the train and knocking Nanao backwards.

'Well, imagine my luck meeting you here,' says the Wolf with glee. 'What a treat!' His nostrils are flaring eagerly.

'Some other time. I'm getting off.' Nanao keeps his voice low, worried that speaking loudly might attract attention from the bag's owner.

'Think I'm gonna let you get away? I've got a score to settle with you, buddy.'

'Settle it with me later. I'm working. Or better yet, don't settle it at all, I forgive you your debts.'

No time for this, and just as the thought flashes through Nanao's mind the doors swish closed. The Shinkansen pulls away, heedless of Nanao's predicament. He hears Maria's voice somewhere, *See what a simple job this is?* Nanao wants to scream with frustration. The job is going south, just like he knew it would.

THE PRINCE

HE OPENS THE TRAY TABLE and sets his water bottle down, then opens a packet of chocolates and pops one in his mouth. The train leaves Ueno and returns to the world above. A few clouds float in the sky, but mostly it's just clear blue. *The sky's as sunny as I am,* he thinks. He sees a driving range, with its backstop like a giant green mosquito net. It flows off to the left and a school slides into view, a string of concrete rectangles, uniformed students hanging around the windows. He can't tell if they're his age or a little older, and Satoshi 'The Prince' Oji spends a moment trying to figure it out, but almost immediately decides that it doesn't matter. They're all the same.

Whether it's schoolkids like him or adults, everyone's all the same. All so predictable. He turns to Kimura sitting next to him. This man is a prime example of how disappointingly boring humans are.

At first he was thrashing around, even though he was all taped up and couldn't go anywhere. The Prince pulled the gun he had taken from him, holding it close between them so no one else could see. 'Calm down, this'll only be for a little while. I'm telling you, if you don't listen to the

28

story until the end, Mr Kimura, you'll wish you had.' That had settled him down.

Now the Prince asks, 'I've been wondering, didn't you at any point think that something felt strange? Me riding the Shinkansen all by myself, and you being able to find out where I was sitting so easily? It never occurred to you that it was a trap?'

'You put that intel out there?'

'Well, I knew you were looking for me.'

'I was looking for you because you disappeared. Lying low, not showing up at your school.'

'I'm not hiding. I couldn't go to school, my whole year is on sick leave.' It's true. Even though there was still a while till winter, flu had broken out in his class and they were told to all stay home for a week. The epidemic showed no signs of slowing down in the following week, and they were told to stay home again. The teachers didn't stop to consider how the flu spreads or its gestation period, or what percentage of cases become severe, no, they just had an automatic system where if a certain number of kids are off sick then the whole class has to stay home. The Prince thought it was ridiculous. Just blindly following a set of rules to avoid assuming any responsibility, avoid taking any risks. Enacting sick leave without a moment's hesitation, the teachers all seemed like fools to him, fools who had shut off their brains. Zero consideration, zero analysis, zero initiative.

'Do you know what I've been doing while school's been out?'

'Don't care.'

'I was finding out about you, Mr Kimura. I figured you must be pretty mad at me.'

'I'm not mad.'

'Really?'

'I'm a whole lot fucking worse than mad.' Kimura spits the words like spitting out blood, causing a smile to crease the Prince's cheeks. People who can't control their emotions are the easiest to handle.

'Well, anyway, I knew you wanted to get me. I figured you'd look for me and come at me when you found me. So I knew it would be dangerous for me to stay at home, and since you were coming for me, I figured I'd find out everything I could about you. You know, when you want to go after someone, or bring someone down, or use someone, the very first thing you have to do is gather information on them. Start with their family, their job, their habits, their hobbies, that'll tell you what you need to know. Same way the tax bureau does it.'

'What kind of schoolkid looks up to the tax bureau? You're the fucking worst.' Kimura sneers. 'What can a kid find out, anyway?'

The Prince furrows his brow in disappointment. This man isn't taking him seriously. He's being fooled by age and appearance, underestimating his enemy. 'If you pay, you can get information.'

'What, did you break open your piggy bank?'

The Prince is utterly disenchanted. 'Or it might not be money. Maybe there's a man who likes schoolgirls. Says he's willing to play private eye if he gets to feel up a naked teenager. He might find out that your wife left you, that you got divorced and live alone with your cute little kid, that you're alcohol-dependent, that kind of thing. And maybe I have some friends, girls, who wouldn't mind taking their clothes off if I asked them to.'

'You'd make a schoolgirl get with an adult? Force some insecure girl into doing it?'

'I'm just saying for example. Don't get so excited. I'm just saying money isn't everything, people have all kinds of desires and do things for all kinds of reasons. It's just about leverage. Push the right button in the right way and even a schoolkid can make anyone do anything. And you know, sexual desire is the easiest button to push.' The Prince makes sure to sound mocking. The more emotional someone gets, the easier they are to control. 'But I was impressed when I heard about the dangerous stuff you used to be involved in. Tell me, Mr Kimura, have you ever killed anyone?' The Prince drops his eyes to the gun in his hand, still pointed at Kimura. 'I mean, you had this. Really cool. This thing you had on the end is so the gun doesn't make any noise, right? Really professional.' He holds up the silencer, now removed. 'I was so scared I almost cried,' he says in a dramatic sing-song, but of course it isn't true. If he's about to cry it's from the effort of holding in his laughter.

'So you were just waiting for me here?'

'I heard you were looking for me so I spread around that I'd be on this Shinkansen. You hired someone to find out where I was, right?'

'An old acquaintance.'

'From when you were still in the business. And he didn't think it was weird that you were looking for a teenage boy?'

'At first he did. He said, I didn't know you were into that. But when I told him my story he got heated, wanted me to find you. Nobody's gonna do that to your boy and get away with it, he said.'

'But in the end he betrayed you. I found out he was asking around about me so I made him a counter-offer so he'd tell you the information I wanted you to have.'

'Bullshit.'

'Once he found out he could do whatever he wanted to a teenage girl he started breathing all heavy. I thought to myself, are all adults this way?' The Prince loves this, scratching the membrane of people's feelings, his words like claws. It's easy to build up your body, but developing emotional resistance is tough. Even when you think you're calm, it's almost impossible not to react to the pinprick of malevolence.

'I didn't know he was into that.'

'You shouldn't trust old acquaintances, Mr Kimura. Doesn't matter what you think they owe you, they'll eventually forget about it. Our trust-based society is long gone, if it ever even existed in the first place. But still, you actually showed up. I couldn't believe it. You're just such a trusting fellow. Hey, I've been meaning to ask, how's your son doing?' He devours another chocolate.

'How the fuck do you think?'

'Keep it down, Mr Kimura. If someone comes over here you'll be in trouble. You've got a gun and everything.' The Prince whispers theatrically, 'Stay cool.'

'You're the one holding the gun.'

The Prince is continually disappointed with how Kimura never once sets foot outside of the bounds of predictability. 'I'll just say I managed to wrestle the gun away from you.'

'And what about tying me up?'

'That doesn't matter. You're an ethanol addict, a former security guard, currently unemployed, and I'm a typical school student. Whose side do you think they'll take?'

'The hell is ethanol? I'm addicted to alcohol.'

'Ethanol *is* alcohol, it's what makes drinks alcoholic. You know, I have to say I'm impressed that you managed to quit drinking. I'm serious, that's hard. Did something happen that helped you quit? Like your kid almost dying?'

Kimura glares with fanatic malice.

'Anyway, I'll ask again, how's your cute little kid doing? What's his name? Can't remember his name but I know he likes rooftops. But he should be careful. When little kids go to high places by themselves they sometimes fall. The railings on the roofs of department stores aren't always solid, and kids always find the dangerous spots.'

Kimura looks like he's about to start shouting.

'Quiet, Mr Kimura, or you'll be sorry.' The Prince turns to look out the window, just as a Tokyo-bound Shinkansen hurtles past in the opposite direction, so fast it's nothing but a blur. The whole train trembles. He feels a quiet thrill at the overwhelming speed and force. Against a giant metal object travelling at more than two hundred kilometres an hour, a human being would be powerless. *Imagine putting someone down in front of an oncoming Shinkansen, they'd be splattered to bits.* The overwhelming power differential fascinates him. *And I'm just as dangerous. I may not be able to move at two hundred kilometres an hour, but I can destroy people just the same.* A smile appears, unbidden.

The Prince's friends had helped him take Kimura's son out on the department store roof. Strictly speaking, they were the Prince's classmates who followed his orders. The six-year-old boy was frightened, frightened because he had never encountered cruelty before.

Hey look, over there by the railing, look down from there. You don't have to be scared, it's safe.

He had said it with a warm smile, so the little boy believed him.

It's okay? I won't fall?

He pushed him, and it felt intensely good.

Kimura scowls. 'Weren't you worried, sitting here, that I might get the drop on you?'

'Worried?'

'You know what kind of work I used to do. You had to figure I'd have a gun. If the timing worked out differently I might have killed you.'

'I wonder.' The Prince is actually wondering. He hadn't felt the least bit of fear. He was more keyed up with anticipation, waiting to see if things would play out as he was betting. 'I didn't think you'd shoot me or stab me right away.'

'Why not?'

'With the way you must feel about me, getting it over with so quickly wouldn't be enough.' He shrugs. 'I didn't think you'd be satisfied if you just snuck up on me and killed me. You'd want to scare me, threaten me, make me cry, hear me apologise, right?'

Kimura neither affirms nor denies. *Adults always keep their mouths shut*, thinks the Prince, *when I'm right.*

'Anyway, I was guessing I could get you first,' and he pulls the home-made taser from his backpack.

'A regular fucking electrician.'

The Prince savours the last reverberation from the passing Shinkansen, then turns back to face Kimura. 'Mr Kimura, when you were still in the business, how many people did you kill?'

Kimura's bloodshot eyes narrow to pinpoints. *Ah, he may be tied up but he's about ready to come at me anyway.*

'I've killed people,' the Prince tells him. 'The first time was when I was ten. Just one person. In the three years since then, nine more. Ten total. Is your number higher than that? Or lower?'

Kimura looks taken aback. The Prince is once again let down by his reaction. *It takes so little to throw this guy off.*

'But I should clarify, I only killed one person myself.'

'The hell does that mean?'

'It's stupid to put yourself at risk. Right? I want to make sure you don't mistake me for someone dumb enough to do that.'

Kimura twists up his face. 'I don't know what the fuck you're talking about.'

'Well, the first one,' begins the Prince.

Back when he was in school, after coming home from class he went out again, rode his bike to the big bookstore to buy a book he wanted. On the way home he came to a main road and stopped his bike at the crossing, waiting for the signal to change. Next to him was a man in a sweater wearing headphones and staring at his phone, but no one else was around. There was barely any traffic, either – the road was so quiet that it was easy to hear the music seeping out of the man's headphones.

There wasn't any deep reason why he started pedalling out when the light was still red. He just thought that it was taking a long time to turn green and there didn't seem to be any cars so there was no point in dutifully waiting for the light to change. He nudged his bike out into the road and started across. A moment later there was a cacophony behind him – screeching brakes, and the sound of impact, although actually the thud of the collision came first and the grating squeal of the brakes afterwards. He turned to look and saw a black minivan stopped in the middle of the road, a bearded man clambering out of the driver's seat. The man in the sweater was on the ground, his phone smashed to bits.

The Prince wondered for just a moment why the man would have crossed when a car was coming, but he immediately pieced together a likely scenario: he himself had biked across, and the man just assumed that the light had turned green. Headphones in, eyes glued to his phone, he must have sensed the Prince's bicycle move out into the road and just followed along reflexively. And then he got mowed down by a minivan. The sudden appearance of the van was more surprising to him than the man's death, given how deserted the road had seemed, but in any case the man was dead. Even from across the street, the Prince could see that he wasn't breathing. The cord from the headphones trailed out like a line of blood.

'I learned two things from that.'

'What?' Kimura growls. 'That you should always obey traffic signals?'

'The first was that if you're careful how you do it, you can get away with killing someone. The whole episode was handled like a typical traffic accident. No one even paid any attention to me.'

'Guess not.'

'The second thing was that even though it was my fault that someone died, I didn't feel bad at all.'

'Lucky you.'

'That's when it started. When I got interested in killing. What it's like to kill someone, how someone reacts when you're killing them, that kind of thing.'

'You wanted to try out the ultimate sin, was that it? Did you think you were special because you could imagine yourself doing something so awful that the thought never enters into normal people's minds? Listen, everyone has those thoughts, even if they don't do anything about it. Why is it wrong to kill people, or how can everyone be so calm when every living thing is going to die, oh, life is so empty! Everyone thinks this stuff. It's like standard teenage angst.'

'Why is it wrong to kill people?' The Prince tries asking. He isn't being cynical or making a joke, he actually wants to know the answer. He wants to meet an adult who can give him a satisfying answer. He knows that Kimura won't be the one. He can imagine Kimura's unconsidered position: killing someone is no problem, long as it isn't me or my family, otherwise, who cares.

Then Kimura gives a stubbly grin. 'I don't think there's anything wrong with killing. I mean, as long as we're not talking about killing me or my family. But otherwise, sure, have a blast, kill and be killed.'

The Prince sighs heavily.

'Impressed?'

'No, just disappointed at such a predictable answer. Anyway, as I was saying, after that episode I made up my mind to experiment. First I wanted to kill someone a little more directly.'

'And that was the person you did yourself.'

'Exactly.'

'So when you pushed Wataru off the roof, was that an experiment too?' Kimura's voice is quiet but tight, dripping venom.

'No, no. Your kid must have wanted to play with us or something. We told him to leave us alone but he wouldn't. We were exchanging trading cards in the car park on the department store roof. It's dangerous up here, we said, don't run around, but he toddled off towards the stairwell. Before we knew what was happening he fell.'

'You and your friends *pushed* him!'

'A six-year-old? From the roof?' The Prince brings his fingertips to his open mouth in a cheesy gesture of fake shock. 'We could never do something so horrible! The thought would never even cross my mind. Adults think the scariest things.'

'I'll fucking kill you.' Kimura's hands and feet are bound but that doesn't stop him from lurching towards the Prince, snapping his jaws.

'Mr Kimura, stop.' The Prince holds his hands out in front of him. 'What I'm about to say is important, so listen carefully. It could mean your son's life. Just settle down for a minute.' He sounds completely calm.

Kimura is all worked up, nostrils flaring with rage, but the mention of his son's life stops him, and he falls back into the seat.

Then the carriage door opens behind them. It must be the snack trolley, because they hear someone say excuse me, followed by the sounds of a transaction. Kimura twists round to look.

'Don't try anything funny with the carriage attendant, mister.'

'Anything funny. You mean like ask her on a date?'

'I mean like asking her for help.'

'Just try and stop me.'

'That would defeat the whole point.'

'Defeat what point? What fucking point?'

'That it would be so easy to open your mouth and ask for help, but you can't. I want you to feel that powerlessness. If I physically forced you to keep your mouth shut, it would defeat the purpose. I want you to feel what it's like not to do anything even when you could. I want to see you squirm.'

Kimura's eyes take on a different cast, shift from anger to a mix of disgust and fear, as if he had just discovered some new horrible insect. He forces a laugh to cover his discomfiture. 'Sorry, but the more you tell me I can't, the more likely I am to try. That's just the way I am. Always have been. So when the girl comes by with the cart I'm gonna throw myself at her, I'll scream and shout, do something about this schoolkid. If you're saying you don't want me to, then I definitely will.'

How is this middle-aged man so stubborn? Even with arms and legs bound, even with his weapon taken from him, even with the power dynamic between us made crystal clear, how is it he can still talk down to me? The only possible explanation is that it's because he's older than I am. He's lived longer than me, that's all. The Prince can't help but feel sorry for Kimura. *And where have his thousands of wasted days got him?*

'I'll put this as plainly as I can, Mr Kimura, so that you can understand. If you don't follow my instructions, or if something happens to me, your little son in the hospital will be in trouble.'

Kimura is silent.

The Prince feels a mix of satisfaction and dejection. He tries to focus on the pleasure of watching someone at a complete loss. 'I have someone standing by near the hospital in Tokyo. The hospital where your son is, understand?'

'Near means where?'

'Maybe it means inside the hospital. All that matters is that he's close enough to do the job as soon as he needs to.'

'The job.'

'If he can't get in touch with me, he'll do it.'

Kimura's anguish shows plain on his face. 'What do you mean, if he can't get in touch?'

'He's going to call at the time we're supposed to be pulling into each station – Omiya, Sendai, then Morioka. To see if I'm okay. If I don't answer, if he figures that something's wrong . . .'

'Who is it – one of your friends?'

'No, no. Like I said before, people do things for all different reasons. Some like girls, some want money. Believe it or not, there are grown-ups whose sense of right and wrong is totally skewed, and they'll do pretty much anything.'

'So what's your guy gonna do?'

'He apparently used to work for a medical equipment company. It wouldn't be hard for him to do something to mess up the machine your son is hooked up to.'

'Wouldn't be hard, my ass. He wouldn't be able to do anything.'

'Well, we won't know until he tries. Like I said, he's waiting somewhere very close to the hospital. Waiting for the signal. All I have to do is call him and give him the green light, and he'll do it. And if he calls me, even if it's not one of the scheduled calls at each station, and it rings more than ten times without me answering, that's a green light too. If that happens, my guy will go to the hospital and start messing with your son's respirator.'

'Some set of rules. Basically all green lights. What if we're somewhere your phone gets no service?'

'They've been installing antennas in train tunnels so I don't think it will affect my service. But you're probably better off praying that it doesn't, just in case. Anyway, if you try anything funny, I just won't pick up when my guy calls. Maybe I'll get off at Omiya, go to the movies, turn my phone off for a couple of hours. By the time I get out of the cinema something terrible will have happened to your son's life-support machine.'

'You're full of shit.' Kimura stares daggers.

'I am not full of shit. I'm always deadly serious. I think maybe you're the one who's full of shit.'

Kimura's flaring nostrils show that he's on the brink of an explosion, but it finally seems to dawn on him that there's nothing he can do. His rigid body goes slack, he slumps back in the seat. The attendant is pushing the snack trolley by and the Prince makes a point to stop her and buy more chocolates. Somehow she doesn't notice that Kimura's hands and feet are bound. Watching Kimura sitting next to him with mouth clamped shut and face red with rage feels exquisite.

'You should be paying attention to my phone, Mr Kimura. If I get a call and it rings ten times, you won't be happy about what happens.'

FRUIT

'TANGERINE, WHAT DO WE DO?' Lemon looks down at Little Minegishi, who sits there eyes closed, not moving. The mouth hangs open in a stupid gape, like he's making fun of them. It makes Lemon feel uncomfortable.

'What can we do?' Tangerine is rubbing his cheeks busily. Seeing Tangerine off balance for a change is a slight comfort to Lemon. 'This is all because you let him out of your sight. Why did you leave the kid alone?'

'I had to. You were on my case about the bag so I wanted to go and check up on it. What'd you expect me to do, after giving me such a hard time?'

'The bag was stolen for sure.' Tangerine sighs. 'Everything with you is sloppy, your words, your actions, your way of thinking. You're such a typical B.'

Lemon snorts. 'Don't try to sum me up by my blood type. There's no scientific proof for that. Talking seriously about that stuff just makes you sound stupid. If it were true, that would make you organised and precise just because you're an A.'

'I *am* organised and precise, and when I do a job I do it nice and neat.'

'Big talk. Listen, my failures are my own. They have nothing to do with my blood type.'

'Yeah, you're right,' Tangerine says brightly. 'Your failures come down to your character and your lack of judgement.'

Tangerine is getting self-conscious standing in the aisle, so he leans down and hoists Little Minegishi's body over to the window seat, propping it up against the window with head tipped slightly forward. 'Guess we just have to make it look like he's sleeping, for now.'

Tangerine takes the middle seat, and Lemon eases down into the aisle seat muttering darkly. 'Who the fuck did this? How did he even die?'

Tangerine starts feeling around the body. There are no obvious cuts, no blood. He opens the kid's mouth wide and peers inside. He doesn't want to look too closely, though, in case there's something poisonous in there. 'No obvious marks on the body.'

'Poison?'

'Could be. Or maybe an allergic reaction and he went into shock.'

'What could he have been allergic to?'

'Don't know. I'm not the creator of allergies, remember? Hey, it could be that all of this was too much for him, getting kidnapped then rescued, no sleep, totally exhausted, and his heart just gave out.'

'Is that medically possible?'

'Lemon, have you ever seen me reading a medical textbook?'

'You're always reading something.' Tangerine does take a book with him wherever he goes, even on jobs, and starts reading whenever there's any downtime.

'I like fiction, not medical books. How should I know if there are medically established cases of people's hearts giving out?'

Lemon pulls at his hair. 'But what are we going to do? Just show up in Morioka and go to Minegishi, Sorry, sir, we rescued your son but he died on the Shinkansen?'

'Don't forget that the ransom money was stolen too.'

'If I were Minegishi I'd be pretty angry.'

'I would be too. Furious.'

'But it's like, all he did was sit around in his villa!' They didn't know for certain, but there was a rumour that Minegishi was on holiday with his mistress and their illegitimate daughter. 'There's a whole fiasco with his son getting kidnapped and all but he goes on a family trip with his girl-friend. It's bullshit.'

'The little girl's still in school, supposed to be really cute. And then you have his heir, this rich kid here. A lightweight, a nobody. It's not hard to guess which one he loves more.' Tangerine doesn't sound like he's making a joke.

'Well, now he's a lightweight nobody who's also dead. But hey, maybe this works out for Minegishi and he'll go easy on us.'

'No way. Say you have a car that you don't really like – if someone else wrecks it you'd still be pissed off. And there's the matter of his reputation.'

Lemon looks like he's about to wail about the tough spot they're in, so Tangerine quickly holds up a finger and says *Shh*. 'We'll just have to fig-ure something out.'

'Figuring things out is your job.'

'Moron.'

Lemon starts to move around, checking the area by the window next to the body, checking the trays attached to the seats in front of them, flip-ping through the magazines in the seat-back pockets.

'What are you doing?'

'Thought there might be some kind of clue. But there's nothing. Stu-pid rich kid.'

'Clue?'

'Like maybe he wrote the killer's name in blood or something like that. That could happen, right?'

'It could happen if this were a murder mystery novel. Not in real life.'

'I guess you're right.' Lemon puts the magazine back despondently, but still pokes and prods the seat and walls around the corpse.

'I doubt he had time to leave any kind of clues before he died. There isn't even any blood, how could he have written a message in blood?'

Lemon looks irritated by Tangerine's logic. 'Well, dying like this doesn't help the people trying to solve the case at all. Just for future reference, Tangerine, if you think someone's about to kill you, make sure you leave behind some useful clues.'

'What kind of clues would you like me to leave?'

'Like the identity of the killer, or the truth or something. At the very least make it clear whether it was murder or suicide or an accident. Otherwise it'll be a pain in the ass for me.'

'If I go, it won't be suicide,' Tangerine proclaims in no uncertain terms. 'I like Virginia Woolf and Mishima, but suicide doesn't sit right with me.'

'Virginia who?'

'Those trains you're always talking about are much harder to keep straight than books. Why don't you try reading one of the books I recommend to you?'

'I've never been into books, not even when I was a kid. You know how long it takes me to finish a book? And what about you, you never even try to remember all the *Thomas and Friends* characters, no matter how many times I tell you. You don't even know which one Percy is.'

'Which one is Percy again?'

Lemon clears his throat. 'Percival is a small, green engine. He is rather cheeky and loves to play tricks, though he is very serious when it comes to his work. He often pulls pranks on his friends, but is also somewhat gullible.'

'I always wonder how you can memorise all these.'

'It's on the trading card from the toy model. Pretty cool, huh? It's a simple explanation, but it also has depth. Percy often pulls pranks on his friends, but is also somewhat gullible, see? It's kind of touching. Makes me get a little emotional, even. I bet your books don't have the same kind of depth.'

'Just try reading something and see. Start with, I don't know, *To the Lighthouse*.'

'What'll it tell me?'

'How insignificant we all are, how we're all just a single existence among the countless other existences. It'll make you feel how small you are, how you're lost in the limitless expanse of the ocean of time, swallowed by the waves. It's powerful stuff. We perished, each alone.'

'The hell does that mean?'

'It's a line from one of the characters in the novel. It means that everyone dies, and they're alone when they do.'

Lemon sneers. 'I'm not gonna die.'

'You'll die, and you'll die alone.'

'Even if I do die, I'll come back.'

'Yeah, it's like you to be so stubborn. But I'm going to die someday. Alone.'

'And I'm telling you, when you do, leave me some kind of clue.'

'Okay, okay. If by some chance it looks like I'm about to be killed, I'll do my best to leave you a message.'

'When you're writing the killer's name in blood, do it clearly, make it legible, okay? No initials or mysterious abbreviations.'

'I'm not going to write anything in blood.' Tangerine stops to think for a moment. 'Here, how about this? Say I have a chance to talk to the killer before he does me, I'll give him a message.'

'A message?'

'I'll say something that'll stick with him. Like, "Tell Lemon the key he's looking for is at the baggage check at Tokyo Station," something like that.'

'I'm not looking for any key.'

'Doesn't matter. I'll say something that will pique the killer's curiosity. I bet eventually he'd show up and pretend not to know you and ask politely if you're looking for a key. Or maybe he'd just go to the baggage check at Tokyo Station.'

'Something that'll interest him, huh?'

'And if you ever meet someone like that, you'll know that's the person who killed me. Or at least they have something to do with it.'

'That's a pretty damn unclear message.'

'Well, I'm not going to give the killer a message that's easy to understand, am I?'

'But hey.' Lemon suddenly looks serious. 'I'm not gonna die easy.'

'No, I guess you won't. And if you do, you're stubborn enough to come back.'

'You too, Tangerine. You and me, if we die, we'll come back for sure.'

'Like trees bearing fruit every year?'

'We'll both be back.'

The Shinkansen sways gently as it begins to dip underground, signalling the approach to Ueno. The view out the window goes dark and the scene inside the train appears reflected in the glass. Lemon pulls a magazine from the pocket in the seat-back in front of him and begins to read.

'Hey,' Tangerine says almost immediately, 'this isn't the time to start pleasure reading.'

'I've already said it a bunch of times. Thinking is your job. Leave the mochi sales to the mochi salesman, right?'

'If I'm the mochi salesman, what's that make you?'

The train begins to slow. First there are lamps in the tunnel, then suddenly they're in a brightly lit space. The platform appears. Tangerine stands up.

'Toilet?' Lemon asks.

'Let's go.' Tangerine tries to push past his partner.

'Where are we going?' Lemon doesn't understand what's happening, but he sees the fearsome look on Tangerine's face and stands up to go with him. 'Are we getting off? Don't you think taking the Shinkansen just one stop a bit extravagant?'

The automatic door opens onto the gangway. No one else there. The platform glides by out the doors on the left-hand side.

'Exactly.'

Lemon furrows his brow quizzically.

'Getting on the Shinkansen at Tokyo and getting off at Ueno *is* extravagant. You could just take a local train. But someone might be getting off after all.'

'Who?'

'Someone who stole a bag on the Shinkansen and wants to get away as soon as possible.'

Lemon nods in dawning comprehension. 'Oh, I get it.' He steps closer to the door and taps the window with his finger. 'If someone gets off at Ueno, that's the thief.'

'It'll be easy to tell if the person is carrying our suitcase, but there's a chance they stuffed it inside another bag. Still, it'd have to be a pretty big bag. Either way, anyone who gets off here is our prime suspect. If you see someone, go after them.'

'Me?'

'Who else am I talking to? Leave the mochi sales to the mochi sales-man, right? You might never have sold mochi, or used your head for that matter, but I know you've chased down thieves.'

The brakes sing as the train slows to an almost complete stop. Lemon stares at the platform, suddenly concerned. 'What do I do if there's more than one?'

'Guess you'll have to go after whoever looks more suspicious,' Tanger-ine says curtly.

'What if there's more than one person who looks suspicious? These days everybody looks suspicious, dammit.'

The train stops and the door opens. Tangerine steps onto the platform with Lemon close behind. They stand just outside the train, peering down the length of it to see if anyone is getting off. It's a straight shot all the way down the platform, as long as they pay close attention it should be easy enough to tell if someone is exiting the train. Lemon and Tanger-ine both have sharp eyes. If something's moving, even if it's far away, they'll notice.

No one gets off.

They do see a guy two or three cars up standing right in front of the door to car five or six and pointing inside, someone they don't recognise, wear-ing a flat cap, but other than that there's nothing particularly noteworthy.

The train stretches into the distance, and Tangerine realises he can't see all the way to the end after all. 'It's hard to tell what's going on at the front,' he grumbles.

'I doubt the thief is in any of those cars. Everything past car eleven is the Komachi, headed for Akita. We're in the Hayate. The Komachi is connected to our train for now, but there's no passing between the two.'

'Well, that's confusing. Trains can be a pain in the ass.'

'Hey, Tangerine, it's not nice to say something's a pain in the ass.'

Music sounds on the platform, signalling the train's departure. A handful of people get on, but no one gets off. What do we do? asks Lemon. Nothing we can do, says Tangerine, but get back on the train.

No sooner do they get back on than the Shinkansen starts to move, up the gradual slope, making for the light of day. A tinkling version of the departure music plays inside the train as well. Lemon whistles along as he returns to his seat, but his mood darkens as soon as he sees Little Minegishi propped up against the window. It's like suddenly being reminded of an unpleasant task that needs to be taken care of, which makes sense, because this whole thing needs to be taken care of, and it's most certainly unpleasant.

'Well, here we are again.' Lemon sits back down in the aisle seat and crosses his legs. 'What do we do now?' His reliance on the mochi salesman is like an article of faith.

'Chances are the thief is still on the train.'

'Do I have any bullets left?' Lemon pulls his gun out of the shoulder holster concealed under his jacket. He had used a lot of ammo rescuing the rich kid. 'Only got one clip.'

Tangerine checks his piece too. 'Same here. Almost out. I didn't think I'd need any for the train. Should have known better.' Then he reaches into a pocket and pulls out a different gun. 'I do have this,' he says somewhat sheepishly.

'Where'd you get that?'

'One of the guys holding the kid had it. I thought it was cute so I took it.'

'Cute? Guns aren't cute. It's not like they have *Thomas* stickers on them. *Thomas and Friends* is for kids. Cute stuff and gun stuff are totally separate.'

'No, not that kind of cute,' Tangerine says with a smirk. 'It's rigged. It won't shoot bullets. Look.' He turns the muzzle towards Lemon, who jerks his face away.

'Hey, watch it. That's dangerous.'

'No, I'm telling you, this thing won't shoot. It looks like a normal gun but the barrel's stopped up. It's an exploding gun.'

'It shoots explosives?' The thought of explosions reminds Lemon about a movie he saw a while back, *Runaway Train*. The movie didn't particularly interest him, but he liked watching the trains and locomotives in it. That got him excited – the sound of the wheels clacking, the movement of the rods, the muscular plume of smoke billowing from the smokestack, the screech of the rails, and most of all the overwhelming force of the steel train barrelling along. He doesn't remember the plot of *Runaway Train*, but he can still picture the main character standing bravely on top of a train raging through a snowscape. *That guy must have loved trains too.*

'No, no, if you try to shoot it, it explodes.'

'Why would you need something like that?'

'It's a trap. The guy who had it really looked like he wanted me to take it off him. Which I did, but if I'd pulled the trigger, bang, it would've gone off in my hand and he'd have had the last laugh.'

'Good thing you noticed. How come you're so careful?'

'I'm not careful, you're just careless. If there's a button you push it, if there's a string dangling you pull it. You get a mysterious envelope in the mail and you open it and are infected with anthrax.'

'If you say so.' Lemon unfolds his legs and stands up, looks down at Tangerine. 'I'll go and have a look,' he says, gesturing towards the front of the train with his chin, 'see if there's anyone suspicious-looking. Whoever has our bag must be here somewhere. We've got some time before we get to Omiya.'

'Whoever has it might have hidden it somewhere and is sitting there trying to be casual. Anyone who looks funny, check them out.'

'I know.'

'But don't look like you're trying to check them out. We don't want to cause a scene. Nice and easy, understand?'

'You're a pain in my ass.'

'I hear it's not nice to call someone a pain in the ass,' Tangerine shoots back. 'Get moving. If we don't find it by the time the train gets to Omiya, there'll be trouble.'

'Really?'

Tangerine looks exasperated. *How can he forget stuff like this?* 'One of Minegishi's men is waiting for us, remember?'

'Really?' As Lemon says it, the details creep back to him: someone will be at the station to make sure Little Minegishi and the ransom money are both safe and sound on the Shinkansen. 'Oh, right. Trouble.'

NANAO

WELL, FANCY MEETING YOU HERE, the Wolf's glittering eyes seem to say as he grabs Nanao's collar and shoves him back against the opposite door.

The train bursts out of the Ueno subterrane, picking up more speed as it moves. The city scenery goes flying by.

Nanao starts to sputter his protest that he was trying to get off at Ueno, but the Wolf clamps his forearm over Nanao's mouth and pins him against the window. The suitcase is by the other door, unattended. Nanao is worried that the swaying of the train will cause it to roll away.

'Thanks to you I'm missing some of my back teeth.' Saliva bubbles at the corner of the Wolf's mouth. 'Missing my *teeth*!'

I knew it, thinks Nanao. *I knew something like this would happen.* His jaw hurts from the Wolf's arm, but more than anything he's dismayed at the turn of events. *Why can't any of my jobs ever go smoothly?* Now he has to stay on the train until Omiya, and there's a good chance he'll run into the bag's original owner.

And to top it all off, here's the Wolf spewing imprecations and shaking his head back and forth, causing a blizzard of dandruff to rain down from the long hair that spills out under the cap. Revolting.

The train lurches and the Wolf staggers, releasing the pressure on Nanao's jaw. 'I'm sorry, I'm sorry,' Nanao says as quickly as he can, 'let's not get violent, okay?' He holds both hands up, looking like he's doing a miniature cheer. 'We don't want to make a scene on the Shinkansen. Let's just go to Omiya, get off together and discuss it then.' But even as he proposes this, Nanao has the sinking sensation that missing his chance to get off at Ueno will be the start of things going steadily downhill.

'You're in no position to be making demands, Ladybird.'

This makes Nanao mad. His head momentarily buzzes with heat. More than a few people in the business call him Ladybird. He doesn't have anything against that particular insect – he thinks they're cute, tiny and red with a little constellation of black dots on the back, and being as unlucky as he is he especially likes the ladybirds with seven spots because he thinks they might be good luck. But it's all too clear that when other people in the business grinningly call him Ladybird they're making fun of him, likening him to a weak, tiny insect. He can't stand it.

'Back off. What do you want with me anyway?' As Nanao says this the Wolf pulls a knife. Nanao quails slightly. 'Hey, put that thing away. If someone sees you, you'll be in trouble.'

'Shut up. We're going to the toilet. I'm gonna slice you up good. But don't worry, I got a job to do, so I won't have time to do you slow like I want. If I had time I'd make you squeal, I'd make you beg me to let you die, but I'm gonna cut you a break.'

'I don't like toilets on trains.'

'I'm glad to hear it, because your life is gonna end in a train toilet.' The eyes under the brim of the flat cap sparkle malevolently.

'I'm on a job.'

'Me too. A big one, unlike you. Like I said, I don't have a lot of time.'

'You're lying. No one would give you a big job.'

'No, it's true!' The Wolf's nostrils flare in indignation at the blow to his bloated pride. The hand without the knife fishes around in his coat pocket and pulls out a photograph. It's of a girl. 'Know her?'

'Why would I know her?' Nanao grimaces. The Wolf always carries around photos of his victims, one from the client and one that he himself takes when the job's done. He's got a whole collection of before and after shots – before and after beating, before and after death – and he loves to show them off. Something else that Nanao can't stand. 'How come it's always girls? Looking for your Little Red Riding Hood?'

'Guess you don't know who this one is. She's no ordinary girl.'

'Who is she?'

'This one's revenge, man, revenge. A blood vendetta. And I know exactly where she is.'

'Getting back at an old girlfriend who dumped you?'

The Wolf screws up his face. 'Hey, man, don't be such a jerk.'

'Says the guy who beats up women.'

'Think what you want. Anyway, I shouldn't be wasting time talking to you, someone might beat me to it. I'm like Hideyoshi going after Akechi Mitsuhide.' Nanao doesn't see how the historical reference fits the situation. 'I gotta get a move on, so I'll take care of you real quick.' The Wolf presses the blade up to Nanao's throat. 'Scared?'

'Yes.' Nanao doesn't feel the need to bluff.

'Don't do it.'

'*Please* don't do it.'

'Please don't do it, Mr Wolf, sir.'

Nanao knows that if any other passengers show up there'll be a scene. Even if they don't see the knife, they'll see two men pressed up against each other and think something's wrong. *What do I do, what do I do?* The thought spins around his head. The knife is on his neck, he could be cut at any moment. The feel of the blade on his skin almost tickles.

Keeping one eye on the knife, he steals a look at the Wolf's stance. Nanao is a good deal taller, and reaching up to hold out the knife has the Wolf off balance. *He's wide open* – as soon as Nanao thinks this he sidesteps and whips round behind the Wolf, catching him under the arms and behind the head in a full nelson. He grinds his chin into the back of the Wolf's skull. The Wolf is rattled by the sudden turnaround. 'Hey, wait, time out!'

'Keep quiet,' Nanao says into his ear. 'You're going to go to your seat. I don't want any trouble.' Nanao knows how to break necks. When he was first starting out he practised the technique over and over again, like someone might practise juggling a football, until he could do it without thinking. If you can get a hold of someone's head, it's just a matter of accounting for angles and speed – give it a good twist and the neck goes snap. Of course, Nanao has no intention of breaking the Wolf's neck. He doesn't want things to get any more complicated than they already are. It's enough for him to keep a firm grip on the other man's head and threaten, I'll do it, stay still.

'Okay, okay, let me go,' the Wolf stammers.

The train lurches again. It doesn't feel like very much movement, but maybe Nanao doesn't have secure footing from maintaining his hold, or maybe the Wolf's shoes have bad traction – whatever the reason, the two topple over.

The next thing Nanao knows his butt is on the floor, his face red from embarrassment at having fallen. Then he realises he still has a tight grip on the Wolf's head, holding him by a fistful of hair. The Wolf is also down on the ground. Nanao worries for a moment that the Wolf might have stabbed himself in the fall, but a glance at the knife still clutched in the man's hand shows no blood on the blade. He exhales with relief.

'Get up.' Nanao untangles his fingers from the Wolf's hair and gives him a sharp push on the back. The Wolf's head lolls crazily, like a baby that can't yet hold its own head up.

No. Nanao blinks several times. He scuttles around in front of the Wolf. The facial expression doesn't look right at all – eyes bugged, mouth hanging open. And of course there's the sickening angle of the neck.

'No no no.' But saying this doesn't change anything. He had fallen with his arm around the Wolf's head, and the momentum had broken the neck clean in two.

Nanao's phone vibrates. He answers without bothering to check the caller ID. Only one person ever calls him.

'I really think there's no such thing as a simple job,' he says while getting to his feet. He hauls the Wolf's body up as well, leans it up against himself until it's balanced – trickier than he would have thought. Like handling a giant puppet.

'Why haven't you called me? What's with you?' Maria sounds angry. 'Where are you? You got off at Ueno, right? You have the bag?'

'I'm still on the Shinkansen. I've got the bag.' He tries to keep his voice as casual as he can. His eyes are on the suitcase, up against the opposite door. 'I didn't get off at Ueno.'

'Why not?' Her tone sharpens. 'What happened?' Then she lowers her voice, apparently doing her best to keep her cool. 'Getting on a train at Tokyo and getting off at Ueno, was that too tough a job for you? What exactly *can* you do? Can you work a cash register? No, probably not, it's a pretty complicated job, lots of little variations and real-time adjustments. I guess you can handle a job that only involves getting on a train at Tokyo Station. You can get on fine, it's getting off that's tough for you, is that it? From now on I'll bring you easy jobs like that.'

Nanao tamps down the urge to smash his phone on the ground. 'I tried to get off at Ueno. The door was open, I had only one step to go, but there he was, he forced his way onto the train. He was on the platform, standing right in front of my door.' He looks down at the Wolf, leaned up against him. 'Now he's here with me.'

'Who the hell are you talking about? The God of the Shinkansen? Did he stand in front of you and say Thou shalt not disembark?'

Nanao ignores the jibe. 'The Wolf,' he says quietly. 'You know, the creep who only takes jobs hurting girls and animals.'

'Oh, the *Wolf.*' Maria's voice changes; she finally sounds concerned. But probably not about whether Nanao is okay, no, she's worried about the job. 'He must have been thrilled. He's got a score to settle with you.'

'He was so happy he threw his arms around me.'

Maria falls silent. She must be trying to process the situation. Nanao wedges the phone between his shoulder and ear as he holds up the Wolf, thinking of where he can put the body. *The toilet, like where he wanted to put me?* But he immediately decides against it. It would be easy to stash a corpse in the bathroom, but he knows he would be paranoid about whether or not it had been discovered, and would keep getting up from his seat to check, which would probably draw unnecessary attention.

'So are you going to tell me what happened?'

'Well, at the moment I'm trying to find a place to hide the Wolf's body.'

More silence from the other end of the line. Then, 'But what *happened?* The Wolf got on and hugged you. And now he's dead. What happened in between?'

'Barely anything. Basically, he pulled a knife on me and had it at my throat.'

'Why?'

'Like you said, he's not a big fan of mine. Then I got around him and put him in a hold, threatened to break his neck. But I was just threatening, okay? I didn't mean to do it. Then the train swerved.'

'The train will do that. So that's how it went down.'

'I just can't believe that idiot showed up at that exact moment.' Nanao lets his frustration creep into his voice.

'Don't speak ill of the dead,' she says earnestly. 'You didn't need to kill him, you know.'

'I didn't mean to kill him! He slipped, we fell, his neck broke. It wasn't a mistake, it was an act of God.'

'I don't like men who make excuses.'

'Don't speak ill of the living,' he jokes, but she clearly isn't in the mood. 'Anyway, I'm holding up the Wolf now, and I'm at a complete loss. You know, as to what to do with his body.'

'If you've got your arms around him you might as well just stay there in the gangway and make it look like you're kissing.' She sounds a bit desperate.

'Two men embracing on the train, all the way to Omiya. Doesn't sound like a realistic plan.'

'If you want a realistic plan, how's this: find a seat and put him there.

Just be careful nobody notices you doing it. You could put him in your seat, or find his ticket and put him in his seat.'

Nanao nods. It sounds sensible. 'Thanks. I'll give it a shot.'

He notices the Wolf's mobile phone peeking out of the chest pocket of the cheap-looking jacket and grabs it, thinking it might come in handy. He puts it in his cargo pants pocket.

'Don't forget the suitcase,' Maria adds.

'Good thing you reminded me, I was about to.'

Maria sighs audibly. 'Just take care of it. I'm going to sleep.'

'It's the middle of the day.'

'I was up all night watching movies. Every single episode of *Star Wars*.'

'I'll call you later.'

KIMURA

KIMURA TWISTS AND FLEXES HIS wrists and ankles, hoping to find some way to squirm out of the heavy straps and duct tape that bind him, but they show no signs of loosening.

'There's a trick to it, Yuichi.' A sudden welling up of memory from his childhood. Someone talking to him. A scene he hadn't pictured for years, maybe not even once since it first happened, his house from when he was growing up, a man in his twenties with arms and legs tied up. His dad was laughing, Let's see you try to escape, Shigeru. His mum standing nearby, she was laughing heartily too, and a kindergarten-age Kimura joined in. Shigeru was a former co-worker of his father's who still came by to visit now and again. He seemed honest and sincere, and there was something dashing about him, like a professional athlete. Shigeru regarded Kimura's father as something of a mentor, and he doted on little Kimura.

'You know your dad was pretty scary on the job, Yuichi. Everyone called him the Condor.' Kimura's father and his younger friend actually shared the first name Shigeru, which was how they started to become close.

Kimura remembered that when his father and Shigeru drank together, the younger man would often complain about his job. 'It's a hustle, you know? I'm thinking of looking for something else.' Hearing that made Kimura realise that adults have problems too, that they aren't always as strong as they seem. At some point they lost touch with Shigeru. What Kimura is remembering now is the time Shigeru imitated an escape artist they were watching on TV. 'I can do that,' he said after seeing the person wriggle out of being tied up.

Kimura's eyes had drifted back to the television, and in the moments he wasn't looking Shigeru managed to untie the rope.

How did he do it? How can I do it now?

He digs at the mountain of memory, hoping to excavate some crucial bit of information, some clue as to how Shigeru had escaped, but finds nothing.

'I'll be right back, Mr Kimura. I'm just going to the toilet.' The Prince stands and steps into the aisle. Kimura looks at him in his blazer, clearly a kid from an upper-class family, raised with every opportunity. *I can't believe I'm taking orders from this brat.* 'Oh, should I get you a drink?' the Prince asks snidely. 'A little can of sake?' Having launched this barb, he walks off towards the back of the train. It occurs to Kimura that there's a closer bathroom in the other direction, but he doesn't say anything.

No doubt about it, rich kid, everything handed to him. Rich schoolkid with a rotten soul. He thinks back to the first time he met the Prince, a few months ago.

He returned home from working the night shift at the hospital in Kurai-cho that morning as towering cumulonimbus clouds filled up the sky. When he got home, Wataru was complaining of a stomach ache, so Kimura took him straight to the paediatrician. Normally he would drop him off at nursery school and get into bed, but he had no chance that day and his head was heavy with fatigue. The doctor's office was unexpectedly crowded. Of course he couldn't have a drink in the waiting room. He noticed his hands were trembling.

All the kids in the waiting room looked to him to have lighter symptoms than Wataru. He grew increasingly angry as he stared at them in their face masks – *damn fakers, they should let the kids who are actually suffering go first.* He glared at the other parents one by one. Each time the nurse came and went his eyes lingered on her ass.

It turned out that Wataru's symptoms were light as well. Just before they were called, he turned and whispered sheepishly, 'Daddy, I think I feel better.' But after waiting all that time Kimura didn't want to go home without seeing the doctor, so he made Wataru pretend his stomach still hurt, got some medicine from the doctor and left the clinic.

When they were outside, Wataru asked uncertainly, 'Daddy, were you drinking?' Once Kimura knew that his son was feeling better he had felt a wash of relief and taken a nip from his flask. Wataru must have seen him.

He had taken his flask from his pocket, turned to face the wall so the other people waiting for the doctor wouldn't see and had a tiny swig. He kept the flask filled with cheap brandy and carried it with him when he was at work so he could have a sip when he needed to. He told himself that it was the same as someone with allergies carrying nasal spray. If he didn't have alcohol, his concentration would falter and he wouldn't be much use as a security guard. His hands would shake, he might fumble his torch, and that wouldn't be good. Having a drink ready to go was like keeping his medicine handy, medicine for his chronic ailment. He convinced himself that he needed alcohol to do his job.

'Wataru, did you know that brandy is distilled spirits, and distillation goes all the way back to Mesopotamia?'

Of course Wataru didn't know what Mesopotamia was. All he knew was his father was making excuses again, but it was a fun word to try to say, Meso-po, Meso-pota-pota.

'In French they call distilled spirits eau de vie. Know what that means? It means water of life. Isn't that cool, the water of life!' Saying it made him feel better. *That's right – every sip is a lifesaver.*

'But the doctor was surprised because you smelled like drinking, Daddy.'

'He had a face mask on.'

'But even with a mask he could smell it.'

'It's the water of life, who cares if it smells? The doctor knows that,' Kimura muttered.

As they were walking through the shopping arcade on the way home, Wataru said, 'Daddy, I gotta pee.' They went into the nearest building, full of clothing stores popular with teenagers, to look for a toilet. There weren't any on the ground floor, and Kimura grumbled a stream of curses as they took the lift to the first floor and had to walk past seemingly endless shops to get to the bathrooms at the back of the building.

'You can go by yourself, right, buddy? I'll wait right here.' He gave Wataru a little slap on the butt, then settled down on a bench near the bathrooms. The accessory shop right opposite had a salesgirl with big breasts and a low-cut shirt, and he intended to sit there and take in the view.

'Yeah, I can go by myself,' Wataru declared proudly, and went in.

He came back out after what seemed like just a moment. Kimura looked down at his own hands and realised that he was holding the flask. *When did I take it out? Don't remember, but the cap's still on, so I can't have had any.* It was like he was piecing together someone else's actions.

'Well, that was quick. Did you go?'

'I did go. It was full!'

'Full? Full of pee?'

'No, there were lots of big boys.'

Kimura stood up and stepped towards the bathroom. 'Lemme see.'

'They were kind of scary,' Wataru said, grabbing Kimura's hand. 'Let's go home.'

Kimura shook him off. If it was a bunch of teenage boys, they were probably hanging out smoking cigarettes or horsing around, or else planning some shakedown or shoplifting, and he thought he might like to go in and have a little fun with them. He was feeling grouchy from lack of sleep and lack of drink and he wanted to blow off some steam. You wait here, he told Wataru, and left him by the bench.

Inside the men's he found five kids in school uniform, young-looking.

It was spacious, with urinals on two walls and four cubicles on the third. The kids were huddled by the cubicles. They glanced up when Kimura came in but almost immediately turned back to each other and continued their little conference. Kimura casually stepped up to the closest urinal to them and began to piss. He tried to make out what they were saying. Probably some meaningless discussion, planning some stupid prank. *Let's mess with 'em a little.* He had retired from the rough stuff he used to do for a living, but that didn't mean he'd gone off causing trouble.

'What are we gonna do?' The kid sounded angry. 'Somebody's gotta explain it to the Prince.'

'Yeah, but who? You were the one who pussied out and ran.'

'No way. I was ready to do it. It was Takuya who pussied out. He said his stomach hurt.'

'My stomach *did* hurt.'

'Tell it to the Prince. Oh, I had a tummyache, I couldn't do what you told us to!'

'No way. I could barely take the shock last time. Any stronger I bet I'd die.'

Then they all fell silent, which Kimura didn't fail to notice.

Kimura didn't know the particulars of what they were talking about, but he could guess at the basic contour of it.

These kids had a leader. Maybe a classmate, maybe a senior, could even be an adult, but someone was giving them orders. This person they were calling the Prince. Stupid name. So they didn't do what his highness the Prince ordered them to. They let him down. The Prince was probably angry. And now these kids were in the men's room trying to figure out what to tell him, who would take the fall. That seemed to be the size of it. *The peasants didn't collect enough taxes to satisfy their precious Prince,* he thought derisively. Meanwhile, his stream of piss just wouldn't stop.

But there was one thing he couldn't figure out: the one kid mentioned a shock. Was he talking about an electric shock? Kimura pictured the electric chairs they use for executions in America. Somehow he didn't think that was what the kid was talking about. But then he had said that if it was any stronger he would have died, and this stuck with Kimura.

Teenagers often talk about dying or killing each other or something killing them, without any of the weight that the words should hold, but this felt different. This felt like the kid was actually aware of the possibility of his own death.

He finally finished peeing. Pulling up his zip, he stepped over to the boys. 'What are you kids doing hanging out in a filthy place like this? You're blocking the way. So – who's gonna be the one to apologise to his highness the Prince?'

He reached out and wiped his unwashed hand on the shoulder of the nearest kid, the smallest one.

They quickly changed formation from a huddle to a line facing Kimura. They had the same uniform on, though they all looked different. One was tall and pimply, one had a buzz cut, one was fat and stupid-looking. They tried to be menacing, but to Kimura they just looked like little kids.

'You guys aren't gonna figure out anything by talking about it in here. Shouldn't you just go and apologise to your Prince?' Kimura clapped his hands once, making all the kids jump.

'None of your business.'

'Get outta here, old man.'

Kimura couldn't help but smile at them trying to look mean when they were still so obviously innocent kids. 'You guys practise those tough faces in the mirror? I mean, I did, when I was your age. Scrunch in your eyebrows all mean? The fuck *you* looking at? Like that. It takes practice. But I'll tell you, it's not worth your time. Once you're done puberty and you look back on it, you'll laugh. Better off looking for porn online.'

'This guy stinks of booze,' said the one with the buzz cut. He was pretty well built, but the exaggerated gesture of pinching his nose shut made him look like a little boy.

'So what were you guys trying to figure out, anyway? Go ahead, you can tell me. Let the old man help with your problems. What did your Prince want you to do?'

The kids seemed confused. After a moment the one on the end asked, 'How'd you know about that?'

'I overheard your little conference when I was pissing.' Kimura looked at each of the schoolkids. 'How about it, you want my advice? I'm happy to help. Tell the old man all about the Prince.'

The kids were silent. They exchanged glances with each other, like they were having a silent meeting.

Then Kimura bellowed, 'Ha, did you really think I'd listen to your problems? I was just messing around. Why would I give advice to a bunch of brats like you? Anyway, I'm sure he just wanted you to sneak into a sex shop or beat someone up.'

But the kids didn't relax at all, they actually looked even more serious. Kimura raised his eyebrows. *Why are they so stressed out?* He stepped over to the sink and washed his hands. He saw in the mirror the boys re-form their huddle and resume their discussion, more agitated than ever.

'Sorry I made fun of you guys. Later.' He wiped his hands on one of their jackets, a different one from the first one he did it to, but they barely seemed to notice.

Kimura emerged from the toilets. 'Okay, Wataru, Daddy's back.' But Wataru was gone. He cocked his head. *Where the hell . . .?* He looked down the walkway between the shops, but didn't see his son anywhere.

He half ran over to the big-breasted salesgirl. 'Hey!' She tossed her highlighted hair as she looked up at him with her big eyes, a distasteful look on her face, though he couldn't tell if it was from the brusque way he addressed her or because he smelled of booze. 'You seen a little boy, about this tall?' He held his hand at hip level.

'Oh,' she said, a bit dubiously, 'I saw him head that way,' and pointed towards the corridor out the back of the store.

'Why would he go back there?'

'I have no idea. But he was with another kid.'

'What do you mean, another kid?' Kimura's voice had an edge. 'Another kid in kindergarten?'

'I thought maybe it was his older brother. Good-looking kid, kind of fancy.'

'Fancy? Who was it?'

'How should I know?'

Kimura ran off without saying thank you. Down the corridor, round a corner, looking around wildly. *Wataru, where'd you go, where are you?* He pictured his ex-wife's contemptuous look when she had asked him if he could really take care of a child. Anxiety turned to a rush of sweat, his pulse started to hammer.

When he finally found Wataru by the escalators he was so overcome with relief that he almost sank to his knees. His son was holding hands with a boy in a school uniform.

Kimura barked at them and rushed over, wrenching Wataru's hand away. Despite the violence of it the boy in the uniform seemed unfazed. He looked placidly at Kimura. 'Aha, is this your daddy?'

The kid was about five foot four, on the skinny side, with fine hair that was longish but didn't seem to have any weight to it. His eyes were large and clear, shining like a cat's eyes in the dark. *Looks almost like a girl,* Kimura thought. He felt the thrill of being stared at by an attractive woman and laughed at himself uncomfortably.

'What the hell do you think you're doing?' Kimura squeezed Wataru's hand and pulled him over to his side. He had said it to the kid in the uniform, but Wataru seemed to think his father was yelling at him.

'He said that my daddy was over here,' the little boy said timorously.

'How many times have I told you not to talk to strangers?' Kimura's voice was forceful, but as soon as he said it he thought about all the times his parents, Wataru's grandparents, had scolded him specifically for not telling the boy things like that. He turned to look fiercely at the schoolboy with his well-proportioned face. 'Who are you?'

'I'm a student at Kanoyama School.' The kid was calm and composed, as if he was just doing what his teachers had told him to. 'My friends are hanging out in the men's room, and I thought they might scare this little boy, so I figured I would take him a little way away. Then he said he didn't know where his father was, so I was taking him to the information desk.'

'I was in the men's too. Wataru knew that. Don't try to feed me that load of crap.' Wataru seemed certain his father was angry with him and he just cowered and trembled. 'Well, that's odd, he didn't tell me he knew where you were.' The kid looked completely unruffled. 'Maybe he thought the way I was talking was too scary he couldn't speak up. I was worried about him so maybe I spoke a little too roughly.'

Kimura didn't like it. More than the fact that this kid had walked off with Wataru, it bothered him how calm the boy was, that he didn't seem the least bit affected by Kimura's aggressive questioning. It wasn't that the kid was rude or a smart-ass, no, there was something more unsettling about him, something sly and cunning.

As he was about to leave with his son, Kimura said, 'Those kids in the toilets kept talking about a Prince. They were having some kind of secret meeting.'

'Oh, that's me,' the kid said lightly. 'My last name is Oji, spelled with the Chinese characters for prince. Weird name, huh? Lots of people make fun of me for it. Satoshi Oji, but they call me Prince Satoshi, or just the Prince. Um, just so you know, my friends and I might have been hanging out in the loos, but we weren't smoking or anything.' Goody two-shoes to the hilt. He walked off towards the toilets.

The Prince re-enters the train car and sits back down, shaking Kimura from his recollection.

Hands and feet still tied, Kimura brings up the episode. 'What were you gonna do with Wataru that time we first met?'

'I wanted to check something,' the Prince answers sweetly. 'I was just listening in on my classmates in the men's room.'

'Listening in? You mean you bugged the toilets?'

'No, one of my friends hid a device in his coat pocket.'

'You had a spy?' It feels a little childish to say. 'Worried that people are trashing you?'

'Not quite. I don't mind if people talk about me. But if they find out that they were being listened to, or if they're worried about who's a spy, it'll mess with them. They'll stop trusting each other. That's good for me.'

'What's any of this have to do with anything?'

'Like I said, all I was doing was listening in on their conversation. I was planning to let them know later that there was a spy, which would make them all paranoid. And actually that's exactly what eventually happened. But when I was there listening I spotted your boy looking at me. He seemed interested in me, so I thought I would play with him a little.'

'He's six years old. I can't imagine he had anything particular in mind when he was looking at you.'

'I know. But there he was, and I wanted to play with him. I wanted to see what it would do to a little kid.'

'What what would do?'

'An electric shock. I wanted to see how a kid that age would react to high voltage.' The Prince points to his backpack and the taser inside. 'I thought I would test it out, but you came along, Mr Kimura, and ruined everything.'

FRUIT

LEMON BEGINS HIS SEARCH TOWARDS the front of the train, heading first to car number four. He tries to remember what the stolen suitcase looks like.

Back when he was in junior school his teacher had told his grandparents that he only ever remembered things he was interested in. He can recall exactly which gadgets Doraemon used in every issue of the comic, the teacher had said in frustration, but he doesn't know the name of the school's principal. Lemon couldn't understand what the teacher was so upset about. Between the principal's name and Doraemon's gadgets, it was blindingly obvious which was more important.

The suitcase must have been around a half metre tall and a little less across. It had a handle. It had wheels. It was black, made of some tough material that was cold to the touch. It also had a lock with a four-digit code, but Lemon and Tangerine didn't know the combination. 'If we don't know the combo, how are we supposed to do the trade with the kidnappers?' Lemon had been unable to resist asking Minegishi's man when they got the bag. 'We can't show them we actually have the money, so how do you expect us to get the job done?'

It was Tangerine who answered, sensible as usual. 'It's not the bad guys they're worried about, it's us. They think we might make off with the cash.'

'Well, what the fuck? If they don't trust us why should we even work for these assholes?'

'Don't worry about it. If you did know the combination, wouldn't you want to open it?'

Later Tangerine had suggested they mark the case somehow. He pulled a kid's sticker out of his pocket and stuck it near the lock.

That's right, the bag had Tangerine's sticker on it.

In front of the entrance to car four he finds the young woman with the snack trolley.

She seems to be checking the inventory, punching something into a little hand-held device.

'Hey, you seen somebody with a black suitcase, about this big?'

'Huh?' She looks startled, 'A suitcase?' The blue apron over her uniform makes her look domestic.

'Yeah, a suitcase, like a bag for carrying stuff, you know? A black bag. I had it on the luggage rack but it's gone.'

'I'm sorry, I really couldn't say.' She seems unsettled by his gaze and moves behind the cart so it's between them.

'Really couldn't say, huh? Guess not.' Lemon moves on, entering car four. The gentle hiss of the door swiftly sliding open reminds him of the inside of a spacecraft he saw in a movie once.

There aren't many passengers. He moves up the aisle, checking left and right under the seats and on the overhead racks. There aren't many bags either, which makes it easy enough for him to see that the black one he's looking for isn't there. But he does spot a paper bag that catches his eye on the right-hand overhead rack. A paper bag of considerable size, on the rack halfway up the car. He can't see inside, but he wonders if maybe someone put his suitcase in this bag. Once the thought enters his head he acts without any hesitation, steps up to the row where the bag is. A man sits in the window seat, and the other two seats in the row are empty.

At first glance Lemon figures the man is a little bit older than himself, maybe around thirty. He's reading a book. Could be a postgrad student, though he's wearing a suit.

Lemon sits down in the aisle seat, then turns to the man. 'Yo,' he says, putting his hand on the armrest next to the man and leaning towards him. 'That bag up there –' he points at the luggage rack – 'what's that all about?'

It seems to take a moment for the man to realise that someone is talking to him. He finally turns to look at Lemon, then up at the rack. 'Ah, that's just a paper bag.'

'Yeah, I know it's a paper bag. What's in it?'

'Sorry?'

'My suitcase is missing. I know it's still somewhere on this train so I'm looking around for it.'

The man processes this for a second. 'I hope you find it.' Then he appears to realise what Lemon is getting at. 'Oh, your suitcase isn't in my bag. I didn't take it. My bag's full of sweets.'

'Pretty big bag. You got big sweets?'

'No, just a lot of them.'

The man looks like he'd be a buttoned-up, timid individual, but he seems remarkably unperturbed.

'Well, let's see 'em.' Lemon half stands and reaches up to the rack for the bag. The man doesn't show any signs of anger or concern. He just turns back to his book. There even seems to be the glimmer of a placid smile on his face. His composure is unsettling to Lemon.

'Once you check inside, I'd appreciate it if you put the bag back where it was.' Lemon brings the bag down to the seat and opens it. Inside are a whole lot of sweets, probably purchased at Tokyo Station. 'These all gifts for people or what? You sure bought enough.'

'It was hard to decide so I got a lot of different ones.'

'Nobody cares that much what you bring them.'

'Sorry I can't be of any more help.' The man smiles gently. 'Will you put the bag back now?'

Lemon stands and tosses the bag carelessly back onto the rack. Then he sits down again, this time in the middle seat right next to the man. He rocks back and forth in agitation. 'You sure you don't know where my suitcase is?'

The man looks at Lemon but says nothing.

'You know, usually most people would get either scared or pissed off from someone showing up suddenly and going through their bags. But you're just sitting there all calm. It's like you were expecting me. You're like a criminal with an alibi who doesn't get nervous when the cops are questioning him. Oh no, detective, I was at so-and-so bar at that time. Same thing. You knew exactly what to say when I came. Right?'

'Don't be absurd.' Now the man's eyes narrow into a piercing gaze. At that moment Lemon notices what the man is reading: *Hotel Buffets,* with photos of food underneath. 'That's like in a witch trial when they said that the woman denying she was a witch was proof she was a witch. You think there's something suspicious about me because I'm not afraid of you?' He closes his book. 'I certainly was surprised. You sit down next to me out of nowhere and demand to look inside my bag. I was so surprised I didn't know how to react.'

Sure don't look surprised, Lemon thinks, and then says as much. 'What do you do, anyway?'

'I'm an instructor at an exam-preparation school. A small one.'

'A teacher, huh? I never got along with teachers. But also, every teacher I ever had was afraid of me. None of them were as relaxed as you. What, are you used to dealing with juvenile delinquents or something?'

'Do you want me to be afraid of you?'

'I mean, no, not really.'

'I'm just trying to be a normal human being. It's not like I'm trying specifically not to be afraid.' The man sounds slightly bewildered. 'But if I'm not afraid,' he continues, 'it might be because of some rough stuff I got wrapped up in some time ago. Ever since then I've felt a little reckless. Maybe I'm desensitised.'

Rough stuff? Lemon furrows his brow. 'One of your bad students beat you up?'

The man narrows his eyes again, his face creasing, followed by a broad smile. It makes him look like a little boy. 'My wife died, I met some scary people, a lot happened. But hey,' he says, his voice suddenly back to how it sounded before, 'crying about it won't do any good. I'm just trying to live like I'm alive.'

'Live like you're alive? What's that supposed to mean? How could you live any other way?'

'Actually, most people live pretty aimlessly, wouldn't you say? Sure, they talk and have fun, but there's got to be something more, I don't know –'

'What, like howling at the moon?'

The man beams at this, nods vigorously. 'Exactly. Howling at the moon would definitely make you feel alive. And eating lots of good food.' He opens the book and shows Lemon a photo spread of a hotel buffet.

Lemon doesn't know what to say, and realises that he doesn't have time to sit here talking to this man. He stands up and steps into the aisle. 'You know, Teach, you remind me of Edward.'

'Who's Edward?'

'One of Thomas the Tank Engine's friends. Engine number two.' Lemon launches automatically into the character description he'd memorised. 'A very friendly engine, kind to everyone. He once helped push Gordon up a hill and another time saved Trevor from almost being scrapped. Everyone on the Island of Sodor knows they can count on Edward.'

'Wow. Did you learn all that by heart?'

'If Thomas was on the college entrance exams, I'd have got into Tokyo U.' With that Lemon walks on, exiting car number four.

He checks the luggage rack in the gangway.

Nothing.

In the middle of car six he meets the kid.

He didn't even see him, the kid just seemed to show up out of nowhere, and suddenly they were standing facing each other in the aisle. Looks like he's thirteen or fourteen, one of these pretty-looking kids you see nowadays. Clear eyes, well-proportioned nose – like a little doll that you can't quite tell if it's supposed to be a boy or a girl.

'Whaddayou want?' Lemon isn't sure of how he should act to make this kid think he's tough. The kid feels too wholesome, reminds him of Percy the green engine.

'Are you looking for something? I saw you peeking in the bathroom.'

The kid gives off a vibe like he's a grade-A student, which makes Lemon feel uncomfortable. He's never been able to get along with eggheads. 'A suitcase. Black, about this big. You seen it? Probably not, I guess?'

'Oh, actually, I did.'

Lemon gets right in the kid's face. 'Oh yeah? You saw it?'

The kid leans back a little, but he isn't scared. 'I saw someone carrying a bag that size,' he says, miming the dimensions with his hands. 'A black bag.' He pokes his finger towards the front of the train, which picks up speed just at that moment, causing Lemon to stagger slightly.

'What'd he look like?'

'Um,' the kid says, touching his fingers to his chin and cocking his head, looking upward and making a show of trying to remember. The performance looks like something a teenage girl might do. 'Um, let's see, he wore dark-coloured trousers and had a denim jacket on.'

'A jean jacket, huh? How old?'

'Late twenties or early thirties, I'd say. Oh, and he had black glasses on. Kind of handsome.'

'Thanks for the tip.'

The kid waves off the thanks, no, it was nothing, and flashes a smile so dazzling it lights up the whole car.

Lemon smiles too, wryly. 'You grinning like that because you've got a heart of pure gold or because you're making fun of a grown-up?'

'Neither one,' the kid answers without hesitation. 'It's just the way I smile.'

'You trying to get the other kids on the Shinkansen to smile like you, innocent and sparkly-eyed?'

'Do you like the Shinkansen, sir?'

'Who doesn't like the Shinkansen? I mean I liked the 500 series best. But I think the Hayate's great too. But if you wanna know what train I like best, it's the Duke of Boxford's personal train.'

The kid makes a puzzled face.

'What, you don't know Spencer? Don't you watch *Thomas and Friends*?'

'I think I used to when I was little.'

Lemon snorts. 'You're still little, dammit. Got a face like Percy.' Then he starts to make his way towards the next car to look for the person the kid described but stops when he sees the digital ticker on the wall above the cabin door. The letters on the display flow to the left, spelling out 'Top Stories'. Distracted, Lemon pauses to watch. The first item tells him that a snake was stolen from a Tokyo pet shop. Apparently a rare breed of snake. There was no known motive, but Lemon mutters to himself that someone was probably looking to sell the snake. Then comes the next story:

'Thirteen dead in the Fujisawa Kongocho killing. Security cameras at the scene had been sabotaged.'

Was it thirteen? The thought doesn't trigger any particular feelings one way or the other. It had been dark in the underground room, and he had shot down one armed man after another, so he wasn't clear on the numbers. All that spraying blood and torn flesh, but seeing it written out like that makes it seem so dull.

'Rough stuff,' says the kid. He's standing behind Lemon, apparently also reading the news. 'Thirteen people.'

'I did at least six, probably more. Tangerine did the rest. It's more than a couple, but it's not that much.'

'What?'

Lemon immediately regrets thinking out loud. He tries to change the subject. 'Hey, know what that thing's called? Officially? A traveller information broadcast device. Did you know that?'

'Sorry?'

'That thing with the news on it.'

'Oh.' The kid nods. 'Yeah, I wonder where they get the news from.'

Lemon feels himself smile. 'I shall tell you,' he says with a flare of the nostrils. 'There are two kinds of information. One is whatever they write in the conductor's cabin, and the other comes from the central depot in Tokyo. The kind from inside the train is like, you know, "We will soon be passing by so-and-so station," that kind of thing. Everything else, advertisements, news, all that, that gets beamed in from the central depot. Like when there's an accident somewhere and it messes with the timetables? That kind of real-time info gets typed up back in Tokyo and shows up on our train. And the news too. News from the six major newspapers comes in rotation, which is pretty cool. And that's not all –'

'Um, I think we're in the way,' says the kid firmly, bringing Lemon back to himself. The snack trolley is right behind them. The attendant recoils when she sees Lemon, as if alarmed that this man keeps showing up everywhere she goes.

'But I had lots of other cool stuff to tell you.'

'Cool stuff.' It's clear that the kid has doubts.

'You didn't think it was cool? About the traveller information broadcast device? It didn't move you?' Lemon is utterly sincere. 'Well, anyway, thanks for the help. If I find my suitcase it'll be because of you. Next time I see you I'll buy you some sweets.'

NANAO

A PASSENGER IS WALKING IN Nanao's direction, a smallish kid in a blazer. Nanao closes his flip phone and puts it away in the rear pocket of his cargo pants, working all the while on calming himself down. He's propping the Wolf's body up against the window: if he doesn't support it properly the head will flop around unsettlingly.

'Is everything all right?' The kid stops next to Nanao to ask. His teachers at school must have taught him to check in with people who look like they might be having trouble. Which is the last thing Nanao needs.

'Oh, yeah, everything's fine, he just had a bit too much to drink and his head was spinning.' Nanao makes sure not to speak too quickly. He nudges the body slightly. 'Hey, wake up. You're scaring the children.'

'Do you want some help getting him back to his seat?'

'No, no, it's fine. Having a great time.' *Who's having a great time? Me? Hugging a corpse and taking in the scenery?*

'Um, looks like someone dropped something.' The kid looks down.

It's a Shinkansen ticket. Probably the Wolf's, which fell on the floor.

'Sorry, could you get that for me?' Nanao asks because it would be tough for him to lean down while holding up the body and also because he has the sense it would be good to satisfy this kid's apparent urge to be kind to people.

The kid scoops the ticket right up.

'Thanks a lot,' Nanao says with a head bob.

'Alcohol sure is scary. The man I'm travelling with today can't stop drinking either. He causes all kinds of trouble,' the kid says cheerily. 'See you later,' and he turns towards the entrance to car six. But then he notices the lone suitcase standing by the opposite door. 'Is this yours too, sir?'

What school does this kid go to anyway? Nanao wants him gone as soon as possible, but the kid seems determined to stick around and help as much as he can. *Where do they teach kids to be so helpful?* Even as Nanao's frustration grows he thinks that if the day ever comes where he has children of his own he'd try to send them to this kid's school. But at the moment it's just more bad luck. In this particular situation, a chance encounter with a kid brimming with charity and benevolence is an unfortunate turn of events.

'Yes, it's mine, but you can just leave it there. I'll get it later.' He feels his tone getting a shade harder and tries to regulate it.

'But if you leave it there someone might take it.' The kid's persistent. 'If you leave yourself open people will walk all over you.'

'Well, that's unexpected.' Nanao speaks his thought out loud. 'And here I was thinking your school taught you to have faith in people. The doctrine of inherent human goodness.'

'Why would you think that?' The smiling kid seems familiar with the doctrine of inherent human goodness, which makes Nanao feel slightly embarrassed. *I only just learned about the idea, from Maria.*

'It's hard to say why, exactly.' *Because it seemed like your school might be full of well-behaved students, I guess.*

'I don't believe that people are born inherently good or bad.'

'They just become one or the other, is that it?'

'No, I think good and bad depend on your point of view.'

This is some kid. Nanao is taken aback. *Do teenagers really talk this way?*

The kid offers again to help with the suitcase.

'It's all right, really.' If the kid keeps pressing, Nanao might lose his temper. 'I'll take care of it.'

'Um, what's inside it?'

'I'm not actually sure.' An honest answer in a careless moment, but the kid laughs, apparently thinking it's a joke. His teeth gleam in a perfect white row.

The kid seems to want to say something else, but after a moment gives a bouncy goodbye and heads into car number six.

With a rush of relief, Nanao hugs the Wolf's body to himself and steps over to the suitcase. He has to figure out what to do with the body first and then the bag, and fast. The bag's owner in car three may not yet have realised that it's missing, but if they do they're sure to search the train. Nanao knows that if he's carrying the bag around in the open chances are he'll be found out.

With one arm around the corpse and the other hand gripping the suitcase handle, he looks left and right, at a loss. First the body, which should probably go in a seat. His eyes fall on the trash receptacle in the wall. There's a hole for bottles and cans, a narrow slot for magazines and paper waste, and a large flap for the rest.

Then he notices a small protrusion on the wall, right next to the magazine slot. It looks like a keyhole, but there's no opening, just a little circular bump. Before he knows what he's doing he reaches out and pushes it. A small metal fitting pops out with a click. *What do we have here?*

He twists it.

What he thought was a wall is actually a panel that now swings open. There's a large space inside, like a locker. A shelf divides the space into two levels. The bottom part has a heavy-duty plastic bag hanging there, where the trash collects when people deposit it. Opening the panel like this must be how the cleaning staff collects the trash.

But of greatest interest to Nanao is the fact that the top shelf is empty. Without stopping to think he tightens his hold on the body and hoists the bag up one-handed, using muscle and momentum to swing it crashing onto the shelf. In the next instant he closes the panel.

Nanao feels his worried mind ease ever so slightly at unexpectedly finding a hiding place. Then, turning his thoughts back to the body in his arms, he checks the ticket that the kid picked up for him. Car six, row one. That is, the closest row in the closest car to him. Perfect for putting the body down without raising suspicion.

It's happening. Things are going my way. And then he thinks: *But are they really?*

Two lucky breaks for a guy usually mired in bad luck – one, finding the trash box panel to hide the bag, and two, the Wolf's seat being so close. One part of him is ringing alarm bells, shrieking that the other shoe's going to drop any minute, and another part of him is lamenting that these two windfalls are as far as his luck will go.

The scenery flies by out the window. Cranes on the roofs of buildings under construction, rows of linked apartment buildings, jet contrails in the sky, all disappearing at a uniform speed.

He adjusts the body against his own. Carrying a grown man over his shoulders is sure to attract attention, so he stands the Wolf up next to him, shoulder to shoulder like they're practising for a three-legged race. He takes a few awkward steps. This doesn't look very natural either, but there's no other way he can think of.

The door to car six slides open. Nanao enters and spills himself and the body into the two-seater directly to his left, wanting to get down and out of sight. He sets the Wolf up by the window and settles into the aisle seat. Luckily, there's no one in the seats across the aisle either.

He allows himself a sigh of relief. Then the Wolf sways and comes lurching towards him. He hastily pushes the body back up against the window, arranging the arms and legs as best he can for balance. He has never quite got used to the sight of lifeless bodies. He tries to stabilise it so it will stop flopping around. First he attempts to prop the elbow on the windowsill, but the Wolf is a bit too short because it doesn't look at all natural. After several minutes of trial and error, he finds a position that seems like it might work, but only a few moments later the body starts to sag and collapse like an avalanche in slow motion.

Nanao fights down his rising temper and once more tries fastidiously to arrange the body. He leans him up against the window and tries to make it look like the Wolf is sleeping. Then he pulls the flat cap down low for good measure.

A call comes in from Maria. Nanao gets up and returns to the gangway. He stands next to the window and puts his phone to his ear.

'Make absolutely sure you get off at Omiya.' Nanao smiles acidly. There was no need to tell him that. 'Well? Are you enjoying your ride on the Shinkansen?'

'I haven't had any time to enjoy it. I'm scrambling here. I finally got the Wolf into his seat. Looks like he's sleeping. I hid the bag, too.'

'Well look at you.'

'You don't know anything about the bag's owner?'

'Only that he's in car number three.'

'Nothing else more specific? If I knew what kind of person to watch out for it would be a big help.'

'If I knew anything I would tell you. But that's all I've got, really.'

'Mother Maria, help me.' Standing by the door, he can feel the vibrations of the train on the tracks. The phone is pressed to his ear, his forehead is pressed to the window. It's cold. He watches the buildings flow by.

The door from the rear of the train opens and someone enters the gangway. Nanao can hear the toilet door open; then whoever went in comes out again right away. There's an exasperated click of the tongue.

Someone looking for something in the toilet?

He risks a glance. A man, long and lanky. Wearing a jacket, a grey shirt underneath. His hair sticks up randomly, like he just got out of bed. An aggressive look in the eyes, like he's ready to pick a fight with anyone he meets. Nanao recognises him. 'Hey, that reminds me,' he says into his phone, trying to keep his voice natural, like he's just a regular passenger having a conversation and looking out the window. He keeps his back turned to the man.

79

'Something wrong?' Maria doesn't miss the sudden change in Nanao's voice.

'I mean, you know, it's like . . .' He stalls for time until the man enters car six and the door closes behind him. Then Nanao's voice returns to normal. 'Saw someone I know.'

'Who? Someone famous?'

'One of those twins. You know who I'm talking about. Twins in the same line of work as us. Not Lemon and Lime.'

Maria's voice gets tight. 'Lemon and Tangerine. They're not twins. They kind of seem similar so everyone assumes they're twins, but actually they're totally different.'

'One of them just passed by.'

'Lemon is the one that likes Thomas the Tank Engine, and Tangerine is the serious one that likes reading novels. Lemon's a classic B blood type and Tangerine's a classic A. If they ever got married it'd definitely end in divorce.'

'Hmm. I couldn't tell his blood type just by looking at him.' Nanao says it lightly, to cover his nerves. It would have been easy to tell which one it was if the guy had been wearing a T-shirt with a train on it. Then he gives voice to his growing sense of foreboding: 'You think the suitcase is theirs?'

'Could be. Could also be that they aren't here together. Used to be that they worked individually.'

'Someone once told me that those two are the most dangerous operators in the business.'

It was a while back, when he was meeting in an all-night cafe with a well-known go-between, a decidedly chunky man. This man used to do all kinds of work, contract kills and other dangerous jobs, but when he began to put on weight he slowed down the pace, got tired of working, and got into the go-between business. When he started it was still a new-ish thing, and since he was persistent and kept up good relations with people he was able to carve out a solid niche for himself. He kept growing plumper into his middle age, so getting out of the field was probably the right move. 'I was always best at making connections,' he told Nanao with self-satisfaction. 'I think I was meant to be a go-between.' It didn't make much sense to Nanao.

Then the man made him a proposition. 'Would you take on work that didn't come from Maria? Because I've got a job for you. There's good news and bad news.' This guy was always talking about good news and bad news.

'What's the good news?'

'It pays extremely well.'

'And the bad news?'

'You'd be up against some tough customers. Tangerine and Lemon. I'd say that right now, they're the people in the business most guaranteed to get a job done. Most violent, for sure the most dangerous.'

Nanao turned it down without thinking twice. It wasn't that he had a problem working with someone besides Maria. It was this man's repeated use of the word 'most'. He had no intention of going up against that.

'I really don't want to get involved with those two,' Nanao wails into the phone.

'You may not want to, but that won't stop them. If it *is* their suitcase, that is.' Maria sounds calm. 'Anyway, declaring someone the most dangerous in the business is pretty much the same as picking the favourites for this year's Academy Awards – people just say whatever they want to. There are a lot of candidates to choose from, after all. Like the Pusher. You've heard about him, right? The one who pushes his victims in front of cars or trains and makes their deaths look like an accident. Some people say he's the best in the biz. And for a while everyone was talking about the Hornet.'

Nanao knows the name. Six years ago, the Hornet made a name for himself overnight by sneaking into the offices of Terahara, the big wheel in the underworld, and killing the boss. He used a poison needle to prick people in the neck or the fingertip. Some rumours said the Hornet was actually two people working together.

'But no one ever mentions the Hornet any more, do they? Flash in the pan. A one-hit wonder. Just like a bee, I suppose, only one good sting.'

'I wonder.'

'Most of what you hear about the old professionals is just a bunch of tall tales.'

This reminds Nanao of something else the rotund go-between had said. 'I always get excited when I watch old movies. I think, how did they make it look so good when they didn't have any CGI or special effects? Like the German movies from the silent era, they're so old but they've got such a glow!'

'Don't you think the glow is because they're so old? Like with an antique?'

The go-between shook his head with theatrical flair. 'No, no. It's *despite* the fact that they're so old. Look at *Metropolis*. In the same way, professionals in the old days were seriously tough. I want to say they were more *solid*, harder. They were on a different level.' He spoke with passion. 'And you know the reason why those old-timers never lose?'

'Why's that?'

'Because they're already dead or retired. Either way, they'll never lose again.'

'Guess you could say that.'

The go-between nodded grandly, then launched into tales about his friends among the legends.

'Maybe if I retire now,' Nanao says into his phone, 'I'll become a legend too.'

'Oh sure,' Maria shoots back, 'you'll go down in history as the man who couldn't get off the train at Ueno Station.'

'I'll be getting off at Omiya.'

'Good idea. That way they won't call you the man who couldn't get off the train at Omiya.' Nanao hangs up and goes back to his original seat in car four.

THE PRINCE

'HEY, MR KIMURA,' THE PRINCE says conspiratorially, 'things might be getting a little interesting.'

'Interesting. No such thing.' Kimura has long since been feeling reckless. He lifts his bound hands to his face and scratches his nose with his thumb. 'What, you had a divine revelation? You realised that you're a sinful boy? That's an eventful trip to the toilet.'

'There's actually a bathroom right next to our car, but I went in the wrong direction, so I had to go through car six to the bathroom in the gangway between six and five.'

'So even his highness the Prince makes mistakes.'

'But things always go my way.' As the words leave his mouth, the Prince wonders why it is that everything always goes his way. 'Even if I mess up, it ends up working out for me. It turns out to have been a good thing that I went to the further bathroom. Before I got there, I saw two men in the gangway. I didn't pay them much attention, just went to the bathroom. But when I came out they were still there. One of them had his arms around the other one.'

Kimura guffaws. 'Somebody being held up by their friend is usually a very drunk somebody.'

'Exactly. And the one holding the other up said the same thing. This guy had too much, he said. But it didn't look that way to me.'

'What do you mean?'

'He wasn't moving, but he didn't smell of alcohol. But mostly, the angle of the head didn't look right.'

'The angle of the head?'

'The one guy, with the black glasses, he was trying his best to cover it up, but I'm pretty sure the other guy had a broken neck.'

'Okay,' Kimura says with a long sigh. 'There's no way that's what was going on.'

'Why not?' The Prince looks past Kimura, out the window, working out his next move. 'Because if someone was dead there'd be a big fuss right about now.'

'The guy didn't want there to be a fuss, so he was making up all kinds of excuses. He lied right to my face.' He pictures the man with the black glasses. Kind-looking, but the offer to help carry the supposedly drunk man had flustered him. It was obvious he was trying to keep a cool facade but inside was frantic. The Prince almost felt sorry for him. 'And this guy had a suitcase.'

'So, what, you think he was trying to put the body inside the suitcase?' Kimura sounds flippant.

'Oh, that would have been a good idea, actually. But it probably wouldn't have fitted. The guy in his arms was pretty small, but I don't think it would have worked.'

'Go and tell one of the conductors. There's a passenger with a broken neck, tell 'em, is that typical? Is there a discount ticket if you have a broken neck? Go and find out.'

'No thanks,' the Prince answers flatly. 'If I did that, they'd stop the train. And . . .' He pauses for a moment. 'It'd be *boring*.'

'Well, we certainly wouldn't want his majesty to be bored.'

'There's more.' The Prince grins. 'I was on my way back here, but I couldn't stop thinking about it so I turned back again. When I was in car six I saw a different man. He was looking for that suitcase.'

'So?'

'He was checking the aisle, the seats, searching for something.'

'And this was a different guy from the one with the black glasses and the drunk friend.'

'Yes. Tall and slim, with kind of crazy eyes. He seemed pretty rough around the edges, didn't exactly look like a productive member of society. And then he asked one of the passengers, hey, what's in your bag! Weird, right? He seemed desperate, and it was pretty easy to see he was looking for a bag.'

Kimura makes a show of yawning. *This old man's desperate too*, the Prince thinks coldly. Unable to grasp what the Prince is getting at, unsure why he would be sharing all this, the man's getting anxious. He doesn't want his much younger antagonist to notice his anxiety, so he fakes a yawn to cover taking a deep breath. *Just a little more.* Kimura is on the brink of accepting his powerlessness, the futility of his situation. *Just a tiny bit more.*

People need to find a way to justify themselves.

A person can't live without being able to tell themselves that they're right, that they're strong, that they have value. So when their words and actions diverge from their view of themselves, they start looking for excuses, to help reconcile the contradiction. Parents who abuse their children, clergy who engage in illicit affairs, politicians who suffer disgrace – they all come up with excuses.

Being forced to submit to someone else's will is the same. It makes people try to justify themselves. In order to avoid acknowledging one's impotence, one's abject weakness, people try to find some reason. They think, this person must be something really special to beat me so thoroughly. Or, anyone would be powerless in this situation. This gives some small satisfaction. The more confidence and self-regard someone has, the more they need to tell themselves something like this. And once they do, the power relations are set in stone.

Then all you have to do is say two or three things that stroke the person's ego and they'll do whatever you tell them. The Prince has done it many times with his schoolmates.

I see it works just as well on adults as it does on kids.

'Basically, one man is looking for a suitcase, and the other one has it.'

'So you should tell him. That guy with the black glasses has the bag you're looking for.'

The Prince glances at the carriage door. 'Actually I lied to him. The man with the black glasses and the bag is behind us, but I told the man looking for the bag that he was further up the train.'

'What are you trying to do?'

'It's just a hunch, but I bet the bag is pretty valuable. I mean there's someone doing everything they can to find it, so it has to be worth something.' As he's talking, something occurs to the Prince: if the man looking for the bag was coming in this direction, wouldn't he have encountered the black glasses man? It wasn't a suitcase that could be folded up and hidden somewhere, so if they crossed paths then the man looking for it should have discovered it immediately. Could he have overlooked it? Or maybe the man with the black glasses hid inside the toilet with the suitcase.

'I'll share something with you. It was back when I was seven,' the Prince says to Kimura with a smile. He smiles so broadly it scrunches up his cheeks. Whenever he does this, adults make the mistake of assuming he's an innocent kid, totally harmless, and they let down their guard. He relies on it. And sure enough, Kimura's face seems to soften a bit at the Prince's smile. 'Robot cards were really popular. All my classmates were collecting them. You could buy packs at the supermarket for a hundred yen, but I didn't see what everyone was getting so excited about.'

'My Wataru can't buy cards so he makes his own. He's adorable.'

'I don't see what's adorable about that.' No need to lie. 'But I can understand it. Rather than buying some generic card that somebody else made for commercial reasons, it seems a whole lot more worthwhile to make your one for free. Is your kid good at drawing?'

'Not at all. It's really cute.'

'He's not? Lame.'

Kimura stares blankly for a second, and then has a delayed flash of anger at the insult to his son.

The Prince always chooses his words carefully. Whether the words are violent or easy-going, he never says them without considering their effect. He always wants to be in control of exactly what he says and how he says it. He knows that the casual-seeming use of impolite words with his friends, words like lame, worthless, trashy, establishes a kind of power relation. Even if there's zero basis for calling something lame or trashy, it has an effect. Saying things like Your dad's so lame, or You've got such crappy taste, these function as a vague denial of someone's foundation, and it's effective.

There are not that many people who have a solid set of personal values, who have real confidence. And the younger someone is, the more their values shift around.

They can't help but be influenced by their surroundings. That's why the Prince frequently displays his own certainty, using words of derision and contempt. More often than not his subjective opinion takes on object-ive force, reinforcing his superior status.

People think, that guy's got a way of looking at the world, he knows what he's talking about. He gets that sort of deference without even hav-ing to ask for it. If you take the position in a group of the one who sets the values, the rest is easy. In the Prince's circle of friends, there are no clearly laid out rules like in football or baseball, but they all follow his orders as if he were the referee.

'One day I found a pack of cards in the car park of a store. It was unopened, so I'm guessing it fell when a shipment was being delivered. It turned out to have a really rare card inside.'

'Lucky you.'

'Exactly. That was lucky for me. When I brought the card in to school, all those young aficionados lit up. Can I have it? they all said. I didn't need it, and I was just going to give it to someone. But too many people wanted it. I didn't know who to give it to, and then suddenly, and this is true, I really wasn't planning anything, but without thinking about it too much I said, well, I can't just give it away for free. So what do you think happened then?'

'What, you sold it to the highest bidder?'

'You're so simple, Mr Kimura. It's cute.' The Prince chooses these words intentionally. It didn't matter whether or not what Kimura said was cute. What mattered was that the Prince had made a judgement. He guessed that Kimura would now feel like he was being treated like a child. Now he'll be wondering what about him exactly is childish, he won't be able to escape the fact that his thoughts might be juvenile. Of course, there's no way for him to answer this, because nothing he said was actually cute. So then he'll start to think that the Prince knows the answer, and he'll start to pay attention to the Prince's values and standards.

'Anyway, it looked like there would be an auction, people started naming prices. But somebody said, hey, Prince, what about something besides money? I'll do whatever you want. That's when the whole situation changed. That kid must have thought that it would be easier to do something for me than to pay. Probably didn't have any money. So then everyone else starts saying the same thing, I'll do whatever you want. That's when I realised. I could use the situation to control the class.'

'Sure, why not.'

'To make people compete with each other, to make them suspicious of each other.'

'So that's when his majesty the Prince started thinking he was hot shit.'

'That was when I realised that people want things and that I could benefit if I had the things they wanted.'

'You must have been so proud of yourself.'

'Not at all. Just that I started wanting to see how much I could affect other people's lives. Like I said before, it's the lever principle, I can push just a little and make someone depressed, I can ruin their lives with minimum effort. It's kind of amazing.'

'I can't say I've ever felt the same way. And so, what, that led you to start killing people?'

'Even if I don't kill anyone, hmm, okay, say I'm at the tail end of a cold, still coughing, right? And I happen to pass a mother in the street pushing her baby in a buggy, and when the mum isn't looking I lean in and cough in the baby's face?'

'Doesn't sound like such a big deal.'

'Maybe the baby hasn't been vaccinated yet and gets a virus. With my little cough it could mess up the baby's life, and the parents' too.'

'Did you actually do that?'

'Maybe. Or say I go to a funeral home and bump into the bereaved when they're transporting their family member's ashes. Pretend I tripped and fell. The ashes spill everywhere, it's a huge mess. Such a simple little thing, but it puts a blot on someone's memory. No one thinks kids have any malice in them, so no one would be that harsh with me. And I'm too young to be punished by the law. Which means that the family who dropped the ashes is even more sad and frustrated.'

'Did you do that?'

'I'll be right back.' The Prince stands up.

'Where're you going?'

'I want to see if I can find the suitcase.'

Walking through car six to the back of the train, he glances around. The man with the black glasses isn't there. Up on the luggage rack there are large backpacks and paper bags and small suitcases. None are the same shape or colour as the one he saw before. He's fairly certain that the black glasses man isn't further up the train than car seven where he and Kimura have been sitting. He had been on the lookout and hadn't seen the man come through. Which means that the man is further back on the train, somewhere between cars five and one.

He exits car six, his mind working.

No one in the gangway. There are two toilets. The closer one is locked. Someone else must be using the sink area because the curtain is pulled.

The man with the black glasses might be hiding in the toilet with the bag, maybe planning to hole up in there until the train reaches Omiya. Wouldn't be a bad idea. It's possible someone could complain that the bathroom has been occupied for a long while, but the train isn't that crowded so it probably wouldn't turn into anything big. The man could very well be in there.

The Prince decides to wait for a while and see. If whoever's inside doesn't come out soon he can ask the train staff to open it. He would just do his honours student routine, full of kindness and respect for the rules – oh, excuse me, the toilet has been in use for a while now, do you think there might be something wrong?

The train attendant likely wouldn't think twice before opening it up.

As he's thinking this the curtain by the sink snaps open, startling him. A woman emerges, who looks at him mildly and apologises. The Prince almost apologises back reflexively, but he holds it in. Apologies create obligation and hierarchy, so he never makes them when he doesn't have to.

He watches the woman walk away. She's wearing a jacket over a dress, medium height and build, looks to be late twenties. He suddenly thinks of his class teacher from three years ago. Her name was Sakura or Sato, he can't remember. Of course he knew her name at the time, but once he graduated he didn't feel the need to hold on to it so he just let it go. Teachers are just that, a teacher at school, occupying a role. It's like how baseball players wouldn't bother learning the names of the other team's fielders and just refer to them by position. He used to say, 'The teacher's name and personality don't matter. Their beliefs and goals are all basically the same. When it comes to personalities and mindsets, at the end of the day there are really only a handful of patterns. The teachers are all looking for ways to get on our good side. We might as well have a chart: we do this and they move like that, we act like that and they react like this. They're just like mechanical equipment. Equipment doesn't need a proper noun.'

When he would say that, most of his classmates would stare uncomprehendingly. At best they would agree, yeah, I guess the teachers' names don't matter. They should have been asking the Prince if he thought that they were just equipment too, or at least wondering, but no one did.

That teacher always thought he was a smart, capable boy who could help her bridge the gap between teacher and students. She even once told him appreciatively, 'If it weren't for you, Satoshi, I would never have known there was bullying in the class.'

He actually felt a little sorry for her for thinking he was her innocent little ally. One time he gave her a hint that he wasn't what she thought. It was in a report he wrote about a book on the Rwandan genocide. The Prince preferred books on history and world affairs over novels.

His teachers were surprised that he would read a book like that at his age.

They were impressed, how precocious, they said. The Prince thought that if there was one thing he was especially gifted at it was reading. He would read a book, digest the contents, his vocabulary would improve, his knowledge would increase, and he would go on to read something more difficult. Reading helped him put words to human emotion and abstract concepts, enabled him to think objectively about complex subjects. From there it was an easy step to helping someone express their fears and anxieties and frustrations, which made them feel indebted to him, come to rely on him.

He learned all sorts of things from the Rwandan genocide.

In Rwanda there were two ethnic groups, the Hutu and the Tutsi. Physically they were more or less the same, and there was no shortage of marriages between people from the different groups. The distinction between Hutu and Tutsi was completely man-made and artificial.

In 1994, when the Rwandan president's plane was shot down, the Hutu began their genocide of the Tutsi. Over the next hundred days some eight hundred thousand people were killed, many of them cut down by machete-wielding neighbours who they had lived beside for many years. A rough breakdown of the numbers puts it at eight thousand people killed every day, which is five or six every minute.

This unmitigated slaughter of man and woman, young and old, wasn't some ancient happening divorced from any sense of reality, no, it happened less than twenty years ago, and this is what most fascinated the Prince.

'It was hard to believe something so horrible could happen,' he wrote in his book report, 'and I thought that we can't ever forget this tragedy. It was not just something that happened in a far-off country. I learned that we all have to face up to our weakness and fragility.' He knew that it was the sort of vague but palatable statement that worked best for these reports. All surface, ultimately meaningless, sure to win the grown-ups' approval. But he also hid some truth in the last sentence.

He did learn something: just how easily people can be whipped up into a frenzy. He came to recognise the mechanism that makes atrocities difficult to stop once they've started, the mechanism that makes genocide possible.

For example, America was reluctant to acknowledge that there was genocide taking place in Rwanda. That's what the book said. Rather, they were frantically trying to find reasons why it *wasn't* a genocide, without paying heed to the facts on the ground. Even though there was reporting on the ever increasing numbers of slain Tutsi, America took an evasive position, claiming that it was difficult to determine what exactly constitutes a genocide.

Why?

Because if they recognised a genocide, the UN would call on them to take some sort of action.

And the UN acted the same way. They basically did nothing.

It wasn't just the Rwandans who expected the Americans to act a certain way. Most Japanese people think that if there's ever a major problem, America or the UN will deal with it. A feeling like the police are on the job and will take care of everything. When in reality, the US and UN determine their course of action based not on any sense of mission or moral obligation, but on a calculation of profit and loss.

The Prince knew instinctively that none of this was unique to the story of a small African country. It could easily be transplanted into his school.

If a problem occurs among the student body, say, an epidemic of violent bullying, then that stands in for the genocide, and the teachers are the US and the UN.

In the same way that the Americans resisted the notion of genocide, the teachers don't want to recognise the bullying problem. Once they do, they'll have to take action, which would lead to all sorts of mental and logistical strain for them.

He thought it would be interesting to try to turn this around on the teachers, to make them recognise that there was bullying but not treat it as a problem worth addressing. He got the idea from a section in the book about a mass killing that took place in a Rwandan technical school. When he first read about the episode, his body trembled with excitement.

UN peacekeeping troops were stationed at the school, and people started to say that the UN would keep people safe from the genocide. Some two thousand Tutsi took refuge in the school, believing they'd be protected. Unfortunately for them, the UN troops didn't have orders to protect the Tutsi, but rather to help foreigners in Rwanda evacuate. By extension, the troops were being told that they had no obligation to save the Tutsi.

This came as a great relief to the UN troops. They didn't have to get involved. If they tried to protect the Tutsi, chances were that they themselves would face mortal danger. When the Hutu surrounded the school, the UN troops claimed that their mission didn't include direct engagement, and they retreated.

The two thousand Tutsi in the school were immediately butchered.

The presence of a peacekeeping force had led to even more victims.

Utterly fascinating.

Regardless of how the students acted on the surface, somewhere deep down they all believed that the teacher would maintain order in the classroom. Their parents thought the same thing. They trusted the teachers, invested them with responsibility, and so they felt secure. The Prince knew that if he could control the teacher he could make life miserable for the rest of the students.

He devised a plan.

First he tried to sow the seeds of anxiety about what would happen if the teachers took action against bullying. He gave his class teacher reason to fear that she herself could be in danger. Then she started to form justifications for her decisions, telling herself that she was doing what was best for the students even though she wasn't taking direct action.

He addressed this in his book report too, touching on the foolishness and self-serving logic of the US and the UN. He thought that the teacher might realise what he was doing, that he was really writing about her, that he was a dangerous boy. He gave her clues.

But of course she didn't pick up on them. 'You really read this hard book, Satoshi? That's so impressive,' she fawned. 'Tragedies like this really are terrible. It's hard to believe that human beings could do this to one another, isn't it?' The Prince was disappointed.

It was easy for the Prince to understand how a genocide could occur. It was because people make decisions based on feeling. But those feelings are extremely susceptible to outside influence.

He read in a different book about a famous experiment. Groups of people were gathered and given problems to solve, questions with easy answers. They answered one by one, and everyone heard how everyone else answered. But actually, there was only one real test subject in each group, and everyone else was instructed to give the wrong answers on purpose. Amazingly, the individual answering according to their own free will chose the incorrect answer that everyone else was giving one out of three times. In total, seventy-five per cent of test subjects gave at least one answer that they knew to be wrong.

Human beings are creatures of conformity.

There have been other similar experiments. One of them isolated the optimum pattern for conformist behaviour: when the stakes are high but the question is difficult and the right answer isn't obvious.

When this happens, people are much more likely to adopt someone else's opinion as their own.

When the question is easy to answer people tend to have more faith in their own decision.

It's also relatively easy as long as the stakes are low. People feel no hesitation with giving their own answer.

The Prince understood it like this: when people have a difficult decision to make, one that may go against their code of ethics, they conform to the group, and even come to believe that the answer is correct.

When he thought about it in those terms, it became easy to see the mechanism by which the genocide not only was difficult to stop but by which it fuelled itself. The people doing the killing didn't trust their own judgement, but rather went along with the group, believing that was right.

He hears a noise in the bathroom, the sound of the toilet flushing. The door opens, but the person who comes out is a middle-aged man in a suit, who heads over to the sink. The Prince swiftly opens the door and pokes his head inside. Just a drab toilet, nothing else.

Nowhere the suitcase might be hidden. Next he checks the other bathroom. It's a ladies' room, but that doesn't stop him.

No suitcase.

He cocks his head. *Where could it be?*

It's too big to fit under any of the seats in the train. It isn't on any of the luggage racks, nor is it in the bathrooms.

He doesn't have any particular reason for drifting over towards the trash receptacles, other than that he's checked everywhere else. He inspects the openings for bottles and cans and the slot for disposing of magazines, bringing his face closer, even though he knows there's no way the bag would fit inside. He peers in the hole – all he can see are discarded containers.

Then he notices the little protrusion.

There, right next to the slot for paper waste. *I wonder.* He pushes it and a handle clicks out. He twists it without hesitation. The panel swings open before him, making his heart flutter in his chest. He had no idea there was a panel there. Inside is a shelf, with the garbage bag on the bottom, and a suitcase on top. No doubt about it – it's the suitcase he saw when he met the man with the black glasses.

I found it. He closes the panel and resets the handle. Then he exhales slowly. There's no need to be hasty. The man with the black glasses isn't likely to move the bag any time soon. *He probably thinks he can leave it here until he gets where he's going, and no one will find it.*

How can I make this even more interesting?

Relishing the sense of accomplishment from finding the suitcase, he starts back towards car number seven. *I really am lucky.*

KIMURA

KIMURA CAN'T STOP GOING THROUGH all the memories he has related to the Prince.

The first time he met him in the mall, he thought he'd never see this schoolkid again.

But within two weeks he found himself involved with the Prince once more, as if there was an invisible force pulling him in.

That time, too, Wataru was with him. It was on the way back from seeing his parents off at the train station.

They had come to Tokyo a day earlier for a class reunion and stayed at a small hotel near Kimura's apartment. After Wataru was back from kindergarten for the day, they took him to a toy shop, offering to buy him whatever he wanted. It wasn't like Wataru to ask for things, and he was clearly a little overwhelmed by his grandfather urging him to pick something, pick something. He seemed satisfied enough with the balloon that the shopkeeper gave him. Kimura found himself on the receiving end of another overblown scolding from his father: 'He's afraid to ask for something because you never buy him anything! Poor kid, oh, poor little guy.'

'Wataru's always been that way,' Kimura explained, but his father wouldn't listen.

Instead he brought up Kimura's ex-wife.

'When she was around the boy was more interested in toys, like a little kid should be,' he said unkindly. 'She left because you're such a mess.'

'That's not true. I told you. She racked up a ton of debt and ran off.'

'She just couldn't stand living with you and your drinking.'

'I wasn't drinking so much then.' It wasn't a lie. He had always been on the lazy side, but when his wife was still around he could live without alcohol just fine. If he had been drinking as much back then there's no way he would have got custody of Wataru.

'Well, now all you do is drink.'

'You're just saying that, you don't know.'

At which his father's face grew hard. 'I can tell by looking at you. I can tell by *smelling* you.' It had been his line since Kimura was a boy. He would puff up and declare that you can tell just by looking at someone, the bad parts always show. Kimura had never liked it, wrote it off as the prejudices of the old. His father's old friend Shigeru once laughed and said, 'Mr Kimura's always saying, this guy stinks, that guy stinks.'

To which Kimura's mother responded, 'But he's always the one farting!'

After they found a toy for Wataru they went to a park with a large playground. Kimura sat on a bench watching his mother scramble breathlessly after Wataru as the little boy ran for the tall slide. He was glad for a moment's break from being his son's main playmate. He reached into his pocket for his flask, but his father grabbed his hand. He hadn't even noticed his old man sit down next to him.

'The hell you think you're doing?' Kimura said, his voice thick with anger, but his father was unmoved. Despite the white hair, the old man was still solid and strong. He tightened his grip until it hurt. Kimura let go and his father took the flask.

'Do you know what the definition of alcoholism is?'

'You're gonna say it's me and my life, right?'

'You're still on the cusp, but if you continue like you are then you'll be a full alcoholic, no doubt about it. I'm asking, do you know what alcoholism actually means?' He handed back the flask, which Kimura snatched up.

'It means you like drinking and you drink a lot.'

'That's putting it roughly, yes, but it means addiction, which means it's a disease. It's different from someone who appreciates a drink or who can hold their alcohol. It means that if you take one sip, you just keep drinking. Then it's no longer a question of resilience or restraint. Alcoholism means you can't stop. It has to do with your physiology. When someone like that takes a drink, it's all over.'

'It's hereditary, so I'd guess you're the same as me. Or maybe I got it from Mum?'

'Neither one of us drinks. And why is that? Because we both know that there's no recovery from being an alcoholic.'

'Of course you can recover.'

'There's a cluster of nerve cells in the brain, the A10 cluster.'

Oh God, Dad, a science lecture? Kimura started rooting around in his ear to show his lack of interest.

'They did an experiment, with a machine, and if you pushed a lever it would stimulate the A10 cells. And what do you think happened?'

'I give up.'

'People kept on pushing the lever.'

'So?'

'When the A10 cluster is stimulated, the brain releases pleasure signals. If someone pushes the lever, they get an easy buzz. So they keep doing it, over and over. Like how monkeys won't stop masturbating, same idea. Apparently this good feeling is similar to the one we get from eating something delicious, or from completing a job well done.'

'So what?'

'Drinking alcohol stimulates the A10 cells.'

'So what?'

'When you drink you get a feeling of having done something worthwhile, even though you haven't done anything at all. This is easy, you say.

It's easy, and it feels good. So then what do you suppose happens? You just keep drinking, like the people who keep pushing the lever. And as you go on like that, eventually, your brain starts to change shape.'

'What do you mean, your brain changes shape?'

'Once that happens, there's no changing it back. It develops a switch that flips the moment alcohol enters the system. Say there's an alcoholic who hasn't had a drink for a long time. The symptoms of addiction have vanished, he's able to lead a normal life again. But if he takes even one sip, he'll go right back to being unable to stop. Because his brain is still wired that way. It has nothing to do with his willpower or resolve. It's just the way his brain works. Like how a man's pupils will dilate reflexively when he sees a naked woman. There's nothing he can do to help it. That's the mechanism of dependence.'

'Mechanism of dependence. Real fancy talk, Dad. Anyway, what about the fact that brandy dates back to Mesopotamian culture?'

'We don't even know if that's actually true. Don't believe everything you hear, it'll make a fool of you. Listen, there's only one way to beat alcoholism, and that's to give up drinking entirely. One sip and it's all over. You shouldn't be looking to alcohol or drugs for a sense of accomplishment. What you should be doing is good, honest work. Taking your satisfaction the easy way leads the human body to form dependencies.'

'Again with the fancy talk.'

'You should do like I do and work a proper job,' the old man said forcefully. 'That'd give you a healthier sense of accomplishment.'

'A proper job? You've worked a supermarket stockroom my whole life.' As long as Kimura could remember his parents had lived humbly. They worked at a supermarket near where they lived, basically glorified part-time jobs. They worked meekly, earned meekly. Kimura had always looked down on them for it.

'The stockroom is important work. I have to manage stock, place orders.' His father exhaled sharply through rounded nostrils. 'What about you? You've never held an honest job in your life!'

'Uh, you mean except for the job I have now with the security company.'

'Oh, well, yes. That's a good job. Sorry.' The apology sounded sincere. 'But you never worked before that.'

'Forget about the past. I mean, what, are you gonna accuse me of not having a job when I was in school? No one did! Anyway, I had a job before I was a security guard.'

'What kind of job?' His father peered into his face and Kimura looked away. What kind of job? Someone would hire him, he would get his gun, he would mess with other people's lives.

Not exactly humanitarian work. But if he told his father that, the old man would feel like he had failed as a parent. He almost told him, just to make his father feel as bad as he himself was feeling, but he hesitated. It didn't seem worth it to burden his father with that kind of hurtful information on top of the natural challenges of getting older. 'I guess the kind of job you can't talk about in polite company, is that it?'

'What, you can tell just by looking?'

'That's right.'

'You'd have a fit if I told you, Dad, so I'll spare you the pain.'

'Hey, I got into my share of trouble when I was young.'

'I think mine was on a different level,' Kimura said with a bitter smile. Nothing's as boring as when old folks brag about how hard things used to be or how much hell they used to raise.

'Forget all that. Just stop drinking, that's all.'

'I appreciate you worrying about my health.'

'It's not you I'm worried about, it's Wataru. You're tough enough, if a giant shoe stomped on you you'd probably survive.'

'What am I, a cockroach?' He chuckled. 'If a giant shoe stomped on me I'd die like anybody else.'

'Listen, if you care at all about Wataru you'll stop drinking.'

'Hey, I've thought about quitting, you know, for Wataru's sake.' Even as he said it he was unscrewing the cap on the flask.

'But you just said – and now you're –' wailed his father. 'I'll tell you again, the only way to overcome dependency is to cut yourself off completely.'

'Guess I'm just a no-good lush.'

The old man stared at him. 'If you were just a lush that might be okay. But if you're no good as a person, then there's no hope for you.' His lips trembled slightly.

'Yeah, yeah.' Kimura opened the flask and brought it up to his mouth. With his father's warning echoing in his head he felt some shame, and only took a small sip. He could feel the alcohol hit him, could feel his brain changing shape like a sponge being twisted. He shuddered.

Later that day, after dropping his parents off at the train station, Kimura led Wataru back the way they came, through the old shopping arcade and into the residential neighbourhood.

'Daddy, someone's crying.' Wataru tugged on Kimura's hand as they were passing by an alley alongside a closed-down gas station. Kimura was in a bit of a daze, holding his son's hand but not really there, haunted by his father's words. He kept hearing it over and over again: *there's no cure for alcohol dependency*. Up until then he had thought that even if you had a dependency you could get treatment, get better and still drink. Like if you get gonorrhoea, your dick gets inflamed, and until you take care of it you can't have sex, but once you get it cleared up you can do it again. He was sure that alcoholism worked the same way. But if what his father said was true, then alcoholism was different from gonorrhoea. There's no cure, and you can never drink again.

'Look, Daddy!' He heard his son calling him again, looked down at the boy's face, then followed his gaze. Between the shuttered gas station and the next building over was a group of kids in school uniform, four in all.

Two of them had another one pinned by the arms so that he couldn't go anywhere. The fourth one stood facing the others. The one being held looked desperate. 'Come on, *stop*.' He was crying.

'What's happening, Daddy?'

'Don't worry about it. It's just some big boys doing their big boy thing.'

Kimura wanted to keep walking. When he thought back to his own schooldays, there was always someone pushing someone else around, getting up to something bad. Kimura was usually among those doing the pushing, so he knew that most of the time it happened for no particular reason. People just feel better when they can put themselves above other people. By grinding someone else down, you prop yourself up. That's the way people work.

'Wait. *Wait!* It's just as much your fault as it is mine!' The kid being held was almost shrieking. 'How come I'm the only one who's getting it?'

Kimura stopped walking and looked again. The kid had short hair dyed brown and a uniform that was too small. He looked fit and strong – this wasn't picking on the weak, it seemed to be more like friends kicking someone out of their group. Kimura's interest was piqued a little.

'What'd you expect, man? He jumped because you overdid it,' said the kid holding Brown-hair's right arm. This one had a round face and a broad brow, looked a bit like a boulder, but still with the innocence of youth.

I guess teenagers are still basically kids, thought Kimura. Seeing kids so young acting so hard felt surreal somehow.

'But we were all in on it. And anyway, even before I put the video online he was all, I wish I were dead, I wanna die.'

'We were supposed to get him up to the point of suicide, but not actually have him do it. The Prince is really pissed off,' said the one on Brown-hair's left arm.

The Prince. The name rang a bell. But more than that, why were they talking about death and suicide?

'Once you've had your shock it'll all be over, so just deal with it.'

'I don't want it!'

'Think about it,' said the fourth one, the tallest. 'What'll happen if you don't take it now? Then we all get shocked. That's what. So it'll happen to you either way. But if we get it too then we'll all be angry with *you.* If you just take what's coming to you now then we'll be thankful. If you're gonna get it either way, which way would you rather have it? You want us to be angry with you or to thank you?'

'Well, what if we just pretended you did it? We'll tell the Prince I got the shock.'

'You think he'll fall for that?' The tall one gave a pained smile. 'You think you can trick the Prince?'

'Excuse me, young men.' Kimura put on a phoney formal tone as he entered the alley, leading Wataru by the hand. 'Did your bullying cause the death of a classmate?' He nodded encouragingly. 'I certainly am impressed.'

The schoolboys looked at one another. Their three-against-one formation dissolved and they hastily became a foursome once again, eyeing Kimura warily.

'Can we help you?' said the tall one darkly. His face was red, either from anxiety or anger, Kimura couldn't tell which, but it was obvious they were trying to look tough. 'You lost something?'

'Did I lose something? I can see that something's going down here,' Kimura said, pointing to the kid being restrained. 'What do you mean, shock? Electric shock? What are you up to?'

'What are you talking about?'

'You were being really loud, I heard everything. You guys bullied a classmate until he killed himself. Well, that's kind of fucked up. So, what, now you're having a review meeting?' As Kimura was talking, Wataru started to tug on his hand. He whispered that he wanted to go home.

'Shut up, old man. Take your kid and get outta here.'

'Who's the Prince?'

As soon as he said that all four boys went white. It was like someone had invoked a terrible curse. Their reaction made Kimura even more curious. At the same moment he recalled meeting that student in the department store.

'Ah, right, now I remember the Prince. And you guys, too – I saw you in the toilets. You were having a secret meeting. You were all worried, oh no, the Prince will be angry, what are we gonna do!' As he ribbed them, he thought back to the kid he met who called himself the Prince. 'You're actually scared of that little goody two-shoes?'

All four of them were silent.

The tall one held a plastic bag from a convenience store. Kimura took a quick step closer and plucked it out of his hand. The boy was taken completely unawares, suddenly becoming frantic, clawing at the bag to get it back. Kimura dodged easily, then grabbed the kid's outstretched hand and twisted hard on the pinkie. The kid yelped.

'Don't think you can mess with me, buddy, I'll break your finger. I've been around a whole lot longer than any of you. I've toughed it out through many more boring hours of life than you have. Know how many times I've broken someone's fingers?' Despite what he was saying he spoke nonchalantly. He handed the bag over to Wataru. 'What's in it?'

The schoolkids buzzed in protest.

'One move and I'll break this one's pinkie. Just try me.'

'Daddy, what is this?' Wataru took some sort of appliance out of the bag. It was fairly low-tech, like the remote control for a toy car, with wires and switches on it.

'Yeah, what is this thing?' Kimura let go of the kid's hand and took the device. 'Looks like the power pack for a train set.'

One of Kimura's school friends, a kid with a rich dad, had lots of model train sets that he loved to show off. This thing looked like the power pack that channelled electricity to the train tracks. Or maybe that's exactly what it was. It had a few wires coming out of it and one end was taped up. A power cord dangled from the other end. 'What's this for?'

The kids left his question hanging in the air unanswered.

Kimura stared at the device. Then he looked around and noticed an outlet low on the wall of the gas station. Probably for when the station attendants had to use some power tool. It had a cover over it to protect it from the rain.

'Wait, you were gonna plug this in and then, like, press the wires on his body and give him an electric shock? Is that it?' As he pieced it together Kimura started to feel a little unsettled. When he was in school he had hurt people too, but it was only ever just hitting them. He never even thought of using electricity. And this device looked like it had been specially modified for exactly that purpose. He got the feeling that it was used on a fairly regular basis. 'You guys do this often?' Using electrical appliances seemed to him like next-level bullying, verging on torture. 'This is, what, the Prince's idea?'

'How do you know about the Prince?' the brown-haired one who had been held by the others asked with a quaver in his voice.

'I met him in the department store after I first saw you guys. When you were all scared and crying in the toilets about the Prince being angry with you. I was there, remember?'

'Oh wait –' Recognition dawned on the tall one as he looked at Kimura's face. Then it seemed to hit the others, this was the booze-reeking man who butted in on their deliberations.

'That time it was Takuya whose turn it was to get punished.' Somehow the name he'd heard in the toilets popped into Kimura's head. 'Takuya was scared because he didn't follow his majesty the Prince's orders and the Prince was mad. You were all, Oh no, oh no, what'll we do, right?'

The kids looked at each other again, exchanging some silent message. Then the round-faced one spoke quietly. 'Takuya's dead.'

The other three whipped round to glare at him for revealing this to a stranger, their faces drained of colour.

'What do you mean, dead? Is that a metaphor?' Kimura spoke tauntingly so he wouldn't have to admit to himself that he was starting to get scared. 'You mean like how rock and roll is dead? Pro baseball's dead, Takuya's dead?'

Strained, sickly smiles spread on the schoolkids' faces, not because they were making fun of Kimura, but because they both identified with and were disheartened by how shaken the man looked.

'You mean he's actually *dead*? So the person you mentioned before, who jumped, that was Takuya?' Kimura sighed. He didn't expect things to take such a dark turn. 'You know when someone dies, that's it, they're gone.'

Wataru kept tugging on his hand, and Kimura himself began to think it wasn't such a good idea to have gotten involved. He turned to leave.

But then he heard one of the kids shout behind him: 'Wait, sir, help us!' He turned back round. The four boys all looked pale. Their cheeks were quivering. 'Please,' said the tall one, and at the same moment the one with the round face said, 'Do something,' and the other two both said, 'Help us.' Of course they hadn't planned this chorus, as if it were a rehearsal for the student arts festival. They all just broke at the same time, finally realising they had to reach out for help, their voices layering over one another, making their pain seem all the more poignant.

'First you try to act tough and now you're asking for help? Which is it?'

By that point they were nothing more than frightened little boys. Their entreaties came pouring out as if a dam had burst.

'You don't look like you're some dumb salaryman, mister.'

'You gotta do something about the Prince!'

'He's gonna kill us all!'

'It's like everything's gone crazy, our whole school's crazy, all because of him!'

Kimura couldn't believe this was happening. He waved his hand, leave me alone, what do you expect me to do? He felt like a fisherman who casually throws in a line and hooks a monster fish that may well pull him into the water. He felt afraid.

'All right, fine, I'll get rid of the Prince for you,' he said, half in desperation, not meaning it. The kids lit up, like a beam of light shone down on them. This upset Kimura even more. He looked around. It was a narrow alley, but it was clearly visible from the street. To anyone passing by it would have looked like nothing so much as a man and his child being mugged by some teenagers. Or maybe a man with child in tow giving a sermon to some students. 'I'll do it if each of you pays me a million yen.'

He threw that in to make it clear it would never happen, but amazingly the schoolboys seemed willing to take him up on it, beginning to discuss how they could get the money together. 'Come on, guys,' Kimura said frantically, 'I was obviously joking. Talk to your parents. If you're having so much trouble with the Prince, go cry to mummy and daddy. Or to your teachers.'

They were all mumbling and whimpering, on the verge of tears.

'Look at you. You guys are too much. Leave me out of it.' Kimura looked down and saw Wataru staring back at him. But the boy wasn't looking at his face; his eyes were locked on the flask in Kimura's hand. *When did I . . . ?* He screwed the cap shut. Which meant that he must have opened it. He hadn't even realised it. He had taken the flask out, unscrewed the cap and had a drink, all without noticing. He tried to keep himself from clicking his tongue in frustration. There was concern in Wataru's eyes, and also sadness.

Well, these schoolkids were leaning on me so heavy. Kimura cast around for his excuse. *Of course I'm going to want to have a little drink, they got me all stressed out.* He needed a drink to keep his wits about him, so he could take care of Wataru. The moment the alcohol hit him was like rain falling on parched earth, nourishing all the nerves in his whole body, making his head clear and sharp. *See, what's so bad about alcohol?* He even started to feel a touch of pride. *Whether it's poison or medicine it all comes down to how you use it, and I know how to use it right.*

'Takuya,' croaked one of the kids. 'Last month his dad was fired.'

'Huh?' Kimura's brows knitted together at the sudden change in direction. 'You mean Takuya who died?'

'It was before he died. His dad was arrested for touching one of the girls in our school. When the story got out he was fired.'

'Well, if he was involved with a teenage girl then he got what he deserved.' Kimura's nostrils flared as he spoke, but then he noticed the kids looking uncertain, searching for what to say next. 'Wait a minute.' He felt a doubt worming around. 'Did you guys have something to do with it? Are you telling me you set up Takuya's dad?'

They didn't deny it, which made Kimura think it was true.

'Was his dad innocent?'

Again, they said nothing.

'How would you even do something like that? How does that work?'

'We just did what the Prince told us to,' muttered the round-faced one. 'Same with the girl. It was because Takuya's dad was trying to find stuff out about the Prince.'

'So the Prince had you guys cook up a sexual misconduct case? He would do that? Smart kid. Ruthless.' Kimura was half joking, but the four schoolboys nodded vigorously. They were all too familiar with the Prince's ruthlessness.

'He's got rid of three teachers too,' said one of them darkly.

'One got depressed and quit, one was caught groping a student, one had an accident.'

'Don't tell me you guys did those too.'

No answer.

'You know, you shouldn't be so afraid of him. Just gang up on him and kick the shit out of him. I bet you'd have no problem if you worked together. Right?' The Prince didn't look particularly strong. And even if he happened to be a martial arts prodigy or something they could still overwhelm him with numbers.

Their reaction was peculiar. Their eyes all popped open, like this man had suggested something unthinkable. Like they couldn't even process what he was saying.

The thought's never even occurred to them. It was clear that they had never once considered trying to topple the Prince.

Kimura thought back to a job he once did. He was assigned to guard a man who had been kidnapped and was being kept half naked in a dingy old apartment. The man said nothing, just lolled about in a daze. Kimura sat in the next room watching TV, drinking, passing the time. But there was something about it that he just couldn't wrap his head around. The man wasn't tied up and the door wasn't locked. The man could have left if he wanted to. So why didn't he?

Kimura got an answer from the next guard who came to take over for him. 'Ever heard about learned helplessness?' asked the guy.

'Learned . . . ?'

'They did an experiment where they shocked a dog, right? And it had this set-up where if the dog jumped it wouldn't get a shock. So you'd think the dog would jump, right? But before that they put the dog in a situation where it got a shock no matter what it did. So then it didn't even try to jump to escape the shock.'

'It gave up, huh?'

'Basically they taught it that it was helpless. So it stopped trying, even when it could have avoided pain by just trying a little. It's the same with humans. Same with like domestic violence. The wife just keeps taking the beating. Because that sense of helplessness takes root, you know?'

'So that's why,' Kimura had said, looking at the man being kept in the room.

'Yup. He won't run away. He thinks he can't. Human beings don't operate on logic. Deep down we're built just like animals.'

This situation with the schoolkids was the same. They had long since decided that there was no way they could beat the Prince. Or had they been taught that? They had seen all the suffering that both their classmates and adults had met at the hands of the Prince, time and again. It must have built up to the point where they were convinced that they were powerless. The electric shocks were probably part of it. Kimura didn't know how the shocks were delivered, or what kind of orders the Prince gave exactly, but he could see that the shocks were getting to these kids on a deep level.

He took another good look at them. They really were young. They might have spent time on their hairstyles, they might have tried to look cool and tough, but they were like frightened puppies. Carving out their status in their little world was, to them, a matter of life and death.

It probably isn't that hard to control these kids, Kimura thought. And then he reflected that he shouldn't get involved. When a stray dog slinks towards you with sad, moist eyes, it's best to ignore it. 'Figure it out for yourselves.'

'Sir, please,' said Round-face, 'you gotta *help* us!'

Wataru squeezed his hand anxiously, pulling him away from the alley, back towards home.

'Not my problem.' Kimura realised with a start that at some point he had drained his flask. 'I'm sure you'll grow up into fine, upstanding adults.' Then he walked away.

*

'Hey, Mr Kimura.'

Kimura opens his eyes at the voice. It takes him a few moments to register that he's on the Shinkansen. He hadn't been fully asleep, but neither was he fully awake, and the sudden appearance of the Prince's face right next to him seems like a phantom swirling up out of memory.

'Mr Kimura, now's not the time for your beauty sleep. Aren't you at least a little worried about what's going to happen to you?'

'Even if I were worried I couldn't do anything about it all tied up like this. So, you know.'

'Still, you should have some kind of sense that you're in danger. I was waiting for you to meet me on the train, but it sure wasn't so that we could take a fun trip together.'

'Oh no? But why not? Let's do it. We can go for cold noodles in Morioka. My treat.'

The Prince doesn't crack a smile. 'There's something I want to ask you to do.'

'No thanks.'

'Don't say that. I'd be so sad if anything happened to your little son in the hospital.'

Kimura feels a leaden weight in his stomach and a boiling rage in his blood. 'What do you want me to do?'

'I'll tell you when we get closer to Morioka.'

'For now you just want me to stew?'

'I'm guessing if I asked you to kill someone you wouldn't want to hear about it.'

Kimura bites his lip. Such casual talk about killing seems at the same time childish and adult. 'Who? Who do you want me to do?'

'I'll just let you savour the anticipation.' As the Prince says this he bends down and starts to loosen the ties on Kimura's legs.

'You're letting me go?'

'If you try anything funny your son's going to be in trouble, okay? Just because I'm taking these off doesn't mean you're free. Don't you forget it. If my guy can't get in touch with me it'll be bye-bye baby boy.'

Kimura's body quakes with fury. 'Hey, are you even checking your phone?'

'Sorry?'

His face twists up. 'You said it'll go badly for me if you don't answer your phone.'

'Oh, that's right. If it rings ten times and I don't pick up then yes, it'll go very badly for you indeed.'

'I don't wanna hear that you just missed a call because you weren't paying attention. Then it'll fucking go badly for *you.*'

'Don't worry about that, mister.' The Prince seems utterly unconcerned. 'In the meantime there's something else I want your help with.'

'What, you want a back rub?'

He points towards the rear of the train. 'I want you to go with me to get a suitcase.'

MORNING GLORY

THE LIGHT IS GREEN AT the main intersection in Fujisawa Kongocho. Cars flow by one after the other. People crowd by the kerb, waiting for the pedestrian crossing signal.

Morning Glory stands thirty metres away in front of a chain bookstore. He watches the light. He watches the people. Male, tall, thin, thirties, no. Male, heavyset, twenties, no. Female, no. Male, short, twenties, no. Female, no. Male, school uniform, no. He waits for his target.

The light changes. The mass of people move into the crossing. They go in all directions, straight, to the side, diagonal. Before long the walk signal starts to flash, then turns red. The traffic light turns green again. He memorises the timing. The key is when the light turns yellow, and when it's about to turn red. Cars go faster on a yellow than they do on a green. They abandon caution, they come charging in.

I think the Pusher is like one of those weasel spirits from the stories, you know, the *kamaitachi*. A woman had said that to him once. She was looking to hire for a job. Morning Glory met with her, saying he was the Pusher's representative.

Someone suddenly gets a cut on their arm or their leg, said the woman, and they scream, a *kamaitachi* got me! But really it was just a sharp wind. I think the Pusher must be the same sort of thing. Someone gets hit by a car or jumps in front of a train and people say it was the Pusher that did it. Couldn't it just be a made-up story?

People often make that mistake about the *kamaitachi*. But the cuts don't come from any wind. Blaming it on the wind, that's the made-up story. Morning Glory told the woman that, and she didn't like it.

She could have gone home then, but she pressed even harder, asking all sorts of questions about the Pusher, digging for scraps. Morning Glory decided he disliked her, turned down the job, and walked off. But she stubbornly came after him, so he pushed her into the road, just as the light was about to turn red in the night. A pickup truck barrelling through the intersection smashed into her. The only regret Morning Glory felt was that he had done it for no fee.

Male, short, forties, no. Female, no. Male, heavyset, twenties, no. Female, no. Female, no. Male, heavyset, forties. His eyes lock on to the passing man. Pinstriped grey suit. Short hair, broad shoulders. Morning Glory starts to follow. The man heads for the intersection. He steps into the crowd of people waiting for the walk sign. Morning Glory follows. He's fully aware and in the moment, but it doesn't quite feel like he's guiding his own movements.

The traffic light turns from green to yellow. The man stops on the edge of the crossing.

Cars come from the right. Black minivan, female driver, short hair, child seat in the back. The timing's off. The next car is coincidentally the same type of minivan. The light changes. The car surges forward. Morning Glory casually moves his hand, touches the man's back.

There is the sound of impact, then the screech of the tyres clawing at the road. No one screams yet. The people's shock is like a silent, transparent explosion.

Morning Glory is already gone. He walks fluidly back the way he came, like floating on a current. Behind him he hears cries of Ambulance! but his heart is calm, like the surface of a lake where no pebble has been cast. His only thought is the vague recollection that he had once done a job at this same intersection, a long time ago.

FRUIT

1 2 3 4 5 6 7 8 9 10

'HEY, TANGERINE. TRY TO NAME some characters from *Thomas and Friends*.' Lemon came back from searching for the suitcase empty-handed, but instead of offering an explanation he just sat down casually in the aisle seat. And now he asks this.

Tangerine looks over at Little Minegishi's body in the window seat. Lemon is acting so relaxed that it seems he doesn't want to acknowledge the gravity of their situation. They still have a corpse on their hands, and they haven't got any closer to figuring anything out. But Lemon insists on starting a nonsense conversation.

'Did you find the bag?'

'Which of the *Thomas* characters do you know? Name me the most obscure character you can think of.'

'How does that have anything to do with the bag?'

'It doesn't.' Lemon juts out his chin, looking slightly peeved. 'Why are we even worrying about the damn bag?'

Guess he didn't find it. It's been five years since Tangerine teamed up with Lemon. He was an ideal partner for their sort of rough trade from the standpoint of physical ability and the fact that no matter what kind of trouble they got into he never panicked, always kept his cool – you could almost say he was emotionless – but on the other hand he was terrible with details, was irresponsible and sloppy. And even worse, when he made a mistake he was quick to spout excuses, he never wanted to own up to his own failures. Like now, when they're facing a situation that's getting steadily more serious, his attitude is Hey, why worry about it. He ignores the facts, actually tries to forget them. Tangerine knows all too well that it'll always be his job to clean up Lemon's mess. Trying to change that would be like pissing in the wind.

'Gordon,' says Tangerine with a sigh. 'He's a character, right? Gordon? One of Thomas's train friends?'

'Oh come on. Gordon's one of the most well-known characters. Like basically a main character. The challenge is to try to name an *obscure* character.'

'What do you mean, the challenge?' Tangerine looks up at the ceiling. Dealing with Lemon is harder than doing a job. 'Fine, whatever. You tell me. Give me a sample answer.'

Lemon's nostrils twitch as he struggles to control his pride. 'Well, I suppose I'm looking for an answer like Sir Handel, formerly known as Falcon.'

'Is that one of the characters?'

'Ned would work too.'

'There sure are a lot of trains.' Tangerine has no choice but to play along.

'He's not a train, he's a construction vehicle.'

'Who's not a train? You're losing me.'

Tangerine looks past the body out the window at the scenery. A mammoth apartment building flies by.

'Hey,' he says firmly to his partner, who is now humming a little tune as he flips through a magazine. 'You don't want to own up to your mistake. I get it. But now's not the time to relax. You hear me? Minegishi's son is no longer breathing. His body's getting cold. And the suitcase has disappeared. We, we're like good-for-nothing kids someone sent to the grocery store, but we didn't get the vegetables and we lost the wallet.'

'The grocery store? I can never follow your explanations.'

'Basically, we are fucked.'

'Yeah, I know, three words that describe our current situation.'

'It doesn't look like you know. That's why I'm reminding you. We should be more worried, all right? Or no, I'm plenty worried, it's you who should be more worried. I'll ask you again. You didn't find the bag, did you?'

'Nope.' For some reason Lemon seems pleased with himself. Tangerine is about to berate him again when Lemon adds, 'That little punk lied to me and sent me on a wild goose chase.'

'A little punk lied to you? What are you talking about?'

'The man with the bag you're looking for went that way, he said, and he seemed like a good kid, so I believed him, I walked all the way to the end of the Hayate looking for this guy.'

'Maybe the kid didn't lie to you. Someone's definitely got the bag, and maybe the kid really did see the guy. Could be that you just didn't find him.'

'It's weird though, I don't know how a bag that size could just disappear.'

'Did you check in all the bathrooms?'

'Basically.'

'Basically? What do you mean, basically?' Tangerine can't help raising his voice. When he realises Lemon isn't kidding it only makes him madder. 'It doesn't count unless you check *all* of them! Whoever has the bag could be hiding in one!'

'If the toilet's occupied I can't check inside, now can I?'

Tangerine can't even bring himself to heave a sigh. 'There's no point in checking if you don't check them all. I'll go myself.'

He looks at his watch. Five minutes until the train pulls into Omiya Station. 'Shit.'

'What's wrong? Why shit?'

'We're almost at Omiya. Minegishi's man will be waiting for us.'

Minegishi was suspicious of everyone, didn't trust anyone, probably because he had been running an underworld organisation for so long. He firmly believed that when someone has a chance to betray you, they will, guaranteed. That's why even when he hires someone to do a job he makes sure he can keep tabs on them so they don't stab him in the back.

With this job, he was concerned that Tangerine and Lemon would turn on him, that they'd take the money and run. Or that they might re-kidnap his son and take him somewhere to re-ransom him.

'I'll be keeping a close eye on you two,' he said at their last meeting, telling them to their faces that he didn't trust them. He'll have one of his underlings waiting for them at station stops along the way, to make sure that Tangerine and Lemon are actually on the train to Morioka with his son, that it doesn't look like they're up to anything funny.

Of course when he told Tangerine and Lemon this, they had zero intention of betraying him, they planned to simply get the job done as ordered, so they had no problem with it. 'By all means keep an eye on us,' they said genially.

'I never thought things would go like this.'

'Accidents happen. There's even a song about it in *Thomas and Friends*. It goes, "Accidents happen, just don't take it all to heart."'

'You should take it to heart at least a bit.'

But Lemon seems not to have heard Tangerine, because he starts singing the song happily, adding snippets of commentary, It's so true, *Thomas and Friends* is really pretty deep. 'Hey, wait a minute.' He finally looks up at Tangerine. 'Minegishi's guy is waiting for us on the platform. Think he's gonna get on the train?'

'I wonder.' They didn't get any details. 'Could be he's just going to stay on the platform and check on us through the window.'

'If that's how it is,' Lemon says, leaning forward and pointing to the corpse by the window, 'we just make it look like this one's asleep, we wave and smile, and the guy never knows the difference.'

Tangerine is instinctively reluctant about Lemon's optimistic proposal, but he can see how it might work. It actually could work, as long as Minegishi's man doesn't get on the train.

'I mean, if the kid's sitting right here they'd have no reason to guess he was dead, right?'

'You could be right. I wouldn't guess that either.'

'Right. So, there you go, he'll never know the difference.'

'But if for some reason he suspects something, he might get on the train.'

'The train only stops at Omiya for like a minute. He won't have time to make a leisurely inspection.'

'Hmm.' Tangerine tries to imagine what sort of orders he would give if he were Minegishi. 'I bet the guy is supposed to stay on the platform, check up on us through the window, and if he thinks something's up he'll give Minegishi a call.'

'Boss, your boy looked like shit. Passed out, must have got pretty drunk. Huh. And then what do you think'll happen?'

'Minegishi would work out that his son isn't drunk and start to wonder if something funny was going on.'

'You think he'd figure that out?'

'Big shots like him have a sixth sense with these kinds of things. Then I guess he'd have a whole gang of his men waiting for us when we make the next stop at Sendai. They'd have no problem piling on the train and nabbing us.'

'What if we steal the phone from the guy who's supposed to call in to report? If he doesn't get in touch with Minegishi then Minegishi won't be angry with us. This kid isn't dead until it gets out that he is.'

'Someone like Minegishi will have more ways to get in touch with his men than just a phone.'

'Like foot messengers?' For some reason Lemon seems taken with the idea and repeats it a few times, yeah, he'll have foot messengers, he's gotta have those.

'Like you know those digital billboards? Maybe his guy could write a message on one of those. It could say, Your son has been killed.'

Lemon blinks several times at Tangerine. 'You serious?'

'I'm joking.'

'Your jokes are dumb.' But he seems pretty excited by the idea. 'We should try that though – next time we finish a job let's use the big screen at a baseball stadium to make our report to the client, Job Done, Great Success!'

'I don't see why we would ever do that.'

'Because it'd be funny!' Lemon grins like a little kid. Then he pulls a piece of paper from his pocket and starts to write on it with a pen that he's produced from somewhere. 'Here, take this.' He holds it out to Tangerine, who takes it.

It's the supermarket giveaway ticket. 'No, look at the back,' says Lemon, so Tangerine flips it over to find a drawing of a train with a round face. It's hard to say whether the picture is well done or not.

'What the hell's this?'

'It's Arthur. I mean, I wrote his name down too. A shy maroon-coloured train. Very diligent in his work, he's proud of the fact that he's never had a single accident. You know, zero accidents, perfect record. He's trying hard to keep it up. I didn't have a sticker of him, so I drew him for you.'

'And why are you giving me this?'

'Because he's never had an accident! It'll be like a good-luck charm.'

Not even a child would put their faith in something so flimsy, but Tangerine is too exasperated to fight about it, so he just folds it in half and shoves it into his rear pocket.

'Although, eventually Thomas tricks Arthur and he does have an accident.'

'Then what good is he?'

'But Thomas says something smart.'

'And what's that?'

'Records are made to be broken!'

'Not a very nice thing to say to someone whose personal record you've just broken. Thomas sounds like a real jerk.'

NANAO

NANAO IS BACK IN THE first row of car four. According to what Maria told him, the owner of the bag is in car three. He didn't like being so close, but he felt that anywhere on the train was too close, so the simplest thing to do would be to sit in his ticketed seat.

He thinks about Lemon and Tangerine.

Are they the ones looking for the bag? He has a feeling of his seat sinking into the floor and the ceiling collapsing down on him. The two of them are cold and ruthless, violent in both outlook and method. He remembers the portly go-between telling him that.

He had considered moving the suitcase somewhere closer to his seat, like to the trash receptacle panel in the gangway between cars four and three, but decided against it. If he were to move it there was a good chance someone might spot him. It seemed best to keep it where it was. *It'll be all right, it'll work out fine.* He keeps telling himself this. *No more unforeseen developments.* Oh really? the other self inside him whispers tauntingly. Whenever you do anything, there are always twists and turns you never imagined, it says. Hasn't it always been that way, your whole life? Ever since you were kidnapped on the way home from junior school.

The snack trolley rolls by and he signals to the attendant. 'I'd like an orange juice.'

'Sold out. We usually have it, but just now we ran out.'

Nanao is impassive. I should have guessed, he almost says to her. He's used to this kind of low-grade bad luck. Every time he goes to buy shoes they're always sold out of his size in the colour he likes. When he gets in line to pay, the next line over always moves much faster.

When he kindly lets an elderly person get on a lift before him, he steps on and then the overweight alarm goes off. It's part of his daily routine.

He asks for a sparkling water and pays.

'You're always so jumpy and paranoid, it's like you bring bad luck on yourself,' Maria once said to him. 'You need to relax. When you think you might get worked up, have some tea, take some deep breaths, practise tracing Chinese characters with your finger on your palm. Do something to calm yourself down.'

'I'm not jumpy because I have a nervous nature or because I get stuck in my own head or anything. It's purely from experience. I've had rotten luck my whole life,' he replied.

He opens the can of sparkling water and takes a gulp. The tingling bite shoots through his mouth, making him swallow quickly and sending the fluid down the wrong pipe.

I hid the bag. We'll be at Omiya soon. If I just keep calm it'll be done soon, and basically according to plan, other than the fact that I'll have got off at Omiya instead of Ueno. I'll meet up with Maria, complain to her about how the job turned out not to be so simple, and that'll be that.

The more he tells himself this, the more anxious he becomes.

Nanao reclines his seat and tries to relax. He takes a breath, opens his left hand and starts to practise tracing Chinese characters with his right finger. But it's unexpectedly ticklish, and his hand reflexively jerks away.

Which knocks his can of sparkling water over. The can rolls with a cheerful clatter across the floor to the other end of the car, propelled by the movement of the train. Nanao springs up and chases after it.

He wasn't so optimistic as to hope that the can would come to a stop, but even he is surprised by how it skitters erratically left and right. He scrambles around, bending over to grab at it, apologising to the other passengers, generally making a scene.

It finally slows down, and Nanao swoops in and seizes it. Sighing, he starts to stand when he feels a sharp pain in his ribs. A groan escapes his lips. *That's it, they got me. Probably the owner of the bag.* A cold sweat wells up, but then he hears an old woman's voice, 'Pardon me, young man,' and he knows it's not an assassin. Just a diminutive granny. It looks like she was trying to get up and thrust out her cane for support, not noticing Nanao crouched down in front of her and catching him in the ribs with the end. It must have hit a particularly vulnerable spot because it's surprisingly painful.

'Excuse me,' she says, making a mighty effort to hoist herself into the aisle, paying very little attention to Nanao other than to make sure he knows she wants to get by. 'If I could just pass.' She hobbles off.

He leans on a nearby seat for support, massaging his rib and trying to catch his breath.

It hurts too much for him to just push past it and he writhes uncomfortably. As he squirms he notices the man in the seat behind the one he's holding. Same age as him, or maybe a little older, wearing a suit that makes Nanao think he's a straight-laced company employee. He can imagine the guy being good at numbers, accounting or finance or something like that.

'Are you all right?' The man looks concerned.

'I'm fine.' Nanao tries to stand up straight to show that he is indeed fine, but a stabbing pain jolts him and he crumples over, crashing down into the seat next to the man. 'I guess it hurts a little. I had a little collision with that woman. Was trying to get this can.'

'That was bad luck.'

'Well, I'm used to bad luck.'

'You always have bad luck?'

Nanao glances at the book the man's holding. Must be a travel guide, since there are lots of pictures of hotels and food.

The pain finally starts to subside and Nanao is about to get up when he has the urge to talk more. 'For example,' he says to the man, 'when I was eight I was kidnapped.'

The man raises his eyebrows in surprise at the sudden revelation, but he also smiles slightly. 'Is your family rich?'

'I wish.' Nanao shakes his head. 'We were about as far from rich as you can get. The only clothes my parents bought for me were my school uniform, and I was always jealous of the toys that my friends' parents bought for them. I was so frustrated I would chew on my fingers. There was another kid in my class, a rich kid who had the exact opposite situation as me. He had all the toys, what seemed like an unlimited allowance, tons of manga and action figures. He was what you'd call a lucky guy. My lucky friend. One time my lucky friend said to me, your family's poor, so you should try to be either a football star or a criminal.'

'I see,' the man murmurs. He looks like he's really feeling sympathy for the young Nanao. 'There are definitely kids for whom that's true.'

'I was one of them. Pretty limited range of options, become a pro footballer or choose a life of crime, but I was an obedient kid and I thought he was smart, so I did both.'

'Both? Football, and ...?' The man raises his eyebrows again and cocks his head.

'And crime. My first crime was stealing a football. I practised football and stealing all the time and got pretty good at both. It ended up shaping the course of my life, so in a way I owe that lucky friend a debt of gratitude.' Nanao is surprised at himself for opening up to a stranger when he's normally cagey, but there's something about this man, kind-seeming but somehow inert, that makes him seem like he'd be a willing listener. 'What was I going to tell you about?' Nanao searches for a moment, then remembers. 'That's right, my kidnapping.' *Am I really going to talk about this?*

'Your lucky friend seems like a much more likely candidate for being kidnapped,' says the man.

'Yes!' Nanao's voice goes up in pitch. 'That's exactly right! They took me by accident. They thought I was him. I mean the kidnappers. I was walking home together with my rich friend. But I lost at rock-paper-scissors so I was carrying his bag for him. He had a different bag from the rest of us.'

'A special bag?'

'Yeah, something like that. Custom-made for rich folks.' Nanao chuckles. 'And I was carrying it, so they took me. What a mess. I kept telling them I wasn't the rich one, they had the wrong kid, but they didn't believe me.'

'But eventually you were rescued?'

'I escaped.'

The kidnappers demanded a ransom from the parents of Nanao's lucky friend, but the parents didn't take it seriously. Which makes sense, because their son was safe at home with them. The kidnappers were furious, and started to treat Nanao more and more cruelly. He kept insisting he wasn't the kid they were looking for, until they eventually listened to him. They called his parents, figuring that as long as they got at least some money it didn't matter where it came from.

'My father gave the kidnappers a piece of unassailable logic.'

'What was that?'

'A man cannot give what he hasn't got.'

'Aha.'

'That upset the kidnappers, they told my father he was a terrible parent, but I understood what he was saying. A man really can't give what he hasn't got. He may have wanted to save his son, but he didn't have the money to do it. There was nothing he could do. I realised that I would have to save myself. So I escaped.'

The compartments of the storage cabinet in his mind start swinging open, thwack, then closing again, thwack. The scenes from the past that he glimpses inside may have been covered in dust but they maintain a vividness, scenes from his childhood that nevertheless seem immediate and tangible. The carelessness of the kidnappers, his youthful energy and determination, the well-timed lowering of a railway crossing arm and arrival of a bus. He remembers feeling a wash of relief when the bus pulled away coupled with fear about not having any money to pay the fare. But he did it, he escaped all on his own, Nanao the eight-year-old.

Thwack, thwack, more cabinet doors fly open inside his mind. By the time he warns himself that there may be memories he doesn't want to dredge up, it's too late, a door that should have stayed closed is already open. He catches sight of another little boy, eyes pleading, saying *Help me*.

'What's wrong?' The man in the suit picks up on the change in Nanao.

'Just some trauma,' Nanao answers, using the word Maria had teased him with. 'There was another boy who was kidnapped, too. He didn't get out though.'

'Who was he?'

'I never knew.' It was true. All he knew was that the other boy was being held with him. 'It was like some sort of storehouse for kidnapped children.'

The unfamiliar boy with the buzz cut realised Nanao was going to escape on his own. 'Help me,' he had said. But Nanao didn't help him.

'Thought he might slow you down?'

'I don't remember why I didn't do it. Might have just been an instinctive thing. I don't even think I thought about it.'

'What happened to him?'

'No idea,' Nanao answers honestly. 'He became my personal trauma. I don't really want to think about it.' *I wonder why I did*, he muses, closing the cabinet of memory. If he could, he would lock it shut and throw away the key.

'What about the kidnappers?'

'They were never caught. My father never even filed a report with the police. Said it would be more trouble than it was worth, and I didn't particularly care. I was just proud that I escaped. That was how I learned I could do things for myself . . . What made me tell you this story in the first place?' He finds it truly bizarre that he felt moved to talk on and on like this. Like a robot that had its talk button pushed. 'Oh, ever since I was kidnapped, my whole life's just been one mishap after another. When I was taking my high school entrance exam, even though I studied so hard, the kid in the next seat kept sneezing, and I ended up failing.'

'He disturbed your concentration?'

'No, no. On one huge sneeze a huge gob of his snot or phlegm or whatever came flying at me and landed on my answer sheet. I freaked out and tried to wipe it off, which smeared all the answers I had worked so hard to fill in. Even my name was illegible.'

Nanao's family couldn't afford to pay for his school so he needed to get a good enough score to win a scholarship, but thanks to some random kid's runny nose his chances were ruined. Nanao's parents never got too emotional about anything, though, so they weren't particularly angry or distraught.

'You really do have bad luck.'

'Wash your car and it rains. Except for when you wash your car in the hope of bringing rain.'

'What's that mean?'

'It's that Murphy's Law they used to talk about on TV. Story of my life.'

'Oh, right, Murphy's Law. I remember when the book came out.'

'If you ever see me in line for a cash register, go to the next line over. Whichever one I'm not in will move much faster.'

'I'll remember that.'

Nanao's phone buzzes. He checks the caller ID: Maria. He has a mixed feeling of relief and irritation at the interruption to this unusual conversation.

'That hit I took in the ribs feels a little better now. Thanks for listening.'

'I didn't do anything special,' the man says politely. There's nothing the least perturbed about his expression, but it's not quite relaxed either. It's as if the plug was pulled on a key emotional circuit.

'I think you might just be good at getting people to talk,' Nanao opines. 'Anyone ever tell you that?'

'But –' The man seems to think he's being criticised. 'But I didn't do anything.'

'Kind of like a priest who gets you talking just by being there. You're like a walking confessional booth, or maybe a walking priest.'

'I think most priests walk. Anyway, I'm just a plain old instructor at an exam-prep school.'

The words follow Nanao as he walks off into the gangway. He puts the phone to his ear and immediately hears Maria snap, 'Took you long enough to answer.'

'I was in the toilet,' he says loudly.

'Well, aren't you just having a grand old time. Although with your luck the toilet was probably out of paper or you got piss all over your hands.'

'I won't deny it. What's up?'

He hears what he thinks is Maria's annoyed breathing, though it could also be the thrum of the Shinkansen. He stands atop the coupling that connects the cars. The layered plates move like the joint of a living creature.

'Oh, What's up, he says. You seem awfully relaxed. The train's almost at Omiya. Make sure you get off this time. What'd you do with the big bad Wolf's body?'

'Don't remind me about him.' His legs sway with the train but he manages to keep his balance.

'Well, even if the body's discovered, I don't imagine anyone could connect his death with you.'

Exactly, thinks Nanao. Nobody knows much about the Wolf, including his real name. He guesses the police will have a tough time even identifying the body.

'So, what, make sure I get off at Omiya, right? Got it.'

'It'll be fine, there'll be no problem. I just wanted to put a little pressure on you, just in case.'

'Pressure?'

'I just spoke to our client. I told him my star player has the bag but wasn't able to get off at Ueno. I mean, I don't think it's a major problem that you're getting off at Omiya, but I figured I should keep him in the loop. It's just good business. Like how they teach new employees to report any problems or cock-ups to their supervisors.'

'Was he angry?'

'He went as white as a sheet. I couldn't see his face, but I could tell the blood was draining from his face.'

'Why would he go white?' Nanao could at least understand it if the client was angry. Whereas this reaction gives him a sense of foreboding, a premonition that this is much more than just a simple job.

'Our client is taking his orders from another client. That is to say, we're subcontractors for a subcontractor.'

'That happens often enough.'

'Indeed it does. But the main client who first ordered the job is a man in Morioka, name of Minegishi.'

The train lurches from side to side. Nanao loses his footing and has to grab on to a nearby handhold. He puts the phone back to his ear. 'Who did you say? I missed that.' As soon as he asks, the train enters a tunnel. The view out the windows goes dark. A rush of noise envelops the train, low and loud, like an animal growling. When he was little, Nanao was petrified any time he was on a train that went into a tunnel. He felt like there was a giant monster snuffling around in the dark, bringing its face up to the train, inspecting the passengers for the choicest morsels. He would feel it turn towards him, leering lasciviously, Any naughty children, any children ripe for the plucking, so he would curl up into a ball and try to remain perfectly still. Now he realises it was probably residual fear from being mistakenly kidnapped. Back then he thought that if there was any unlucky passenger likely to be taken by the monster it was him.

'Minegishi. You've heard of him – yes? You must at least know the name.'

For a moment Nanao doesn't follow what Maria is saying, but then it clicks, and the moment it does his stomach tightens. 'Minegishi. You mean *that* Minegishi?'

'I don't know what you mean by *that*.'

'The one who maybe cut off a girl's arm for being late.'

'Five minutes. Just five minutes late.'

'He's one of those characters who's always popping up in stories we tell to scare young criminals. I've heard rumours. They say he hates it when people don't do their jobs properly.' As the words leave his lips Nanao feels a wave of dizziness. Together with the swaying in his legs from the train and it's almost enough to make him topple over.

'See?' says Maria. 'See what I mean? We're in trouble. We didn't do our job properly.'

'This feels like it isn't really happening. Are you sure the main client is Minegishi?'

'Not a hundred per cent, but it definitely feels that way.'

'If it just feels that way, then we don't know for certain.'

'That's true. But our client sounds terrified, like he's worried what Minegishi will do to him. I told him that if you get off at Omiya it won't be that big of a problem, that he should keep calm, nothing to cry about.'

'Do you think Minegishi knows what happened? I mean that I didn't get off at Ueno. That I didn't do the job right.'

'I don't know. I guess it all depends on how our client handles it. Whether he's too scared to make a report, or if he runs off to confess because he's worried what'll happen if he doesn't.'

'Hey, wasn't there someone who called you with the intel on where the bag was?' The detail comes back to Nanao: right after the Shinkansen left Tokyo Station Maria got word that the suitcase was in the storage area between cars three and four. 'Which means that the person who gave you the information might still be on the train.'

'Could be. So what?'

'So that person is on my side, on team steal-the-bag. Right?' The thought of having an ally on the train is heartening to Nanao.

'I wouldn't count on it. That person's job was just to confirm the location of the bag and call me. They probably got off at Ueno.' He has to admit she's probably right. 'Well, are you feeling a little nervous? Like you'll be in trouble if you don't do the job right?'

'It was always my intention to do the job right.' As he says it Nanao nods resolutely. *I can't think of anyone else who tries as hard as me to do things right. I mean, depends on your definition of doing things right, but I never had my head in the clouds, I always put one foot in front of the other, I never complained about how poor my parents were, I never gave in to despair, I just stole that football and tried to get better and better at kicking it. I wouldn't be surprised if other people look up to me.*

'You do do the job right. But you're unlucky. I never know what's going to happen.'

'It'll be fine.' Of course, he isn't responding to Maria so much as telling himself, insisting on how things are supposed to go. 'I hid the bag. We're almost at Omiya. When I get off there, the job's over. Minegishi will have no reason to be mad.'

'I hope you're right. But I've learned an important lesson since we started working together: life is full of bad luck, just lying in wait. A job that feels like it's impossible to mess up can go unexpectedly wrong. Or even if the job doesn't go wrong, something else terrible can happen. Every time you go out, I discover a new way for things to fall apart.'

'But every time you still say it's a simple job.'

'Which is always true. It's not my fault that trouble follows you around. You could be about to cross a foot bridge and try stomping on it just to make extra sure it was stable and you'd end up hitting a bee that was resting on the bridge and it would sting you and you'd fall into the river. It's always like that with you. I bet you've never played golf, right?'

What? 'Uh, no.'

'Don't. You'd get the ball in the hole, and then you'd reach in to get the ball back, and a rat would pop out and bite your finger.'

'That's ridiculous. Why would a rat live in a golf hole?'

'Because *you* played golf there. I'm telling you. You're a genius at finding ways to mess things up.'

'You should get me a job where the mission is to mess up the job. It would probably go well,' Nanao jokes. But Maria doesn't laugh.

'No, because then you wouldn't mess up.'

'Murphy's Law.'

'Are you talking about Eddie Murphy?'

But anxiety suddenly clutches at Nanao. 'I should go and check on the bag.' He looks towards the front of the train.

'Good idea. With you involved, the hidden bag going missing sounds like a distinct possibility.'

'Don't make this any worse, please.'

'Careful. I bet you going to check if the bag is still there will mess something up.'

Then what the hell am I supposed to do? Nanao wants to scream, but he has to admit that Maria's probably right.

THE PRINCE

HE TAKES THE DUCT TAPE off of Kimura's wrists and ankles, setting the man free, but he isn't at all concerned. If Kimura lets his feelings get the better of him, turns violent, it'll put his son in danger. The man knows this by now. He doesn't think the Prince is bluffing. He knows that the Prince isn't one to lie about something like that. And now the Prince is asking for Kimura's help, which suggests that if he does a good job his son might escape danger. There are lots of things Kimura could do to get himself out of his current situation, but the chances that he would willingly put his son's life in danger are extremely slim. As long as a person believes things could still work out, they tend not to try anything desperate.

'What do you want me to do?' Kimura asks sullenly, rubbing his ankles where they had been taped up. It has to be humiliating for him to ask orders from someone he hates, but he's working to suppress his emotions. The Prince finds it extremely amusing.

'We're going to go together to one of the gangways a little further back. You know how there's a trash bin in the wall? The suitcase is in there.'

'It fits in the trash bin?'

'No, I didn't know this either but the wall with the trash is actually a panel and it opens up.'

'And that's where the guy with the black glasses hid it, huh? Okay, so we get the bag, and then what? It's a suitcase, right, so it's not exactly small. We bring it here and keep it by our seats, it'll be seen.'

The Prince nods. The bag isn't that large, but they wouldn't be able to hide it anywhere near the seats.

'There are two things we could do,' he says as they move from their car into the gangway. Then he steps over to the window and turns to face Kimura. 'The first is to have the conductor hold it.'

'The conductor?'

'Yes. Take the bag to the conductor, explain the situation, and have him hold on to it. I imagine there's a crew room or something where he could store it. If it's in there the owner will never find it.'

'What, you'd say you found a random bag? Or that it fell off the rack? They'd just make an announcement on the PA and everyone on the train would know. You'd have the people who want this suitcase lining up in front of the crew room.'

'I'd come up with a better story than that. Like this is my suitcase, but the man sitting next to me keeps eyeing it and I'm afraid he wants to steal it, so could you please hold on to it until I get off the train, something like that.' When he mentions the man sitting next to him, he points at Kimura.

'Oh, no, that doesn't sound suspicious at all.'

'Not if it comes from an honest-looking schoolkid like me.'

Kimura snorts, making a show of disdain for the plan. But it's plain to see that he's realising the Prince probably could con the conductor without too much trouble. 'Still, if you give the bag to the conductor then you won't have it.'

'I can get it back when we get to Morioka, and if that seems problematic I can just leave it there. I want to know what's in it, but it's more important that it's hidden. That way I can have influence over the people who want it.'

'What, like with your classmates and the robot cards?'

'Exactly. But I also thought of another thing I could do with it. Which would be to just take the contents.' The bag that the man with the black glasses seemed so concerned about has a four-digit combination lock. 'Keep trying different combinations and eventually it'll open.'

'You're gonna try every single possible combination? Do you have any idea how many there are? Good luck, kid.' Kimura clearly thinks it's a stupid idea cooked up by a child. The Prince feels sorry for the man and his inability to escape his prejudices.

'It won't be me doing it, it'll be you. You'll take it into the bathroom and start trying combinations.'

'Like hell I will. Do that in the toilet? No way.'

The Prince bites back his laughter at how easily Kimura loses his cool.

'Mr Kimura, I'm getting tired of telling you this over and over again, but if you don't do as I say your son will be in trouble. It'll be much better for you to just take the suitcase into the bathroom and play with the combination lock. Much, much better.'

'If I'm in the toilet for that long the conductor'll notice.'

'I'll come by and check the scene every once in a while. If people are lining up I'll let you know. You can come out, wait until it clears, and then go back in. It's not like you're doing anything wrong by turning the dials on a combination lock. There's all sorts of workable excuses.'

'I'll be turning dials till I die. I got no intention of sitting turning dials until I'm old and grey.'

The Prince starts walking again. He enters the next car, makes his way down the aisle, imagining what Kimura must be thinking as he follows. The man is close behind, staring at the back of the very person who pushed his son off a roof. No doubt he wants to pounce. His desire to do violence is palpable. If the setting allowed for it, he would grab the Prince by the arm, pull him close, strangle him to death. But Kimura can't do any of that. It's far too public here in the Shinkansen, but more than that, his son's life hangs in the balance.

Just picturing Kimura's teeth-grinding frustration fills the Prince with warmth and well-being.

'Mr Kimura,' he says, glancing back over his shoulder as they pass through car number six. Sure enough, Kimura's face is twisted into an ugly mask at having to keep his rage in check. The Prince finds the sight delectable. 'It won't take as long as you think to find the combination. It'll be something between 0000 and 9999, so that's ten thousand possible combinations. Say you try one combination per second, that's ten thousand seconds. About one hundred sixty-seven minutes. Less than two hours and fifty minutes. And I bet it won't even take that long. You'll probably be able to do more than one per second, and also –'

'You do all that maths in your head? What a clever boy.' Kimura says it mockingly, but this just makes him sound even more stupid to the Prince.

'– and also, you'd be surprised at how lucky I am. Even when I act more or less randomly, usually it works out for me. I win raffles and things like that all the time. It's always been like that for me, my whole life. It's almost bizarre. So I bet you'll find the right combination relatively quickly. Maybe even in the first thirty minutes, somewhere between 0000 and 1800.'

They emerge into the next gangway. It's deserted. The Prince walks right up to the trash bin in the wall.

'What, here?' Kimura steps up beside him.

'Look.' He points at the round protrusion. 'Push that, then give it a pull and a twist.'

Kimura does as he's told, extends his hand, pushes, pulls, twists. The panel swings open. He makes a little noise of surprise. The Prince leans closer and they look inside together. There it is on the top shelf: the black suitcase.

'That's it. Go ahead, grab it.'

Kimura is slightly dazed by the revelation of the secret compartment, but the Prince's words snap him back to attention. He reaches in and lifts the bag out. As he lowers it to the floor the Prince shuts the panel neatly.

'Okay, Mr Kimura, get in there and get opening.' The Prince points to the toilet door. 'We should set a signal. If there's a problem, I'll knock. Some other passenger might try knocking, so ours has to be a special one. So, if people are waiting in line and you should come out for a little, I'll knock five times, knock-knock-knock-knock-knock. I doubt anyone else would knock five times. And if someone who looks like trouble is nearby, I'll go knock-knock, knock. Three times, with a pause.'

'Who do you think might look like trouble?'

'Maybe the man with the black glasses.' As he says it the Prince pictures the worried-looking man. Then he thinks that even if this man accuses him of stealing the bag, he could almost certainly talk his way out of it. Some people are tough to handle, but others are simple. It has a little to do with their smarts and abilities, but it's mostly based on their fundamental character and psychology. People who let themselves get pushed around don't get any savvier as they get older. That's why there will always be opportunities for scammers and con artists. 'Or the other taller man who was looking for the suitcase.' That man seemed more dangerous, like he could get violent at a moment's notice. 'If someone like that comes along, I'll knock twice, then again.'

'Knock-knock, knock. And then what do I do?'

The Prince can't stop himself from smiling. Kimura's already relying on him, looking to him to make the decisions. He almost wants to encourage the man to think for himself.

'It'll depend on the situation. Just wait inside and stay alert. When the person goes away I'll knock again, just once.'

'And what about if they don't look like they're gonna go away?'

'I'll figure something out. Anyway, I don't think anyone would guess that you're inside trying to figure out the combination, so I doubt they would wait around too long.'

'I gotta say, I didn't expect such a vague plan from you.'

Kimura intends it as a jab, but the Prince doesn't take it to heart. He doesn't see any need for a complex plan. It's more important to be flexible, to keep calm when something happens and choose the next move.

'All right, Mr Kimura, you're on. Find that number. Open the case. Ready, set, go.' The Prince tugs Kimura's sleeve in the direction of the toilet.

'Hey, don't get all high and mighty with the orders. You think I'm just gonna do whatever you say?'

'I do. If I come back and you're not in the toilet, if you try to run off somewhere, I'll just make a phone call. You know, to my friend at the hospital. And that'll be the end of your boy. Aren't phones dangerous? You can do all sorts of things with a phone.'

Kimura glares with fury but the Prince pays him no mind. He just opens the door to the bathroom. Kimura enters grumbling. The lock clicks into place.

The Prince checks his watch. Almost at Omiya, but still a fair amount of time until Morioka. He has a feeling they'll have the case open before then.

As the Prince waits there in the gangway, the door to car five towards the rear of the train opens with a sound like a gust of wind.

The man with the black glasses steps through. He looks smart in his jean jacket and cargo pants. He has creases next to his eyes that make him look kind, like he smiles often. The Prince is careful to look natural as he steps over to the toilet door and knocks twice, then a third time. He tries to make it seem as if he's been waiting a bit to use the toilet but is finally giving up. Then he turns, as if just noticing the man with the black glasses. 'Oh, hey,' he says. 'Is your friend who drank too much okay?'

'Oh, you again.' A trace of irritation creeps onto the man's face, barely noticeable, but the Prince doesn't miss it. *He thinks I'm a pain,* he notes. It's not an uncommon reaction. Some adults are impressed by an honours student, but to some there's nothing in the world as annoying as a high-achieving kid. 'He passed out. Still sleeping. Drunks sure are trouble, huh?' He comes to a stop, scratching his temple. Then he turns towards the bin in the wall, glancing back at the Prince as he does.

'Something wrong?' the Prince asks solicitously, though he knows exactly what the man wants to do next: check that the bag is still there. He only hid it a short while ago; the Prince would have guessed it might be a bit longer before the man came to check on it.

He's more nervous than I thought. The Prince adjusts his appraisal of the man. Probably the type who starts worrying as soon as he leaves the house about whether he locked the door and turned off the gas.

'Uh, it's nothing.' The man clearly wants the Prince to leave him alone and go somewhere else. He doesn't lose his temper, but he's agitated.

The Prince makes a show of looking at his mobile phone, as if a call was coming in. 'Excuse me,' he says, pretending to start talking on the phone, and steps away towards the door. He reasons the man will try to open the panel if he thinks he's not being watched. Sure enough, he registers in his peripheral vision the man's nervous movements in front of the bin.

There's a slight clang, probably the panel swinging open. He forces himself not to look, but he can picture the man's shocked face upon discovering that the suitcase is gone. He fights back a smile.

'You've gotta be kidding me!' wails the man. The Prince ends his fake phone call and ambles back to the toilet door. When he innocently asks the man again if something's wrong, the man just stands there going pale and gaping at the open panel, not having bothered to close it.

'Oh wow, the wall opens,' the Prince says airily.

The man pulls at his hair, then takes his glasses off and rubs his eyes. The gesture is such a clichéd pantomime of consternation that the Prince wouldn't even expect to see a character in a manga do it, but the man clearly isn't trying to be funny. He's utterly bewildered. The only thing that the Prince doesn't understand is what the man says next: 'I knew it.'

'You knew it? Knew what?'

Apparently overcome with shock, the man doesn't bother to dissemble. 'There was a bag in here, the bag you saw me with before, my, my bag, I put it in here.'

'Why would you put it in there?' The Prince assumes the role of the naive, well-intentioned student.

'It's a long story.'

'And now it's gone? So what did you mean when you said you knew it?'

'I knew this would happen.'

He knew it would be stolen? The thought makes the Prince a bit uncomfortable. *Is he saying he knew I would steal it?* The possibility that the man might have seen through his plan seems so unbelievable that he almost accuses the man of lying, but he checks himself. 'You knew the bag would go missing?'

'Not specifically that, no. If I knew that then I wouldn't have put it in here. Just that something like this always happens. Everything I do ends up going wrong. As soon as I think, wow, it would be terrible if that happened, I really hope that doesn't happen, it happens. I was thinking I would be in trouble if the bag disappeared, so I came to check on it, and of course it's gone.' As he speaks the man seems to edge closer and closer to bursting into tears.

Aha, so that's it. The Prince is relieved. 'That sounds tough,' he says kindly. 'You said you'll be in trouble if you lose the bag?'

'Big trouble. Really big trouble. I was supposed to get off at Omiya.'

'Can you not get off if you don't have the bag?'

The man looks straight at the Prince, blinking rapidly. Apparently the possibility had never occurred to him. Then he seems to be imagining what might happen if that was the move he made. 'I guess I could, if I wanted to live the rest of my life on the run.'

'Whatever's in the bag must be really important.' The Prince touches his fingers to his mouth in a gesture he knows is hammy, but he calculates it will reinforce the image that he's just a harmless kid. 'Oh-h-h,' he says, pitching his voice up and drawing the syllable out, 'now that you mention it, I saw it just a little while ago. Your bag, I mean.'

'What?' The man's eyes pop. 'Wh-where?'

'When I was on my way to the bathroom. There was a man with a black suitcase. He was tall, wearing a jacket. His hair was kind of long.'

The man with the black glasses listens with a suspicious air, but after a moment his face turns into a scowl. 'Lemon or Tangerine.'

It's not clear why the man is naming fruits.

'Which way did he go?'

'I didn't see.'

'Oh.' The man looks back and forth towards the front and back of the train, trying to decide where he should begin his search. 'Which way do you think he went? Your gut instinct.'

'Huh?' *Why would he care about my gut instinct?*

'Everything I do goes wrong. If I go towards car six, then whoever has the bag will probably have gone the other way, and if I start in car five, then they'll be in the other direction. Whatever I choose, it'll get turned around.'

'Turned around by whom?'

The man swallows, at a momentary loss. Then he snaps, 'By someone, okay? Like maybe there's someone looking down on us, pulling the strings on all our lives.'

'I don't believe that,' says the Prince. 'No one's pulling any strings. There's no god of fate, and if by some chance there is a god, I feel like he just tossed all us humans into a display case and forgot about us.'

'So you're saying my bad luck isn't God's fault.'

'It's hard to explain. Say you have a board resting at an angle, and you drop some BBs or pebbles on it. Each one will roll in its own direction, find its own course down, but that's not because anyone set the course for it or changed its direction partway down. Where it falls depends on the speed and shape, so that it would naturally go that way on its own.'

'So what you're saying is I'm just unlucky by nature, it'll never change, no matter what I do, no matter how hard I struggle.'

The Prince was hoping his words would needle the man, make him lose his temper, but he didn't expect his reaction to be so completely dejected.

'What's your favourite number?'

'Why?' The man seems thrown off by the question. But despite his confusion he answers clearly, 'Seven. It's the Nana in my name, Nanao, Seven Tails. Although you'd think seven would be a lucky number.'

'Then why not try car number seven?' The Prince points to the front of the train.

'I feel like that'll end up being the wrong way,' the man says. 'I'll go in the other direction.' He starts towards the rear. The train will arrive at Omiya any moment.

'I hope you find it!'

The Prince steps closer to the toilet door and knocks once. *The bag you're looking for was in here all along, but you just walked on by. You really are unlucky.*

FRUIT

1 2 3 4 5 6 7 8 9 10

THE MELODY SIGNALLING THE TRAIN'S imminent arrival at Omiya starts to play in the carriage, followed by a station announcement. In the next seat over, Lemon is grinning. 'Feeling nervous?'

'A little, yeah. Aren't you?' Minegishi's man will be waiting for them at Omiya.

'Nope. Not really.'

Tangerine sighs. 'I'm jealous. It must be great to be so simple-minded. You know, it's your fault we're in this mess.'

'Sure, why not,' Lemon says, munching on some crackers. 'Though it's not all my fault. I mean, yeah, it's definitely probably my fault we lost the bag, but the fact that this kid is dead isn't on you or me, it's on him.'

'Him?' Tangerine looks at the corpse by the window. 'You mean it's his fault he's dead?'

'Yeah. He shouldn't have just gone and died. Selfish. You don't think so? He didn't even leave any clues.'

The Shinkansen starts to drop speed. Tangerine stands up.

'Hey, where you going?' Lemon sounds worried.

'We're pulling into Omiya. I have to report to Minegishi's guy, tell him everything's going smoothly. I'm going to wait by the door.'

'You're not gonna get off and make a run for it, right?'

I hadn't thought of that, realises Tangerine. 'Running would probably just make things worse.'

'If you run, I'll call Minegishi, I'll tell him it's all your fault, I'll offer to bring you in. You know, I'll lick his boots, I'll wag my tail, Oh, Mr Minegishi, I'll get that bastard Tangerine, just please forgive me, spare me my life! Like that.'

'Somehow I can't picture it.' He squeezes past the still-seated Lemon and steps into the aisle.

The train's brakes are kicking in. Tangerine sees a stadium out the left-hand window. It looks like a fortress, overwhelmingly large and somehow unreal. To the right a department store slides by.

'Don't be too confident,' Lemon says from behind, having followed. 'That's in the *Thomas* song too. Your best-plans can go wrong if you get too confident,' he sings, 'if you don't concentrate on what you're doing, accidents happen, just like that!'

'Sounds like a load of sunny crap to me,' Tangerine says. 'Anyway, you're the one who needs to listen to the message of that song.'

'I'm never overconfident. My confidence is exactly where it should be, no more, no less.'

'I mean the part about concentrating on what you're doing. You do everything sloppily, everything's a chore to you. No powers of concentration, no attention span.'

'Hey, don't tell me I've got no attention span. I'll give you an example. Take *Thomas and Friends*...'

'For fuck's sake.'

'There are two characters named Oliver, did you know that? There's the tank engine that Douglas rescued, and then there's the shovel car. Most people only think of the tank engine when they say Oliver, but strictly speaking there are two Olivers.'

'So what?'

'So, I'm saying that I pay attention to things like that. My attention's great.'

'Yeah, yeah.' Tangerine waves him away. He wants to point out that if that's the kind of thing Lemon cares about, there are three characters named Nikolai in *Anna Karenina*, but he knows all too well that Lemon will just spout some nonsense, like there's no Anna in *Thomas* but there is an Annie and do you realise that Karenina sounds like a combination of car and Nina but there's no Nina in *Thomas* either.

The train pulls in to Omiya Station.

As Tangerine enters the gangway an announcement says that the doors on the left side will open. He positions himself accordingly. The platform slides by on the left. A scattering of people await the train's arrival.

Tangerine doesn't know what Minegishi's man will look like, or even if it's just one man. *Am I even gonna find this guy?* He wonders uncertainly, but at that very moment, just as the train is easing to a stop, he glimpses a man through the window, a man who obviously has nothing to do with the society of law-abiding, workaday people, clearly someone whose world is the backstreets and dark alleys. *There he is.* The man is tall with slicked-back hair. He wears a black suit and a loud blue shirt, no tie. He's only visible for a moment as the train floats along its last few metres, so Tangerine doesn't get a clear look at the man's face.

With a sound like an exhalation, the door trembles, then opens.

Tangerine steps onto the platform without any hesitation. He turns and sees the man in the suit and blue shirt step up to the Shinkansen and bring his face up to the window, his hands framing his eyes to make a shade. He peers inside the train, ignoring the two young women who seem scandalised by his peeping. He must be checking up on Minegishi's kid, seated across the aisle by the opposite window.

'Yo,' Tangerine calls out. The man turns, scowling. Tangerine sees now that this guy isn't some flashy punk. He has a dignified bearing, in his forties – if he were a normal working citizen he'd probably be in management. Actually kind of handsome. Sharp look in the eyes, no visible paunch. He electrifies the air around him just by standing there, making Tangerine's nerves stand on end.

'What can I do for you, buddy?' The man resumes looking through the train window, tossing a few more glances towards Tangerine.

'I'm Tangerine. I guess you're the fellow Minegishi sent to make sure my partner and I have his son.'

Blue-shirt's scowl eases with recognition, but a moment later his face turns grave again. 'Everything going smoothly?'

'More or less. You know, three men squeezed in together isn't the most comfortable.' He points at the window and looks in. Lemon, still in his seat, notices them and waves his hand with childish enthusiasm. All Tangerine can do is pray, *Don't mess this up.*

'Is he sleeping?' Blue-shirt jerks his thumb towards the window.

'Who, the kid? Yeah, when we found him he was tied to a chair and hadn't had any sleep. He must be worn out.' Tangerine tries his utmost to keep his voice sounding natural. The train won't be stopping at the station much longer. He needs to get back on.

'That tired, huh?' Blue-shirt crosses his arms, a dubious look on his face as he peers back in once more. The young women make pained faces and contort their bodies to avoid his gaze. Lemon just keeps waving.

'Hey, I was wondering something about Minegishi,' Tangerine says. He doesn't want this guy to look too hard at the dead rich kid.

'You mean *Mr* Minegishi.' Blue-shirt is basically pressing his nose against the window. His mild tone carries an undeniable authority.

'Sure, Mr Minegishi. Is Mr Minegishi as rough as they say? I mean I've heard all kinds of rumours, but I don't know what's really what.'

'He's not rough if people do their jobs properly. People who don't do their jobs properly tend to find his treatment rough. Which is perfectly fair, wouldn't you say?'

The melody signalling the train's departure starts to play on the platform. Tangerine tries to hide his relief. 'Guess that's my signal.' *Stay cool now.*

'Sounds like it.' Blue-shirt steps away from the window and looks straight at Tangerine.

147

'Tell Minegishi we're on top of it.'

'*Mr* Minegishi.'

Tangerine turns on his heel and heads back to the Shinkansen door. *Bought ourselves a little time, at least until we get to Sendai,* he reassures himself, but he feels Blue-shirt's eyes boring a hole in his back. *Keep it together.* His hand floats to his rear pocket, where he feels the giveaway entry Lemon gave him, the one with the drawing of the train that's never had an accident. *Wonder if this thing works.*

'Oh, hey,' Blue-shirt calls from behind. Tangerine halts in mid-stride, with one foot already on the train. Trying to act natural, he steps his other foot into the train and turns round.

'What's up?'

'You've got the suitcase, right?' Blue-shirt's expression doesn't show any doubt or suspicion. He just seems to be doing his administrative duty, checking an item off his list. Tangerine attempts to keep his breathing steady.

'Of course.'

'And you didn't do anything stupid like store it somewhere you couldn't keep an eye on it.'

'No, it's right there by our seats.'

Tangerine turns slowly and steps further into the train, just as the door slides shut. He re-enters car number three and returns to his seat. His eyes meet Lemon's. 'No sweat,' Lemon says, giving a playful thumbs up.

'Cut it out,' Tangerine hisses. 'He's probably still watching.'

Lemon turns reflexively to the window, but his movements are jerky, making him look nervous. Before Tangerine can scold him again he follows Lemon and looks towards the window. Blue-shirt is just on the other side, staring in at them.

Lemon waves again. Tangerine can't tell if he's just being paranoid but it seems that Blue-shirt looks more sceptical than before. 'Come on, man, don't push it. He suspects something's up.' Tangerine tries to move his lips as little as possible.

'Relax. The train's leaving. Once a train starts moving no one can stop it. Unless you're Sir Topham Hatt, forget about it.'

As the train inches forward, Blue-shirt stares penetratingly in at them. Tangerine gives a brief wave, like you would to a co-worker.

Blue-shirt opens one hand and twitches it as if to say See you later, following along as the train departs. Then his face goes rigid and his eyes widen, which makes Tangerine's brow furrow in consternation. *What happened?* He wonders, then turns his head and sees something he doesn't quite believe: Lemon lifting up Little Minegishi's dead hand and waving it, like he was playing with a giant doll. With the kid's head against the window and his body slumped on the wall the angle of the waving hand looks completely bizarre.

'What the fuck are you *doing?*' Tangerine wrenches Lemon's arm away. Which makes the body lurch towards Lemon. The head flops forward, chin to chest. It does not look at all like someone sleeping peacefully. Frantic, Tangerine tries to prop the body up.

'Ohhh shit.' Even Lemon seems concerned.

The Shinkansen picks up speed and Tangerine looks back at the receding platform. Blue-shirt's face is deadly serious as he lifts his phone to his ear.

They somehow manage to get the body upright and stable.

Tangerine and Lemon collapse back into their seats simultaneously.

'We're fucked.' Tangerine can't help stating the obvious.

Lemon just starts to sing quietly, 'Accidents happen, don't take it a- a-all so h-a-ard!'

NANAO

AS NANAO WATCHES OMIYA STATION disappear into the distance, he wonders vaguely what the hell is going on. There's a smokescreen swirling around inside his head, preventing his thoughts from circulating.

It seems like he should be doing something besides going back to his seat, so he stays in the gangway and stares at his phone. He knows he should call Maria, but he can't quite work himself up to it. But he also knows that it'll only be a matter of time before she calls him.

He makes up his mind and dials.

She answers before it even rings, like she was hovering over her phone waiting to pounce. It gives Nanao a heavy feeling. Even Maria, usually so optimistic and flexible, is apparently on edge. Probably because she knows how dangerous Minegishi is.

'What train did you catch back to Tokyo?' There's a forced casualness in her voice though she's dying to confirm his homeward status.

'Same train as before. I'm on the Hayate.' He says it so matter-of-factly that it almost sounds flippant. He also has to speak louder than usual due to the noise of the tracks in the gangway. Maria's voice is difficult to make out.

'What do you mean? You haven't got to Omiya yet?'

'We passed Omiya. I'm still on the Hayate.'

Maria falls silent in momentary confusion. But then she heaves a sigh, guessing from her previous experiences with Nanao that something's gone wrong. 'Yeah, I thought that might happen, but I didn't *really* think it would happen. Guess I shouldn't underestimate you.'

'The bag's gone. So I couldn't get off.'

'Didn't you hide the bag?'

'Yeah. Now it's gone missing.'

'Time for you to get married.'

'Sorry?'

'To the god of bad luck. You two should really get married at this point, since you're so cosy. I should be pleased, but I'm just too pissed off.'

'Why should you be pleased?'

'Because I was right that you wouldn't be able to get off at Omiya. It's satisfying to be right, you know? But in this case I'm just depressed.'

Nanao doesn't appreciate her mockery, and he considers jabbing back, but he doesn't want to waste the time and energy. Most important is figuring out how to handle their immediate predicament.

'Next question. I get that you don't know where the bag is. I'm not happy about it, but I accept the facts of the situation. But why didn't you get off at Omiya? If the bag's missing that means somebody probably took it. Now the Shinkansen stopped at Omiya, so I'd say there are two possibilities. One, that the person who took it is still on the train, or two, that they took the bag and got off.'

'Right.'

Nanao had considered this in the moments before the train pulled into Omiya, as if he was scrambling to put together a rush construction job: should he get off the train, or stay on and keep looking for the bag?

'So why did you decide not to get off at Omiya?'

'Two options, and I had to pick one. I went with the option that seemed to have better odds, even if only a little.'

He had tried to anticipate which option would give him a higher chance of getting the suitcase back. If he had got off at Omiya and tried searching for whoever had it, he wasn't sure he'd be able to find them. If whoever it was got on a different train or slipped off into the streets, there wouldn't be much he could do. On the other hand, if he stayed on the train, and the person with the bag was also on board, there was at least some chance he could get it back. The thief wouldn't be able to get off for a while, so if Nanao went through the train with a fine-tooth comb he might very well be able to catch them. Based on these calculations, Nanao decided it would be better to stay on the train. In no small part it was also the fact that as long as he remained on the train he could reasonably say he was still on the job. If Minegishi got in touch to check on the status, Maria would be able to say that Nanao was on the train, fighting the good fight. At least he hoped that was the case.

He did get off for a minute, though. He thought he should at least scan the platform to make sure no one was running off with the bag. If someone looked like a likely suspect he would have chased them. Given how long the train was and the curve of the platform he couldn't see all the way to the front, but he was resolved to do what he could, and he stood there swivelling his head back and forth, watching.

A few cars back, maybe car three or four, two people caught his eye. The taller one wore black clothes and had long hair for a man. Tangerine, or maybe Lemon.

Whichever one it was, the tall man stood with his back to Nanao, facing someone else who was apparently waiting on the platform. An older guy, with a vivid blue shirt. His hair was pulled back in a way that made Nanao think of an old lady's hairstyle in a foreign film. Kind of endearing.

The taller man got back on the train. Nanao glimpsed his profile and couldn't tell if it was Lemon or Tangerine or even someone else entirely. The man in the blue shirt stayed on the platform and leaned towards the train, peering in at the window. It didn't look like he was seeing the taller man off. In fact it wasn't at all clear what the blue-shirted man was doing. All Nanao could say for sure was that it was car three and not four. He had counted.

'You said the bag's owner was in car three, right?' Nanao checks with Maria after recounting what he had seen on the platform at Omiya.

'Yeah. At least that's what I was told. And you're saying you spotted Tangerine or Lemon in car three?'

'Someone who looks like he could be one of the two of them. Which gives more strength to the theory that they were the bag's original owners.'

'I think it's a little more certain than a theory.'

'Sorry, what was that?' He's paying attention, but it's difficult to hear her. The Shinkansen is known for being a smooth ride, but the swaying can be intense in the gangway; he has to focus on keeping steady, and he's distracted by the incessant racket of the tracks. It's as if the train is trying to prevent him from connecting with Maria, his only ally. 'Either way, I decided that staying on the train gave me a better chance to get the bag back.'

'Well, you're probably right about that. So you think that the fruit twins stole it back from you?'

'I stole it from them first. Then they stole it back from me. That seems the most likely. If there were a third party involved things would start to get complicated. I really hope that isn't the case.'

'If that's what you hope, then it probably is the case.'

'Come on, stop trying to freak me out, please!' His hopes and dreams never come true, but everything he fears always does.

'I'm not trying to freak you out. This is just the story of your life. The god of bad luck is totally in love with you. Or the goddess, I guess.'

Nanao tries to steady himself against the swaying. 'Is the goddess of bad luck good-looking?'

'Do you really want to know?'

'I guess I'll pass.'

'Okay, but really, what *are* we going to do?' He can hear her anxiety plainly enough.

'What indeed.'

'How about this?' As she says this the train bucks and he loses his balance, then catches himself. 'For starters, you steal the bag back from the two fruits.'

'How?'

'Doesn't matter how. You just have to do it, no matter what. Get that bag. That's the first order of business. Meanwhile, I'll make something up to tell our client.'

'Like what?'

'Like we have the bag, but you missed getting off at Omiya, and the Shinkansen doesn't stop again until Sendai so he'll just have to sit tight until then. That's what I'll tell him. The important part is that we have the bag. I mean I'll be casual, but I'll make it clear that you're doing your job. You just weren't able to get off the train, unfortunately. That'll probably be good enough.'

'Good enough for what?'

'Good enough to keep Minegishi from flipping out.'

Makes sense, thinks Nanao. Rather than being the kids sent to the grocery store who don't buy any vegetables, it's better to be the kids who bought the vegetables but got held up on the way home due to roadworks. They'd still seem reliable enough, and probably get in less trouble.

'By the way, do you think Tangerine and Lemon would recognise you?' Maria's voice is tight. She's no doubt starting to imagine a confrontation.

Nanao thinks back. 'I don't think so. We've never worked together. Once I was in a bar and someone pointed them out to me. That's Tangerine and Lemon, baddest guys in the business, he said. I remember thinking they looked dangerous, and actually they ended up tearing the place apart. It was pretty hectic.'

'Well then, the opposite could be true too.'

'Meaning what?'

'Maybe somebody once pointed you out to them. That guy in the black glasses, he's still young but he's by far the unluckiest guy in the biz. So they might recognise your face too.'

'I – that's –' But Nanao swallows his words. He can't say for sure that it wouldn't have happened. Maria seems to sense what he's thinking.

'Right? That's exactly the kind of thing that would happen to you. Because you're her favourite,' she says knowingly, 'the dog-faced goddess of bad luck is madly in love with you.'

'Now she's dog-faced?'

'Beggars can't be choosers. Okay, go on, get over to car three.'

Then Maria lets out a cry of dismay. 'Maria? What happened?'

'No way. Are you kidding me?'

Nanao presses his ear against the phone. 'What happened?'

'I am just so over this,' she groans.

He hangs up in consternation.

KIMURA

WHY DO THEY GOTTA MAKE train toilets so nasty? Kimura grimaces as he hunches over the suitcase and fiddles with the lock. The toilet gets cleaned regularly, and isn't particularly dirty, but the whole situation feels repugnant.

He's working on the combination lock. Rotates one dial by one digit, tries to open it. It doesn't budge. *Next,* he flips the dial again, one more digit, tries to open it. Tries again, but it still doesn't cooperate.

The Shinkansen sways back and forth rhythmically.

The walls of the tiny room start to press in, make him feel like his spirit is being crushed. He thinks back to how he was not too long ago. Couldn't stop drinking, and if he went even a little while without a drink he would get anxious and crabby. More than once Wataru hid all the alcohol in the apartment on his grandparents' instructions, but Kimura just ransacked the place looking for it, and if he didn't find it he'd get desperate, almost ready to drink his hair tonic. He's just glad that he never got violent with Wataru. He knows that if he ever hit his son his

156

remorse would fester in him until it filled his whole body up, killing him dead.

And now that he's finally stopped drinking, now that he's clawed his way out of the dark forest of alcoholism, his son's lying in the hospital in a coma. It makes him want to scream. *How come now that I beat this thing Wataru isn't around to see it?* He feels like his new beginning has been robbed of meaning.

The bucking train tosses his body around.

His finger scrapes the dial. He puts pressure on the handle to open the suitcase. But it doesn't open. He's got from 0000 to 0261 and he's already sick of the tedious task. *How come I gotta do this bullshit job for that fucking Prince?* His humiliation and rage mix and mount until he explodes, savagely kicking the toilet bowl. It happens three more times. Each time, he manages to get a hold of himself, telling himself he has to stay calm. *Keep calm, make a show of following the Prince's orders, wait for my chance. Sooner or later I'll get my chance to punish that little son of a bitch.*

But before long his nerves start to twist and fray, and he wants to lash out again. Rinse, wash, repeat.

A bit earlier the Prince gave him a signal. Two knocks, then a third, knock-knock, knock. They agreed that meant someone looking for the bag was just outside, maybe the guy in the black glasses. He tried to make out what was going on outside the door, but all he could really do was keep trying combinations. Eventually there was another knock, just one, meaning the guy had left.

When he gets the dials to 0500 he reflexively reads it as five o'clock, which makes him think of that one evening when he remembered looking at the time just when it displayed 5:00.

He was home with Wataru, who was watching a kids' show on TV. Kimura lay sprawled on the couch behind his son, pulling from a bottle of booze. It was a Monday but he was off work so he spent the whole day loafing around drinking. Then at 5 p.m. the doorbell rang. *Probably a newspaper subscription guy,* he guessed. He usually had Wataru get the door, since most people preferred being greeted by a friendly little kid than by a middle-aged drunk.

But that time Kimura went to see who it was. Wataru was into his show, and Kimura felt like he should be getting up soon anyway.

There was a kid at the door in school uniform.

Kimura couldn't figure out why a schoolboy might be ringing his doorbell and for some reason he thought it might be a pitch for a religious group. 'We're already saved, thanks.'

'Sir.' The boy's tone was familiar, definitely not how you would talk to someone you're just meeting for the first time, but it wasn't a rude familiar. It was vulnerable. The kid looked like he was on the verge of tears.

'Whaddayou want?' The alcohol in Kimura's system made it feel like he was seeing something that wasn't really there, a mirage of a schoolboy. But then he remembered: he had seen this kid before, it was coming back to him. This was one of the boys he had crossed paths with twice before. The kid was gangly with a pale face and an oblong head that made Kimura think of a cucumber. His nose jutted out crookedly. 'What the hell are you doing here?'

'Sir, I need your help.'

'Oh come on, seriously?' Kimura wanted to close the door, wanted nothing to do with this, but it also bothered him enough to want to know what was going on. He stepped outside and grabbed the kid's collar roughly, jerked him forward and threw him down. The cucumber-headed kid toppled over and sat on the ground snivelling. Kimura didn't feel sorry for him. 'How'd you know where I live? You're one of those kids I've seen around. How'd you find me here?'

'I followed you,' he wailed, but it was a resolute wail.

'You followed me?'

'When I go for exam-prep lessons I ride by here on my bike. I saw you walking one time and I followed you back. That's how I know where you live.'

'How come sexy chicks never follow me? Or maybe that's what you're after. You like older guys or something?' Kimura cracked a dumb joke to cover his fear, his sense that this kid was an ill omen, bringing some-thing dark to his door.

'No way. I just, there's no one else that can help but you.'

'The Prince again?' Kimura exhaled roughly, down in the kid's direc-tion. He didn't know if there was booze on his breath, but the kid's expression made him think he must smell pretty foul.

'. . . gonna die.'

'No one's gonna die from inhaling alcohol breath. It's not like it's cig-arette smoke.'

'No, Takeshi's gonna die.'

'Who's Takeshi? Another one of your classmates?' Kimura sounded fed up. 'Last time it was someone who committed suicide. What kind of school do you go to, anyway? I'm definitely not sending my kid there.'

'This time it isn't suicide,' Cucumber-head said urgently.

'I don't care what the hell you kids do.' He was about to aim a kick at the kid and shout at him to get lost, but the boy spoke up quickly.

'He's not a person, he's a dog. Takeshi is Tomoyasu's dog.'

This hit Kimura differently.

'Wha? What do you mean, he's a dog? You kids keep it confusing,' he said, but now he was interested. He called back into the apartment, 'Wataru, I'm going out. You just watch TV like a good boy, okay?' Wataru answered back obediently. 'All right, kid, tell me what's going on.'

Kimura often went to the park at the edge of the neighbourhood. There was a playground and a sandpit for the kids in front of a small wood of mixed trees. It was a nice park, uncommonly large for a residential neighbourhood.

The kid filled Kimura in on the situation as they walked to the park.

It started when one of their classmates whose father was a doctor and ran a private clinic said that they had a medical device that admin-istered electric shocks. It was like an AED, for shocking a stopped heart back to life, but it was a prototype, stronger than the typical defibrillator.

159

It was as straightforward to use as a normal AED. It had two electrode pads that were pressed on the chest to either side of the heart, and the pads fed data to an electrocardiogram. If the device determined that the heart needed a shock, you just pushed a button and let the current flow.

'As soon as the Prince heard that, he was like, let's see how strong it is.'

Kimura made a sour face, like he'd swallowed an insect. 'Your Prince sure is a noble guy to come up with an idea like that. So what happened?'

'The kid with the doctor dad said the machine's automatic, so it wouldn't work on a human who was healthy.'

'That how it works?'

Cucumber-head frowned and shook his head. 'He thought that saying that would make the Prince give up.'

'But that's just the kinda thing the Prince would wanna try, huh?' The kid gave a pained nod.

That day the Prince made the doctor's kid steal the shock device. 'So they're gonna do it in the park?'

'Everyone's there.'

'The machine's for restarting a stopped heart, right?'

'Yeah.'

'So what would happen if you used it on a healthy person?'

The kid's face crumpled. 'I asked the doctor's kid that, you know, secretly. He said his dad said that it'd kill the person.'

'Hmm.'

'AEDs are automatic, so it wouldn't work, but this one's a prototype, and it's stronger.'

Kimura grimaced at the thought. 'And now the Prince wants to use Takeshi the dog as a test subject. Makes sense. I guess the Prince doesn't have the balls to go ahead and try it on a human first.'

Cucumber-head shook his head slowly. It wasn't a gesture of denial, but one of disappointment that Kimura was underestimating the Prince. A gesture of despair at the realisation that this man probably couldn't help after all.

'No. At first the Prince was gonna try it out on Tomoyasu.'

'What, Tomoyasu messed up?' It wasn't hard to imagine. He thought back to his own experiences with gangs and criminal organisations. Usually when the higher-ups got violent with members of their own group it was to make an example of them. Doing that served to tighten up the group through fear. It was a good way to force obedience. The Prince, who won his position over his classmates through fear, probably relied on the same tactics. He used electric shocks to dole out punishments and remind everyone that he was the one with the power.

'Tomoyasu's kind of slow. You know, he moves slow. The other day we were stealing manga from the bookstore and he fell behind and almost got caught.' He explained that the clerk had chased Tomoyasu down and grabbed him, but the others ran back and kicked the clerk to the ground, giving their classmate a chance to get away. 'Even after the guy was down we kept kicking him until he was knocked out. I think he was hurt pretty bad.'

'If you're that worried about getting caught you shouldn't bother shoplifting.'

'It's always something like that with Tomoyasu, but he also talks kind of big.'

'Moves slow and talks big. No wonder the Prince is annoyed with him. What, does he brag about his dad being a hotshot lawyer or something?' Kimura just hit on the idea of a lawyer randomly. Cucumber-head looked surprised.

'Actually, yeah. His dad is a lawyer.'

'Yeah, well, lawyers aren't such a big deal. And something tells me laws don't much matter to the Prince.'

'But Tomoyasu's dad has some scary friends, or at least that's what Tomoyasu always says.'

'Ah, now that is annoying. Nobody likes to hear someone brag, but bragging about who you know is the worst. People who do that deserve to be taken down a peg or two.'

'Tomoyasu was picked to be the test subject for the shock thing, but of course he didn't wanna do it. He cried and begged and kissed the Prince's shoes right here in the park.'

'And what'd his majesty do?'

'He said he'd spare him but Tomoyasu had to go and get his dog instead. His dog Takeshi. I've known Tomoyasu since we were little and he's had that dog his whole life. He really loves him.'

Kimura chuckled. Now he could see what the Prince was up to. At this point testing out the defibrillator was secondary. It was more about savouring Tomoyasu's sacrifice of his beloved dog just to save his own skin. And by doing that he could grind Tomoyasu down, break his spirit. It was clear enough what the Prince was after. But even though he understood it, Kimura was also unsettled by the thought that the Prince would actually do it. 'His highness really is something else. You know, if he's that rotten it actually makes him kind of predictable.'

'Sir, I wouldn't start thinking the Prince is predictable if I were you.' As he said this the park entrance came into view.

'Uh, I shouldn't go with you any further. I'll split off and go home from here. If the Prince thinks I snitched I'll be in trouble.'

Kimura couldn't bring himself to make fun of the kid, call him a chicken. He could tell the kid was desperate. And if his friends found out that he went for help, who knows what would happen to him. At the very least he'd become the new test subject for the defibrillator. 'Yeah, all right, get outta here. I'll make it look like I was just walking by.' He waved the kid away.

Cucumber-head nodded like a frightened child and started to leave. 'Hey, wait,' Kimura called to him. The kid turned, right into Kimura's fist, slamming full force into his jaw. He staggered, went down, his eyes rolling wildly.

'You've done your fair share of bad stuff too, right? Consider this your punishment. Just be thankful that's all you get,' Kimura snarled. 'But why me? How come you came to me for help? You don't know any other grown-ups?' Looking for help from a drunk with a kid didn't seem like the best of choices.

'No one else,' the kid said, rubbing his jaw and checking for blood. He didn't look angry. He actually seemed relieved at the thought that he could get off with just a solid punch to the jaw. 'There's no one else who could do it. Who could stop the Prince.'

'Try the police.'

'The police . . .' The kid hesitates. 'No, that'll never work. They need like proof to do anything. The police only go after people who are obviously bad.'

'What does that mean, obviously bad?' But Kimura knew what it meant. Laws work for people who steal things and beat people up. The authorities can cite legal verse and administer the appropriate penalty. But when things aren't so clear-cut, when dealing with a vaguer sort of evil, laws don't work as well. 'I guess laws don't apply to princes. Princes make their own laws.'

'Yeah, exactly.' The kid started to move away again, still rubbing his jaw. 'But you don't seem like laws matter to you, sir.'

'You mean cos I'm a drunk?'

The kid didn't answer, just melted away into the twilight.

Kimura made his way into the park. *I can walk straight.* At least that's what he thought, but he wasn't sure if he was actually walking straight or not. He imagined his parents berating him, telling him he had never walked a straight line in his life. He breathed into his palm to check for alcohol, but he wasn't sure he could smell that either.

He came to the trees and began picking his way through them in the settling gloom.

Further in, he could hear something, not quite voices or identifiable noises, just a dark murmur.

The ground sloped gently downward to a depression in the wood where fallen leaves collected. Shadowy figures stood in a huddle. The black school uniforms made them seem like members of a cult conducting a ritual.

Kimura hid behind a tree. His shoes on the leaves made a sound like crumpling paper, but was still a little way off from the group and no one noticed his approach.

He peeked his head out once more and watched the schoolkids. About ten of them were tying up a dog. At first he couldn't tell what they were tying it to, but after a moment he realised they were tying it to another boy. Probably the dog's owner, Tomoyasu. The kid was hugging the mutt to himself and the others were wrapping them both in duct tape. Kimura could hear Tomoyasu trying to calm the dog, It's all right, Takeshi, everything's all right. The sight of the kid trying to ease his dog's fear made something tighten in Kimura's chest.

He ducked back behind the tree. The other students surrounding Tomoyasu and the dog were all silent. Air charged with breathless anxiety. Kimura thought it was odd that the dog wasn't barking, and he poked his head out again. He saw that the dog was muzzled with a tightly wrapped length of fabric.

'Hurry up and put 'em on,' one of the students said. They were sticking on the defibrillator pads.

'They're on, look.'

'Is this thing really gonna work?'

'Of course it's gonna work. You calling me a liar? What's your problem? When we were beating up Tomoyasu before I heard you saying sorry. You don't even want to be doing this. I'm gonna tell the Prince.'

'I didn't say sorry. Don't make shit up.'

The Prince really has these kids under his thumb. They're completely powerless. Kimura was impressed. When you lead a group by fear the rank and file lose trust in one another. The stronger the fear, the weaker the trust. The anger and resentment at the despot is turned on people who should be allies, making the spark of rebellion less likely. Everyone just wants to keep themselves safe, their only goal is to avoid being punished, and they start watching one another. When Kimura used to carry a gun and do his illegal work, he often heard about the man named Terahara, and how the members of Terahara's organisation were all suspicious of one another. They tried to avoid mistakes in the hope that Terahara's wrath would be directed at someone else. It eventually led to them all turning on each other, looking for someone to serve as a sacrificial offering.

Sounds exactly like what we've got here.

Kimura scowled. The schoolkids crunching around in the fallen leaves as they prepared their sinister experiment didn't seem to be having any of the fun Kimura remembered from when he was younger and pushing other kids around. All he sensed from them was terror. They were torturing someone just to protect themselves.

He looked down at his feet and noticed for the first time that he was wearing sandals.

Given what he could imagine might happen once he confronted the kids, his preparations seemed to be sorely lacking. *Should I lose the sandals? No, if I'm barefoot that makes it harder to get around. Should I go and get my gun? That'd wrap this up quick, but it'll be a pain in the ass to go back.* As he ran through his options, Tomoyasu cried out.

'Wait, guys, stop. You can't do this. I don't want Takeshi to die!' The vegetation in the wood seemed to absorb his pleas, but Kimura heard them clearly enough. Rather than giving the others pause, Tomoyasu's wailing only goaded them on. Hearing a sacrifice beg must have finally given them a flash of sadistic thrill.

Kimura stepped out from behind the tree and ambled down the slope towards the group. 'Hey, it's you,' one of the students said, recognising him immediately. Kimura couldn't recall the kid's face but he figured it was one he had met before, like Cucumber-head.

He edged closer, sandals crunching leaves. 'Hey now, what do you think you're doing to that dog? Don't worry, doggie, I'll save you.' Kimura glared at the group. The medical device lay on the ground. Two cords ran from it and attached to pads, which were taped to the dog. 'Poor doggie, look at you. This just isn't right. Well, don't worry, a drunk old man is here to rescue you.'

Taking advantage of the fact that the kids were standing around at a loss, Kimura strode in among them and pulled the pads off the dog. Then he ripped off the tape that was binding the dog to his master. The adhesive was strong and it pulled at the fur, making the dog thrash around, but Kimura somehow managed to get it off.

'This is bad,' he heard someone say behind him. 'We gotta stop this guy.'

'There you go, get mad, kid. I'm messing with your mission – if you don't do something quick his highness the Prince'll be angry.' Kimura smiled viciously. 'Hey, where is the Prince anyway?'

A calm, clear voice rang out. 'Wow, sir, you sure seem pleased with yourself.'

Kimura looked up. A short distance away was the Prince's dazzling smile. Then a rock came hurtling out of the darkness.

Click, goes the lock, and the suitcase opens, interrupting Kimura's recollection. The dials read 0600. *Guess his majesty really is lucky.* Considering how many possible combinations there were, he's arrived at the correct one quickly. He hoists the bag up onto the toilet and opens it all the way.

It's filled with neatly stacked sheaves of 10,000-yen notes. Kimura isn't all that impressed. The notes aren't new, they're used and wrinkled, and though there's a fair amount of money in there it isn't enough to move him especially. He had transported far larger sums in the past.

He's about to close the bag when he notices several cards in the webbing. When he pulls them out he sees they're debit cards, five of them, each from a different bank. They all have pin numbers written on the back in permanent marker.

Some kind of bonus, like use whatever's in these accounts. It seemed like a fancy touch on top of a pile of cash. *Guess this is how the criminals do it nowadays.*

He has a sudden urge, and he peels off one 10,000-yen note. 'Doubt anyone'll miss this.' Then he tears it to pieces. He has always wanted to try that. He closes the suitcase, moves it off the toilet, and tosses the shreds of money into the bowl.

A wave of the hand in front of the sensor lets loose a hearty gush of water. He exits the bathroom. The Prince is there waiting. Kimura doesn't even realise that somewhere in his mind he's hoping the Prince will praise him for a job well done.

FRUIT

'WELL, MY DEAR TANGERINE, WHAT shall we do now?' Lemon is sitting in the middle, squeezed between the body by the window and Tangerine in the aisle seat. 'Hey, switch with me. I don't like the middle.'

'What the hell was that back there?' Tangerine looks angry, and he clearly has no intention of switching seats.

'What do you mean?'

'Lemon, you knew that Minegishi's guy was there on the platform.'

'Sure I knew. I'm not stupid. That's why I waved.'

'You waving would have been fine,' Tangerine says in a spitting whisper, doing his best to contain his rage. 'Why did you wave *his* hand too?' He points at Little Minegishi, eyes closed by the window.

Lemon sniggers uncontrollably. 'You're talking like that thing on TV where they sneak into people's bedrooms while they're still sleeping. You know, whispering like that.' Saying this reminds Lemon of something he heard once. 'Hey, speaking of sneaking into bedrooms, you ever heard about the professional who hated being woken up?'

Tangerine doesn't seem like he's in the mood for idle chatter, but he answers curtly, 'Yeah.'

'When someone woke him up, he'd flip out and shoot the person who woke him. They say he got pissed off just watching someone wake *someone else* up.'

'Yeah, yeah, he even got angry at his partners and clients when they tried to wake him. Soon everyone started contacting him indirectly, without actually going to his place. I've heard the damn stories. They'd leave messages for him on the train station blackboard.'

'What, like Ryo Saeba?' Lemon doesn't think Tangerine will get the reference to the old manga. Sure enough, Tangerine asks who that is, and Lemon responds, 'Another badass from back in the day. Speaking of back in the day, do train station blackboards even exist any more?'

'The point, since you always miss the point, is that communication can be the trickiest thing in our line of work. Figuring out how to get information to someone securely and without leaving any evidence. If things get too complicated it usually doesn't work.'

'I guess so.'

'Like what we were talking about before, communicating using digital billboards? Say we wanted to try something like that, either we'd need to plant someone in the operation that programmes the billboards, or we'd need to lean on whoever's in charge of programming them.'

'Yeah, but when you put it that way, all we have to do is get control of the place that programmes the billboards, and it'd work out.'

'That's what I mean. Way more trouble than it's worth.'

'Anyway, that guy who hated being woken up, he was supposed to be pretty awesome. That's what I heard. They say he was tough as nails. A legend.'

'Legends start because someone makes them up. He probably never even existed. Saying someone's a legend is basically the same as saying they're a myth. Probably some guys thought too hard about how to pass messages and one of them ended up dreaming about this killer who didn't like to be woken up. I'm telling you, the guy never gets woken up because there's no such guy.' As he talks Tangerine's voice gradually gets louder.

'I never wake you up, because I'm such a nice guy.'

'No, it's because you always sleep later than I do.'

'Listen, I thought it would be a good idea to make this kid move so that he didn't look like he was dead.'

'When someone looks like they're sleeping and suddenly they wave their hand, they're either a giant puppet or a dead body that's waving because someone else is moving their hand.'

'Oh, come on. I bet you it worked pretty well.' Lemon starts jiggling his legs nervously. 'That guy with the slicked-back hair probably called Minegishi and summed up the situation in three words: Everything's A-okay. A-okay counts as two words.'

'He definitely called him. Mr Minegishi, there was something strange-looking about your son. I think there might be something wrong.'

'Wait, I couldn't count how many words that was.'

'That doesn't matter!'

Lemon looks at Tangerine's profile and notes the severe expression. *Why's he always so stressed out?* 'Fine, whatever. Give me your take on the situation.'

Tangerine checks his watch. 'If I were Minegishi, I'd send my men to the next station. Dangerous men, armed to the teeth. I'd have them wait on the platform and make sure the two on the train who he hired don't try to make a run for it. And if those two stayed on the train, I'd have my men board. Luckily this Shinkansen has lots of empty seats. Right about now I'd be buying up every single one.'

'I feel bad for the two guys on the train.'

'Yeah, I wonder who they could be.'

'So you think when the train gets to Sendai, a bunch of lowlifes are gonna swarm the train. That could be bad.' Lemon imagines the train filling up with bearded men wielding guns and knives. He finds the image annoying. 'You don't think Minegishi has any girls working for him? Who could attack us in bikinis?'

'It doesn't matter who they are if they've got guns. While you're busy admiring their tits they'd shoot you dead.'

The door at the front of the train car slides open. A young man enters, coming from the direction of car four.

'Mr Lemon.' Tangerine says it quietly, which makes Lemon take notice.

'What is it, my good Tangerine?'

'Would you like to hear a funny story?'

'No thanks. When a serious guy like you says he's got a funny story, ninety per cent of the time it's a dud.'

Tangerine continues undeterred. 'The other day I bumped into someone I know from the neighbourhood.'

Now Lemon knows what his partner is getting at. He forces himself not to smile. 'Ah. Yeah, I know him too.'

'Do you now.'

And the conversation ends there.

The scenery flows by outside the window. Lemon watches a driving range and an apartment building slide past and recede into the distance. He starts thinking of Thomas.

'Hey, in *Thomas and Friends*, the head of the Sodor Railway, Sir Topham Hatt, tells Thomas and Percy and everyone, "You are very useful trains." That's what he says.'

'Who's that? Sir Topham Hatt.'

'I've told you before, the Fat Controller. How many times are you gonna make me say it? The director of the Sodor Railway, who always wears a black silk hat. He praises trains who work hard and scolds those who don't. He is widely respected by the trains. You know, he's like the boss of all the trains on Sodor. So that's a pretty great thing to hear from a guy like him.'

'What is?'

'You are very useful trains. Anyone would be happy if someone told them they were useful. I'd love for someone to tell me that, hey, you're a great train.'

'Then you should make yourself more useful. I mean, you and I, today, we're about as far from being useful trains as can be.'

'That's because we're not trains.'

'You're the one who brought up trains in the first place!' Tangerine exhales sharply. 'Lemme see those stickers I gave you before.'

'I already gave them back to you.'

'Oh, right.' Lemon takes the folded sheet of stickers from his pocket. 'Which one's Percy?'

'Don't know, don't care.'

'How many years we been working together? A long time. Do me a favour and try to remember who's who in *Thomas and Friends*. At least their names.'

'What about you? Have you read any of the books I recommended? *Forbidden Colours*? How about *Demons*?'

'I told you, I'm not interested. The books you recommend have no pictures.'

'And everything you recommend is just a bunch of steam locomotives.'

'There are diesel engines too. Anyway. More important. I got a flash of inspiration.'

'And what's that?'

'A plan.'

'When a sloppy guy like you says he's got a plan, ninety per cent of the time it's a dud. But I'm listening.'

'Okay, it's like this. You're saying that we need to find whoever killed Little Minegishi. Or else we need to find the missing bag. Because Minegishi's pissed off with us.'

'That's right. And we haven't found either.'

'But we're barking up the wrong tree. Or no, not the wrong tree, we're just doing it wrong. But that's no reason to get upset. Everyone messes up once in a while.'

'Is there actually a plan here?'

'Yes indeed.' Lemon's lips twitch with the hint of a smile.

Meanwhile, Tangerine's face hardens. 'Hey, don't let our friend from the neighbourhood hear.'

'I know,' Lemon replies. 'Pop quiz. Here's a famous quote: "Don't look for a culprit. Create one." Know who said it?'

'Uh, I'm guessing Thomas or one of his friends.'

'Not everything I say has to do with Thomas. It was me. I said it! That's my quote. Don't look for a culprit. Create one.'

'And what does that mean, exactly?'

'We pick someone on the Shinkansen, anyone really, and we make them the culprit.'

A change comes over Tangerine's face. Lemon doesn't fail to notice. *Well, well, look who likes my plan.*

'Not bad,' Tangerine mutters.

'Right?'

'That doesn't mean Minegishi will buy it.'

'Who knows. But it's better than sitting around doing nothing. Me and you, I mean you and me, we messed up our job. We let the kid get killed, and we lost the bag. Of course Minegishi'll be mad. But if we can get the killer for him that oughta mean something.'

'And what about the bag?'

'I guess we'd say that the killer got rid of it or something. I mean, I don't think this'll solve everything, but if we can make it look like someone else was the cause of all of this, it'll, you know, what do you call it.'

'Quell Minegishi's fury?'

'Yeah, that's exactly what I was gonna say.'

'Who do we use?'

Lemon is happy that Tangerine is willing to go along with his plan and wants to get started right away, but at the same time he's annoyed at actually having to go through with it. 'Wait, we're really gonna do this?'

'It's your idea. You know, Lemon, if all you're willing to do is screw around then eventually I'm gonna get mad. There's a passage in a book I like. "I despise that man. For even as the earth splits beneath his feet and rocks tumble down on his head he shows his teeth in a smile. He checks to see his pancake make-up is undisturbed. My scorn becomes a storm, and I devastate this place, because of him." '

'Okay, okay.' Lemon waves his hand back and forth. 'Don't get angry.'

Lemon knows all too well how dangerous Tangerine can be when he's angry. Usually Tangerine is content to read his novels and keep violence to an absolute minimum, but once he loses his temper he becomes ruthless and nearly unstoppable. It's impossible to tell from his demeanour whether he's angry or not, which makes him even more dangerous. He erupts all at once, without any warning, terrible to behold. But Lemon knows that when Tangerine starts quoting books and movies, it's time to be wary. It's as if in his frenzied state the box of memories inside his head gets tipped over and the contents spill out, making him start quoting his favourite lines. It's the surest sign he's about to get violent.

'I get it. I'll be serious.' Lemon lifts his hands slightly. 'I know just the guy we can pin this on.'

'Who?'

'You know. A guy who probably knows who Minegishi is.'

'Our friend from the neighbourhood?'

'Exactly. The guy we know from around the way.'

'Yeah. Yeah, that's a good idea.' Tangerine stands up. 'I have to go to the toilet.'

'Hey, wait. What's up?'

'I have to take a leak.'

'What do I do if I see an opening before you come back? You know, an opening to talk to our friend from the neighbourhood. What if you aren't here?'

'Then it's up to you. You're okay on your own, right? It'll probably be quieter if there's just one of us anyway.'

Lemon is a little tickled that Tangerine's trusting him with this. 'Yeah, okay.'

'Don't make a scene.'

Tangerine exits the car and Lemon follows him with his eyes. Then he leans in to Little Minegishi's corpse and takes hold of the back of the head, nodding it up and down like he's operating a puppet. 'Lemon, you are a useful train,' he says, doing his best ventriloquist act.

NANAO

NO TIME TO LOSE WORRYING, Maria had said. But Nanao is worried. He heads towards car three, worrying all the way.

He thinks about Tangerine and Lemon. Immediately his stomach starts to hurt. He's used to dangerous work, but he also knows how scary high-level professionals can be.

The second the door to car three slides open Nanao shores up his resolve. *They're in here. Act natural,* he tells himself. *Like I'm just a normal passenger on the way back from the toilet, nothing suspicious about me.* He tries his best to be nonchalant. There are plenty of empty seats, perfect for him to calmly choose where he wants to sit, but less than ideal for blending in. He looks around, keeping his face composed. *There they are.* On the left side as he's looking in, a three-seater halfway down the car with three men together. The man in the window seat leans against the window, sleeping like the dead, but the other two are awake. The one in the aisle seat looks serious as he talks to the man in the middle, seeming to pepper him with questions. They're the same

176

height and they look alike. Long hair, lanky, their legs barely able to fold into the seats.

Nanao can't tell which one is Tangerine and which one is Lemon.

He makes a split-second decision to sit near them. The row right behind them is open. So is the row behind that. Sitting further from them would help him stay safe, but keeping close will let him get a handle on the situation more quickly. Maria had thrown him off with talk of Minegishi, and he's feeling unsteady from his streak of mishaps. For a moment he pictures a footballer who makes a risky play, the sort he would never normally try, in the hope of making up for mistakes earlier in the game. A desperate gambit to regain good standing. Nanao realises he's never seen it work. Failure only begets failure. But a player in the hole has to try.

He sits in the row behind them. He's encouraged by the fact that when he entered the car he briefly locked eyes with Tangerine, or Lemon, and they didn't seem to recognise him. *Good, they don't know me*, he thought with relief. He also knows from experience that people tend not to pay much attention to the seats behind them.

Holding his breath, doing his best not to draw any attention, he pulls a magazine out of the seat-back pocket and opens it. It's a mail-order catalogue with a range of products. As he flips through it, he tries to listen in on the conversation between the pair in front of him.

Nanao leans forward slightly. Though he can't quite make out everything, he can hear well enough.

The man in the middle seat is saying something about Thomas and trains. Maria had said she thinks Lemon is the one who likes *Thomas and Friends*, which would make the man sitting next to him Tangerine, who likes literature.

His nerves buzzing as he tries to maintain a low profile, Nanao turns the page of the catalogue to see a selection of suitcases. *If they were selling Minegishi's bag I'd buy it right now.*

'Okay, it's like this. You're saying that we need to find whoever killed

Little Minegishi. Or else we need to find the missing bag. Because Minegishi's pissed off with us.'

Nanao almost jumps up when he hears what Lemon's saying. *They don't have the bag either.* And he doesn't miss the name Minegishi. But not Minegishi, Lemon said Little Minegishi. *So who's that?* Sounds like it might be Minegishi's son. *Does Minegishi have a son? Did Maria say anything about that?* He can't remember. But he definitely heard Lemon say that Little Minegishi had been killed. Which meant that someone killed Minegishi's son. A chill crawls down Nanao's spine. *Who did it? Who could have done something so crazy?*

He recalls one time when he was in an *izakaya* and the bartender said to the patrons at the bar, There are two types of people in this world. Nanao smiled wryly, as that sort of set-up always seems so tired, but he politely took the bait. 'What are the two types?'

'People who've never heard of Minegishi, and people who are terrified of him.' Everyone at the bar fell silent. Seeing that, the bartender continued. 'And then there's Minegishi himself.'

That's three types, the customers all pointed out.

Even as Nanao laughed at the other patrons making fun of the bartender, he reflected that everyone he knew seemed terrified of Minegishi, that fearing the man seemed to be the safest thing to do. There in the bar, he felt more certain than ever that he should keep his distance.

'Pop quiz,' Lemon says, raising a finger and sounding self-important. Nanao can't quite make out the next words, but he catches the word 'culprit', and then, 'create one'.

After a bit more discussion that's too low to hear, Tangerine suddenly stands up, startling Nanao. 'I have to go to the toilet.' Tangerine starts towards the front of the car, in the direction of the bathroom in the gangway between cars three and four.

Lemon stops him. 'Hey, wait. What's up?'

'I have to take a leak,' answers Tangerine.

'What do I do if I see an opening before you come back? You know, an opening to talk to our friend from the neighbourhood. What if you aren't here?'

'Then it's up to you. You're okay on your own, right? It'll probably be quieter if there's just one of us anyway.'

'Yeah, okay.'

'Don't make a scene.' With that, Tangerine turns away and exits car three.

The car is plunged into silence. At least that's how it seems to Nanao. Of course the train is still swaying and the wheels are clacking on the tracks as the scenery glides by, but Nanao has the weird sensation that the moment Tangerine and Lemon's conversation ended the train car became deathly still and time stopped.

He flips a page in the catalogue. He runs his eyes across the words, but doesn't comprehend them. *Now or never,* he thinks as his eyes slide over the page. *Lemon's alone. If I'm going to talk to him, now's my chance.*

'And what will talking to him do?' asks a voice inside his head. 'You have to find the bag, and they obviously don't have it, so what's the point?'

'But there's no one else who can help me.'

'You really think they'll help you?'

'If I bring up Minegishi, they might listen. What's that saying, the enemy of my enemy is my friend?'

He doesn't know everything that's going on, but it's clear that Tangerine and Lemon were transporting the suitcase for Minegishi. And Minegishi hired Nanao to steal the same suitcase. Which means that they're both working for the same client. It isn't hard to imagine that Minegishi has some sort of plan. Nanao's betting that if he tells Lemon he's also working for Minegishi, even if Lemon is wary of him and doesn't want to believe him, they might be able to strike a deal. They both have the same goal: to find the bag. If Lemon and Tangerine are willing to overlook the fact that Nanao stole it from them in the first place, they could conceivably join forces. They could form a team, like a couple that works past a one-off infidelity and manages to make it work. At least that's what he wants to propose.

Nanao closes the catalogue and reaches out to put it back in the seat pocket. It doesn't quite slide in at first but he manages to force it. He steadies himself. If he can get the drop on Lemon he'll have a good chance of immobilising him. Then he'll explain the situation. *Here goes,* he thinks, and stands up.

To find Lemon, looking right at him. 'Well, hello there.'

Nanao isn't immediately able to process what's happening. 'Well, hello there, how've you been?' Lemon sounds like he's talking to a long-time acquaintance. He stands in the aisle next to Nanao's seat, blocking the way.

Before Nanao can address the question mark in his brain his body starts moving. First he ducks, and not a moment too soon, because Lemon's fist smashes air where his head just was. If he had hesitated at all he would have taken the hook straight on the jaw.

Nanao stands upright and snakes his hand out to grab Lemon's right wrist. He wrenches it around behind Lemon's back, all the while trying to contain his movements as much as possible so as not to call attention to himself. Causing a commotion won't do him any good. If the police or reporters get involved it would make it harder to hide his failure from Minegishi. He still needs to buy himself more time.

Luckily, Lemon also seems to want to avoid making a scene. Keeping his movements compact, he makes his hand tremble like he's having a spasm, causing Nanao to lose his grip.

Nanao knows that he can't afford to give his opponent any openings, but he's so concerned about being noticed that he risks a glance around the train car. Most of the passengers are asleep or looking at their phones or magazines, but at the back of the car is a toddler standing on the seat, staring at them with great interest. *Not good.* He pops his elbow into Lemon's chest, not to do damage but to disrupt his balance. While Lemon staggers slightly Nanao slips backwards and down into the window seat. If they stay standing, sooner or later someone will notice them.

Lemon sits too, in the aisle seat, and they start throwing punches over the empty middle seat. The middle seat in front of them is reclined a fair amount, making it hard to aim a clean strike, but they do the best they can. Neither one has ever had a sit-down fistfight before.

They twist their bodies and throw punches at each other, leaning and blocking.

Lemon fires a vicious uppercut at Nanao's ribs, but Nanao slams the raised armrest down and Lemon's fist crashes into it with a dull thud. He makes a frustrated noise. Nanao's spirits rally, but only for a moment, because he notices that Lemon has a knife in his other hand. It's a small knife, but it gleams cold as it slices through the air. Nanao grabs a magazine from the seat-back pocket and spreads it open in the blade's path. The knife slashes through photographs of lush rice paddies. He tries to fold the magazine around the blade but Lemon yanks it back.

I'm just glad he didn't pull a gun. It could be that Lemon thinks a knife is better than a gun for this kind of close-in fighting, or maybe he's not even carrying one. Nanao isn't that concerned with the reason.

The blade comes once more. Nanao tries to catch it in the magazine again but he mistimes it and takes a slash on the left arm. There's a flash of pain. Nanao's eyes drop to his arm for a moment. It's not deep. He looks back at Lemon and makes a quick grab, getting him by the wrist of his knife hand. He jerks the hand towards himself and drops a heavy elbow strike on it with his free arm. Lemon groans and the knife clatters to the floor. Nanao presses his advantage, thrusting two fingers at Lemon's eyes. Past the point of holding back, he fully intends to blind his opponent, but Lemon flinches at the last moment and the fingers just miss, catching him on the sides of the eyes instead of dead centre. He screws up his face in pain and Nanao is about to try again, readying his fingers for another strike, when Lemon's hand flies towards his own chest and into his jacket. Nanao blinks, and in the split second his eyes are closed a gun appears. Lemon holds it low, but it's aimed right at Nanao.

'I didn't wanna have to use this, but I've just about had enough,' he says quietly.

'If you shoot you'll give yourself away.'

'Got no choice. Emergency measures. Tangerine'll understand. Any-way, it's pretty hard to fight without getting noticed.'

'How did you know who I am?'

'I clocked you the second you walked into the car all nervous. You were basically screaming, here I am, the sacrificial lamb.'

'Sacrificial lamb? What do you mean, sacrificial lamb?'

'You're the guy who works with Maria, right?'

'You know Maria?' As he speaks, Nanao looks between Lemon's face and the gun at his hip. He knows he could be shot at any moment.

'We're all in the same line of work. McDonald's knows all about Mos Bur-ger. Bic Camera knows about Yodobashi Camera. Same thing. And our world is pretty small. There aren't too many people who'll take on any job someone needs doing. I heard about you and Maria from that old fat go-between.'

'Who, Mr Good News-Bad News?'

'Yeah, that's right. Although most of the time with him it's bad news. But I hear about Maria all the time. And I heard that for the past couple of years she's been Glasses Guy's manager.'

'What do people say about Glasses Guy?' Nanao doesn't want to let his guard down for even an instant, but he tries to make it look like he's unconcerned.

'They say he isn't bad. To put it in terms of *Thomas and Friends*, I guess I'd say he's like Murdoch.'

'Is that one of the characters?'

'Yeah. He's pretty cool, Murdoch.' Lemon pauses for a moment, then: 'A very large engine with ten wheels. Quiet by nature, he likes peaceful places. But he also enjoys chatting with his friends back at the depot.'

'Sorry?'

'That's Murdoch's character description.'

Nanao is thrown off by the sudden recitation, but he also smiles to himself. *It's true that I like peaceful places. All I want is some peace and quiet. But,* he reflects with a touch of bitterness, *here I am.*

'I've seen a photo of you before, Glasses Guy. But I didn't expect you to come wandering in here. Just a coincidence?'

'It's a kind of coincidence, but also not.'

'Oh, wait, I get it.' Realisation dawns on Lemon. 'You're the one who stole the bag. Well, good. Now I don't even need to frame you, since you actually did it.'

'First hear me out. Minegishi hired you to bring him the bag, right?'

'So you *are* involved. You know what's going on.'

'I'm also working for Minegishi. He hired me to steal the bag.'

'What are you talking about?'

'I don't know why, but Minegishi hired me without telling you guys.'

'You sure about that?'

Lemon doesn't offer any counter-arguments other than that simple question, but it's enough to unsettle Nanao. After all, Nanao doesn't know for certain that it's even Minegishi he's working for.

'Why would Minegishi want you to steal the bag from us? We're supposed to be bringing it to him.'

'I know, it's weird, right?' Nanao wants to emphasise that something doesn't add up. 'So, say Thomas has some freight to carry, but he gets another train to haul it for him. Way I see it, there would only be two reasons: either Thomas is broken down, or someone doesn't trust him.'

'And are you and your partner broken down? I don't think so. So that's not the reason.' Lemon clicks his tongue. 'You're saying Minegishi doesn't trust us.'

The barrel of the gun twitches slightly. Lemon is obviously displeased, and his displeasure is making his finger tighten on the trigger. 'You better give us the bag back, and fast. Where is it? I'll shoot you, get it? And while you're wriggling around I'll go through your pockets and find your ticket. When I go to your seat, I'll find the bag. Right? So just give me the bag before I shoot your ass.'

'Wait, you don't understand. I'm looking for the bag too. It's not at my seat.'

'Looks like you wanna get shot.'

'I'm telling you the truth. If I had the bag, I wouldn't come looking for you guys. I thought you definitely had it. That's why I came to this car, even though I knew it would be dangerous. And it turned out to be really dangerous.' Nanao keeps his voice low and tells himself over and over to stay calm. Showing any fear or agitation will just encourage Lemon. And though he's still coming to terms with his lifelong bad luck, he's used to looking down the barrel of a gun. Guns don't scare him all that much.

It's clear enough that Lemon doesn't believe him, but he appears to be thinking. 'Okay, then who has it?'

'If I knew that I wouldn't be here talking to you. But the simplest answer is that there's someone else, or some other group, that wants it.'

'Some other group?'

'Besides me and the two of you. And now that other party has it.'

'And do they work for Minegishi too? What the fuck's he thinking?'

'I'll say it again, I don't know exactly what's going on. I'm not the smartest.' *I'm just good at football and dangerous work.*

'How come you wear glasses if you're not smart?'

'Aren't there any trains who wear glasses?'

'Yeah, Whiff does. A tank engine with glasses, a nice guy who doesn't get mad even when people gossip about him. But yeah, I suppose he isn't so smart either.'

'My guess is that Minegishi doesn't trust contract workers like us.' Nanao is sharing these thoughts as they occur to him. He figures that as long as he's talking there's less of a chance he'll be shot. 'So maybe he hired a few different people to make sure the bag gets back to him.'

'Why would he go to all that trouble?'

'When I was a kid there was a man in my neighbourhood who used to ask me to go shopping for him.'

'What does that have to do with this?'

'He told me if I went to the station to get his newspaper and magazines for him he'd give me a little cash, so I ran off to do it. When I got back, he said, look at this magazine, it's bent, I'm not giving you anything.'

'So?'

'He never had any intention of giving me a tip, so he had an excuse ready. I bet Minegishi has the same thing in mind for you guys. What happened to the bag, he'll want to know. And then he'll say, you messed up, and now you're going to pay.'

'So that's why he had you steal the bag from us?'

'Could be.' As he says it Nanao thinks that it really might be true. Minegishi might hate the thought of saying good job and having to pay full price. By setting up a situation like this he can make the people he hired feel like they owe him, instead of the other way round.

'Now you're gonna pay – what do you think that means, exactly?'

'Maybe he'd make you give him money, or maybe he'd have you shot. I bet he's thinking, I want someone else to do my dirty work, but I don't want to have to pay for it, wouldn't it be great if I could hire someone and then get rid of them.'

'But if he hired someone else to mess with our work, wouldn't that cost him money too? There'd be no point.'

'If it's an easier job he could hire someone for less. It would probably work out cheaper for him in the end.'

'When a train works hard, you gotta make it feel good, tell it it's a useful train.'

'Some people would rather die than praise someone else. Could be that's how Minegishi is.'

Nanao is still wary of the gun, still trying to make it look like he doesn't care. He's doing his best to distract Lemon from the possibility of pulling the trigger.

'Your partner Tangerine, is he still in the toilet?'

'He has been gone a while.' But Lemon doesn't look at the door, he keeps his eyes on Nanao. 'Maybe there's a queue.'

A thought occurs to Nanao. 'Is there a chance he's double-crossing you?'

'Tangerine wouldn't do that.'

'He could have hidden the bag somewhere.' Nanao's doing a balancing act, he wants to shake Lemon up a bit, but not so much that he pulls the trigger.

'Nah, Tangerine wouldn't screw me. Not because we share some deep mutual trust or anything. He's just a cool customer. He knows that if he turned on me it'd be a whole mess of trouble for him.'

'And you're not mad that while you're here fighting me he's just taking his time in the toilet?' Nanao keeps looking for ways to sow doubt in Lemon's mind.

But Lemon just makes a disparaging face. 'Tangerine knows you and me are in here together, bud.'

'What?'

'The second you came in, he said I saw someone I know from the neighbourhood. All of a sudden, you know? Which is our code. For when someone we know shows up. We say it that way so that the person doesn't know we know. When Tangerine got up to go to the toilet he said he'd leave you to me.'

'Oh, oh really?' Nanao is struck with a feeling of incompetence. Everyone in the business uses secret codes and messages. He tries to think back to the conversation he overheard. He can't recall having noticed anything that stood out, but he figures Lemon is probably telling the truth.

There's also a new rush of urgency. If Tangerine knows Nanao's here, he could come back at any moment, and two against one is not good odds.

'Hey,' Lemon says suddenly, 'you don't hate being woken up, do you?'

'Being woken up?'

'I heard about somebody in the biz who hates being woken up. Supposed to be a beast. I thought for a second it might be you, but I guess not.'

Nanao had never heard about anyone like that. It seemed like kind of a silly thing for a professional to be known for. 'He's tough, huh?'

'He's like the legendary train City of Truro. Even Gordon was too slow to beat City of Truro.'

'Sorry, I don't know the reference.'

'Listen, you're not gonna be able to beat me, bud. And if somehow you manage to kill me, I still won't die.'

'What do you mean by that?'

'I mean that the great Lemon is immortal! Even if I die, I come back. I'll appear before you and scare the shit out of you.'

'No thanks,' Nanao says, scowling. 'I'm not into the afterlife and I don't like ghosts.'

'I'm worse than a ghost!'

At that moment Nanao notices another Shinkansen passing in the opposite direction across the aisle and out the far window from where they're sitting. It roars by, and the two trains seem to be jostling one another, as if to say that there's no peaceful passage through life, everything is a struggle.

'Hey, maybe that's Murdoch,' Nanao mutters absently, not intending anything in particular. It isn't a ploy, and if it were he wouldn't expect it to work. He just noticed the other train and wondered what model it was, and spoke his thoughts aloud.

But Lemon, without any scepticism whatsoever, excitedly says, 'Where?' and turns to look. Nanao is astonished. Lemon has a gun on him, but he looked over his shoulder as if they were just having a friendly conversation. *Not going to get another chance like this,* Nanao realises. He grabs the gun hand and forces it down, at the same time ramming his other fist into Lemon's chin. Snap back the chin, rattle the brain, knock the opponent unconscious. It was another of the techniques Nanao had practised over and over again in his teens, just like he practised football. He hears a sound like a muscle popping or a large switch being flipped.

Lemon's eyes roll back and he slumps over in his seat. Nanao hauls the long body across to the window seat and arranges him against the window. For a moment he wonders if he should break Lemon's neck, but something stops him. After the Wolf, it feels too risky to kill again. And he's also sure that if he takes Lemon's life he'll have to deal with an enraged Tangerine. He needs to try to keep these two from becoming his enemies. It's hard to imagine that they'd become allies, but he knows he doesn't want to provoke them more than necessary.

Now what do I do? What now? What now?

His head feels like it's heating up. The gears start spinning faster.

He takes Lemon's gun and secures it in his belt under his jacket. He also takes Lemon's phone. Then he leans down and looks at the knife on the floor. He thinks about grabbing it, but decides not to.

What next? The pulleys and blocks of thought work furiously, hoisting up one idea after another. The ideas appear and then vanish. *What are you going to do?* whispers a voice inside.

Should I go to the front of the train or to the back? Tangerine will be here any minute. As soon as he thinks that and remembers where Tangerine's coming from, he knows he can't go forward. The only choice is towards the rear.

His mind buzzes with options and fragments of escape plans. *Even if I go towards the back Tangerine will just come for me. Both ways are dead ends.* He has to figure out some way to get past Tangerine.

He opens his waist pack. First he takes out a tube full of first-aid cream, unscrews the cap and spreads some where Lemon slashed him. It isn't bleeding heavily, but it seems like a good idea to try to stop what bleeding there is. The arm throbs with pain both from being cut and from blocking punches. Bruises are already forming where he was hit. Lemon had got a few good blows in, pounding Nanao's flesh and bones. Every move stings, but there's nothing he can do about it.

Next he takes out a digital wristwatch. *No time to think.* He sets the alarm volume to max and picks a time. *How long will I need? Too early won't help, too late is no good either.* Just in case, he decides to set a second alarm on a different watch, ten minutes later than the first.

He places one watch on the floor under Lemon's seat and the other on the luggage rack above his head.

Nanao is about to leave when he glances at the row in front, the three-seater where Lemon and Tangerine had originally been sitting and where the third man still sits motionless by the window. Something seems off about the man, so Nanao moves closer and touches him warily on the shoulder. No response. *No way,* he thinks. He lays his fingers on the man's neck. No pulse. *Who is he?* Nanao sighs, overwhelmed by the unknown, but he knows he can't hang around any longer. Just before he steps away he notices a plastic water bottle, half empty, in the seat-back pocket where Lemon had been sitting. He hits on a sly little idea and takes a packet of powder from his waist pack. Water-soluble sleeping medicine. He tears it open and pours it into the bottle, then shakes the bottle up and replaces it in the pocket. He has no idea whether Lemon will drink it or if it will even work, but he reasons it's best to plant seeds wherever he can.

Then he hurries towards car number two. *Okay. What now?*

THE PRINCE

JUST AS HE'S THINKING MAYBE he should go back to his seat, the toilet door opens and Kimura steps out wearing an agitated look.

'What was the combination?'

'How'd you know I got it open?'

'I could tell by the look on your face.'

'Well, you don't look surprised or even happy. You're just used to being lucky, is that it? It was o600.' Kimura glances down at the suitcase under his arm. 'I locked it back up for now.'

'Let's go.' The Prince turns and leads the way, Kimura following with the bag. If they bump into the bag's owner it'll be easy enough to blame everything on the older man.

They arrive at their seats and the Prince has Kimura sit by the window. *This next part's critical,* he thinks, readying himself. He'll feel much safer if he can manage to get Kimura tied up again.

'Mr Kimura, I'm going to retie your hands and feet, okay? Your son's well-being is at stake so I imagine you won't try anything stupid, but we might as well do you up like before.'

I don't particularly care if you're tied up or not, either way is fine by me – the Prince is trying to project this attitude. When in fact the difference between whether an opponent is bound or free is considerable. Kimura is much bigger than he is. Even if the man knows his son's life hangs in the balance, something could make him snap, launch a desperate suicide attack. If that happens, the Prince might not be able to stop him. Things don't always go as expected when the situation turns violent. The best way to ensure his safety is to put things back how they were before. But he also has to make sure Kimura doesn't realise all this.

The Prince knows this is the key to exerting control over someone else. If someone understands that the moment of truth has come, that if they're ever going to make a move to change the situation then now's the time, then they'll most likely take action, regardless of what kind of person they are. If they know for certain that this is their only chance they might fight with a wild abandon. That's why if you can prevent someone from knowing this, you're much more likely to win. Lots of rulers do it. They hide their true intentions, as if they were taking a horde of passengers on a train journey with no information about where the train is going and yet this state of affairs was the most natural thing in the world. The passengers could get off at any of the stations along the way, but they're never allowed to realise this. The conductor just keeps the train going, perfectly calm. By the time people start to regret not having got off earlier, it's too late. Whether it's war, genocide, or revisions to the law, in most cases people don't notice until it's already happening, and they feel like they would have protested earlier if they only knew.

That's why when the Prince finishes re-securing Kimura's hands and feet with the bands and tape, he feels considerable relief. Kimura doesn't even seem to notice that his chance to fight back slipped away.

The Prince puts the suitcase at his feet and pops it open, exposing the sheaves of notes. 'Look at that.'

'Not much of a surprise. Nothing special about a bag full of cash. The bank cards thing is new though.'

The Prince takes another look, and sure enough in the webbing on the inside of the suitcase he finds five debit cards. Each one has four digits written in marker on the back. 'I'm guessing these are the codes to make a withdrawal.'

'Probably. Two kinds of payment, cash and card. Pain in the ass.'

'I wonder, if you used the cards then could the owner of the bag find out the location where you made the withdrawal . . .'

'No way, they're not the cops. Anyway, nobody involved with this bag makes a straight living, not the carriers and not whoever it's going to. They probably have some arrangement worked out so one doesn't screw the other.'

'Hmm.' The Prince thumbs through a few notes. 'Hey, Mr Kimura, you took one of these, right?'

Kimura's face stiffens and his cheeks go red. 'What makes you say that?'

'I just have the feeling that when you saw this you'd want to try something, like take a note or two and tear them up and flush them down the toilet. Did you do that?'

The Prince notices the blood drain from Kimura's frowning face. *Looks like I guessed right.*

Now Kimura starts to move his hands and feet. Unfortunately, they're already all bound and taped up. *If he was going to make a move, he should have done it before.*

'Mr Kimura, in this life, do you know what's right?' The Prince slips off his shoes and pulls his knees into his chest. He leans back in his seat and balances on his tailbone.

'Yeah. Nothing.'

'Exactly! That's one hundred percent correct.' The Prince nods. 'In life, there are things that are *said* to be right, but there's no saying if it's *actually* right. That's why the people who can say, *This* is what's right, those people have all the power.'

'Over my head, your majesty. Talk so that the commoners can understand.'

'Like there was that documentary in the '80s *The Atomic Cafe.* It was pretty famous. There's a part where soldiers are doing training for a strata-gem involving nuclear arms. The soldiers have to enter an area where a nuclear bomb has just been set off. In the briefing before they go, a high-rank-looking guy is writing on the blackboard and explaining the operation to the soldiers. There are only three things you have to be wary of, he says. The blast, the heat and the radiation. Then he says, the radiation is the new threat, but it's also the one you need to worry about the least.'

'How could they not need to worry about radiation?'

'It's invisible and odourless. The solders are told that as long as they follow procedure, they won't get sick. The nuke is detonated, and the soldiers start marching straight towards the mushroom cloud. In their normal uniforms!'

'You kidding me? And the radiation didn't hurt them?'

'Don't be ridiculous. They all got radiation sickness and suffered horribly. Basically, if people hear an explanation they want to believe it, and when someone important says with full confidence, Don't worry, everything's fine, people go along with it. When really, the important person has no plans to tell everyone else the whole truth. In the same movie there's an educational video for kids, with a cartoon turtle in it. He says, when there's a nuclear blast, make sure you hide right away! Duck down under the table and hide!'

'That's stupid.'

'*We* think it's stupid, but when the government calmly and confidently declares it to be so, we have no choice but to believe they're right. Right? And maybe it even is right, for that time and place. Like, for example, asbestos. It's prohibited to use it in construction now due to health haz-ards, but it used to be prized for its flame-retardant and heat-resistant qualities. There was a time when everyone thought that using asbestos when building buildings was the right thing to do.'

'Are you really fourteen? How are you talking like that?'

What a moron, the Prince thinks as he laughs through his nose. *How's a fourteen-year-old supposed to talk? If you read enough books and gain enough knowledge, your way of speaking naturally evolves. It has nothing to do with age.* 'Even after there were reports that asbestos was dangerous, it still took years until it was outlawed. Which probably made most people think, if it's really dangerous, there would be more of an outcry and they'd pass a law banning its use, but since that hasn't happened, everything must be fine. Now we use different materials, but don't be surprised when you start hearing that those are health hazards too. Same with pollution, food contamination, unsafe medication. There's no way anybody can be sure of what to believe.'

'The government's rotten, politicians are the worst, everything's a mess. Is that it? Not the most original opinion.'

'That's not what I'm saying at all. My point is how easy it is to make people think that something wrong is actually right. Although in the moment even the politicians probably think it's right, and they're not actually trying to trick anyone.'

'So . . . so what?'

'So, the most important thing is to be one of the people who decide what people believe.' *But even if I explain this to you I doubt you'll ever understand it.* 'It's not politicians who control things. Bureaucrats and corporate leaders, they're the ones who call the shots. But you'll never see them on television. Most people are only familiar with politicians who appear on TV and in the newspapers. Which works out well for the people who stand behind them.'

'Shitting on bureaucrats isn't hard either.'

'But say someone thinks that bureaucrats are worthless, they don't actually know who the bureaucrats are, so there's nowhere to direct any anger or discontent. Just a set of faceless pronouncements. Whereas politicians have to work in the public eye. Bureaucrats make use of that. The politicians absorb all the fire and the bureaucrats stand safely behind them. And if a politician causes any trouble, it's a simple matter of leaking sensitive information to the media.' The Prince realises he's talking too much. *I'm probably just excited about getting the suitcase open.* 'Basically, the person who has the most information and can use it to further their goals is the strongest. Like this suitcase, just by knowing where it is I can control the people who want it.'

'What are you gonna do with the cash?'

'Nothing. It's just money, after all.'

'Well, yeah. Exactly. It's money.'

'It's not like you want it, Mr Kimura. No amount of money will help your stupid kid get better.'

The lines in Kimura's face deepen and shadows harden around the edges. *Too easy,* thinks the Prince.

'Why are you doing this?'

'You need to be more specific. What do you mean by "this"? Are you talking about the suitcase? Or my tying you up and taking you with me to Morioka?'

Kimura doesn't answer at first. *He doesn't even know what he's asking,* notes the Prince. *He asks why without being sure of what he wants to find out. Someone like him will never be able to turn his life around.*

Finally Kimura settles on his question. 'Why did you hurt Wataru?'

'I already told you, little Wataru followed me and my friends up to the roof and just fell. Let me play, he said, let me play. Careful, it's dangerous, I said. I warned him.'

Kimura's face turns so red it gives off heat. But he suppresses his rage. 'Whatever. Not interested in your bullshit story. What I'm asking is, why Wataru? Why him?'

'Well, of course, it was to get at you,' the Prince says with great humour. Then he holds a finger up to his lips and whispers, 'But don't tell anyone.'

'You know what I think?' Kimura's mouth hangs open in a half-smile. All at once the tension vanishes from his face, his expression comes alive, his eyes flash. He seems to be young again, a teenager, as if he too were in school. The Prince is overcome by the sudden sensation that he's dealing with an equal. 'I think you might've been scared of me.'

The Prince is used to being underestimated. There is no shortage of people who look down on him because he's a schoolboy, because he's small and weak-looking. He relishes turning that underestimation into fear.

But right now he's the one feeling unsettled.

He thinks back to that evening a few months ago.

In the park, among the trees of a small wood, at the bottom of a gentle dip in the terrain, the Prince and his classmates were getting ready to test the medical device. He proposed that they use it to shock Tomoyasu, that flat-footed dimwit. Although it wasn't really a proposal, it was an order. Unlike an AED, if used on someone whose heart was still functioning this defibrillator could conceivably kill. The Prince knew this, but he didn't tell the others. He only ever gave them the barest minimum of information. He also knew that if Tomoyasu did happen to die it presented an opportunity: the others would all panic, and in their discombobulated state they would look to him for answers.

Tomoyasu was screaming and crying so annoyingly that the Prince agreed to use the dog as a test subject instead. At that point his interest shifted away from the effects of the defibrillator. Instead the Prince wanted to see how it would affect Tomoyasu to sacrifice his faithful dog, which he had raised since he was a boy.

Tomoyasu loved the dog, but he was ready to subject it to pain and suffering. How could he justify it? No doubt he was casting around for justification, trying to convince himself he was not a bad person.

The first step in gaining control over his classmates was to destabilise their sense of self-worth. He made them realise how flawed they were as humans. The quickest way to do this was to exploit their sexual urges, find out their secret desires, expose and humiliate them. Or in some cases he would confront them with their parents' sexual activities, sullying their image of the people they depended on most. Even though there's nothing unusual about sexual desires, having them exposed never fails to make someone feel shame. The Prince couldn't help but be surprised at how well it worked.

The next step was to get them to betray someone. It could be a parent or a sibling or a friend. When they turned on someone important to them, their self-worth plummeted even more. This was what the Prince was hoping to do with Tomoyasu and his dog.

But just as they had the dog tied down and were ready to administer the shock, Kimura showed up.

The Prince immediately recognised him from the time they met at the local department store. He had struck him as a grown-up juvenile delinquent with a kid, vulgar and boorish, the sort of man who can only think in straight lines.

'Hey now, what do you think you're doing to that dog?' Kimura simply seemed to want to rescue the dog and the boy. 'There you go, get mad, kid. I'm messing with your mission – if you don't do something quick his highness the Prince'll be angry. Hey, where is the Prince anyway?'

He didn't like the way Kimura was laughing. 'Wow, sir, you sure seem pleased with yourself.' Then he threw a rock at the man's face. It hit full force, knocking him over backwards. 'Shall we try to hold him?' the Prince said quietly. His classmates obediently sprang into action.

They hauled Kimura up and held his arms on both sides. A third came from behind and clamped an arm around his neck.

'Ow, that hurts,' the man bellowed.

The Prince moved closer. 'I guess you didn't notice me there, sir. You should pay better attention.'

The dog started barking, drawing the Prince's eye. Tomoyasu and his dog stood off to the side. He must have got up while everyone was busy with Kimura. His legs were shaking. The dog didn't try to run away, it just waited loyally by its master, barking bravely. *So close,* the Prince thought bitterly. It would have only taken a bit more to shatter the bond between them, just a bit more pain, a bit more betrayal.

'Hey, your majesty, you get off on ordering your friends around like this?' Even though his assailants were just schoolkids, the two boys holding his arms and one gripping his neck made it difficult for him to move.

'Look at the position you're in,' the Prince replied. 'And you're still talking tough? Hilarious.'

'Positions change. It all depends on what happens.' Kimura appeared totally calm, unfazed by the fact that he was being held fast.

'Who wants to punch this old man in the stomach?' The Prince eyed his classmates. A gust of wind blew through the trees, kicking up the leaves on the ground. The schoolkids, confused by the sudden command, looked at one another warily, then all at once pushed to be first in line to attack Kimura. They punched him with glee, one after the other.

He grunted with what sounded like pain, but then he said, 'I been drinking, you're gonna make me puke,' and his voice was quite relaxed. 'You guys know that you don't have to do what he tells you.'

'I've got an idea. Why don't you be our test subject, sir?' The Prince looked over at the defibrillator on the ground. 'How do you feel about an electric shock?'

'Sounds great,' Kimura said lightly. 'Happy to give my body to science. I always thought the Curies were cool.'

'I wouldn't be so laid back if I were you.' *What an imbecile*, thought the Prince. *How has he survived this long? I bet he's never worked hard, never suffered, always just done whatever he felt like.*

'Yeah, you're right, I should take it more seriously. Oh no, I'm scared, your majesty!' Kimura's voice went up an octave. 'Save me, your majesty! Then give me a kiss!'

The Prince didn't think it was funny, but neither did he get angry. He was mostly just dumbfounded at how Kimura had made it this far in life.

'All right, let's give it a shot.' The Prince looked at his classmates again. After punching Kimura, they had just been standing there dumbly, awaiting the next instructions. At the Prince's word several of them moved to pick up the defibrillator and carry it closer to Kimura. They would need to affix the electrode pads to his chest. One of them leaned in and pulled Kimura's shirt up, about to stick on the pad, when Kimura spoke again.

'Hey, you should be careful of my legs. No one's holding them, I'll kick the shit outta you. Your highness, tell these idiots to get my legs!'

The Prince couldn't tell if Kimura was trying to seem unconcerned or if the man was just crazy, but he took the suggestion and ordered one of his classmates to hold Kimura's legs.

'Don't you have any girls in your gang? I'd rather have girls grabbing me. You guys all reek of jizz.'

The Prince ignored this and told them to stick on the pads.

And if this kills him, he thought, *we'll just tell the police that this drunk stranger showed up with a defibrillator and hooked it up to himself.* He guessed that no one would bat an eyelid if a slovenly alcoholic were to wind up dead.

'Here we go,' said the Prince, gazing at Kimura. With the way the four boys were holding him, he looked like Jesus nailed to the cross.

'Wait a second,' Kimura said mildly. 'Something's been bothering me.' He turned his head to face the schoolkid holding his left arm. 'I think I have a pimple on my lip – does it look bad?'

'Huh?' The kid blinked in confusion and leaned in. Kimura spat violently at him, hurling a gob of saliva right into his face. The kid flinched and pawed at the spit on his face, letting go of Kimura's arm.

Kimura immediately swung his fist downward, bashing the kid holding his legs on the top of the skull. The kid squinted hard and held his head with both hands, freeing Kimura's legs.

Then Kimura kicked backwards, smashing his heel into the shin of the student behind him. Last he punched the kid holding his right arm straight in the face. In just a few moments he was free, leaving four schoolboys moaning with pain.

'Ta-daaa. Did you see that, your majesty? Send all the classmates you want after me, it won't matter. Look, not even a scratch. Now it's your turn.' He advanced on the Prince menacingly.

'You guys, take care of this old man,' the Prince ordered. 'Don't be afraid to hurt him.'

Aside from the four hapless kids Kimura had just shaken off, there were three more.

They were clearly terrified, after seeing what he had just done to their friends. 'Anybody who doesn't fight like they should gets to play a little game later. Or maybe I'll make your brothers or sisters or parents play.'

It was all the Prince needed to say to get them moving. At the mere hint of getting an electric shock they followed orders like programmed robots.

Kimura dealt with them easily. Two of them had knives, but he administered swift beatings all round, handling them roughly, yanking them by their collars into his fists, sending the buttons from their uniforms flying. He didn't hold back. One went down, bleeding from the mouth, but he kept smashing the kid's face with his elbow and palm heel. The two others, he purposely broke their fingers. By the end his legs were wobbling, either from alcohol or from fatigue, but it only made him look even more monstrous.

'What do you say, your majesty? You think you're so fucking tough, but you can't even handle one old man!' Kimura's face shone here and there, as if flecked with spittle.

Before the Prince knew what was happening, Kimura was on him. He grabbed two fistfuls of the Prince's uniform and wrenched it apart, tearing the fabric in two. Suddenly he was about to affix the electrode pads to the boy's naked chest.

The Prince flailed his arms in defence.

'Yeah, I think you might've been scared of me.' Sitting here now in the Shinkansen, Kimura sounds almost triumphant. 'That's why you came after my kid. You wanted to get me back for scaring you.'

The Prince almost sputters *That's not true!* but he swallows the words. He knows that showing emotion is a sign of weakness.

Instead he stops to ask himself, *Was I scared?*

It's true that Kimura's berserk rampage in the park cowed him. Kimura was strong and raging and not the least bit bound by propriety or common sense. Encountering such purely physical dominance came as a shock to the Prince, who relied on book-learning to make up for his lack of life experience. The sight of Kimura beating his classmates bloody made him feel like he was observing humanity in its true form, while he himself was just a painted prop in a cheap stage production.

That's why he turned and ran. At the time he told himself he was going after Tomoyasu and the dog.

Naturally it wasn't long before he regained his composure. He knew that Kimura was nothing but a loser who easily resorted to violence without considering the consequences. But that moment of terror and confusion Kimura made him feel, that stuck in the Prince's craw, and his desire for revenge grew with each passing day. He knew he wouldn't feel satisfied until he had terrorised Kimura in return, until he could bring the man to his knees.

And if he couldn't do that, he would have felt like he had reached the limit of his powers.

He saw it as a challenge, a test of his skills and abilities.

'I wasn't scared of you, Mr Kimura,' he replies. 'What happened with your son was just part of a test. Like an aptitude test.'

Kimura doesn't seem to understand what this means, but he gathers that the Prince is making light of his comatose son. His face reddens again and the confidence he felt a moment ago vanishes. *That's better*, thinks the Prince.

He lifts the bag up to his seat and dials the combination back to 0600, then opens it.

'So now his highness wants the money? Guess your parents don't give you much allowance.'

He ignores Kimura's taunt and reaches in, takes the debit cards, tucks them into his pocket. Then he closes and locks the bag and grips it by the handle.

'What are you doing?'

'I thought I would put the bag back.'

'What the hell does that mean?'

'Exactly what it sounds like. I'm going to put it back where it was, in the panel over the garbage bin. Oh, or maybe I'll put it somewhere easier to find. That's probably better. I could just leave it on the luggage rack.'

'Why would you do that?'

'I found out what's in it. Now I don't really care about it any more. It'll be more fun to watch the other people who want it fight over it. And I took the debit cards, so that should cause some problems for someone down the line.'

Kimura stares, flummoxed. He can't seem to wrap his head around what motivates the Prince. *I bet he's not used to people doing things for any reason besides money or bragging rights. He can't relate to my desire to figure out how people work.*

'I'll be back.' The Prince stands and steps towards the door, wheeling the suitcase behind him.

MORNING GLORY

⟨ 1 │ 2 │ 3 │ 4 │ 5 │ 6 │ 7 │ 8 │ 9 │ 10 ⟩

HE MAKES A PHONE CALL and reports, The job's done. At the other end of the line is a man who could be called a go-between. He used to do jobs too, years ago, but he put on weight and slowed down, and now that he's into his fifties he's established himself as a contract broker.

Morning Glory used to handle his own contracts, but these days he's been getting jobs from the go-between. He had grown tired of negotiating jobs, ever since the byzantine arrangements around the large-scale operation to bring down the Maiden organisation six years back.

That whole affair started at the same large intersection. The memories reawaken. A man who worked as a tutor, two children and a woman, Brian Jones, pasta, the images bubble up without context or order. They cavort through his head, then settle like dust, then fade.

The go-between says, Good work, and then, While I have you.

He gets a sinking feeling.

The go-between continues, I've got good news and bad news.

He smiles acridly. The go-between always says that.

I'm not interested in either.

Don't say that. Okay, bad news first, says the man. I just got an urgent call from someone I know. There's a job, could be a bit of a pain, and it has to be done right now.

Sounds rough. Morning Glory's voice is neutral, he's merely being polite. Now for the good news. The site for the job is right near where you are.

Morning Glory stops walking. He looks around. A broad avenue and a convenience store, not much else.

Those both sound like bad news to me.

The client, well, we go way back, this is someone who's helped me out before. I'm not in a position to say no, confesses the go-between.

That's got nothing to do with me. It isn't that Morning Glory is against the work itself, but he prefers not to pull two jobs in one day.

This guy who's asking me, he's like a big brother, he showed me the ropes back in the day. And he's the real thing, a classic, the go-between says with some excitement. If he were a video game he'd be Hydlide or Xanadu, one of the greats.

You'll have to use an analogy I understand.

Okay, if he were a band he'd be the Rolling Stones. Ah, them I know. Morning Glory smiles slightly.

Or no, more like the Who. Because they broke up, but they get back together every once in a while.

Yes, well, regardless.

What, you don't like the classics?

Anything that's existed for a long time deserves respect. Survival is proof of superiority.

What kind of job is it, anyway?

He decides to at least hear the man out. The go-between sounds happy, apparently taking this as a sign of assent.

Morning Glory listens to the job description and almost laughs out loud. Not only are the details extremely vague but it's not at all the sort of work he's suited for.

Why would you say that? What makes you think you're not right for the job?

I only work where there are cars or trains going by. Vehicles don't pass through buildings. Indoors isn't my field. Ask someone else.

I understand that, but there's no time. And it's right near where you are. No one else could make it in time. I'm actually on my way there right now. I've been arranging jobs for other people for years now, it's been forever since I actually worked a job, but I've got no choice. I have to get out there for this one.

Should do you some good. And like you said, you're not in a position to refuse.

I'm a little nervous, says the go-between, his voice quavering slightly, like a recent graduate confessing their fear of going out in the real world. It's been a long time since I worked, so I'm nervous. That's why I'm asking you to come with.

Even if I did, what could I do? People call me the Pusher. This job doesn't require any pushing. It's like asking a shot-putter to run a marathon.

All I'm asking is for you to come with me. I'm almost there.

I'll be praying for you.

Really? Thanks, Morning Glory. I owe you one.

Morning Glory is left wondering how exactly the man interpreted that as agreeing to come along.

FRUIT

TANGERINE EXITS THE BATHROOM AND steps up to the sink, in no particular rush.

He immediately recognised the man who had entered car three as someone from their world. The man looked a bit younger than Tangerine and Lemon, and his black-framed glasses gave him an intellectual air. He also seemed somehow naive, trying to act natural, but obviously jumpy. When he passed by their seats he had to make a serious effort not to look their way.

Tangerine, in turn, had to make a serious effort not to laugh.

The timing couldn't have been any more perfect.

Here's our sacrificial offering, right on cue. If they were going to pin their failure on someone else, as Lemon suggested, they couldn't ask for a more ideal victim than this particular individual. His arrival was like a ray of light shining into a dead-end alley.

Tangerine left Lemon alone with the man for no reason other than that he had to go for a leak. He didn't want to be worrying about holding it in when things got more serious and figured he would relieve himself while

206

they still had some breathing room. It didn't seem likely Lemon would have a problem handling this guy on his own.

The man with the black glasses – he's the one who works for Maria. While he was pissing he recalled what he knew about this character. Same field as him and Lemon, which is to say, not especially picky about what jobs he takes, a jack of all trades. They had never worked a job together, but the rumours said he was good, despite being relatively new to the game.

Even if he is good I doubt he's a match for Lemon, Tangerine muses as he washes his hands carefully. *I'm sure by now he's taken his beating and is behaving nicely.* He scrubs his fingers one by one, then turns off the water and waves his hands in front of the dryer.

The slim mobile phone in his rear pocket starts buzzing quietly. He recognises the number on the caller ID: it's Momo, a fat woman who runs a hole-in-the-wall adult bookstore in Tokyo. She carries the whole range, from the merely suggestive to the hardest of hardcore, an exhaustive selection of adult magazines for old-fashioned people who still preferred their porn in print. While she has enough regular customers to stay in business, sales are never phenomenal. But her shop also happens to be a hub for underworld intel. The extralegal crowd comes to her for information, and they have to give information in exchange. Over the years Momo has become a central node in the criminal information network. Depending on the job Tangerine and Lemon will go to her to buy information, and sometimes to sell it.

'Tangerine honey, are you in trouble?' she asks him over the phone.

The racket from the tracks makes it tough to hear, and Tangerine steps over to the window and speaks loudly, feigning ignorance. 'What are you talking about?'

'I hear Minegishi is looking to get a bunch of people together. In Sendai, in Morioka.'

'Sendai? Why would Minegishi be getting people together in Sendai? Is it one of those online friends IRL meet-ups I'm always hearing about?'

He hears Momo sigh. 'Lemon's right, your jokes really are terrible. There's nothing less funny than a serious man trying to be funny.'

'Gee, sorry.'

'It's not just people in Minegishi's outfit, either. He'll take anyone reliable who can get to Sendai in a hurry. Lots of people are getting in touch with me about it. Trying to get a bunch of people together in Sendai in the next half an hour doesn't sound like an ordinary job.'

'And you're calling to see if we want in?'

'Not exactly, no. I hear that you were spotted with Minegishi's son. I thought maybe you two were picking a fight with Minegishi.'

'A fight?'

'Like maybe you kidnapped his son and you're holding him for ransom.'

'No way. We know how dangerous it is to cross Minegishi.' Tangerine grimaces. He knows it all too well. And that's exactly the situation in which he finds himself. 'It's the other way around. Minegishi hired us to rescue his son from kidnappers. Now we're on the Shinkansen taking him home.'

'Then why is Minegishi getting people together?'

'I guess to make a welcoming party for us.'

'I sure hope so. I like you guys. I was worried you were in some kind of a jam so I figured I'd get in touch and let you know what's going on. It feels good to help people, doesn't it?'

Tangerine is about to ask her to call again if she finds out anything else when a thought occurs to him. 'Hey, do you know the guy who works for Maria?'

'Sure, Ladybird.'

'Ladybird?'

'His name's Nanao. Seven in his name, seven spots on a ladybird. He's a cutie, I like him too.'

'You know they say that people in my line of work who you like, Momo, they tend to disappear.'

'Like who?'

'The Cicada.'

'Oh, that really was too bad.' She sounds sincere.

'This Ladybird, what's he like?'

'I can't tell you for free, honey.'

'What happened to the woman who just said it feels good to help people? Bring her back.'

Momo's laughter mingles with the rattling of the door. 'Let's see, Nanao's courteous and polite, a little timid-seeming, but don't underestimate him. He's a tough cookie.'

'Tough, huh?' He didn't look tough. He looked better suited for office work.

'Tough, or maybe fast is more like it. That's what people say, anyway. Like, I was about to hit him but he got me first, that sort of thing. Moves like he's spring-loaded. You know how it is, the more even-keeled someone is the more dangerous they are when they get going. A higher threat level than rougher-seeming people. That's how Nanao is. Mild-mannered, but if he gets worked up, watch out.'

'Okay, sure, but he's probably no match for Lemon.'

'Just don't take him lightly is all I'm saying. There are more than a few people who did and ended up regretting it, probably enough of them for a good-sized meet-up IRL.'

'Ha ha.'

'You've caught a ladybird before, right? I mean the actual insect. And if you raise your index finger, it climbs up to the top?'

Tangerine can't quite place how he felt about insects when he was younger. He has memories of killing them wholesale, but also remembers crying over dead ones and giving them miniature funerals.

'Then when the cute little ladybird gets to the tip of your finger, what happens next?'

He recalls the sensation of the insect working its way up his young finger, a mix of alien creepiness and ticklish pleasure. *Oh, now I remember.* Upon reaching the summit of his finger the ladybird would pause, like it was gathering its breath, then spread its wings and float into space. 'It flies.'

'Exactly. That's Nanao. He flies.'

Tangerine doesn't know how to answer. 'Uh, humans can't fly.'

'Of course they can't. Come on, Tangerine, you really are too uptight. It's a metaphor. I mean when he gets cornered he flies. As in, he takes off.'

'He goes crazy or something?'

'More like he goes into turbo mode. Super focus. When his back's against the wall, his reaction time, or his computation speed, whatever you want to call it, it goes off the charts.'

Tangerine ends the conversation and hangs up. *There's no way,* he thinks, but a finger of uncertainty traces the length of his spine. He's suddenly starting to worry if Lemon is all right. His feet speed him back to car three. The door opens and the first thing he registers is Lemon, eyes closed, sitting one row back from where he had been, now directly behind the empty husk of Little Minegishi. Lemon isn't moving. *He lost.* He steps over and sits down in the next seat to lay his fingers on Lemon's neck. There's a pulse. But he isn't napping: Tangerine forces Lemon's eyes open, but there's no response. Unconscious.

'Hey. *Lemon.*' He speaks directly in Lemon's ear, to no effect. Then he slaps his cheeks. Nothing.

He stands and looks around. No sign of Nanao.

The snack trolley happens to be passing by, though, so he stops it and buys a can of sparkling water, keeping his voice as level as he can.

As the trolley exits the car, he presses the cold can up to Lemon's cheek. Then his neck.

Still nothing.

'Come on. This is ridiculous. You're nowhere near being a useful train. More like a totally useless train,' he mutters. 'You're not even a train at all.'

Lemon's body jolts forward. His eyes open but they don't seem to see anything. He grips Tangerine's shoulder. 'Who's a useless train?' he bellows, so loud that Tangerine claps a hand over his mouth. People shouldn't be shouting in the train, and especially not about being trains. But the Shinkansen is passing through a tunnel and the dull roar is enough to absorb Lemon's outburst.

'Calm down. It's me.' Tangerine reaches the can towards Lemon's forehead.

'Huh?' Lemon returns to himself. 'That's cold, man.' He snatches the can from Tangerine, yanks the tab open, takes a gulp.

'What happened?'

'What happened? I took the can. Now I'm drinking it.'

'No, I mean what happened before. Where's our friend?' He realises he has automatically slipped into their code, so to be more precise he tries again: 'Where's Nanao? Maria's guy, where'd he go?'

'Oh, him.' Lemon jerks to his feet and tries to push past Tangerine into the aisle, but Tangerine stops him and forces him back into the seat.

'Wait. First tell me what happened.'

'I let my guard down. Was I out?'

'Like the power was cut. He must have got you good.'

'Hey, he didn't get me. He just cut my power.'

'You didn't try to kill him, did you?' Tangerine had expected that Lemon would do no more than knock Nanao around and tie him up.

'I mean, I got excited. Listen, Tangerine, that guy's wa-a-ay tougher than I thought he'd be. And when I run up against someone tough, I get excited. It's like how Gordon's the fastest train on Sodor Island and when there's a challenger he gets all juiced and goes at top speed. I know exactly how he feels.'

'Momo called and told me a bit about him. Apparently underestimating the guy can be deadly.'

'Yeah, I guess so. I underestimated him. Why would Murdoch have been here, anyway?' Lemon pauses for a moment and looks around. 'Hey, wait a second. This isn't my seat.' He moves to reclaim his spot next to Little Minegishi, unsteady on his feet. It's clear he's still a bit out of it.

'You stay here. Rest for a minute. I'll go and look for him. He's somewhere on the train. He knew I was in the toilet ahead of our car, so it's a safe bet he went towards the back.'

Tangerine heads down the aisle. The door opens to the gangway between cars three and two. No toilet or sink here. One glance is all he needs to tell that there's nowhere anyone could be hiding.

Assuming Nanao came this way, Tangerine figures he'll be able to corner him easily enough between here and the back of car one. Nanao's options are limited: he could be in a seat, or crouched in the aisle, or squeezed up on the luggage rack, and if none of those then somewhere in the gangway, or else in a toilet or by a sink. That's about it. All Tangerine has to do is thoroughly check cars two and one and he'll have his man.

He calls to mind what Nanao was wearing when he spotted him earlier. Black glasses, jean jacket, cargo pants.

Then he steps into car two. A smattering of passengers, no more than a third of the seats filled, all sitting facing the door where Tangerine enters.

Before checking each face he takes in the whole scene at once, like a camera snapping a wide shot. He's looking for any reactions at the moment of his entry. If anyone had stood up suddenly, or averted their gaze, or gone tense, he'd have noticed.

He takes his time walking down the aisle. Without trying to be too obvious, he scrutinises each passenger.

The first one that catches his eye is a man sitting in the two-seater halfway down the car, sleeping by the window with the seat leaned way back. His face is covered with a hat pulled down low, a ten-gallon cowboy hat straight out of a western, bright red. Decidedly fishy. The rest of the row is empty.

If that's Nanao, does he really think he can hide like this? Or maybe he's trying to lure me into a trap?

Tangerine draws closer, alert, ready for an attack at any moment. As soon as he's within arm's reach he whips the cowboy hat off the man's head, expecting Nanao to fly at him, but nothing happens. It's just some man, fast asleep. Different face from Nanao, different age.

I'm too keyed up, thinks Tangerine, exhaling the breath he had been holding in. Then he spots a flash of green through the window in the door to the gangway leading to car number one. The automatic door slides open at his approach. In the gangway is a passenger in a green tube top, reaching for the door to the toilet.

'Hold it,' Tangerine finds himself saying.

'What do you want?' The person who turns to face him is dressed like a woman but is unmistakably male. Tall, broad shoulders, well-defined arms.

Tangerine doesn't know who this person is, but it isn't Nanao.

'Nothing,' he answers.

'You're cute. You wanna join me in the bathroom, have some fun?' The voice is mocking. Tangerine feels the urge to rough up the cross-dresser, but he restrains himself.

'Have you seen a young guy with black glasses?'

The man snorts and smirks, creases forming in the five o'clock shadow. 'You mean the boy who ran off with my wig?'

'Where did he go?'

'I dunno. If you find him, get my wig back for me, will ya? Now excuse me, before I wet my panties.' He steps into the toilet and locks the door. Tangerine bristles at the encounter.

There's another bathroom, unlocked. Tangerine peeks inside. Empty. Same with the sink area and the urinal alcove.

He wonders about the wig the cross-dresser mentioned. *Did Nanao steal it to use as a disguise?* Even if that's what happened no one passed by. Which means that there's nowhere else Nanao could be but car number one.

Just to be sure, Tangerine checks around the luggage rack. There's a suitcase covered with stickers. Next to that is a cardboard box, flaps open. Inside he finds another box, this one made of plastic. It's transparent, looks kind of like a terrarium, but there's nothing inside. He reaches in to lift it up, but stops when the top comes loose. A lid, not secured in place. Tangerine has a flash of fear that the clear box contains some kind of poison gas, but it doesn't, and he's on the hunt, so rather than trying to figure out what it's all about he just closes it back up and moves on.

The door to car one slides open. Once again he takes in the whole interior at a glance, registering the scattered passengers who sit facing him. The first thing that draws his attention is a black shape in one of the three-seaters. He's momentarily confused, taking it for a giant head of hair, but almost immediately sees it for what it is: an open umbrella, compact size, left on an empty row of seats.

Someone is sleeping two rows in front of the umbrella, but it's not Nanao. *So what's with the umbrella? Has to be some kind of decoy,* Tangerine decides. A red herring to distract him from something else. His eyes dart around warily, up, then down: stretched across the aisle, some kind of cord. He steps carefully over it and leans in to examine. It's a length of vinyl packing string, slightly frayed, tied to armrests on either side of the aisle and threaded down under the seats close to the floor to make an improvised tripwire.

Now I get it. He wanted to draw my focus with the umbrella and trip me up with this.

Tangerine smirks at the simplicity of the ploy, but he also reminds himself not to let his guard down. Nanao thinks fast when he's cornered – that's what Momo said. Probably trying anything and everything that occurs to him. It can't have been long since he knocked out Lemon. In that time he rigged up this tripwire, and probably the umbrella too. No doubt hoping to get Tangerine off his feet. And then what? There were two likely answers: attacking his pursuer when he was down, or trying to make an escape. Either way, Nanao would have to be nearby.

Tangerine looks rapidly around. He sees two teenage girls dressed for going out and a bald man who hasn't once looked up from his notebook computer. The girls seem to have noticed Tangerine standing there, but they don't appear especially concerned. There's another couple, a middle-aged man and a young woman who are obviously on a tryst. No sign of Nanao.

By the window in the back-most two-seater is one more person, head ducked down. Tangerine doesn't fail to note that whoever it is had only just now hunched over. He starts down the aisle.

The wig. He can glimpse it on the head in the gap between the seats. It has the glossy shine peculiar to man-made hair. Tangerine can tell that the person felt his gaze and tried to get out of sight as quickly as possible, which only drew more attention.

Is it him? Tangerine checks his surroundings again. All the rest of the passengers have their backs to him, and no one is in the seats immediately nearby.

He closes right in, ready to attack. Just then the wigged head suddenly pops back up and Tangerine reflexively retreats a pace. The man in the wig raises both hands meekly and stammers out, 'Don't hurt me!' He then reaches up to hold the wig in place as it starts to slide off.

It's not Nanao. Doesn't look anything like him – round face, beard, simpering grin.

'I'm sorry, I was just doing what I was told!' He looks nervous. The fingers on one hand are fumbling at the keypad of his phone.

'What you were told by whom?' Tangerine looks back over the car, then grabs the man by the collar. He keeps his voice low. 'Where's the guy who told you to do whatever it is you're doing? A young guy with black glasses, right?' He pulls upward on the cheap-looking striped shirt, lifting the man slightly.

'I don't know, I don't know,' the man squeals. Tangerine hisses at him to keep quiet. The man doesn't appear to be lying, though. 'He tried to steal the wig and I yelled at him to stop but he gave me ten thousand yen,' explains the man, now making an effort to control the volume of his voice. Nonetheless, one of the other passengers picks up on the disturbance and half stands, neck swivelling to get a look at what's happening. Tangerine immediately lets go of the man's collar, dropping him heavily into the chair. The wig slides off completely.

This guy is just another decoy.

Tangerine decides to head back to car number two. Halfway up the aisle of car one he stops next to the middle-aged man on the lovers' getaway and claps a hand on his shoulder. The man nearly jumps out of his skin. 'Did you see who put that umbrella there?' He gestures at the black umbrella, carefully arranged on the seat like a piece of modern art.

The man is visibly terrified. His young lady-friend is much more composed. 'A guy in black glasses left it there just a minute ago.'

'Why would he do that?'

'I don't know. Maybe he wanted to air it out?'

'So where is he?'

'I think he went back that way,' she says, pointing towards the front of the train, that is, in the direction of car number two.

How could he have got past me? Tangerine hadn't seen anyone between cars three and one who looked anything like Nanao.

He turns to look at the door to the gangway and through the window sees the cross-dresser from before exiting the bathroom, swinging his hips as he re-enters car one. *Not this creep again,* thinks Tangerine, and as if on cue the man steps right up to him and lays a hand on his arm. 'Hey, baby, you been waiting here for me?'

Tangerine recoils. 'I hope you washed your hands.'

The cross-dresser looks serene. 'Oh, you know, I completely forgot.'

NANAO

AS NANAO STEPS FROM CAR three into the gangway his mind plays a steady chorus of *What do I do, what do I do?* He figures that Lemon will stay unconscious for at least a little while. But he also knows that Tangerine will be back from the toilet any second, and it won't take him long to piece together what happened. Then he'll come in pursuit. In a perfect world he would start by looking in the other direction, towards car four, but that doesn't seem likely. It's almost certain he'll guess Nanao went towards the back of the train. *He'll be coming this way.*

There's no toilet or sink in the gangway between cars three and two. Nanao steps up to the trash bin and pushes the button to reveal the handle, then opens the panel. There was enough space to hide the suitcase, but it's obvious a person wouldn't fit inside.

I can't hide in here. So where? What do I do? What do I do?

Nanao can sense his field of vision narrowing. His pulse quickens with anxiety, his breathing becomes shallow, his chest starts to tighten. Shakes his head. His mind a cacophony of whispers demanding what he's going to do. The waters rise, then overflow, sweeping away thought in the current. A vortex forms, taking all words and emotions and swirling them around like a washer on a spin cycle. Nanao surrenders himself to the flood. The torrent rages through his head, washing it clean. This all happens in a matter of seconds, the space of a few blinks, but the moment it passes Nanao feels renewed. The muddle in his brain is gone, and without thought or hesitation, he acts. His narrowed field of vision is now wide open.

The door to car two slides out in front of him with a forceful exhalation. Nanao sees all the seats and passengers facing him and steps into the car.

In a two-seater on the right is a sleeping man, middle-aged, salt-and-pepper hair. His seat is leaned as far back as it can go, and his mouth hangs half open as he snores lightly. There's a cowboy hat on the seat next to him, fire-engine red and eye-catching. It clearly belongs to the sleeping man, whether or not it actually looks good on him. As Nanao passes by he scoops up the hat and puts it on the man's head, hoping it doesn't wake him, but the man must be a deep sleeper because he doesn't stir in the slightest.

Will Tangerine see this and stop to investigate? He doesn't know, nor does he know what, if anything, could happen if Tangerine takes the bait. But even if it doesn't work he knows he wants to set up as many distractions as he can. If Tangerine notices them, takes interest, tries to figure them out, it'll slow him down. The more he can slow his opponent down the better his chances of making it out alive.

Nanao proceeds to the gangway between cars two and one and scans the interior, looking for anything he can use. In the luggage storage area there's a suitcase that looks like it's been around the world, dinged up and covered in stickers. He grasps the handle and starts to pull it off the rack, but it's so heavy it barely moves and he decides against it.

Next to the suitcase is a cardboard box bound up with vinyl packing string. Nanao undoes the string and looks inside, only to find another box.

The second box is a transparent plastic case with a length of black rope coiled inside. *Why would someone go to the trouble of packing a rope inside a plastic case? Is that a terrarium . . .?* Nanao leans in for a closer look and then lets out a little yelp. The thing coiled inside isn't a rope. It's a snake. The mottled skin has a glutinous sheen. Nanao jerks backwards and falls on his ass. *What's a snake doing here?* He comes to the forlorn conclusion that it's just another manifestation of his rotten luck. *Maybe the goddess of bad luck is a reptile enthusiast.* Then he realises that when he jostled the case the lid came loose, and before he has a chance to move the snake slides out swiftly. His surprise shifts to alarm.

He watches the snake glide along the floor towards the front of the train, a vague sense he's committed a sin that can't be undone. But even if he could make amends, there's no time to waste chasing after a snake, not when Tangerine is chasing him. He gets up and puts the lid back on the case. He's about to retie the packing string but changes his mind and takes it back off, winding it into a coil that reminds him of the snake, now vanished somewhere. He tries to put it out of his mind. For now he has to find a way to escape.

The bathroom is empty, but not a good place to hide. If Tangerine shows up and finds it locked he'd know that his quarry was inside, leaving Nanao no better than a rat in a trap.

He enters car number one and notes all the passengers, then starts quickly down the aisle. In the three-seater on the left side is a man dozing. On the luggage rack overhead Nanao spots an umbrella, a compact folding model tossed up there carelessly. He plucks it off the rack and opens it. It makes a popping noise and fills the air in front of his face. Several passengers look his way but Nanao ignores them and sets the umbrella down on a seat two rows further in.

Then he starts tying the vinyl string to the armrest of the middle seat. He crouches down on one knee, guides the string under the seat and pulls it across the aisle, then loops it under the seat. When he pulls it taut there's enough length left over for him to tie it to this armrest. Now the string makes a neat little tripwire.

He's extremely cautious when stepping over it. Given his track record, it wouldn't surprise him if he were to get caught up in his own trap. Without looking back he heads to the end of the car and out the door to the observation deck. There's nowhere to hide, though, and nothing that looks usable, so he returns to car number one.

So far all he's done is set up the umbrella and the tripwire. He knows it won't be enough.

He tries to picture Tangerine being distracted by the umbrella and tripping over the packing rope. Then he himself would jump out of a nearby seat and attack, if possible landing a solid blow on the chin to knock Tangerine out and then make his escape towards the front of the train. *Is that realistic?* He knows the answer is no. *Tangerine won't fall for anything this simple.*

Nanao looks all around car number one.

His eyes rest for a moment on the digital ticker over the rear door, with the headlines running across it. He smiles grimly. *Everything that's going on on this train, it's all going to make the news, guaranteed.*

As he suspected, no good hiding places anywhere in the train car.

Moving on, then. He exits car one and heads towards car two. A scene from the platform at Tokyo Station replays in his mind. A certain someone in heavy make-up had complained about not getting to travel in the green car. A man in woman's clothes, throwing a tantrum. And her companion, a small man with a beard, had done his best to calm her down. Green car's too expensive, he had said, But look, we're in car two, row two. Two-two, like February the second.

Your birthday!

Nanao continues past the sink and the toilet. He keeps a wary eye out for the snake, but it doesn't reappear. *Maybe it slithered into the trash bin.*

He steps into car two. There they are, in the second row. The crossdresser is reading a tabloid and the bearded man is playing with his phone. On the luggage rack above them is a shopping bag, the same one Nanao had seen on the platform back in Tokyo. He knows there's a gaudy red jacket and a wig inside. *Maybe I can use those as a disguise.* The seats behind the pair are empty so he slips in, reaches up, gingerly takes the bag and lowers it down. The paper bag makes a small rumpling noise as he takes it, but the pair don't seem to notice.

Nanao hurriedly withdraws to the gangway and steps over to the window where he begins rummaging through the bag. Jacket, wig, also a dress. He takes the wig out. The red jacket is too noticeable. He tries to gauge how well the wig will work as a disguise.

'Get your hands off my shit, you sneaky bitch.'

Nanao jumps at the sudden voice.

He whirls round to see the cross-dresser and the bearded man standing right there, looking aggressive, pressing closer to him. They must have noticed him after all and followed him to the gangway.

Nanao knows he has no time to waste. He instantly grabs the bearded man by the wrist and wrenches him round into an armlock.

'Ow, owww,' wails the man.

'Please keep your voice down,' Nanao hisses into his ear. He can feel the clock ticking, can almost hear Tangerine's footsteps, coming closer. *Any minute now, any second.*

'Hey, seriously, what are you tryna do?' asks the well-built cross-dresser.

'There's no time. Please just do what I ask,' Nanao says as quickly as he can, then tries again, abandoning his usual polite tone. 'Do as I say. If you do, I'll pay. If you don't, I'll break his neck. I'm serious.'

'What are you on?' The cross-dresser looks rattled.

Nanao releases his hold on the bearded man and spins him round so they face each other again. Then he plops the wig down on the man's head. 'Go to the back of car one. Keep this thing on. Someone will be coming soon. When he gets close to you, you call her.'

Nanao realises that he referred to his partner as her, but the pair seem completely comfortable with that.

What next, what next?

His head is whirring at full speed, formulating plans, sketching up blueprints, erasing them, trying again.

'Why do I have to call her?'

'Just let it ring a few times and then hang up.'

'Let it ring and then hang up?'

'You don't have to talk at all. It's just sending a message. Hurry, there's no time. Go.'

'Oh, so I'm just supposed to do whatever you say? Who do you think you are, anyway?'

Instead of arguing Nanao pulls out his wallet and peels off a 10,000-yen note, then stuffs it in the man's shirt pocket. 'This is your reward.'

The man's eyes light up, which comes as a relief to Nanao. People are easy if they can be motivated with money. 'If you do a good job I'll give you twenty thousand more.'

Suddenly enthusiastic despite being threatened only a moment earlier, the man asks, 'How long should I stay there for? Who exactly is coming?'

'A man, tall, handsome.' Nanao gives the man a light shove to get him moving.

'Okay, okay, I got it.' Looking rather absurd in the wig, the man turns and heads towards car one. But halfway there he stops and looks back. 'Hey, this isn't dangerous, right?'

'Not at all,' Nanao says decisively. 'Completely safe.'

Completely untrue, Nanao chastises himself, feeling a pang of guilt.

The man looks uncertain as he shuffles into car one, leaving Nanao feeling the same. He turns to the cross-dresser. 'Come with me.'

Fortunately the cross-dresser shows no signs of resisting Nanao. She even seems excited. She follows Nanao along the gangway to the toilet door. 'You know, honey, you're pretty cute. I'll do whatever you want.' The glint in her eyes makes Nanao shrink a little but he doesn't waste any time worrying.

'The man who's coming is even cuter. Listen to me. He'll be coming from that direction, any second now. You stand here until he does.'

'Ooh, a male model's on the way?'

'When he gets here, you go into the bathroom. Make sure the male model sees you going into the bathroom.'

'Why?'

'Just do it,' Nanao says urgently.

'And then what?'

'I'll tell you in the bathroom.'

'What do you mean, in the bathroom?'

Nanao already has the toilet door open and one foot inside. 'I'll be waiting in here. Then once you seen the man, you come in. And don't let him know I'm in here.'

The cross-dresser doesn't look like she has a firm grasp on the situation, but it's too risky to spend any more time trying to explain it. 'Just do what I said. And if for some reason he doesn't show up in the next ten minutes, then just come in anyway.' Then Nanao steps fully inside and pulls the door shut behind him. He stands beside the toilet and presses himself up against the wall. There's no telling if this will work or not, so he wants to have a good angle to get the drop on Tangerine if he comes in.

After a short while the door opens. Nanao's whole body tenses up. 'Excuse me before I wet my panties,' says the cross-dresser as she enters, then she closes the door and locks it.

'Was it him?'

'Yeah, he was cute all right. He really could be a model, with long legs like that.' *Tangerine.* Even though Nanao was expecting his pursuer, his stomach does a flip. 'Looks like it's just you and me now, and in such a tight space,' she says, wriggling her hips and stepping closer.

'Back off, and shut up,' Nanao says sharply, trying to be as fierce as he can. He's never been good at intimidation, and he can't even tell if she's joking or actually making a pass, but either way he needs to keep her quiet. There's no telling what someone outside can hear.

He tries to picture what Tangerine is doing now. Probably investigating the gangway, and then moving on to car number one. Nanao needs him to get all the way to the far end of the car or the plan won't work. He knows Tangerine will want to check both toilets, but he's betting that having seen the cross-dresser enter this one, he'll check it off the list. From what Lemon said, Tangerine knows what Nanao looks like. Which means that the cross-dresser would register as being not Nanao. And it doesn't seem likely he'd guess right away that there were two people in one bathroom.

Should be in car one by now. Nanao envisions the scene: Tangerine, stopping to investigate the umbrella. Then coming to the tripwire. *Will he notice it? . . . Yeah. He will.* Then he'll conclude that Nanao set it up, which will tell him that Nanao came that way. Which will mean he'll keep going further into the car.

So then it comes down to whether the bearded man follows instructions. He'll need to hide out in the last row, and call when Tangerine approaches. *Come on, beardie, don't let me down.* The moment Nanao utters this silent plea the cross-dresser's bag starts to vibrate with what must be an incoming call. It stops almost as soon as it starts. *Perfect.*

'Let's go,' Nanao says. No time for thinking. Just instinct. 'Leave the toilet and head into car one.'

'What?'

'Get out of the toilet and head straight into car one.'

'And then what?'

'The man who you just saw will probably try to talk to you. Just tell him you don't know anything. Say I threatened you and you just did what I asked.'

'And what are you gonna do?'

'Better you don't know. That way if he asks you, you can say you don't know and you won't be lying.' Nanao knows he'll only get one chance. He'll have to exit the toilet when she does and head in the opposite direction, towards the front of the train. Then even if Tangerine looks towards the gangway, the cross-dresser should be in the way and give Nanao some cover. *At least I hope so.*

'Oh, wait,' he says, pulling a phone out of his pocket and pressing it into her hand.

It's the phone he took off the Wolf. 'Give this to him.'

'Hey, what about my money?'

Nanao had forgotten, but he whips out two 10,000-yen notes from his wallet and hands them over. 'Now let's go.' He unlocks the door.

She turns left towards car one and he breaks right, moving steadily, not looking back.

KIMURA

THE PRINCE WALKS OUT THE back exit of the car, wheeling the suit-case behind him.

Kimura leans towards the window and gazes outside. The sight reminds him just how fast the train is moving. Each building or patch of land he focuses on shoots by and disappears behind the train in an instant. With his hands and ankles bound he can't quite find a comfortable position. The Shinkansen enters a tunnel. A roaring reverberation envelops the train and rattles the windows. A question floats into his head: *Any light at the end of the tunnel?* It occurs to him that for Wataru, lying there in a hos-pital, everything is as black as this tunnel. *All dark, all uncertain.* Thinking about it makes his heart hurt.

He wonders where the Prince went to drop off the bag. *I hope he bumps into the owner.* He smiles at the thought. Some rough customers corner-ing the kid, What are you doing with our bag, you little shit? Kimura hopes they work him over. But almost immediately he remembers that if anything happens to the Prince, Wataru will be in danger too.

Is that really true? Is there really someone waiting by the hospital for the green light? He starts to question. *Couldn't it just be a bluff?* Maybe the Prince is just making it up to keep him docile. Maybe the Prince is laughing at him at this very moment.

It's possible. But no way to know for sure. As long as there's some tiny chance it's true, he knows he has to keep the Prince alive. Just thinking that makes him seethe with rage, makes him want to swing his tied-up hands around and bash everything in sight. It takes a supreme effort to calm his ragged breathing.

I should never've left Wataru alone. Regret washes over him.

Kimura had barely left the hospital in the month and a half since Wataru went into a coma. The boy was unresponsive, so there was no conversation, no way for Kimura to encourage him, but he did everything else he possibly could. Changed his clothes, moved him around on the bed, everything. And it was tough to get a good night's sleep in the hospital, so Kimura's fatigue kept building. There were other patients in the room, as many as six at a time, all little boys and girls, and their parents stayed there too, just like he was doing. None of the other parents made any small talk with the gruff and brooding Kimura, but neither did they make any overt signs of trying to keep their distance. Seeing him sitting next to Wataru, muttering to himself and to the unconscious boy, they could easily guess what he was going through, since they were going through something similar themselves, and they looked at him with sympathetic eyes. In a way, they were all fighting the same battle. As for Kimura, everyone in his life was either an enemy or someone who gave him a wide berth, so at first he didn't know what to make of these other parents, but eventually he came to regard them as being on the same team, all sitting on the same bench.

'Tomorrow I have to be somewhere all day for work, so if anything happens with Wataru, would you please give me a call?'

Yesterday, after letting the nurses know he'd be gone, Kimura had asked this of the other parents with kids in Wataru's room. It felt unnatural for him to make a request so politely.

He had no intention of telling his own parents. They would

undoubtedly read him the riot act, How can you leave Wataru, what are you thinking, where are you even going? What was he supposed to tell them – that he was going to get revenge for Wataru by killing a school-kid? It would boggle their elderly minds.

'Of course, no problem at all,' the other parents had said affably. They had never seen Kimura leave the hospital, so they didn't know how he could be making a living, or if he had taken an extended leave from work, or maybe he was some fabulously wealthy financier but if that were true why wouldn't his son have a private room? They had made all sorts of speculations, so it relieved them to hear him say he had to go somewhere for work. It was an indication that he was a normal, working person. Meanwhile, he knew that the hospital would take care of most of Wataru's needs, but he wanted to be sure that his boy was fully covered, so he had to ask. The other parents were all too happy to help.

'This past month and a half he's just been, you know, sleeping, so I don't imagine there will be any change tomorrow.'

'You never know, the one day you leave could be the day he wakes up,' one mother said brightly. Kimura could tell she wasn't being sarcastic. There was real hope in her voice.

'Sure. Could be.'

'Yes it could,' she said. 'And if your work keeps you out for more than a day, just call. We'll do whatever needs doing.'

'I'll be gone one day,' he responded immediately. What he had to do was simple. Get on the Shinkansen, point his gun at that vicious little bastard's head, pull the trigger. Then back to the hospital. That's all.

Or so he thought. He would never have guessed things would turn out this way. He looks down at his bound hands and feet. He tries to remember how his father's friend Shigeru escaped being tied up, but there's no recalling something that you didn't know in the first place.

Doesn't matter what happens on this train, Wataru's back there, asleep, waiting for me. He suddenly can't bear just sitting there. Before he realises what he's doing, he's up on his feet. He has no plan, but he knows he has to do something, and he wriggles into the aisle.

Gotta get back to the hospital.

He thinks he should make a phone call and reaches for his pocket, but with his hands bound he loses balance and falls, his hip crashing into the armrest of the aisle seat. Pain shoots down his side and he clicks his tongue in frustration, hunching over.

Someone approaches from behind. A young woman, looking both annoyed that Kimura is blocking the aisle and also unnerved at the thought of interacting with him. 'Um,' she says searchingly.

'Oh, hey, sorry.' Kimura hauls himself up into the aisle seat, then has an idea. 'Listen, do you think I could use your phone?'

She blinks, taken aback. It's clear she thinks there's something weird about him. He awkwardly hunches over and puts his hands between his legs to hide the fact that they're tied together.

'I gotta make a call. It's urgent. My phone ran out of juice.'

'Where do you need to call?'

He hesitates. He doesn't know his parents' new number since they changed their service plan. For that matter he doesn't know any number he might want to call. They're all saved on his phone. 'Uh, the hospital,' he says, naming the place where Wataru is staying. 'My boy's laid up there.'

'Sorry?'

'My son is in danger, okay? I need to call the hospital.'

'Oh, okay, um, what's the hospital's number?' Feeling pressured by the urgency in Kimura's voice, she takes out her phone and steps closer to him. Then she looks at him as if he's injured. 'Are you all right?'

He grimaces. 'I don't know the damn hospital's number.'

'Oh. Well, then I guess I'll . . . Um. Sorry.' And she beats a hasty retreat.

Kimura's anger flares, but he decides against going after her. He almost shouts at her to call the police and tell them to protect Wataru, but that won't work either. He doesn't have any information about the person taking orders from the Prince, whether it's a school student or someone medical, or even if it's someone connected to the police, improbable as that seems. But if the Prince finds out that Kimura tried to contact the authorities, it's easy to imagine him exacting retribution.

'What are you up to, Mr Kimura? Going to the toilet?' The Prince reappears, looking down at Kimura in the aisle seat. 'Or are you up to something naughty?'

'Toilet.'

'With your feet tied together? I'm sure you can hold it a little longer. Come on, go back to your seat.' The Prince pushes Kimura out of the aisle seat and eases himself down.

'What'd you do with the bag?'

'I put it back. On the luggage rack where it was originally.'

'Took a long time.'

'I got a phone call.'

'From who?'

'I told you. My friend is waiting near the hospital where your son is. And he calls me to check in. He already called when we left Omiya, as planned, so I was wondering what was up when he called again. When do I get to do it, he asked, how much longer do I have to wait? Let me do it now, let me kill the kid. Seems he's really eager to get the job done. Don't worry, I told him not to. But if I tell him it's time, or if I don't answer when he calls . . .'

'Then he hurts Wataru.'

'He won't just be hurting him,' the Prince says with a laugh. 'Little Wataru, who's doing nothing but breathing right now, would no longer be breathing. If you think about the fact that all he's doing is exhaling CO_2 into the atmosphere, then you could say we're being ecologically progressive. Killing Little Wataru Kimura isn't a sin, no, it's environmentalism.' He cackles ostentatiously.

He's trying to get a rise out of me, Kimura tells himself, keeping his anger in check.

Choosing his words to piss me off. He's started to notice that sometimes the Prince says your son, and sometimes he says little Wataru, and there's a method to it, intended to push buttons. *Don't let him get to you,* Kimura warns himself.

'Who do you have over there, anyway, this guy who's so eager? What's his deal?'

'I bet you'd like to know. But to tell you the truth, I don't know much about him either. I just know he agreed to do the job for money. He could be wearing a white coat and inside the hospital already, for all I know. If he's dressed like a medical worker and walking around like he belongs there I doubt anyone would question him. All he has to do is act natural and no one will suspect a thing. But really, don't worry. It's fine for now. I told him not to do anything to your son just yet. I said, sit, stay. Don't kill the kiddy just yet.'

'Yeah, well, do me a favour and don't let your phone run out of juice.' Kimura says it lightly, but in his heart he's deadly serious. He can't even let himself think about what will happen if the Prince's lackey tries to call and doesn't get through.

He takes a long look at the Prince, like he's staring at something revolting. 'What's your goal in life, anyway?'

'What kind of a question is that? I don't know how to answer it.'

'It's hard for me to imagine you don't have some kind of goal.'

The Prince smiles, so carefree and innocent that for a split second Kimura's disgust is replaced by an urge to care for him, protect him. 'You're giving me too much credit. I'm not that sophisticated. I just want to try as many things as I can.'

'Life experiences, is that it?'

'I'll only get to live once.' It doesn't sound like a put-on. He's being totally earnest.

'Keep pushing it like you do and your precious one life might end quicker than you'd like.'

'You might be right.' There again, that look of unfiltered innocence. 'But I've got a good feeling you're wrong.'

What makes you so sure? Kimura wants to ask, but he stops himself. He knows that the answer won't be some childish prattle. It's all too clear that the Prince was born with a natural sense of authority over other people, a belief in his own power to grant life and death, and that he doesn't have a shred of doubt about his superiority. A royal prince has better luck than anyone else, because he gets to make the rules.

'Hey, Mr Kimura, you know how at the symphony when the performance is done everyone applauds?'

'You been to the symphony?'

'Sure. The applause doesn't come from everyone at once – a few people start it, and then everyone else joins in. The applause gets louder, and then quieter, because fewer and fewer people are clapping.'

'Do I look like I've ever gone to hear classical music?'

'If you were to graph the sound of the applause, it would make a bell curve, right? At the beginning only a few people are clapping, then more, and after it passes the peak it starts to fall off again.'

'Do I look like I care about graphs?'

'And if you were to make a graph of something else entirely, like maybe the diffusion of a particular model of mobile phone, it would look just like the graph of applause at the symphony.'

'What am I supposed to say to this? You want me to tell you your findings are great and you should present your research?'

'My point is that people act based on the influence of those around them. Human beings aren't primarily motivated by reason but by instinct. So even when it looks like someone is acting of their own individual will, they're always taking input from other people. They might think they have an independent, original existence, but once you put them on a graph they're just another data point. See? For example, if you tell someone they're free to do whatever they like, what do you suppose they do first?'

'No idea.'

'They look around to see what other people are doing.' The Prince seems immensely pleased with his pronouncement. 'Even though they've been told they can do whatever they want! They're given free rein, but they worry about what everyone else is doing. And they imitate others most of all when the question at hand is important but doesn't have a clear answer. Weird, right? But that's how human beings are built.'

'Good thing for that.' Kimura gives an offhand reply, because he's already lost the thread of what the Prince is trying to say.

'I'm fascinated by how that works, how people are controlled by such a powerful force without even knowing it. They fall into the traps of rationalisation and self-justification, all the while naturally acting in accordance with what others are doing. It's fun to watch happen. And if you can take advantage of that to control people, that's the most fun of all. Don't you think? If I do it right I could cause a traffic accident, or even a genocide like the one in Rwanda.'

'What, through controlling information?'

'Hey, not bad, Mr Kimura,' says the Prince with a generous smile. 'But that alone isn't enough. It's not just about information. Manipulating human relations is like a game of pool – if you make someone feel anxious, or if you frighten them or get them angry in the right way, it's easy to make them attack someone else, or have them put someone on a pedestal, or have them ignore someone.'

'Is bringing me to Morioka part of your independent research?'

'It sure is.' The Prince sounds confident.

'Who exactly are you expecting me to kill?' As soon as the words leave Kimura's mouth something wells up, something he had put out of his mind so completely it feels like the memory of a tall tale. 'Years ago there was a guy in Tokyo, a big deal, who suddenly went back to the countryside.'

'Oh, you're definitely headed in the right direction. Keep going.' The Prince sounds like he's having fun, but Kimura's face becomes tight and drawn. It feels like his next words are being wrenched out of him.

'Don't tell me you're going after Mr Minegishi.'

The Prince's cheeks pull upwards slowly but surely into a joyous grin. 'Is he really that big a deal?'

'We're not talking about some celebrity here. He's the badass boss of a gang of badass criminals. You wouldn't believe how much money he's got, or how little he cares about rules and morals.' Kimura had never met Minegishi, of course, and when he was still working he had never been hired by Minegishi directly. But in those bad old days, Yoshio Minegishi's grip on the underworld was so tight that virtually any job could be traced back to him, or so people said.

Kimura knew chances were good that most of the work he did was subcontracted out to him by someone working for Minegishi.

'And before him there was a man named Terahara, right?' The Prince sounds like a little kid asking to be told a story of days past, as if hearing about crime lords was the same as his grandma telling him about how she used to do her laundry in the river.

'How do you know about this?'

'It's easy to get information. Only stupid old people think that they can keep their secrets from getting out. It's impossible to keep information contained. If I feel like it I can gather all kinds of info, either by poking around for stray bits or by forcing someone to spill their guts.'

'What, you get stuff on the Internet?'

The Prince's smile takes on a shade of disappointment. 'Of course I use the Internet, but that's just one way. Old people are so black and white in their thinking. They look down on the Net, or they're afraid of it. They put a label on something to make themselves feel better. Even though it doesn't matter whether you get the information online or not, it matters how you *use* the information. And then there are younger people who say that you can't trust anything on TV or in the newspapers and that the adults who swallow it all are morons, but I think that they're the morons for swallowing the notion that everything on TV and in the papers is automatically false. It's so obvious that any source of information is a mix of truths and untruths, but everyone wants to say that one is better than another.'

'And I guess your highness has the magical power to tell truth from lies.'

'Nothing so fancy. It's just a matter of getting information from several sources, isolating what's relevant, and doing your best to confirm it for yourself.'

'So Minegishi's giving you trouble?'

'I don't know if I'd call it trouble,' the Prince replies with a pout, effecting that childlike air. 'There's a classmate I don't like. You know him, the one we were playing with in the park that time. The one with the dog.'

'Oh, him.' Kimura's brow furrows as he digs up the name. 'Tomoyasu, right? You call that playing? More like you were torturing him.' He's on the verge of asking why they're talking about Tomoyasu when another detail comes back to him. 'Wait a minute, didn't he say that his dad had some scary friend who would come after you?'

'I thought he was just making it up, so I didn't pay it much attention, but it turns out he really did go crying to his dad. Pathetic, isn't it? Who goes and complains to their parents? So his dad got angry. Isn't it stupid how worked up parents get over their kids? Dumb lawyer, thinks he's so important.'

'Yeah, I'd never want to be that kind of dad,' Kimura says thickly. 'So what did he do?'

'He went and told on me!'

'To who?'

'To Mr Minegishi.'

Actually hearing it spelled out comes as a momentary surprise to Kimura, but then it all clicks into place and he sees how the Prince is connected to Minegishi. 'Turns out his dad's scary friend really is scary.'

'I have more respect for someone like you who takes care of their own business. Tomoyasu's dad is worthless. I was very disappointed.' The Prince doesn't seem like he's trying to act tough at all. He sounds more like a child who's crestfallen at finding out that Santa Claus isn't real. 'But what was even more disappointing is how lightly that dummy Minegishi took me.'

'What does that mean?' Kimura can scarcely believe that he just heard someone calmly refer to Yoshio Minegishi as a dummy. What's more, that calmness isn't born of ignorance but confidence.

'All he did was call me on the phone. He called my house and said to me, Leave Tomoyasu alone, if you don't I'll get angry and you'll be sorry. Like he was scolding a kid.'

'You *are* a kid.' Kimura barks out a derisive laugh, but he knows all too well that the Prince is no ordinary kid.

'I figured the best thing to do was pretend I was scared. I'm sorry, I said, I'll never do it again. I made my voice sound like I was about to cry. And that was it.'

'Then you got off easy. Minegishi wouldn't waste any time fucking around with a schoolkid. If he really came after you, it'd be a whole lot worse than having to cry some fake tears.'

'Is that really true?' The Prince looks genuinely doubtful. This adolescent boy with his silky hair and his graceful, slim body looks like the classic image of a hard-working honours student. He looks so squeaky clean it's hard to picture him shoplifting or even sneaking a snack on the way home from school. Kimura has a sudden fantasy that he's on a day trip to the north with his refined nephew. 'Is Minegishi really that scary?'

'He's goddamn terrifying.'

'I wonder if that's just what everyone thinks. Like those American soldiers in the movie who are convinced that radiation can't hurt them. Couldn't it be that everyone just takes all the rumours about Minegishi at face value? Or maybe it's like how old people are always talking about how TV shows and baseball players in the old days were so much better. It's just nostalgia.'

'If you underestimate him it'll cost you your life.'

'See, I'm saying that's just like a superstition. Don't cross Minegishi or you'll end up dead! It's like a warped preconception gave rise to a group bias that then warps reality even further.'

'Talk like a normal teenager, okay?'

'When people are told that someone's dangerous, they just accept it and fear that person. Same with terrorism, same with diseases. Nobody has the time or energy to make up their own mind. I'm betting that your Mr Minegishi doesn't have anything going for him besides money, threats, violence, and a numerical advantage in manpower.'

'That'd be enough to scare me.'

'And so he didn't take me seriously. Just because I'm a teenager.'

'And so what are you planning, your majesty?'

The Prince points in the direction of the front of the Shinkansen, towards their destination. 'I'm going to Morioka to meet with Mr Minegishi. Did you know that once a month he goes to see his daughter from his mistress? There's also a son from his wife, and that son is Minegishi's heir, but apparently he's stupid and selfish and basically useless. Maybe that's why Minegishi dotes on his cute little daughter so much. She's still just a little kid.'

'You did your homework, I'll give you that.'

'That's not the point. What's important is that there's a child involved.'

Kimura's brows knit. 'What's that supposed to mean?'

'In kids' shows on TV, no matter how tough the villain is he always has a weak point. When I was a kid I used to think that was too convenient.'

'You still are a kid.'

'But it turns out it's true. Everyone has a weak point, no matter who they are, and usually it's their family or their children.'

'That simple, huh?'

'That's why you came after me, isn't it? Because of your son. People are unbelievably weak when it comes to their kids. And Minegishi has a kid he loves too. If I can press on that, I'll get to his weak point soon enough.'

'You're going to go after Minegishi's *daughter*?' Kimura experiences a swirl of emotions.

One is simple anger, that the Prince would be willing to harm an innocent little girl. Another is doubt as to whether Minegishi would actually expose himself on behalf of his daughter. 'You really think that'll work?'

'I'm not going to do it.'

'You're not?'

'Not yet. Today's just the first step. An introduction, or like a preliminary investigation.'

'You think Minegishi's gonna meet with you?'

'I heard his mistress and their daughter arrived yesterday. They're staying with him in his villa, in a compound near a bunch of farms.'

'How'd you find out where he is?'

'It's not like he keeps it a secret. He's not hiding or anything. He just has tons of security around his villa so nobody can get in.'

'Then what are you planning to do?'

'Like I said, preliminary investigation. But I thought it would be a waste not to try anything. That's why I'm bringing you, Mr Kimura. To put you to work.'

The critical detail comes screaming back to Kimura: the Prince plans to have him kill Yoshio Minegishi. 'That's no preliminary investigation. Sounds to me like the main event.'

'We'll go to his compound and I'll distract the security so you can get in and try to take down the boss.'

'And you think that'll work?'

'It's a toss-up. I'd say there's a twenty per cent chance it'll work. More than likely you'll fail, but that's still okay.'

'Like hell it is.'

'The chances of winning go up when I use his daughter against him. If her safety's at risk I doubt he'd do anything rash.'

'I'd be careful if I were you. There's no telling what an angry parent'll do for their kid.'

'Oh, you mean like you? Willing to die for your child? And even if you die you'll be so worried about the kid that you'll come back again?'

'Damn right.' Kimura has an image of dead mothers clawing their way out of their graves. Given how he feels as a parent, it doesn't seem out of the realm of possibility.

'People aren't that strong.' The Prince laughs. 'Minegishi will do anything for his daughter. And whatever happens to you, I'll be fine. I'll just say that you put me up to it.'

'Nothing's gonna happen to me.' Sheer bluster.

'You know, I heard a rumour. They say that Minegishi doesn't die even if you shoot him,' says the Prince with foppish glee.

'Sounds like a bunch of bullshit.'

'I know, right? He probably just survived being shot at one time. Must be a really lucky guy.'

'If that's what you're going by,' Kimura says, his voice hardening, 'then I was lucky too, back when I was working.' It's not a lie. On two separate occasions a job went sour and it looked like he was done for, but both times he was saved at the last minute, one time by a fellow professional and another time by the arrival of the police. 'It'd be hard to say who has better luck, though, Minegishi or your highness.'

'That's what I want to find out.' The Prince's eyes shine, like an athlete who's finally found a worthy opponent. 'So today I'm going to have you go after Minegishi. A little test to find out just how lucky he is. Whatever happens, I'll learn something about him. At the very least I'll be able to get close to his compound and see what kind of security he has in place. I'll be able to see how he operates. Not bad for a preliminary investigation, I'd say.'

'And what'll you do if I turn on you?'

'You'll do your best, for your son's sake. You are his father, after all.'

Kimura works his jaw left and right, making a popping noise. He really can't stand this kid, with his clever answer for everything. 'Okay, let's just say that you mess with Minegishi, and it goes well, although I'm still not sure exactly what going well would mean to you, but say things go as you plan and you embarrass all the grown-ups –'

'I'm not trying to embarrass them. It's more than that. It's like, how can I put it? I want to make them feel despair.'

That's still pretty vague, thinks Kimura. 'You know, it doesn't matter what you do, you're just a little punk trying to run with the big dogs.'

'That's exactly it, Mr Kimura. That right there.' The Prince opens his mouth, showing his beautiful white teeth. 'Anybody who thinks I'm just a little punk, I want to show them just how powerless they are against me. That's what I mean when I say despair. I want them to realise just how meaningless their lives have been. I want them to give up completely.'

FRUIT

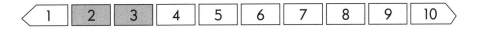

LEMON'S HEAD IS STILL A bit fuzzy. He looks out the window. As he follows the buildings that fly by he reaches up to touch his chin. There was no pain in the moment when it happened, he just blacked out. *Shouldn't have underestimated that little dude just because he wears glasses.*

'That was close, you know, I could've ended up in the same place you are,' he says to Little Minegishi. 'What, now you're ignoring me?'

A sudden thought occurs to him and he pats his side. His gun's gone. He scowls. *Not nice to take someone else's stuff, Murdoch.*

Then Lemon recalls what Nanao had said to him before: that he was working for Minegishi also. But after he stole the bag from them, someone else stole it from him. *So where's the bag now?*

He stands, considers going to see what's up with Tangerine, is about to head towards the rear of the train but decides against it. *Don't really feel like it. I'll just take it easy here for a little longer.* Reaching for his phone to try calling Tangerine instead, he finds that's missing too. *Dammit, Glasses Guy!* He's especially sad to lose the Thomas charm he had dangling from his phone.

He finally notices a noise that's been there for a little while, a digital tone sounding insistently under the train's vibrations. At first he figures it's someone's phone ringing. 'Come on, whoever's that is, answer it already!' But it doesn't stop. Then he realises that it's coming from somewhere closer, and starts to look around, trying to isolate the noise.

Down below me.

He can hear it emanating from under his seat, and a little behind him. He leans over and searches for it, but can't get a good view. He's not crazy about the idea of getting his trousers dirty, but the sound is getting on his nerves now, so Lemon kneels down and peers around in the space between the underside of the seat and the floor. Nothing there. It sounds like it's coming from one row back, so he gets up, changes rows and crouches down again.

The sound is much louder now, and it's not long before he finds the source. A small digital wristwatch. Black band, cheap-looking.

The display is flashing. He wonders if someone dropped it by accident. *Take better care of your stuff, people.* He mutters a stream of invectives. Then he freezes. *Is this part of some trick?* It doesn't seem like a bomb, but it's not hard to imagine that the alarm is a signal that triggers some unforeseen result. Better not to leave it there. He works his long body into the right position and finds a good angle to reach his arm under the seat to grab the watch. It takes some fumbling but he eventually gets it. Then he stands and returns to his seat.

'Hey, rich kid,' he says, flashing the watch in front of Little Minegishi's dead face. 'You ever seen this piece of junk before?' The beeping stops once he pushes the button. It looks like an ordinary watch, nothing special. *Is it a bug?* He turns it over, then brings it up to his ear and listens. *Just a wristwatch.*

As he's deciding whether or not to toss it out, Tangerine enters from the direction of car number two.

'You find Glasses Guy?' asks Lemon. But he can tell the answer just by looking at Tangerine's dour face.

'He got away.'

'So, what, he went the other way? To the front of the train?' Lemon points at the door leading to car four.

'No, he was in car one for sure. But at some point he got away.'

'At some point? What, when you weren't paying attention?' Lemon can feel the corners of his mouth pulling upward. Thinking about his cool-headed and fastidious partner messing up is a distinct pleasure. 'I mean, it couldn't have been that hard. You go from here to car one. Glasses Guy is somewhere between those two points, so he's got nowhere to run. You should have bumped into him somewhere. It'd be harder to miss him than to find him, you know? What happened, Tangerine, did you get stuck in the toilet? Or did you like blink for a really long time and he got away when your eyes were closed?'

'I didn't go to the toilet, and my blinks are short. But he had help.' Tangerine curls his lip. *Oh shit, he's really pissed off,* Lemon realises with some distress. *It's such a pain when Mr Cool-headed is pissed off.*

'Then you should have squeezed his helpers.'

'Apparently he forced them to help. A couple, a guy in drag and an older guy dressed normally.'

'You think that's true, that he forced them?'

'They seemed pretty clueless to me. I don't think they were lying.' He rubs his right knuckles distastefully. *Must have roughed 'em up a little.*

'So that means Glasses Guy escaped and went the other way.' Lemon's eyes go to the front of the train. 'But I didn't see anyone go by.'

'Maybe you were holding a long blink.'

'No way. When I was a little kid I won the school-wide staring contest.'

'Glad I didn't go to your school. Are you sure no one came this way? No one at all?'

'Well, one or two people went by, sure. People move around the train, and there's the girl with the snack trolley. But nobody who looked like Glasses Guy.'

'You were in your seat facing the front the whole time?'

'Sure. I'm not a kid, it's not like I had my face glued to the window.' No sooner are the words out of his mouth than Lemon remembers the wristwatch in his hand. 'Ohh,' he sighs. 'I did bend down to pick this thing up.'

Tangerine immediately looks suspicious. Lemon holds the watch up.

'The alarm on it was going off. It was on the floor down there,' he says, pointing to the seat behind him, 'so I picked it up.' Tangerine's gaze hardens, so Lemon hastens to add, 'That was the only time I wasn't looking!'

'Then that's it.'

'That's what?'

'He must have put it there. Glasses Guy is supposed to be a quick thinker, remember? He must have been planning something.'

'What could he have been planning?'

'He likes to use tools and gadgets. Here, look.' Tangerine holds up the phone in his hand.

'You get a new phone?'

'He gave it to me. She. The cross-dresser. Said it was from Nanao.'

'What's he up to? Maybe he's gonna call crying and ask us to let him off the hook.' Lemon is only joking, but just as he says it the LCD screen on the phone lights up and it emits a gentle melody.

'Huh. Looks like you were right,' Tangerine says with a shrug.

NANAO

AFTER DODGING TANGERINE IN THE gangway between cars one and two, Nanao has made his way to the entrance of car three. He tries to peek through the window on the door but he trips the sensor and the door slides open. *Bad luck again.* From his past experience he knows better than to resist the flow of his fortune. Instead he slips into car three. The first row is empty so he sits quietly to remain out of sight.

Making sure to keep a low profile, he peers between the headrests up the length of the car. There's Lemon, standing up.

Awake. Evidently he didn't drink from the bottle with the sleeping powder in it. That would have made things simpler, but Nanao hadn't really been counting on it to go down that way. It was just one of the little traps he had scattered around in his haste. No sense getting all worked up when one doesn't pan out.

He risks another look.

Lemon is moving. Probably looking for the watch that's beeping. 'Come on, whoever's that is, answer it already,' he says. *It's mine,* thinks Nanao. *My watch that I put there on the floor, for you.*

Since he's used to his rotten luck, he was expecting the alarm not to go off, or for the battery to run out even though those watches almost never run out of batteries, or maybe someone might pick it up before Lemon had a chance to find it, but somehow none of that happened.

Nanao gauges the timing.

The exact moment to stand, the exact moment to move. He worries that Tangerine might appear behind him.

He lifts his butt off the seat slightly, ready to launch, and pokes his head out over the headrest.

The alarm is still beeping urgently. Nanao waits, wondering if Lemon will go after it, betting that he will. Sure enough, Lemon stands back up, moves one row behind, and crouches down.

Now.

Nanao obeys the command inside his head and launches. He proceeds directly up the aisle, not hesitating in the slightest, moving with controlled haste. While Lemon is busy groping around on the floor Nanao zips right by, holding his breath.

He exhales once he's out the door and in the gangway. *Can't stop now. Keep going.*

Through car four, then five. As soon as he exits five he whips out his phone and starts thumbing through the phonebook until he finds the number that he just entered as a new contact, the Wolf's phone, and dials. In the gangway the train sounds like the roar of a wild river but Nanao presses the phone to his ear so he can hear the line ringing. He leans up against the window as his call is answered.

'Where are you?' demands the voice on the other line. 'What's your game?'

'Please calm down. I'm not your enemy,' Nanao says firmly. His first priority is to talk Tangerine down from coming after him. 'I took your bag, but I was only following orders from Minegishi.'

'Minegishi?' Tangerine sounds suspicious. Nanao can hear Lemon saying something in the background. Probably telling Tangerine that he heard the same thing from Nanao earlier. *So they're back together again.*

'I think us fighting each other is exactly what Minegishi wants.'

'Where's the bag?'

'I'm looking for it too.'

'You expect me to believe that?'

'If I had it I'd have got off the train at Omiya. There'd be absolutely no reason for me to get in touch with you. I'm reaching out to you irregardless of how dangerous it is, because I don't have any other options.'

'My father told me something before he died.' Tangerine's voice is cold and cautious, the exact opposite of Lemon's easy-going delivery. He sounds like the wary type who carefully weighs each and every decision. 'He said never trust authors who overuse sentence fragments or conversationalists who use the word irregardless. Want to know what else I think? I think that maybe you weren't just hired to steal the bag from us, but to take us out, too. You trying to connect with us even though you know it'd be dangerous is because you need to get close enough to kill us. You sound nervous because you still haven't got the job done.'

'If I'd been hired to take you out, I would have done Lemon when I had the chance before, when he was unconscious.'

'Or maybe you were waiting until you had us both in the same place. You wanted to wrap it up all at once, Lemon and Tangerine together.'

'What exactly are you getting out of being so distrustful?'

'It's how I've stayed alive so far. Now, where are you? Which car?'

'I switched trains,' Nanao says somewhat desperately. 'I left the Hayate, I'm on the Komachi now.' Even though he knows that there's no gangway between the linked trains.

'That lie wouldn't even fool a preschooler. You can't get from the Hayate to the Komachi.'

'Sometimes lies that don't work on preschoolers work better on adults.' The shaking of the train ratchets up a notch in intensity. Nanao presses the phone hard against his ear and tries to keep himself steady. 'But listen. What's your plan? Neither of us has much room to manoeuvre here.'

'Right, it's like you said, not many options. That's why we're going to offer you up to Minegishi. We'll tell him everything's your fault.'

'You're going to blame me for the bag disappearing?'

'And also for the death of his precious son.'

Nanao is stunned. He thought he'd heard something to that effect when he was spying on their conversation earlier, but now that he knows it's true it takes a moment to digest the terrifying ramifications.

'I guess I forgot to mention. Minegishi's son is with us, but he's dead.'

'What do you mean, dead?' Nanao recalls seeing the body of the young man next to Tangerine and Lemon. Not breathing, not moving, clearly deceased. *So that was Minegishi's son. Why did he have to be on this train? Why is all of this happening to me?* He wants to scream in frustration. 'That, uh, that isn't good.'

'No, not good at all.' Tangerine sounds unconcerned.

Idiot, Nanao wants to shout. Anyone who lost their child would be driven mad with grief, regardless of what kind of person they were. And if they found out who was responsible, their grief would turn into an inferno of rage. Nanao doesn't even want to imagine the intensity of the rage inferno when the source is Yoshio Minegishi. Just thinking about it makes him feel the heat, already blackening and crisping his flesh.

'Why did you kill him?'

At that moment the train lurches sideways. Nanao flexes his leg muscles to keep from tumbling over and tips his body towards the window, pressing his forehead up against it for support. Out of nowhere something wet splats against the outside of the glass right in front of his face. Nanao can't tell if it's bird shit or a clump of mud, but it startles him so much that he yelps embarrassingly and jerks backwards, falling hard on his backside.

There's my crappy luck again, he sighs. The pain in his tailbone bothers him less than his persistent misfortune.

He dropped his phone when he fell.

A man happens to be walking by and stoops over to pick the phone up. It's the man Nanao met earlier, the exam-prep instructor with the placid but somehow lifeless face. 'Oh, hey, teach,' Nanao says without meaning to.

The man looks at the phone in his hand. He hears a voice coming out of it and instinctively puts it up to his ear.

Nanao hastily stands up and holds his own hand out, asking for the phone back. 'Having a hard time staying on your feet again, I see,' the man says genially, handing over the phone. Then he disappears into the bathroom.

'Hello?' Nanao says into the phone. 'I dropped the phone. What were you saying?'

He hears an annoyed click of the tongue. 'I said that we didn't kill Minegishi's kid. He was just sitting there, and suddenly we noticed he was dead. We thought maybe he died from shock or something. But it wasn't us, you hear me?'

'I doubt Minegishi would believe you.' *I don't believe you either*, he says to himself.

'That's why we're going to say it was you. That's believable enough, right?'

'Not at all.'

'It's better than nothing.'

Nanao sighs again. He was hoping to join forces with Tangerine and Lemon, but now that he knows they're planning to pin the death of Minegishi's son on him on top of the loss of the bag, he's regretting reaching out to them. He realises it was a dumb idea, like trying to beat a shoplifting rap by asking murderers to help explain the situation to the police. All wrong.

'Hey, you still there?'

'Yeah, I'm just surprised that you two got yourselves in so much trouble.'

'Not us two. This is all on you, Glasses Guy.' Tangerine doesn't sound like he's making a joke. 'You lost the bag, and you killed Minegishi's number-one son. So we're going to kill you. Minegishi will be angry, sure, but the bulk of it will be directed at you. He might even praise us for a job well done.'

What do I do, what do I do? Nanao's head is whirring at full speed.

'That won't be how it goes down. In any case,' he says, looking through the window at the splattered filth on the glass, now changing shape and spreading out with the speed of the Shinkansen, 'trying to kill each other on the train isn't going to end well for anyone. Can we agree on that?'

Tangerine doesn't answer.

Someone is standing behind Nanao. It's the exam-prep instructor, apparently back from the toilet. He's gazing steadily at Nanao with an inscrutable expression on his face.

'If you don't want to work together, let's at least settle on a temporary ceasefire.' Nanao speaks softly, conscious of the teacher. 'I'm stuck on the train like you, there's nowhere for me to go. Let's just keep things nice and quiet until we get to Morioka. Once we arrive we can settle this. There'll still be time to do that.'

The train bucks sharply.

'Two things,' Tangerine's voice says into Nanao's ear. 'One, when you say we'll settle this at Morioka, it sounds like you think you'll win.'

'What makes you say that? You have the advantage of numbers. Two against one.'

'Irregardless.'

'Hey, you just said irregardless.'

Nanao can almost hear Tangerine smirk. 'Two. We can't wait until Morioka. We have to hand you over at Sendai.'

'Why Sendai?'

'Minegishi's people will be checking on us at Sendai.'

'Why?'

'They want to see if Little Minegishi is all right.'

'Which he isn't.'

'That's why we need to get you by the time we arrive at Sendai.'

'But that's –' Nanao realises that the exam-prep instructor is still standing right there, as if he's discovered students up to no good. He doesn't look like he has any intention of going anywhere. 'Sorry, do you mind if I hang up for a second? I'll call you right back.'

'Sure, we'll just enjoy the scenery while we wait for your call, is that what you want me to say? As soon as you hang up we're coming after you.' Tangerine's voice is cutting, but Nanao also hears Lemon in the background, 'Hey, that sounds nice, let's just enjoy the scenery for a while.'

'We're all on the same train, so there's no rush. There's more than thirty minutes until we reach Sendai.'

'We can't afford to wait that long,' says Tangerine, but once again Lemon pipes up, 'Come on, man, forget about it, just hang up.' Then the line goes dead.

Dismayed at the unravelling of negotiations, Nanao almost calls back, but then he reflects that Tangerine isn't the type for rash action. There's probably no cause to panic. *Stay calm,* he reassures himself, *one thing at a time.* He looks up at the instructor. 'Can I help you?'

'Oh, sorry,' the man says, seemingly just noticing that he's been standing there. He bobs his head in apology, a swift and mechanical movement, like a toy that's just had new batteries put in. 'When I picked up the phone before I heard the person on the line saying something somewhat disturbing, and it got me thinking. Guess I got lost in my own head.'

'Something disturbing?'

'He was talking about someone who had been killed. Scary stuff.'

He must have picked up the phone just when they were discussing Minegishi's son. 'You don't look very scared.'

'Who was killed? Where?'

'It was on this train.'

'What?'

'What would you do if it were true? Probably best to go run and tell one of the conductors. Or get on the PA system. You could make an announcement, Will any police officers on board please come forward?'

'I might as well ask,' he says with a wan smile, barely there, like a line traced by a finger on a watery surface, 'will any murderers on board please come forward?'

Nanao laughs out loud at the unexpected response. *That would be a better idea.* 'Anyway, I'm just kidding. If I knew about a murder on the Shinkansen, I wouldn't be so calm, would I? I'd probably hide out in the toilet until my stop. Or I'd hide behind the conductor and wait til it was all over. If something violent happened in a closed space like this there'd be quite a scene.'

All lies, of course. Nanao had already killed the Wolf and had a fight with Lemon, and there was nothing remotely like a scene.

'But before, you did say that you have terrible luck. So it wasn't that surprising when I picked up your phone and heard someone talking about a murder. Murphy's Law, right? Any time you travel on the Shinkansen you get wrapped up in some trouble, except when you're specifically looking for trouble.' He takes a step closer. There's a sudden glimmer of threat in his eyes. Eyes like hollows in a tree – like a great tree appeared around the man, invisible except for two hollows in the trunk, right where his eyes are, darkly luminescent. Nanao stares at them, feeling like he'll be sucked in any moment, absorbed into the melting darkness beyond.

Overcome with fear, he edges backwards. Those eyes are like an evil omen, but Nanao can't look away, which only makes him feel more afraid. 'Are you also,' he stammers, 'I mean, are you the sort of person who does, um, dangerous jobs?'

'That's a funny thing to ask. Of course not.' The man laughs gently.

'Your seat was at the back of car four. You could have gone to the toilet between four and three. Why exactly did you come all the way up here?' Nanao eyes the man searchingly.

'I just went the wrong way, that's all. Came towards the front of the train. By the time I realised it I had come most of the way, so, rather than run back, you know.'

Nanao murmurs wordlessly, still unconvinced.

'But I have been involved in dangerous situations before.'

'I'm involved in one right now,' Nanao says reflexively. He can feel the words springing up from his throat unbidden. 'A very dangerous man's son has been killed. Not that I saw it happen. No one saw it happen, apparently, but he's dead.'

'The son of a dangerous man.' The instructor seems to be speaking to himself. 'That's right. One moment he was alive, and then he wasn't.'

Nanao can't believe he's talking about this, knows he shouldn't be talking about it, but he can't stop. *This man just makes you want to tell all,* he thinks. *Like he's got some kind of special aura. Like the space around him is a confession booth.* He warns himself not to tell the man anything more, but it's like there's a membrane inside him, shielding him from his own advice. *It's his eyes,* he thinks, but that thought too is muted.

'Now that you mention it, the time I had my brush with trouble there was another dangerous man whose son was killed. The dangerous man was killed too, actually.'

'Who are you talking about?'

'I don't think you'd know the name. Although he was apparently famous in his line of work.' For the first time the man makes a pained face.

'I don't know for sure what line of work you're talking about, but something tells me I'd recognise the name.'

'His name was Terahara.'

'Terahara,' Nanao repeats. 'He *was* famous. Died by poisoning.' He doesn't mean to say it, and as soon as he does he regrets it.

But the instructor isn't perturbed in the least. 'That's right! The father was poisoned. The son was hit by a car.'

The word poisoned stays in Nanao's head, switching on a light of recognition. 'Poisoned,' he mutters. Then the name of the professional who killed Terahara comes back to him. 'Hornet?'

'Sorry?' The man cocks his head.

'I bet Minegishi's son was killed by the Hornet too.' Then before he can stop himself, he points at the man. 'Are you . . . are you the Hornet?'

'Take a good look at me. Do I look like a hornet?' He raises his voice slightly. 'I'm just an exam-prep instructor. I'm just Mr Suzuki.' Then he gives a little self-deprecating laugh. 'I'm a human being. A hornet is an insect.'

'I can see that you aren't an insect,' Nanao says seriously. 'But I still think you're a walking priest.'

The truth is that Nanao has no idea what the professional known as the

Hornet looks like, what his distinguishing features are, or really anything concrete about him. *I bet Maria knows,* he thinks as he takes out his phone and starts thumbing through to her number. When he looks up again the man is gone. He feels a flash of fear that he was just talking to a phantom. As the phone rings he looks through the window on the door into car five. There's the instructor walking away from him. He puts his hand on his hammering heart. *Not a ghost after all.*

Stepping back over to the window where the scenery flows by, he brings the phone up to his ear. The muck on the outside of the glass has been scattered into little droplets.

The phone keeps ringing but Maria still doesn't answer. Nanao gets more and more fidgety, expecting Tangerine and Lemon to appear at any moment. He starts pacing up and down the gangway. The coupling between cars writhes back and forth like a reptile.

'Where are you?' Maria's voice finally sounds in his ear.

'Huh?' Nanao makes a sudden noise of surprise.

'What happened?'

'It's here.' He sounds completely dumbfounded.

'What's where?'

Nanao had called Maria, but now he's forgotten all about that. He's staring at the black suitcase. Right there on the luggage rack, where he first found it. As if it had never gone anywhere in the first place.

'The bag.' The unexpected appearance of the very thing he was searching for doesn't feel quite real.

'By the bag do you mean the one we were hired to get? Where was it? And good work finding it.'

'I didn't find it, really, I just called you and then there it was. On the luggage rack.'

'Where you lost track of it before?'

'No, where I first picked it up at the start of all of this.'

'What do you mean?'

'It came back.'

'Like a dog coming back to its master? How touching.'

'Maybe someone took it from me by accident and when they realised they brought it back.'

'Or maybe they stole the bag from you but were too scared to hang on to it. So they gave it back.'

'Scared of Minegishi?'

'Or scared of you. Maybe they were like, That Nanao's involved, it's too dangerous. He's like a magic lamp that sucks in and stores all the world's bad luck. Either way, good for us, right? Now don't lose it again. And make sure you get off at Sendai.' Maria breathes a heavy sigh of relief. 'I was worried for a moment, this could have been really bad, but everything's okay now. I have a feeling everything's gonna be just fine.'

Nanao's face contorts. 'Maybe, but there's still Tangerine and Lemon to worry about.'

'Did you run into them after all?'

'You were the one who told me to man up and go to car three!'

'I don't remember that.'

'I remember it very clearly.'

'Okay, let's say I did tell you to go to car three, did I tell you to tangle with them? No, I don't think I said that.'

'Yes, you did,' Nanao shoots back, knowing it isn't true. 'I remember it very clearly.'

Maria laughs dismissively. 'Well, what's done is done. I guess you just have to figure out how to get away from them.'

'How?'

'Somehow.'

'Easy enough for you to say, but there are only so many places I can go on the train. Should I just hide out in a toilet?'

'That's one option.'

'But if they search carefully it's only a matter of time before they find me.'

'Sure, but it's pretty hard to force open the toilet doors on the Shinkansen. At the very least it'll buy you some time. You'll be at Sendai before you know it.'

'But if I come out of the bathroom at Sendai and they're waiting to ambush me, then that's that.'

'Okay, well, force your way out.'

Pretty vague, not exactly a strategy, Nanao thinks. But he acknowledges that she's not totally off the mark. The entrance to the toilet is tight, so if they come in after him and he's ready to attack, it could work. Whether he uses a blade or goes for a neck break, he'll have better odds against the pair of them if it's a tight space rather than out in the open. Or else once the train reaches Sendai he could burst out of the bathroom forcefully enough to overwhelm them and make a break for the station platform. Maybe.

'And there could be more than one toilet in use, so it would take them some time to check all of them. If your luck is good then a bunch of the toilets will be in use at once and Tangerine and Lemon will have their hands full figuring out where you are. The train could get to Sendai before they find you.'

'If my luck is good? You must be joking.' Nanao almost laughs. 'You do know who you're talking to, right? Saying to me If your luck is good is basically like saying Here's something that will never happen.'

'Yeah, you're right,' Maria agrees. 'Or, hey, you could use the crew room.'

'The crew room?'

'Or the little room at the end of the green car. The green car is number nine, so in the gangway between nine and ten. People use it for breastfeeding.'

'What should I use it for?'

'Maybe breastfeeding, if you feel like it.'

'Great. If I feel like it I'll have a look.'

'Oh, and one more thing, just in case you didn't know, you can't get from the Hayate to the Komachi while the train's moving. They're linked up externally but there's no passage between them, so don't try to hide in the Komachi.'

'Even a preschooler knows that.'

'Some things preschoolers know that adults don't. By the way, what was it you wanted? You called me.'

'Right. I forgot. When we talked earlier you mentioned the Hornet. Not the insect. The professional, who used poison needles.'

'And who killed Terahara. Although some people say it was the Hornet and the Whale and the Cicada working together.'

'What's the Hornet supposed to be like? Or look like?'

'I can't say for sure. I think it's a man, but I also hear that there was a woman involved too. Maybe a solo operative, or maybe a pair. Either way, I don't imagine they'd stand out in a crowd.'

No, probably not, Nanao thinks. It's unlikely that they would go around wearing something that screams killer for hire. 'I think the Hornet might be on this train.'

Maria is quiet for a moment. 'What do you mean?'

'I can't say for certain. But there's a dead man on board with no visible injuries.'

'Yeah, the Wolf, and it was you who killed him.'

'No, not the Wolf. Someone else.'

'What do you mean, someone else?'

'I mean what I said, there's someone else who was killed, maybe by a poison needle.' He can't bring himself to tell her that it's Minegishi's son. At the same time, her mention of the Wolf triggers something in his mind.

'Oh for goodness sake,' says Maria, sounding more than a bit exasperated. 'I don't know what's going on, but there's something seriously wrong with your train. Nothing but trouble.'

Nanao has no rejoinder. He feels exactly the same way. Tangerine and Lemon, Little Minegishi's corpse, the Wolf's corpse. The train is lousy with underworld characters. 'But it's not the train's fault. It's mine.'

'True enough.'

'What do I do if the Hornet really is on board?'

'I haven't heard anything about him in a long time. I'm guessing he's retired.'

This sparks some speculation on Nanao's part: could it be that the Hornet is trying to re-establish his name by killing Minegishi's son the same way he killed Terahara? At the same time, lingering thoughts of the Wolf come into the mix. Wasn't the Wolf a lackey of Terahara's?

'I can imagine you're scared. Needles are scary. You'd probably cry if you saw one.'

'Actually I used to help an old lady in my neighbourhood with her insulin shots. I did it all the time.'

'That's a medical procedure. I think it's illegal for someone who's not a relative to do that.'

'Really?'

'Yup.'

'Oh, by the way, it seems that Tangerine and Lemon are also working for Minegishi.'

'What do you mean?'

'They're supposed to be bringing the bag to Minegishi.' The pace of Nanao's words speeds up as he shares his theory. 'Minegishi probably doesn't trust anyone. So he hires more than one professional for the same job so that they mess each other up and he comes out ahead. Maybe he doesn't want to have to pay anyone, or he plans to take all of us out.'

Maria considers this. 'You know, if it turns out that's what's going on, don't try to be a hero or anything. You can always give up.'

'Give up?'

'Yeah. Or maybe call it aborting the mission. Forget about the bag, just give it to Tangerine and Lemon in exchange for your life. I bet they'd be satisfied as long as they got it back, and if Minegishi was planning something bigger then it won't really matter that much whether or not we finish the job, right? We'll forfeit the payment and apologise. It'll probably be fine in the end.'

'What's come over you all of a sudden?'

'I'm just thinking that if it's as complicated as it's starting to sound, pulling out might be the best option.'

Of course, it's not just the bag. There's also the not-at-all-insignificant matter of Little Minegishi's death, but Nanao doesn't know how he can tell Maria about that. It would just upset her even more.

'I can't believe what I'm hearing. You're saying that the job comes second, that my safety is priority number one?'

'I'm talking about a worst-case scenario. All I'm saying is that if you get to the point that it looks like you're totally stuck, you can pull out. The job most certainly does not come second. The job is priority number one. But, you know, sometimes you just can't make it work.'

'Okay. Got it.'

'You got it? Then first things first, try to get that bag off the train. Do whatever you can. And then, if nothing you're trying works, plan B.'

'Got it.' Nanao hangs up.

Do whatever I can? No way. One hundred per cent give up.

THE PRINCE

THE DOOR BEHIND THEM OPENS and someone enters the car. The Prince composes himself and leans back in his seat.

A man walks up the aisle with a suitcase. The man with black glasses. He neither slows nor looks around him, just keeps moving quickly for the far door. Kimura seems to notice him too, but he only watches silently.

Then the man in the glasses exits car seven and the door slides shut behind him, as if to seal him away.

'It's him,' Kimura mutters.

'Yes it is. I bet he's pretty excited at having found the bag. And there's another pair looking for it too. They should be after him any minute. He'll just keep going to the front of the train. Things are getting interesting!'

'What are you gonna do?'

'Let's see.' The Prince was just wondering that himself. 'How can we make things even more interesting?'

'I keep telling you, it's dangerous for a kid like you to stick your nose into adult stuff.'

A phone starts buzzing, inside the Prince's backpack. 'It's your phone,

Mr Kimura,' he says, pulling the mobile out. The caller ID says Shigeru Kimura. 'Who's this?' he asks, holding the phone up to his captive's face.

'No idea.'

'Is it a relative of yours? Your dad, maybe?' Kimura purses his lips, which tells the Prince that his guess was right. 'What does he want, I wonder?'

'Probably just checking on Wataru.'

The Prince looks thoughtfully at the still-buzzing phone. 'I've got an idea. Let's play a game.'

'A game? I don't have any games on my phone.'

'Let's see how much faith your father has in you.'

'What the hell are you talking about?'

'Take his call and ask him for help. Tell him you're being held and you need his help.'

'. . . Really?' Kimura looks uncertain.

'But don't say anything about your son. Grandpa will soften right up if he thinks anything's amiss with his grandson.'

The Prince thinks about his own grandmother, recently passed. His family isn't close with their relatives, and his other three grandparents had all passed away in the first few years of his life, so his father's mother was really the only elderly family member he had. She was just as clueless as the rest as far as the Prince was concerned. He acted innocent and well behaved around her and made sure to look happy when she bought him anything. That's a good boy, she always said, her face scrunching up into a smile, You're getting so big, her eyes glistening as she saw her own diminishing future live on in him.

Over summer break when he was eleven he was home alone with his grandmother, and asked, 'Why is it wrong to kill people?' He had tried asking other adults the same question and they didn't even attempt to give him any real answers, or maybe it was more that they couldn't give him any real answers, so he didn't have very high expectations for his grandmother either.

'Satoshi, you shouldn't say things like that,' she replied, looking concerned. 'Killing is a terrible thing.' *Same old stale stuff,* he thought, disappointed again.

'What about in war? Everyone says that it's wrong to kill, but then we have wars, right?'

'War is terrible too. And killing is illegal.'

'But the same government that makes laws against killing goes to war and has the death penalty. Don't you think that's weird?'

'You'll understand when you're older.'

Her deflection only annoyed him. 'You're right,' he said finally, 'it's wrong to hurt people.'

He presses the button to accept the call. An old man's voice comes across the line. 'How's Wataru?'

The Prince covers the microphone and says hurriedly, 'Here you go, Mr Kimura. Remember, no talking about your son. Break the rules and Little Wataru never wakes up again.' Then he holds the phone up to Kimura's ear.

Kimura gives the Prince a sidelong look, trying to gauge what to do. 'Wataru's fine,' he says into the phone. 'But, Dad, I need you to listen to what I'm about to tell you.'

A sardonic grin spreads across the Prince's face as he sits there listening. It would make the most sense for someone to ascertain their situation before jumping in, yet Kimura just goes along unthinkingly. The Prince had said they would play a game but he never explained the rules. Kimura didn't even demand to know the ins and outs before he started playing. The Prince almost feels sorry for him. People want to act of their own free will, but in the end they just surrender to someone else's control. If a train were to suddenly pull into a station and someone said to get on, it would be a good idea to find out where the train was going, to weigh the risks. But someone like Kimura would just get on. The ignorance is astonishing.

'I'm on the Shinkansen,' Kimura continues. 'Headed to Morioka. What? No, this has nothing to do with Wataru. I told you, he's fine. I asked the other parents at the hospital to keep an eye on him.'

It seems that Kimura's father is angry that the boy was left alone.

Kimura tries to calm his father down by explaining the situation. 'Just listen to me. I'm being held. By a bad person. That's right. What? Of course I'm telling the truth. Why would I lie to you?'

The Prince has to bite down to keep from laughing. Kimura's going about it all wrong. His father will never believe him if he goes on like this. To get someone to believe you, you need to be deliberate. About your tone, about what you say, so that you give the other person a reason to trust what you're saying. Kimura isn't doing any of the necessary work, he's just putting it all on his father, saying it's up to him to do the believing.

The Prince tilts the phone towards himself.

'You're drinking again, aren't you?' he hears the old man say.

'No. No! I'm telling you, I'm being held.'

'By the police?'

It's a sensible guess; when someone says they're being held most people would automatically think it was by the police.

'No, not the cops.'

'Then who? What are you trying to pull?' Kimura's father sounds disgusted.

'Trying to pull? What does that even mean? Don't you wanna help me?'

'You're asking for an old man's help, a stockroom manager collecting his pension? And your mother, with her knees she can barely get in and out of the bath. How are we supposed to help you when you're on the Shinkansen? What Shinkansen are you even on?'

'The Tohoku Shinkansen. In twenty minutes it'll get to Sendai. And when I say don't you wanna help me, I'm not asking you to come all the way out here. It would just be nice to know you were on my side.'

'Listen, I don't know what you're up to. But what were you thinking, leaving Wataru behind and hopping on a Shinkansen? I'm your father, but don't understand you at all.'

'I'm telling you, I'm being held!'

'Who would want to hold you? What kind of a game is this?' *Very sharp, grandpa,* thinks the Prince. This is all just a game. Kimura's face screws up. 'Like I said –'

'Let's say you are being held. I have no idea why you would be held on a train. If any of this is even true. And if it is, I'd say you likely brought it on yourself. If you're being held, why would your captor let you answer the phone like this?'

The Prince sees that Kimura doesn't know what else to say. With a triumphant smile he holds the phone up to his own ear. 'Hello, I'm sitting in the seat next to Mr Kimura.' His elocution is refined but his voice still sounds young.

'Who is this?' Kimura's father sounds confused at the new voice.

'I'm just a kid. I'm fourteen. We happened to be sitting next to each other. I think Mr Kimura was just messing around. When your call came in he said Let's pretend I'm in trouble and upset the old folks.'

The elderly man's disappointed sigh comes across the line, hanging in the air. 'I see. Even though he's my son I can't ever seem to understand why he does the things he does. Sorry if he's troubling you. He likes to play tricks.'

'I think he's a very nice man.'

'The nice man isn't drinking, is he? If he looks like he's going to start drinking, do me a favour and try to stop him.'

'All right. I'll do my best,' the Prince says politely, in a tone guaranteed to please adults. After hanging up the phone he grips Kimura by the wrist. 'Too bad, Mr Kimura. You lost. Your father doesn't believe a word you say. Although I don't blame him, with the way you were talking.' As he says this he takes a small bag out of his backpack with his free hand and pulls out a sewing needle.

'What are you doing?'

'You lost the game. Now you have to take the penalty.'

'The game wasn't exactly fair.'

The Prince adjusts his hold on the needle and leans over. People are controlled through pain and suffering. He couldn't risk another electric shock on the train, but a needle would be fine. Much easier to hide, or explain

262

away. By setting the rules and forcing someone to go along with them, he establishes their difference in status. While Kimura sits there looking confused, the Prince inserts the needle under the man's fingernail.

Kimura screams.

The Prince shushes him, like he's scolding a child. 'Keep quiet, Mr Kimura. The more noise you make the more you'll get stabbed.'

'Get the fuck off me!'

'If you scream again, I'll stick the needle somewhere that hurts even more. Take it silently and it'll end much more quickly.' As he says this, the Prince pulls the needle out and starts to slide it under the next fingernail. Kimura's nostrils flare and his eyes bug. He's clearly on the verge of shrieking in protest. The Prince sighs. 'Next time you scream, Little Wataru gets it,' he breathes into Kimura's ear. 'I'll make the call. I'm serious.'

Kimura's face turns beetroot red with rage. But then he remembers that the Prince isn't one to bluff and he immediately goes pale and clenches his jaw shut. He's doing everything he can to keep his fury in check and brace against the coming pain.

He's completely under my control, exults the Prince. The man has been following his orders for some time now. Once someone obeys a command, it's as if they've gone down a rung on the ladder, and the more they obey the further down they go, until they do whatever they're told. And climbing back up is no easy thing.

'Okay, here we go.' He pushes the needle slowly inward, digging between the nail and the flesh. It gives him the same satisfying feeling as peeling a scab.

Kimura whimpers quietly. To the Prince he looks like a toddler trying to hold back tears, and the sight is hilarious. *Why?* he wonders. *Why are people willing to suffer for someone else? Even if it's their child? Taking on someone else's pain is so much harder than pushing your pain onto someone else.*

A sudden impact rocks the Prince, momentarily blinding him. The needle falls from his hand to the floor.

He sits back up.

Unable to bear the pain, Kimura had smashed his knee and elbow into the Prince's head. The man's face is a mix of triumph and horror over what he's done.

The Prince's head starts to throb, but he doesn't lose his temper. Instead he smiles sympathetically. 'Oh, did it hurt too much?' His voice is mocking. 'You're lucky it's me and not someone else. My teacher always praises me for being the most patient and cool-headed student in the class. Someone a little hastier would be on the phone right now, sending a killer after your boy.'

Kimura exhales sharply through his nose. He doesn't appear to know what to do next.

The door behind them opens once more. The Prince turns to look as two men walk past his seat, both thin and long-limbed. They're scanning the car exhaustively as they move through it. When the one with the nastier look in his eye notices the Prince he stops. 'Hey, it's Percy again.' His hair looks like a lion's mane with bedhead. The Prince remembers meeting him before.

'Are you still looking for something? What was it again?'

'A bag. Yeah, we're still looking for it.' He thrusts his face towards the Prince, who gets worried that this man might see Kimura's hands and feet are tied. He stands up quickly to distract them.

'I just saw a man go by with a bag,' he says, trying to sound as naive as he can. 'He had glasses on.'

'You sure you're not lying to me again?'

'I didn't lie before.'

The other man turns towards his partner with the bedhead. 'Come on, let's go.'

'Wonder what's going on up front,' says Bedhead. 'A showdown, probably.'

A showdown? What showdown? The Prince's sense of curiosity sits up and takes notice. 'Murdoch v. the Hornet. Oh, I can call the Hornet James.'

'Does everyone have to have a name from *Thomas the Tank Engine*?'

'James is famous for getting stung on the nose by a hornet.'

'Can't be that famous, because I've never heard about it.'

With that they walk on. The Prince didn't follow a word of what they were saying. Which makes him even more interested.

He turns to Kimura. 'Let's go further up the train, shall we?' Kimura glares silently.

'Looks like everyone's getting together.'

'So what if they are?'

'Let's go and have a look.'

'Me too?'

'You don't want anything to happen to me, do you? You have to protect me. Protect me like you're protecting your own son, Mr Kimura. In a way, I'm the only thing keeping Little Wataru alive. Think about me as his saviour.'

FRUIT

SLIGHT REWIND. BEFORE PASSING BY the Prince in car seven.

As they step out of car five, Lemon glances at his watch. 'Only thirty minutes till Sendai.' They come to a stop in the gangway.

'Ah,' Tangerine drawls, 'but Glasses Guy said there were *more than* thirty minutes.'

The little placard next to the lock of the women's toilet says it's in use. All the other toilets are open; no one inside.

'What are the chances he's hiding in the girls' room?' Lemon looks bored to tears.

'Why would I know the chances? But sure, he could be in there. Our bespectacled friend is desperate, I doubt he'd be particular about hiding in the ladies' room over the men's room.' Tangerine pauses a beat. 'If he's in any toilet, we'll find him soon enough.'

After Nanao's call before, Lemon had said, 'There are only so many places he can go on a train. Even our very talented friend can't hide forever.'

'What do we do when we find him?'

'He took my damn gun, so you'll have to shoot him.'

'Firing a gun on the train is going to attract attention.'

'Then should we get him into a toilet and try to kill him quietly in there?'

'Wish I'd brought a silencer.' Tangerine glumly pictured a tight little suppressor on the barrel of the gun to keep things nice and quiet. He hadn't thought he would need one on this job.

'Maybe we can find one somewhere.'

'Oh yes, maybe they sell them with the refreshments. Or you could ask Santa for one.'

Lemon clasped his hands together. 'Please, Santa Claus, this Christmas I want a silencer for my gun.'

'Enough. We need to figure out what we're doing. First, we want to give Minegishi his son's killer.'

'Which was Glasses Guy.'

'But if we kill him, we'll have to deal with moving the body and not getting caught. Bringing him to Minegishi will be much easier if he's alive. Killing him now will just make it more complicated.'

'Yeah, but if we get him in front of Minegishi, he'll just say I didn't do it, I was framed!'

'Anyone would say they were framed in a situation like that. Nothing to worry about.'

So they decided to search every last inch of the train. If they checked every seat, all the luggage racks, all the toilets and sink areas, they'd find him for certain. If a toilet was in use, they'd wait to see if someone came out.

Now, beside the in-use toilet Lemon says, 'I got this one. You keep going.' He points towards the front of the train, but then, 'I have a better idea – we do the opposite!'

'And what's your opposite idea?' Tangerine knows it won't be anything very good, but he asks anyway.

'I can go around locking all the bathrooms. That way even if I don't find him, he'll have fewer places to hide!'

Just a few minutes ago they had hidden Little Minegishi's body in the bathroom between cars three and four. They didn't think it was a good idea to leave him in the seat while both of them were gone. They propped him up on the toilet, then Lemon used a twist of copper wire to lock the door from the outside. By winding the wire around the knob for the lock on the inside of the door, he could pull the door shut and locked. There's a trick to the angles, and you have to yank down the moment the door closes, but Lemon did it deftly. 'There you go, one locked murder room,' he said proudly. Then he got excited. 'Hey, wasn't there an old movie where they used a giant magnet to open a locked door from the outside?'

'Yeah, *Un Flic*.' Tangerine remembered enjoying the scene, with the oversized U-magnet moving the chain on the lock.

'That the one with Steven Seagal?'

'Alain Delon.'

'Really? You sure it wasn't in *Under Siege 2*?'

'It wasn't *Under Siege 2*.'

After a minute the ladies' room door opens and a thin woman emerges. Her white blouse has a youthful cut, but the heavy make-up and lines on her face give her away. She reminds Tangerine of a wilting plant. He watches her walk off. 'Definitely not Ladybird. At least that one was straightforward.'

They enter car six and scan the passengers one by one, confirm that no one is Nanao, and move on. They check under seats and on luggage racks, even though they doubt they'd find him, or the missing suitcase, in either one of those places. Luckily they can tell at a glance that none of the passengers might be Nanao in disguise – they're all either the wrong sex or the wrong age.

'When I was on the phone with Momo earlier, she told me that Minegishi's trying to put together a squad at Sendai Station.'

'So we're gonna pull in and find the platform packed with bad dudes. Gross.'

'At such short notice, I don't imagine he'd get that many people,'

Tangerine muses as they exit car six. 'Everyone who's any good already has a full schedule.'

'Yeah, but whoever he does get is gonna come on and start shooting. They're not gonna listen to reason.'

'That could happen, true, but I doubt it.'

'Why?'

'Because we're the only ones who might have any idea about what happened to Minegishi's kid. You and I. They can't just kill us immediately.'

'Huh. I guess you're right. We're useful trains.' Lemon nods his agreement. 'No, wait.'

'What is it?'

'If it were me, I'd kill me, or you.'

'I have no idea who's doing what to whom in that sentence. Like bad prose in a novel.'

'I'm trying to say, Minegishi's guys only need to bring one of us in alive if he wants to find out what happened to his kid. Right? And trying to bring in both of us together would also be more dangerous. Better to take one of us out. This train only needs one car.'

A call comes in. Tangerine reaches for his own phone, but it's on the phone he got from the cross-dresser. Not a number he recognises. He answers and hears Nanao's voice.

'Mr Tangerine? or Mr Lemon?'

'Tangerine,' he says. Lemon makes a questioning face at him, so he traces circles in front of his eyes: glasses. 'Where are you?'

'On the Shinkansen.'

'Wouldn't you know it, we are too. Why are you calling? We're not going to make a deal with you.'

'I'm not looking to make a deal. I give up.' He can hear the tension in Nanao's voice.

The shaking and noise are much more intense in the gangway than in the train cars. The roar sounds like they're hurtling along in open air.

'You give up?' Tangerine isn't sure if he heard right. He says it again, louder. 'You're giving up?' Lemon's eyes narrow.

'And I found the bag.'

'Where?'

'On the luggage rack in the gangway. It just showed up, out of nowhere. Wasn't there before.'

Sounds fishy to Tangerine. 'Why would it just reappear? It has to be some kind of trap.'

Nanao is quiet for a moment. 'I can't say that is not a trap. All I can say is that the bag was there.'

'And the contents?'

'Couldn't say. I don't know the combination for the lock and I didn't know what was in it to begin with. But I wanted to turn it over to you two.'

'Why would you do that?'

'I don't think I can keep dodging you here on the train, so rather than worrying about you trying to kill me I thought it would just be easier on my nerves to call it quits. I gave the bag to one of the conductors. Soon there should be an announcement about it on the PA. That's your bag. Will you go and get it and then just go to the back of the train? I'll get off at Sendai and you'll be done with me. And I'll be done with this job.'

'If you don't finish the job, you'll make Maria angry. And I'm guessing your client Minegishi will be even angrier.'

'I'd rather that than be targeted by the two of you.'

Tangerine lowers the phone and turns to Lemon. 'Glasses Guy is giving up.'

'Smart move,' says Lemon with great satisfaction. 'He knows how tough we are.'

'Still doesn't solve our problem with Little Minegishi.' Tangerine brings the phone back up to his ear. 'In our scenario, you're the killer.'

'It'll be more believable if you bring in the real killer.'

'Who do you mean, the real killer?'

'You're familiar with the Hornet?'

Lemon cranes towards the phone. 'What's Glasses Guy saying?'

'Asks if we're familiar with the hornet.'

'Of course we are,' Lemon says, grabbing the phone out of Tangerine's hand. 'When I was little and went out collecting beetles, I got chased by hornets all the time. Hornets are bad news!' Flecks of saliva fly from his mouth. Then his brow knits at Nanao's response. 'What do you mean, I'm talking about real hornets? Are you talking about a fake hornet? Do people make counterfeit hornets?'

Tangerine has put it together. He gestures for Lemon to give him back the phone. 'You mean the professional who poisons people. That Hornet.'

'That's the one,' Nanao affirms.

'So what do I get for getting the right answer?'

'You get the killer.'

At first it's not clear what Nanao's suggesting and Tangerine is about to snarl at him for wasting their time, but then it hits him. 'Are you saying the Hornet is on this train?'

'Whoa, where, I hate hornets!' Lemon immediately starts shielding his face and looking around nervously.

'I think the Hornet may have poisoned Minegishi's son,' continues Nanao. 'That would explain why he doesn't have any visible wounds.'

Tangerine doesn't know exactly how the professional called the Hornet works, but the rumour is that he uses needles to trigger anaphylaxis. The first prick won't kill, just lights up the immune system, but the second needle sets off a massive allergic reaction that causes the victim to die of shock. That's the Hornet's method, they say. Tangerine tells Nanao about it.

'So the second prick is the deadly one?'

'Maybe. Where is he?'

'I don't know. I don't know anything about what the Hornet looks like . . . but I think it's a she. And there's a picture of her.'

'What do you mean, there's a picture of her?' Not knowing where Nanao is going with this, Tangerine starts to get annoyed. 'Get to the point.'

'In the back of car six, you'll find an older man seated by the window. There's a photograph in his jacket pocket.'

'And that photo is of the Hornet, huh? Who's the old guy?' Tangerine swivels round towards car six. He thinks he remembers seeing a middle-aged man sleeping.

'He's in the business. A real sleaze. He said the photo was of his target. Then I thought, that means she must be on this train.'

'What makes you think she's the Hornet?'

'I don't have any real proof. Just that the man with the photo was one of Terahara's underlings. Liked to brag about how much the boss liked him. And Terahara –'

'– was killed by the Hornet.'

'Right. And the man in car six was saying he was on the Shinkansen for revenge. He called it a vendetta. I didn't pay much attention to it at the time, but he was probably talking about getting revenge on the Hornet.'

'That's just speculation on top of speculation.'

'Oh, and he mentioned something about Akechi Mitsuhide. I bet he was saying the Hornet killing Terahara was like Akechi killing Nobunaga. You know, a trusted lieutenant turning on the boss.'

'I can't say I'm convinced, but I guess we'll go and get the picture from the old guy and see what he has to say.'

'Um, you won't get much out of him,' Nanao says hastily, but Tangerine talks over him.

'I'll have a look at the picture and call you back.' He hangs up. Lemon steps over and asks what's up.

'Looks like I was right.'

'Right about what?'

'I guessed that Little Minegishi died from an allergic reaction, remember? Turns out that may have been right.'

They enter car six and stalk down the aisle. Several passengers stare at them, by now wondering what the two rangy men are doing coming and going. The pair ignore the scrutiny, proceeding straight to the back of the car.

A middle-aged man is leaning up against the window of the two-seater. His flat cap is pulled low on his brow.

'What's with Uncle Sleepy?' Lemon frowns. 'This isn't Glasses Guy.'

'Sleeping like the dead.' As soon as Tangerine says it, he realises that the man actually is dead. He sits down next to the corpse and pats down the tracksuit jacket. It feels unclean, even though it's not visibly stained, and Tangerine plucks it open distastefully so he can reach in. Sure enough, there's a photo in the inside pocket. He pulls it out. The head slides off the window and lolls forward. Broken neck. Tangerine rearranges the head against the pane.

'You're just picking his pocket like that?' hisses Lemon. 'And look, he's not even doing anything!'

'Because he's dead,' Tangerine says, pointing at the head.

'Guess it's dangerous to toss and turn too much when you're sleeping.'

Tangerine steps out the door at the back of the car into the gangway. He pulls up the history on his phone and calls the last number. Lemon emerges from the car and stands beside him.

'Hello,' Nanao says.

The train's passage rumbles in Tangerine's ears. 'I got the picture. What's with that guy? Broken necks in fashion this season?'

'Sometimes things like that just happen,' Nanao says gravely, without any further explanation.

Tangerine doesn't bother asking if Nanao was the one who did it. Instead he looks down at the photo. 'So this is the Hornet?'

'Well, I can't see the picture, but I'd be willing to say there's a good chance. If you see anyone on board who looks like her, be careful.'

Tangerine has never seen the woman in the photo before. Lemon leans in to have a look. He asks excitedly, 'How do you beat the Hornet? Insecticide spray?'

'In Woolf's *To the Lighthouse*, they kill a bee with a spoon.'

'How'd they kill a bee with a spoon?'

'I ask myself the same thing every time I read that part.' Then he hears Nanao saying something indistinct. 'What'd you say?' There's no response. Tangerine asks again, and after a moment Nanao answers.

'Sorry, I was buying a tea. The snack trolley came by. I was thirsty.'

'Sure are taking it easy for someone in so much trouble.'

'You have to get your nutrients and fluids when you have a chance. Same with going to the toilet.'

'Well,' Tangerine says, 'I don't necessarily believe you, but I'll keep an eye out for her. It'll take some time to check every passenger, but it won't be impossible.'

Then Tangerine realises with a start that maybe that's Nanao's plan, trying to buy time before the train gets to Sendai.

'He-e-ey,' Lemon says with dawning recognition, pointing his finger at the face in the photo. 'It's her!'

'Who?'

Lemon seems surprised that Tangerine can't place the face. 'The snack trolley girl. The one who's been pushing that cart back and forth this whole time.'

NANAO

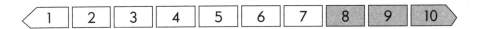

REWIND A BIT FURTHER. NANAO is about to hand the suitcase over to a conductor. On the right side of the gangway between cars eight and nine is a narrow door with a sign that says Crew. Just as Nanao is approaching a conductor steps out of it, and the two nearly collide.

'Whoops, sorry.' *On my way to see a conductor and I almost bowl him over. Bad luck as usual.*

While Nanao is flustered, the surprisingly young-looking conductor in the snappy double-breasted suit uniform is completely calm. 'Can I help you?'

Before he can change his mind, Nanao thrusts the bag forward. 'Could I give this to you?'

The conductor makes a puzzled face. His hat is too large, which makes him look like a little boy who loves trains and somehow got a job on the Shinkansen. His vibe is gentle despite the formality of the double-breasted uniform. 'You'd like me to take your luggage?'

'I found it in the bathroom,' Nanao lies. 'In the gangway between five and six.'

'Is that right?' answers the young conductor, without any apparent suspicion. He examines the bag as he turns it around, tries the clasp and finds it locked. 'I'll be sure to make an announcement about it.'

Nanao thanks him and proceeds into the green car, then beyond to the next gangway, linking the green car to car ten. The end of the Hayate. He's thinking about the Wolf and the Hornet and the connection between the two. After a moment he takes out his phone.

Tangerine answers, and Nanao explains the situation as quickly as he can. About how he's ready to give up, that he turned over the bag to the conductor, his theory that Minegishi's son could have been killed by the Hornet, the fact that the man in the back of car six has a photo of the Hornet in his pocket. Then Tangerine hangs up.

Nanao leans against the window and gazes out, gripping his phone like he's waiting for a call from a lover. The train enters a tunnel. Plunging into the dark feels to him like holding his breath underwater. When the scenery is visible again the air comes rushing back. But almost immediately there's another tunnel. Dive, surface, dive, surface, dark, light, dark, light, bad luck, good luck, bad luck, good luck. He recalls the old saying about fortune and misfortune being inextricably intertwined. *Although in my case it's mostly all misfortune.*

That's when the refreshments girl pushes her trolley into the gangway. The trolley is stuffed with snacks and drinks, a tower of paper cups perched atop.

Nanao orders a bottle of tea just as Tangerine calls back. He wedges the phone between shoulder and ear as he hands some change to the attendant. Tangerine asks what's going on and Nanao explains that he's buying tea.

'Sure are taking it easy for someone in so much trouble.'

'You have to get your nutrients and fluids when you have a chance. Same with going to the toilet.'

The refreshments girl thanks him and starts to push her trolley towards car ten.

'Hey, Nanao,' says Tangerine forcefully. 'Something you'll want to hear. It seems that the snack trolley girl is the Hornet.'

'What?' The sudden revelation catches Nanao so completely off guard that he raises his voice more than he means to.

The snack trolley comes to a stop.

The attendant still has her back to him, but she turns her head to look over her shoulder in his direction. Her full, still-youthful cheeks are arranged in a kind smile, as if to say, Is everything all right? May I be of some assistance? She looks perfectly natural.

Nanao hangs up the phone and stares. *Could she be the Hornet?* It seems hard to believe. He looks her up and down carefully.

'Is something wrong, sir?' She slowly turns to face him. With her vending apron on top of her staff uniform she doesn't look like she could be anything else but the snack trolley attendant.

Nanao puts his phone in his rear pocket. 'Oh, uh, no, everything's fine.' He tries not to let his nervousness show. 'Um, can anyone use this room?' He points to the door on the left that says Multi-Purpose Room. Next to the sliding door is a plate on the wall directing passengers to inform a staff member if they plan to use the room. *Must be what Maria was talking about, with the breastfeeding.* He tries the door and finds it unlocked. A drab space inside, nothing but an empty room and a single seat.

'Most people use it for childcare needs,' replies the attendant, 'but as long as you let a staff member know, you can use it too.' By now her smile seems pasted on, artificial. He can't tell if it's the standard issue customer service smile or a sign of some deeper tension.

Opposite the multi-purpose room is a bathroom, larger than the ones on the other gangways. On the wall next to it is an oversized button to open the door, no doubt for passengers in wheelchairs.

The attendant is still smiling. *What do I do, what do I do?* The refrain reverberates through Nanao's head. *Should I try to find out if it's really her? And if it is, what do I do?*

There's a small ripping sound.

It's the label on the bottle of tea in his hand. He had been picking at it without realising. 'Sorry, but is there a hornet onboard?' He tries to sound as casual as he can, like it just occurred to him. Stepping away from the door to the multi-purpose room, he peels the label off completely.

'Pardon me?' She seems startled by the question. 'A . . . hornet?'

'You know, the Asian giant hornet. The venomous kind,' he presses. 'I feel like there's one on the train.'

'You saw one flying around? Maybe it came aboard at one of the station stops. That could be dangerous. I'll let one of the conductors know.'

He can't tell if she's deflecting or if she really doesn't know what he's getting at. Nothing about how she's acting gives anything away.

She flashes another smile and turns away once more, towards car ten.

Nanao turns too and makes it look as if he's going back to the green car. He focuses all his attention behind him, trying to sense any movement.

He raises the plastic bottle, seeing if he can use the fluid as a mirror.

There, reflected vaguely in the sloshing tea, is the woman, noiselessly coming closer.

Nanao whirls round. She's right in front of him.

He whips the bottle at her face. She dodges the blow but Nanao uses the opening to shove her, fast and sharp and full force. She staggers backwards and crashes into the snack trolley, toppling the stack of paper cups and scattering several boxes of souvenir snacks. Her back against the cart, she slides down and sits hard on the floor.

Nanao notices something else: what looks like a length of cord unspooling from under the cart, wriggling back and forth.

The snake.

The same one he witnessed jump out of the terrarium at the back of the train. It must have been hiding out among the snack boxes under the trolley. It slithers along the wall of the gangway and after a moment Nanao loses sight of it.

The woman grips the cart handle and pulls herself up. Something glitters in her right hand. A needle.

Her form-fitting blue button-down shirt and indigo apron aren't meant for athletics, but that doesn't slow her down in the slightest. She darts forward, no hesitation. The way she's moving gives Nanao no clues as to how she might attack, whether she'll stab with the needle or throw it.

She's almost on him.

Nanao hits the big door-open button for the wheelchair toilet. The door slides open. The woman glances at the opening door.

Nanao doesn't miss his chance. He steps around at an angle and kicks at her as hard as he can, trying to knock her into the bathroom. He knows that it doesn't matter if your opponent is a man, woman or child, if they're a pro there's no room for mercy.

She careers into the bathroom and he follows right behind her. Even with more space than the standard toilets there's not much room for the both of them. They're right on top of the toilet. He launches his left fist at her face but she deflects the blow with her forearm, so he quickly punches with his right, aiming at her ribs. Just as the body blow is about to land she twists and it glances off.

She's quick. Looks slightly concerned, he's making her work, but she's handling his attacks.

He has a feeling that any moment the needle will come flying at him.

The automated door starts to slide shut so Nanao pounds the button inside the bathroom and it reopens. He springs out into the gangway and tries to turn round and secure his footing, backing up hard against the door to the multi-purpose room. A flash of pain shoots up his arm from where Lemon stabbed him earlier.

The gun falls out of the back of his belt, the gun he took off Lemon, clattering to the floor. He scrambles to pick it up when he hears a metallic ping behind him.

Something hits the door and falls. A needle, hurled like a missile.

The woman steps back into the gangway. She kicks the gun away from Nanao's outstretched hand, sending the weapon spinning across the floor.

Nanao scurries over to the cart and scoops up one of the gift-wrapped boxes of souvenir snacks that litter the ground. He holds it up towards the woman, using it as a shield. The instant he raises it a needle comes piercing through. *A split second slower and –* She pulls back her hand, the needle held between the fingers of her closed fist. She thrusts again. Nanao catches it on the box once more.

He wrenches the box to the side, the needle still lodged in it, pulling her arm along.

He aims another kick at her, catching her in the solar plexus with the toe of his shoe. It's a solid hit. She clamps her hands to her midsection and sinks down and back.

That's it, Nanao thinks, closing in to press his advantage.

But just as he's stepping over the coupling between cars the train bucks. It only lasts for a second, but it's intense, like an animal shaking water from its fur. If Nanao were a ladybird on the animal's back he could easily fly away to escape the fleshly quake, but for Nanao the human on the Shinkansen this is impossible. Before he can catch himself he's lost his footing and is spilling to the floor.

Rather than thinking, *Why now?* he tells himself, *Of course. Falling over in the middle of a fight. More proof of love from the goddess of bad luck.*

Nanao starts to struggle to his feet. The woman is still holding her stomach and groaning.

As he tries to use his hands to prop himself up he feels a stab of pain. *What?* Then he feels the blood drain from his face. There's a needle sticking out of the side of his hand. His eyes go wide and the hair on his neck stands up. The needle the woman threw at him bent when it hit the door and the point curved up like the tip of a fishhook. Nanao had put his hand down right on top of it. *And this is no ordinary pinprick,* he knows. The needle is poisoned.

In the next second Nanao's head fills with signals, a blizzard of words and thought fragments. *Rotten luck. The Hornet. Poison. Dying. Always so unlucky.* And then, *Is this really it?* A great heaviness settles on him. *Just like that?*

But at the same time his head is buzzing with the familiar chorus of *What do I do, what do I do?* He can feel his vision narrowing and he looks around wildly, fighting to stay aware. The woman, doubled over. The cart.

The scattered refreshments. He can feel the poison coursing through his body. *How fast is it circulating?* Then it comes: the rising waters, the churn, the overflow. *What do I do? What do I do?* The question fills him up.

An instant later it's done. The waters recede and his field of vision is wide open. His head is clear. He knows exactly what to do.

First he yanks the needle out of his hand.

No time to lose.

There's another needle on the ground next to the woman. Nanao shoots to his feet and advances.

She's finally able to sit up, though she's still clutching at her solar plexus with one hand.

The other is pawing at the floor, trying to grasp the gun that Nanao dropped.

Nanao flies towards her. First he grabs the gun. Then he plucks up the needle and without a moment's hesitation he plunges it into her shoulder, as naturally as if he's clapping her on the back in encouragement. Her mouth snaps open and stays that way, like a chick in the nest waiting for food. Then she sees the needle sticking out of her shoulder and her eyes go round.

Nanao takes one step back, then another.

She's dumbfounded at having been stabbed with one of her own poison needles.

Nanao doesn't know how long it takes the poison to kick in or what symptoms signal its onset. As he stands there waiting he starts to imagine his breath going ragged, his consciousness fading, his life winking out, and terror washes over him. He thinks about the end, swift and sudden, like pulling a plug, and it becomes almost too much for him to stay standing. Cold sweat starts to pour from his skin. *Please, I'm begging you, hurry up.* As if hearing his pleading, the woman starts patting her apron, feeling for the pocket. She pulls out something that looks like a felt pen. She's visibly frantic. Pops off the cap, then pulls her skirt up and exposes her thigh. She moves the pen towards her skin.

Nanao swoops in, leans down, breaks her neck.

He grabs the pen-shaped device. It looks like it's designed to deliver an injection, just like the ones he would use to help the old lady in his neighbourhood with her insulin shots when he was younger. Normally he would fuss over whether this one worked the same as the ones he was familiar with, but right now he doesn't have the breathing room. He hooks his finger into the hole at the left knee of his cargo pants and roughly tears it further open up the leg. As soon as he can see his thigh peeking through he pushes the tip of the pen-injector into his skin, wondering wildly whether it will work as an antidote, whether he's administering it correctly, whether it isn't already too late. The doubts and fears bubble back up inside of him, but he sweeps them aside.

The prick of the needle doesn't hurt as much as he was bracing for. He holds it against his skin for a few moments, then pulls it away. As he tries to stand he feels like his heart is thumping harder than it should, but it may just be nerves.

He lifts the neck-broken woman, carries her into the multi-purpose room and sets her back down, propping her against the wall with her legs extended so that they prevent the door from being opened fully. Then he squeezes out through the gap.

It may not be a perfect solution, but he guesses that if a passenger tries the door and it doesn't open easily they'll assume that it's out of order or in use. He also sets the placard to read Occupied.

Then Nanao replaces all the fallen refreshments on the cart. He doesn't want there to be any signs of a struggle. After tidying up the scene he pushes the cart into one corner of the gangway.

He takes the clip out of the gun and tosses it in the trash. Knowing his luck, it seems quite likely that he would lose the gun and end up in even more trouble. It almost just happened with the woman. He decides that it's safer for him not to carry a loaded weapon.

Now emptied, the gun returns to its place in his belt. Even without bullets, it could work to threaten someone.

He leans back against the wall beside the trash bin and sinks down, bringing his knees up in front of him.

He takes a deep breath in, then out. Then looks at his hand, where the needle had gone in.

A middle-aged man enters the gangway from car number ten. Just a passenger. He glances at the snack trolley off to the side, but doesn't seem perturbed that it's there unattended, and he disappears into the toilet. *That was close,* thinks Nanao. *A minute earlier and he would have seen every-thing.* He keeps asking himself if he was lucky or unlucky, keeps checking to see if he's still there. *Still alive. Still alive. Aren't I?*

The shaking of the Shinkansen radiates upward through his body.

KIMURA

'COME ON, LET'S GO. I'm sure there'll be good stuff happening.' The Prince pushes Kimura from behind. The bands on his hands and feet are off, but Kimura still doesn't feel free. Of course hatred for the Prince suffuses his entire being, but he knows he can't let it burst forth. The part of him that's trembling with rage, muttering *I'll fucking kill you,* feels hazy and indistinct, like it's being viewed through smoked glass, like it's someone else who only looks like him, like the animosity belongs to a stranger and Kimura is just imagining what it feels like.

They head up the aisle of car seven. He knows that the person behind him is just a schoolkid but he keeps getting the unsettling feeling that he's being followed by a monster that could devour him at any moment. *Am I afraid of this kid?* That question too feels like it's obscured by mist. *Does this kid really have the power to threaten people, to make others fear him?* Kimura shakes his head, pushing the thought aside.

When they enter the gangway they find a tall man standing there, leaned up against the wall next to the door, arms crossed and looking bored. His eyes are hard and mean, and his hair is sticking up in a halo, like how a little kid might draw the rays of the sun.

Kimura recognises him as one of the two men who had just walked through car seven. 'If it isn't Percy,' the man says lethargically. Kimura has never heard of Percy but he guesses it's some character from a show.

The Prince asks, 'What are you doing standing around here?'

'Me? I'm waiting for the toilet,' he says, pointing to the closed door. It's too far to see the placard but it must be occupied. 'I'm waiting till the person in there comes out here.'

'Is that your friend in there?'

'Tangerine is heading to the front.'

'Tangerine?'

'Yup,' the man says proudly. 'I'm Lemon, and he's Tangerine. Sour and sweet. Which one do you like better?'

The Prince doesn't seem to get the point of the question, and just shrugs silently.

'So, what, you and your dad always go to the toilet together?'

Oh, right, Kimura realises, *it must look like this horrible kid is my son.* And then he finds himself imagining it.

The Shinkansen rattles and sways. It feels like the train is being buffeted by furious winds. The sensation reminds Kimura of when he gave up drinking cold turkey, when it took every ounce of will to fight off the urge. During those days he would shake even more than the Shinkansen is right now.

'He's not my father,' says the Prince. 'I'll be right back, Uncle Kimura, okay?' As the Prince heads for the urinal cubicle, he flashes a smile of dazzling innocence that makes Kimura's chest feel warm just looking at it. He knows the reaction is just instinctive, not coming from any place of reason, but it makes him want to forgive the Prince for everything. 'Wait here for me.'

Kimura knows that what the Prince really means is wait here and don't say anything you shouldn't be saying. He suddenly feels awkward standing there as the wild-haired man eyes him irritably.

'Hey, buddy,' Lemon says with no overture, 'you're a drunk, right?' Kimura looks away.

'You are, aren't you? I've known a lot of drunks, so I can usually tell. My ma and pa were both drunks. Both parents with the same addiction, no one holding the other back, neither ever hitting the brakes, they just got worse and worse. Like in *Thomas and Friends* when Duck was being pushed by the freight train and couldn't stop and crashed into the barbershop. Like that. Help me-e-e, I can't sto-o-op, you know. Whole life goes down the tubes. There was nothing I could do so I just kept my distance, hid in the corner. My buddy Thomas helped me survive.'

Kimura doesn't get half of what Lemon's saying, but he answers, 'I don't drink any more.'

'Well, yeah. When a drunk has a drink, that's it. I mean, look at me. You can't fight against your genes, so I never ever drink. Just water. Funny, water and alcohol, both are wet and see-through but they're so totally different.' He lifts the bottle of mineral water in his hand with a flourish, unscrews the cap and takes a swig. 'Alcohol messes up your head but water does the opposite, it gets you thinking straight.

Kimura doesn't notice it at first, but the more he looks at the liquid in Lemon's bottle the more it seems to be alcohol, sweet and delicious, disappearing down Lemon's throat. Kimura recoils.

The train doesn't shake rhythmically or mechanically, it writhes like a living creature, every so often bucking upwards, seeming to float for a moment. The sensation of being in mid-air, then the sudden jolts, they threaten to dislodge Kimura from reality.

'I'm back,' says the returning Prince. 'Let's go and check out the green car,' he suggests to Kimura, neither shy nor brazen, just perfectly even. 'I bet we'll see some rich people!' He sounds exactly like an eager kid on holiday.

'Not necessarily,' answers Lemon. 'I mean, sure, the people in the green car are probably a little more comfortable than other people.'

The door to the toilet opens and a man in a suit steps out. He registers Kimura and the others but pays them no special mind, just washes his hands in the sink and returns to car seven.

'Huh. Guess it wasn't Nanao after all,' says Lemon.

'Nanao?' Kimura has no idea who that might be.

'We-e-ell, guess I'll be moving on,' Lemon sighs, and starts towards the front of the train.

The Prince gives Kimura a look that says they'll be going too. Then he calls out, 'I'll help you look for your suitcase.'

'Won't be necessary, Percy. I already know where it is.'

'Where?'

Lemon closes his mouth and stares at the Prince. His gaze is chilly, suddenly wary of the kid. He doesn't look like he would make any special allowances just because he's dealing with a schoolboy. Like a predator in the wild that doesn't care in the least how old its prey might be. 'Why should I tell you? You after the bag too?'

The Prince doesn't appear rattled. 'No, not at all. It's just fun, like a treasure hunt.' Lemon still looks dubious. He glares razor-sharp, like he's trying to stab through the Prince's exterior to scratch at the psychological level.

'Never mind,' the Prince sulks, 'my uncle and I will look for it ourselves.' He's just putting it on, Kimura knows, to seem childish, to show that he has no agenda.

'You stay out of it. Nothing good ever happens when Percy tries something out. Like when, you know, when he rubbed chocolate all over his face so he wouldn't have to get coal-stained. He's always up to something and it never turns out good.' Lemon turns to leave again.

'Well, I hope you'll be happy when we find it first!' The Prince is being as petulant as he can. 'Right, Uncle Kimura?'

Kimura responds without thinking, 'Yeah, I want a share of that cash.' He doesn't even mean it, he just said the first thing that came into his head when the Prince threw the ball to him. Though it's also true that somewhere in his mind is the memory of seeing of all those notes and cash cards.

'How d'you know what's in it?' Lemon swivels round, his eyes stony. Kimura can feel the air crackling.

Even now, the Prince looks calm. He shoots Kimura a thorny look, contempt for failure, but he doesn't seem otherwise concerned, and says to Lemon, 'Whoa, the bag is full of *money*?' His voice is guileless.

There's a pause in conversation, when all they hear are the vibrations of the barrelling Shinkansen.

Lemon glowers at Kimura, then at the Prince. 'I don't know what's inside it.'

'Then it's not what's inside, it's the bag itself that's worth so much! That's why everyone's looking for it.' Standing there listening, Kimura has to admire the Prince's guts and cleverness. They're being interrogated, but little by little the kid is trying to deflect the scrutiny off them. Not everyone could do that, lower an opponent's defences with a mask of innocence.

But Lemon's suspicion is harder to dispel than most people's. 'How do you know that everyone's looking for it?'

For a split second the Prince's face goes rigid. It's the first time Kimura's ever seen the kid look like that.

'That's what you said when I first met you,' the Prince says, once more a carefree schoolboy. 'You said everyone's looking for it.'

'Did not,' Lemon puffs, thrusting his chin out. 'I don't think I like you.' He scratches his head in annoyance.

Kimura is paralysed between choices. If only he could he'd say Hey, this kid is dangerous, get rid of him before he gets you. But he can't do that. If the Prince gets in touch with his accomplice then it could mean Wataru's life. He doesn't know for sure if that's even true, but somehow he feels it is.

'Uncle,' the Prince says, but Kimura is in a daze. 'Uncle Kimura!'

'Uh. What?'

'I think we said something bad. I think Mr Lemon is angry.'

'Sorry about that. We didn't mean to upset you.' Kimura bows his head.

'Uncle Kimura,' Lemon says abruptly, 'you don't look to me like a regular hard-working citizen.'

'Well, I am a drunk.' Kimura is starting to worry what Lemon will do next. He feels sweat seeping down his spine. Back when he was in the business he'd been in this sort of encounter any number of times.

Facing down someone who's sniffing out what kind of a man he is. He can sense a band of tension stretched between himself and Lemon, pulling tighter.

'Got a question for you, unc. You hate being woken up?'

What? The question sounds totally random.

'You get angry when you're sleeping and someone wakes you up?'

'The hell does that mean?'

'So you're okay with being woken up?'

'No one likes being woken up.'

Stars burst. Kimura's head snaps back.

The punch had slammed directly into his mouth. He never saw the arm move or the fist fly. Something small and hard is between his tongue and gums. He moves his tongue around: one of the front teeth is missing. A hand goes up to his mouth, wipes the blood. Then he fishes out the tooth and deposits it in his pocket.

'Hey, why did you do that? Uncle Kimura, are you okay?' The Prince sticks with his naive schoolboy routine. 'That wasn't nice. Why'd you punch him?'

'I figured if you were a proper professional you'd have been able to dodge. But I got you easy. Looks like I guessed wrong about you.'

'Of course you were wrong, my uncle's just an ordinary guy!'

'Huh.' Watching the blood drip from Kimura's mouth, Lemon seems suddenly deflated. 'My gut was telling me this old man was in the business, same line of work as me and Tangerine.'

'Your gut was wrong,' Kimura replies truthfully. 'I used to get into some rough work, but I retired years ago. Now I work as a security guard. To be honest, I'm pretty rusty.'

'Nah, it's just like riding a bike. Even if you take a couple years off your body knows what to do.'

Bullshit, Kimura wants to retort, but he holds it in. 'Did you say you were going on towards the front of the train?' More blood spills from Kimura's mouth.

'Uncle, are you all right?' The Prince shrugs his backpack off and pulls out a handkerchief from the front pocket, offering it to Kimura.

'Ready with a handkerchief,' Lemon says with a little smirk. 'You're a high-class little dude.'

The Prince slides his backpack on again. That's when Kimura remembers that inside the backpack is the gun he brought with him. He could just reach out and unzip the bag, just like that, and pull it out. That's what he tells himself.

Then two questions flash through his head.

The first is what he would do once he had the gun. Threaten? Or shoot? And who should he aim for, Lemon or the Prince? Of course what he wants to do most is point the gun at the heartless teenager and pull the trigger, and that's absolutely what he would do if he could. But nothing has changed with Wataru's situation. His life still hangs in the balance. *Don't worry about that. Just do it.* The train seems to be striking at him with each little jolt, chipping away at his self-restraint. *You've always done things nice and simple. If you want to do something, you do it. Life gets shorter every day. Why hold yourself back? Make this fucking kid suffer. He deserves it. He's just bluffing anyhow. There's nobody waiting by the hospital, Wataru isn't in any danger.* He's been keeping a tight lid on the part of himself that wants to take the easy way out, but now he feels the seal starting to loosen.

And then his second question: *Am I just playing into his hands?*

The backpack is right there in front of him. He is hyper-aware of the gun inside.

Could the Prince have planned that? Is he hoping I'll grab the gun and take on Lemon? Is he just controlling me?

The more he thinks about it the more Kimura sinks into the mire. Doubt piles on doubt. He grasps at a nearby stick to pull himself out of the swamp, but he isn't even sure he can trust the stick to support his weight. And then there's that other Kimura, loosening the lid bit by bit, who wants to act and doesn't care about the consequences. He feels like he's on the verge of being torn to pieces.

'And now we will be inspecting your baggage.'

It's a play-acting voice, and before Kimura realises what's happening Lemon snatches the Prince's backpack away. The Prince gawks. He hadn't seen it coming either. The hand just floated out, traced a gentle line in space and then had the bag.

Kimura feels himself go pale. Even the Prince looks shaken.

'Okay, Percy and his uncle. I don't know what's in this bag, but from how Uncle Kimura was looking at it I bet there's something in here that could give you an advantage in your current situation.' Lemon lifts up the backpack, undoes the zip and looks in. 'Ooh,' he squeals. 'I found something good.'

The gun appears, and all Kimura can do is stare.

'If I had to say how I'm feeling in six words, it'd be Daddy, Santa Claus is real! Or wait, is that five words?' Kimura can't tell if Lemon is talking to himself. The man looks appreciatively at the gun in his hand, with silencer attached. 'If you fire a gun inside a train it'd be so loud everyone would notice. That was exactly our problem. But look, you *can* get a silencer on board! Didn't even have to ask Santa!'

The Prince's eyes are glued to the gun. The situation is deteriorating too quickly for Kimura to even react.

'Now listen up. I got one question for you.' Lemon flicks off the safety and aims at Kimura.

'Me?' Kimura blurts it out, but can't quite say the rest: *Don't shoot me, this kid is the bad one.*

The Shinkansen thrums, amplifying Kimura's anxiety.

'The two of you have a gun. And a silencer, which means you're no amateurs. I never heard of an adult–kid team before, but it's not crazy. There's all kinds of weird team-ups in our biz. What I want to know is, why are you two here? I wanna know, was it your idea, or did someone send you here? What are you after? What's your connection to me and my partner?'

The truth is that there's no direct connection between Kimura and Lemon or Tangerine. Kimura had brought the gun to kill the Prince, and getting involved with the suitcase was all the Prince's initiative. But he doesn't think it's likely that Lemon would believe him.

The Prince regards Kimura. 'Uncle, what's happening? I'm scared.' He makes a face like he's on the verge of tears.

A sense of duty wells up in Kimura, to protect this vulnerable child, but right away he tells himself *Don't let him fool you. This looks like a frightened kid but he's just a psychopath playing a part. A cunning creature pretending to be a schoolboy.*

'I wonder if you guys are working for Minegishi too,' Lemon asks. 'Are you?'

'Minegishi?' Kimura glances nervously at the Prince. *Why's he talking about Minegishi?*

'Here's how it is. I'm gonna shoot one of you. You, or you. If you're wondering why I don't just shoot the both of you, it's cos Tangerine would get angry. He usually gets angry when I kill someone we could have got information from. He's so fussy about that kind of stuff. Typical type A. But then I can't just let both of you live, right? Too dangerous. Gotta shoot one of you. So, I have another question for you.'

Then Lemon lowers the gun. He bends one leg and slouches. 'Which one of the two of you is the leader? I'm not fooled by looks or size, either. I wouldn't say for sure that the kid isn't the leader. So, on three, the leader raises his hand, and the other one points to the leader. If your answers don't match up right, like if you both raise your hand or you both point at the other one, I'll know you're lying, so I'll just shoot you both.'

Kimura feels desperate. 'I thought you'd get in trouble if you killed both of us.'

'What, unc, are you type A too? Fussy. Well, whatever, I don't like it when Tangerine's mad at me but it's not like he's gonna kill me. I'm more interested in having some fun.'

'Is this fun for you?' Kimura's face rumples. Earlier the Prince had said Let's play a game, and now Lemon is having fun playtime. *What's wrong with these people?* He feels like he's the most upstanding one there, able to quietly get his enjoyment from alcohol.

'Okay, here goes. Answer truthfully, now,' Lemon says with puckered lips.

Just then a young mother and her toddler son enter the gangway. Lemon falls silent.

Kimura and the Prince keep quiet too. 'Mama, let's go-o-o,' shrieks the little boy happily, running past Kimura. It makes him think of Wataru. The mother peers at the three of them facing off there in the gangway and can sense that something is wrong, but she just keeps moving towards car seven.

The little boy's voice flips a switch in Kimura. *I've got to live. I've got to get out of this for Wataru. No matter what happens, I can't die.* He repeats it over and over again, like he's trying to hypnotise himself.

The boy and his mother pass through the carriage door, which hovers open for a moment, then slowly slides shut.

Lemon watches it close. 'Who's the leader?' He smiles wide. 'One, two-o-o – three!'

Kimura doesn't think twice. He lifts his hand. A glance to the side reveals the Prince, pointing over at Kimura. He looks back to the front. There's Lemon, and the barrel of the gun.

In the curtained-off sink area next to them, there's the sound of a hand dryer blowing.

Someone must have been in there the whole time. The quiet roar of hot air draws Kimura's eye to the curtain.

The gunshot never goes off. Just a light *ka-cha*, like a key turning in a lock while the dryer's still blowing. *Ka-cha, ka-cha*, the key turns again. It takes some time before Kimura realises it was the sound of the silenced gun. So quiet he didn't even know he'd been shot. Then he notices his chest is warm. No pain, just the sensation of fluid leaking from his body. His vision blurs.

'No hard feelings, unc.' Lemon is still grinning. 'And I guess that's that.'

By the time the words reach him Kimura can no longer see. He feels something hard up against the back of his head. *Am I on the ground?*

Pain spreads through his skull. Then all he can feel is the rumbling of the Shinkansen.

Before his eyes yawns an abyss, then all is black. No sense of space, no up or down.

His mind winks out.

After a bit he has the sense of floating. Or being pulled?

He doesn't know what's happening or how long it's been since he was shot. This isn't at all like falling into a deep sleep. It's much more lonesome.

Being shut up in a close, dark space.

Uncle, uncle, someone is saying, somewhere.

Kimura can feel his consciousness dissolving into mist, to be scattered forever, but his mind is still casting about. He wants a drink. His physical senses are fading. Fear and uncertainty grip the root of his heart. Squeezing harder, excruciating. *But there's one last thing. One thing to make sure.* His love as a father gushes up like magma.

Is Wataru all right? Sure, he must be.

In exchange for my death, my son's life goes on. I can be happy with that. Far away, the Prince's voice is like the wind howling outside your house. Uncle Kimura, you're dying. Are you sad? Scared?

What about Wataru? Kimura wants to ask, but he can't breathe.

'Your son's going to die too. I'll make the call soon. That means you died in vain, uncle. Disappointed?'

Kimura doesn't know what's happening. All he knows is he heard that his son is going to die.

Let him live, he tries to say, but his mouth won't move. His blood is barely flowing. 'What's that, uncle? Is there something you'd like to say?' The Prince sounds casual, and far away.

'You can do it. Just say, Please let my son live, and I will.'

There's no more anger at the Prince. If he's willing to spare Wataru, then Kimura is willing to beg. He makes up his mind even as it's shutting down.

He tries to work his lips. Blood oozes out, and he feels like vomiting. His breath is a rattle. 'Wataru,' he mouths. But he's wrung dry, and his voice won't sound.

'Sorry, what was that? I can't hear you. Hey. Uncle.'

Kimura no longer knows who it is that's speaking to him. *I'm sorry, I'll talk as soon as I'm able, really I will, please just help my son.*

'What a disgrace you are, Uncle Kimura. Little Wataru's going to die. And it's all your fault.' The voice sounds delighted. Kimura feels himself sinking back into the abyss. His soul his screaming out something, but no one hears.

THE PRINCE

'ALL SET,' LEMON SAYS. The Prince watches him straighten back up.

'So now it's locked?'

After they stuffed the barely breathing Kimura inside the bathroom, Lemon used a thin copper wire to lock the door from the outside. He gave the wire a sharp tug just as the door closed. It didn't work the first time, but the lock clicked into place with the second try. The technique strikes the Prince as being somehow primitive. The wire now pokes out of the door frame.

'What about this little dangling part?'

'Don't worry about it. No one'll notice or care, and this way I can reopen it if I pull the wire up. Here, gimme back.' He holds out his hand. The Prince passes him the bottle of mineral water. Lemon gulps down a mouthful. Then he fixes the Prince with a stare. 'I was wondering, though, you were talking all quiet in there, what was that?' When they dragged Kimura into the toilet, the Prince had asked to say one last thing to the dying man and had leaned over to speak.

'Nothing important. He has a son, I was just saying something about his son. And it looked like he wanted to say something to me, so I waited to hear what it was.'

'And?'

'He couldn't really talk.' The Prince thinks back to the scene, moments ago, when he told Kimura that Little Wataru was going to die. Seeing Kimura pale and fading, and then watching the man's face grow even more desperate at the mention of his son – that one instant – it flooded the Prince with indescribable satisfaction.

The Prince feels proud of himself. *I made someone who was already on the verge of death feel even more hopeless,* he thinks. *Not everyone can do that.* The sight of Kimura trying to form the words to beg for his son's life was hilarious, how he was straining so hard and still couldn't say anything.

It reminded him of something he read in the book about Rwanda. The majority of the Tutsi who died were killed with machetes. Many were butchered horribly. Fearing this fate, there was one person who offered everything he had to his assailants so that they would shoot him to death instead. Not please don't kill me, but please kill me less painfully. It struck the Prince as so completely pathetic. The thought of someone being brought so low also excited him.

Death cuts someone's life short, but it's not the worst thing you can do to them. You can also plunge them into despair right before they die. Once the Prince realised this he knew he had to try it out himself. He approached it with the same attitude of a musician attempting to play a difficult piece.

From that standpoint, what happened with Kimura couldn't have gone any better. He keeps wanting to laugh when he thinks how even at the moment of Kimura's own death the man couldn't stop worrying about his child, about another human being. Which gives him another idea: maybe he can use Kimura's death to torment other people. Like Kimura's son, or his parents.

'Alrighty, let's go. Follow me.' Lemon jerks his head towards the front of the train.

Lemon must know how to aim for a clean shot, because barely any blood spurted onto the floor. When they dragged Kimura to the toilet it left a faint trail, like a red slug had crawled that way, but Lemon mopped it right up with a moist towelette.

'Why do I have to go with you?' The Prince tries to project fear, but he makes sure not to overdo it. 'I was just doing what that old guy told me to. He's not really my uncle. I don't know anything. I don't even know what to do with his gun.'

Lemon had returned the gun to the Prince's backpack. 'Yeah, well, I still don't believe you. I think you might be a professional.'

'A professional?'

'Someone who takes money to do a job. Dangerous jobs, you know, like what me and Tangerine do.'

'Me? I'm just a school student.'

'There's all kinds of school students. I don't mean to brag or anything, but I killed some people when I was in school.'

The Prince brings his hands to his mouth to make a surprised face. But on the inside he's disappointed. He has been killing people since he was eleven. He had hoped that Lemon would surprise him, but now that hope is wilting. One more test. 'Why is it wrong to kill people?'

Lemon had started walking but now stops. Another man passes through the gangway, so Lemon steps out of the way, beside the door. 'C'mere, Percy.' The area where they're standing is fairly spacious. 'Why is it wrong to kill people? Percy would never ask anything like that.' His eyes are narrowed. 'That's why kids love Percy.'

'I've always wondered. I mean, we kill people in war, and there's the death penalty. So why do we say it's wrong to kill people?'

'I just killed someone, so it's pretty funny for you to ask me that,' says Lemon, but he doesn't look like he's amused. 'Okay, here it is: people who don't want to be killed made up the rule that it's wrong to kill people. They can't do anything to protect themselves but they wanna feel safe. If you ask me, if you don't wanna get killed, then you should act in a way that keeps you from getting killed. Don't piss anybody off, or get strong, or whatever. There are lots of things you can do. You should take this to heart, it's good advice.'

The Prince doesn't find this answer very deep at all, and he almost laughs with derision. This man may act odd, but he's just doing criminal work because there's no other way he can survive. There are lots of people like him, no philosophy at all. The Prince is actually angry that Lemon didn't live up to his expectations. If someone turns to violence after a thoughtful consideration of who they are as a person, that would be fascinating, but someone who just lashes out is empty, nothing more than a paper cut-out.

'What're you smiling about?' Lemon's voice comes like a slash, but the Prince just shakes his head quickly.

'I'm so relieved,' he explains. For the Prince, making a weave of explanations and logic is a basic technique for controlling people. Giving a reason, withholding a reason, explaining the rules or hiding them – these tools make it surprisingly easy to influence people, or to fool them. 'That old man scared me so much.'

'You didn't seem upset when I shot him to death.'

'After what he did to me . . .'

'Was he really that bad?'

The Prince tries to look frightened. 'He was awful.'

Lemon stares hard at him. His sharp gaze goes below the surface, one layer at a time, like peeling a citrus fruit. The Prince worries that his true self might show in his face, so he pushes it deep down into his chest.

'Sounds pretty fishy to me.'

The Prince's mind starts racing, trying to hit on what to do. Meanwhile he shakes his head piteously.

'You know, this reminds me of an episode.' Lemon's eyes light up and his cheeks relax into a smile.

'What episode?'

'The time when the Diesel came to Sodor Island. The Diesel didn't like Duck, the green steam locomotive. He thought he would get rid of him, so he started spreading rumours about Duck.'

'I don't know that episode.' The Prince keeps a wary eye on the now more animated Lemon, all the while scrabbling for a plan.

'The mean old Diesel went around saying that Duck was spreading nasty rumours about all the other trains! The locomotives on Sodor Island are kind of gullible, you know, so they all got angry at Duck, he said bad stuff about me, like that. Basically, he was set up.'

Lemon is talking excitedly, like he's speaking before a crowd. Even the Prince is drawn in. At the same time, the Prince doesn't fail to notice how as Lemon talks he has the gun in one hand and the silencer in the other, having removed it earlier, now twisting it onto the gun like a sushi chef making a roll. The whole series of movements feels like the preparation for a ceremony, measured and practised. *When did he . . .?* The Prince realises he doesn't even know when Lemon took the gun back out of the backpack.

'Duck was shocked. Before he knew it, everyone was mad at him. When he finally found out that he was framed for being a gossip, you know what he said?' Lemon looks questioningly at the Prince, like a teacher giving a lesson. He gives the silencer one final twist into place and points the gun at the ground. He pulls back the slide to check the chamber.

The Prince can't move. Listening to this man tell a children's story while preparing to murder someone doesn't feel real.

'I'll tell you what Duck said. He said, I could never come up with that stuff! Which is true. Those nasty rumours were too clever for Duck to have come up with them.'

Lemon's right arm dangles, gun in hand. Ready to go, the gun seems to be saying, I can fire whenever.

'And then,' says the Prince, looking away from the gun and straight at Lemon, 'and then what happened?'

'Then Duck said something good. Something you should remember.'

'What did he say?'

'Steam locomotives would never do something so cowardly!'

The barrel of the gun appears in front of the Prince. Lemon's arm is extended, and the gun is pointed straight at the Prince's forehead. The attached silencer seems to float in the air.

'Why?' asks the Prince. He's searching frantically for what to do. *This is bad,* he finally admits.

He considers leaning on the innocent kid routine. Controlling people's emotions depends a good deal on appearances. If babies weren't as cute as they are, if they didn't push that emotional button, no one would go to all the trouble of taking care of them. Koalas are violent creatures, but even if you know that to be true it's hard to feel threatened by an adorable koala bear with a cub on its back. In the same way, if something is grotesque-looking, it doesn't matter how much you care about it, there will always be an instinctive revulsion. It's nothing more than an animal response, and that makes it even easier to take advantage of.

People make decisions based on instinct, not intellect. Physical response is a lever for emotional control.

'Why are you going to shoot me? Before, you said you wanted to leave one of us alive.' This seems like a good first move. Lemon might have forgotten what he said earlier, and it makes sense to try to remind him.

'Yeah, but then I realised.'

'Realised what?'

'That you're the mean old Diesel.'

'What do you mean, I'm the Diesel?'

'Well, it's like –' he begins reciting – 'The Diesel is an engine who came to help at Sir Topham Hatt's railways. He is nasty and vain. He makes fun of the steam locomotives and only ever does things to benefit himself. But in the end his wicked plans are discovered and he is punished . . . That's the Diesel. Same as you. Am I right?' Lemon isn't smiling now. 'You said that your uncle was an awful man, but I think he was more like Duck. He could never come up with all that stuff. Right? He didn't seem like the smartest guy. He was a no-good drunk, sure, but I don't think he was cruel.'

'I don't understand.' The Prince tries to collect himself. He stops focusing on the barrel of the gun. *If I have attention to spare on the gun then I should be figuring out a way out of this instead. You panic, you lose.* He lays out his options: bargains, pleas, threats, temptation. *First I need to buy some time. What will get his attention?* He tries to think about what this man wants the most. 'Um, about the suitcase.'

'Then again,' Lemon says, ignoring the Prince, 'I don't think that guy was a good guy like Duck. But the fact that he was set up, that makes them similar.'

The gun is pointed like it's one of Lemon's fingers, extra long. The barrel stares, unblinking.

'Wait, wait. I don't understand what you mean. And I, uh, about the suitcase.'

'You're not Percy, you're the mean old Diesel. It just took me some time to see it.'

I've been shot. The Prince can't see anything. Then he realises that he's closed his eyes. He snaps them back open.

If I'm going to die here, I want to watch it happen. Shutting your eyes against fear and danger is for the weak.

He's not feeling fear, which is good. All he feels is a mild sense of disappointment that it's happening so abruptly. As if the end of his life is a television being switched off, and someone's telling him that there weren't really any good shows on anyway. The news doesn't bother him that much, though. He's more proud that he's facing his end unperturbed.

'Yeah, you're the Diesel,' he hears Lemon say.

Then he looks hard at the barrel. *The bullet that's going to end my life will come out of that hole.* He doesn't intend to look away.

A few moments pass, and the Prince starts to wonder why he hasn't been shot. Behind the gun, he notices the right arm begin to sag.

He looks up at Lemon, who is blinking and frowning, touching his face and around his eyes with his free hand. It's clear enough something's wrong with him. He shakes his head back and forth, then yawns twice, his mouth opening wide.

Is he falling asleep? That can't be. The Prince takes first one step to the side, then another, away from the barrel.

'What's wrong?' he tries asking.

Medicine. It comes to him in a flash. Once when he was going after a classmate, trying to bring her down, he used strong sleeping meds. This looks exactly the same.

'Fuck.' Lemon waggles the gun. Some flash of danger, urging him to take out the Prince before he goes under. 'I'm pretty *sleepy.*'

The Prince grab's Lemon's arm with both hands, seizing his chance while the other is sluggish, then single-mindedly wrenches the gun away. Lemon snarls and swings his other arm around. The Prince dodges, then backs up against the far wall of the gangway.

Lemon's knees buckle and he lurches into the door. He's wrestling with the sandman, and he's losing. His arms shoot out to the walls and grope feebly, then he's on the floor, like a marionette with the strings cut.

The Prince puts the gun in his backpack, not bothering to take off the silencer.

There's a plastic bottle at Lemon's feet. He steps over cautiously and picks it up. Just an ordinary-looking bottle of mineral water – *maybe the medicine was in here.* He peers in. *Who would have put it here?* Just as the question rises to the surface, another thought paints over it entirely.

I'm so lucky. I'm so lucky.

He can hardly believe it. When it seemed like there was nothing he could do, when he was a hair away from death, to have such a stupendous turnaround.

He circles behind Lemon and grabs him from under the armpits. He's heavy, but not so heavy he can't be moved. *Okay.* He sets Lemon back down and goes over to the toilet door. Careful not to cut himself, he grabs the end of the copper wire and yanks it upward. It unlocks.

He goes back to Lemon, stepping up behind so he can lift and drag him to the toilet.

Then comes the attack.

Lemon looks deep asleep, but both arms fly up and grab the Prince by the lapel of his blazer, then wrench him down. The Prince tumbles forward and slams to the ground. Everything is upside down, he's lost his handle on the situation. He springs back up, his hair on edge at the thought of Lemon's next attack, the one that will finish him.

'*Hey.*' Lemon is still seated. His eyes are pointed in different directions and his hands are pawing at the air in front of him, like a drunk. He slurs, 'You tell Tange*rine.*'

The medicine must be strong if Lemon can't stay awake no matter how hard he tries.

Watching him fight is highly comical to the Prince, like watching a fool struggle to keep one foot on the shore while the boat's already sailing on the tide. This probably wasn't regular sleeping medicine, it must be something nastier. Gun in hand, the Prince steps closer to Lemon. He leans his face in.

Lemon grits his teeth to stay awake. 'Tell Tangerine, the thing he's looking for, the *key*, it's a coin locker in Morioka, you *tell* him.' Then his head falls forward and doesn't come back up.

He looks dead, but the Prince can tell he's still breathing.

When he goes behind to lift the body again, he notices a little picture under Lemon's hand.

It's a sticker, stuck on the floor.

A little green train engine with a face. Some character from a kids' show. *He sure loves that stupid show,* thinks the Prince, but then it occurs to him that it might be some kind of signal for his partner. He peels it off and crumples it up, then tosses it in the trash.

He proceeds to haul Lemon into the bathroom. There's Kimura, on the ground. A red-black stain emanates from his body, the blood mixing with the piss flecks on the floor. The Prince feels a wave of disgust and hisses, 'Gross, Mr Kimura.'

Before anyone can walk by and see what's going on he shuts the door and locks it, then hoists up Lemon's unconscious body and sits him down on the toilet. Next he pulls the gun out of his backpack, and without hesitating presses the barrel up to Lemon's forehead. But he doesn't want to risk chunks splattering on him, so he backs up to the door.

He sets his stance, takes aim, and pulls the trigger, *ga-chin*. The sound leaves a hum in the air. Between the silencer and the rattling of the Shinkansen nobody heard the gunshot.

Lemon's head lolls and hangs. Blood burbles from the hole.

Being shot in your sleep – it seems to be missing something. *I bet he didn't even feel any pain.*

The blood is oozing out feebly, barely flowing now. The Prince smiles wickedly. A toy running out of batteries dies a more dignified death.

I do not want to go like this.

After thinking about it for a moment, he decides to leave the gun in the bathroom. First he was going to keep it on him, but the risk seemed too high. His stun gun he can say is for self-defence, but that won't work for a real gun. And considering that Kimura and Lemon were both shot dead it makes sense for there to be a gun in the bathroom.

He goes back out to the gangway and uses the wire to lock the door.

A few steps towards car eight and he stops again, an idea popping into his head. He pulls a phone out of the front pocket of his bag. It's Kimura's. Finding the last number in the history, he hits call.

It rings for a while. 'Yes?' It's a gruff male voice.

'Is this Mr Kimura's father?' The rumbling of the train makes it difficult to hear, but the Prince doesn't care.

'Sorry?' The man pauses for a moment, then, 'Oh, the, uh, schoolkid I talked to before.' His voice softens.

The Prince can picture the tranquil scene, tea in front of the TV, and he wants to burst out laughing. *Your son was killed while you were enjoying some tea!* 'I wanted to tell you that everything Mr Kimura said before was true.'

Kimura's father doesn't respond. Whenever the Prince is revealing something a thrill runs through him.

'Mr Kimura got himself into a dangerous situation. His son is in danger too.'

'I'm sorry, what? Wataru's in the hospital.'

'I'm not sure that he is.'

'Where's Yuichi? Let me talk to him.'

'He can't come to the phone any more.'

'What do you mean, any more? Is he on the Shinkansen?'

'You know, you and your wife must be relaxing, I probably shouldn't have called.' His voice is flat and colourless, like he's just reporting the facts. 'And I think it's best if you don't talk to the police.'

'What are you talking about?'

'Sorry, that's all I have to say. I'm hanging up now.' The Prince pushes the end button.

That'll work, he thinks. Kimura's parents are probably panicking right now. They have no idea what's happening with their son and grandson and they'll be tormented by worry. All they'll be able to do is call the hospital. But when they call, if nothing's happened yet, then the people at the hospital will say, All's well, no problems here. Beyond that, Kimura's parents can do nothing. He doesn't imagine they'll go to the police. And even if they do, it'll probably just be written off as a prank call.

Then when everything comes to light, then they'll feel despair. An old couple, living out their final years in peace and quiet, only to have their little remaining time filled up with rage and regret. The Prince can't wait. He pictures himself crushing people so he can harvest the juice that comes pouring out. To him nothing else in the world tastes as sweet.

He heads into car eight. *You weren't such a big deal after all, Mr Lemon. No one is.*

Children, adults, animals, all weak, all worthless, all junk.

MORNING GLORY

⟨ 1 ║ 2 ║ 3 ║ 4 ║ 5 ║ 6 ║ 7 ║ 8 ║ 9 ║ 10 ⟩

THE TAXI RIDE ISN'T EVEN long enough for the meter to go up.

He pays the fare and disembarks, then watches the cab disappear. Across the prefectural road, two lanes in each direction, stands a building. It's tall and new-looking.

Is the go-between already here? He's an administrator, working by phone from a desk, and the thought of him nervously venturing out into the field makes Morning Glory smile. It's much more pleasing than someone who finds excuses to hide themselves away.

He makes the call. The go-between doesn't answer. Even though he's the one who said to be here. There's no anger, just a feeling of having wasted time. He considers going home. By the time he realises it, he's crossing the street, towards the building.

Waiting at the traffic island for the pedestrian signal to turn green. He regards the road. To him it looks like a river. His field of vision narrows and colour falls away. The river runs by in front of him, irregular waves peaking and dipping. The guardrail next to the pavement is a bulwark, keeping the murmuring current from spilling over the riverbanks.

Now and again a storm whips by and turns the water to froth, but apart from that the surface of the water barely seems to tremble.

His vision returns to normal. The river vanishes and the road appears. The scene takes on colour and becomes solid.

In the shrubs on the traffic island is a little flag urging pedestrian caution and a small aluminium trash receptacle. He looks down. At the base of the shrubs are some dandelions. Their little yellow flowers have a wholesome vitality, like a child who sleeps when it wants to sleep and plays when it wants to play. The more subdued green stalks hold up the bright flowers, swaying gently.

There are drooping green frills around the yellow flowers. Common dandelions.

The non-indigenous common dandelion pushed out the native Kanto dandelion. He remembers hearing that.

But it's not true.

The Kanto dandelion is disappearing because humans are encroaching on its habitat.

Then the common dandelion just fills in the space where the other dandelions used to be.

Morning Glory thinks the whole thing is fascinating.

People act like the common dandelion is the culprit in the drop-off of the Kanto dandelion, and that humans are merely the witnesses, but the truth is it's the humans who are to blame. Common dandelions just happen to be tough enough to live with humans. Even if the common dandelion hadn't appeared, the Kanto dandelion would still be dying off.

Next to one of the yellow flowers is a speck of red.

No bigger than a fingernail, a perfect red droplet. A ladybird. On the back of the red droplet are neat black spots, like they were painted on by the finest of brushes. Morning Glory looks closer.

Who came up with the design for this insect?

It doesn't seem like an environmental adaptation. Is there any evolutionary use for a red body with black spots? It isn't grotesque or bizarre like some other insects, but it is an appearance that doesn't seem like it should occur in nature.

Morning Glory stares as the ladybird climbs busily up the leaf. He extends his finger and the insect circles behind the stem.

When he looks up the signal is green. He's about to step out onto the crossing.

A call comes in. The go-between.

FRUIT

TANGERINE IS STARTING TO WONDER what's taking Lemon so long, but he forgets about it the moment he steps from the green car into the gangway and sees a man with glasses sitting on the floor.

The train enters a tunnel and the roar of the tracks changes its sound pattern. The surroundings go dark. A sudden pressure bears down on the train, as if it's diving underwater.

Nanao sits up against the wall facing the rear of the train, his knees bent. He looks unconscious at first. His eyes are open but staring blankly.

Tangerine reaches into his jacket for his gun but there's Nanao, aiming a gun back at him before he can draw.

'Don't move,' Nanao says. He's still seated, but the gun is steady. 'I'll shoot.'

The Shinkansen bursts out of the tunnel. Through the window paddies of rice ripe for the harvest stretch into the distance. Almost immediately the train plunges into the next tunnel.

Tangerine puts his hands up slightly.

'Don't try anything funny. I'm not in the mood. I will shoot.' Nanao keeps the gun trained on Tangerine. 'To bring you up to speed – I found Minegishi's son's killer. The Hornet.'

In his peripheral vision Tangerine notices the snack trolley. The attendant is nowhere to be seen.

'Yeah? Easy win? Where is she?'

'In the multi-purpose room. It was a tough win,' Nanao says. 'Now you don't need me for a fall guy. Right? There's no point in attacking me now.'

'I wonder.' Tangerine takes a measuring look at Nanao. *I could find an opening. Could probably get the gun away from him.* He acts it out in his head.

'Like I said before, our best hope is to work together. Nothing good will come of us shooting it out. That will only serve someone else's purposes.'

'Like who?'

'I don't know. But there is someone.'

Tangerine remains still, facing Nanao. He's thinking. Then he nods. 'All right. Put the gun away. Let's have a cessation of hostilities.'

'I never opened hostilities in the first place.' Nanao slowly gets up on one knee and leans a hand on the wall. He places the other hand on his chest and takes several deep breaths. *The fight with that woman must have taken a lot out of him.* He's gingerly checking in with his body. There is a rip in the leg of his cargo pants. On the floor lies something that looks like a toy syringe. When Nanao notices Tangerine eyeing it he scoops it up and throws it in the trash.

Then he puts the gun in the back of his belt.

'Were you shooting up?'

'She was a pro, so I figured she'd have some kind of antidote. I came this close to dying. I was counting on her to bring out the antidote if she got stabbed. It was no sure thing though.'

'How come?'

'I didn't know if it was already too late for me.' Nanao opens and closes his hands a few times, just to be sure. Then he leans over and fiddles with the torn fabric of his trousers.

Tangerine's pocket buzzes with an incoming call. He pulls his phone out and checks the caller ID. A heavy feeling immediately presses down on him. 'It's our mutual client.'

'Minegishi?' Nanao's eyes open wide. Just as he was starting to come back to life, speaking that name makes him go white all over again.

'We're almost at Sendai. He's calling to check in one last time.'

'Check in on what?'

'To make sure I know that if I don't tell him the truth he'll start to lose his temper.'

'But what could you possibly tell him?'

'Maybe I'll give the phone to you and you'll tell him.'

Tangerine answers.

Minegishi doesn't bother to say who it is. 'I got a question for you.'

'Yes?'

'Is my son all right?'

It's so direct that Tangerine doesn't know how to respond.

'I got a call a little while ago,' Minegishi says. 'Saying that something didn't look right with my boy on the train. He said, Your son looked a little odd, you might want to check up on it. So I said, My son isn't on the Shinkansen by himself. I hired two men I trust to accompany him. Nothing to worry about. But then he says, You might want to be careful about trusting those two men. They may be with him, but your son wasn't moving, and I couldn't tell if he was breathing or not.'

Tangerine smiles uncomfortably. 'Your man in Omiya was wrong, sir. Your son was asleep. He might have just looked like he wasn't breathing.' He's terrified that Minegishi will ask him to put the kid on the phone.

Nanao stands watching, looking nervous.

'You know, it occurred to me, sir, as we were talking, that one of the two Chinese characters for the word son is the character for breath. Your son must be breathing.'

Minegishi isn't listening to Tangerine. He's used to giving orders and making demands. The advice and opinions of others may not even reach his ears. All he needs from other people are their reports.

'And so,' continues Minegishi, 'just to be sure, I'm having some people check up on you at Sendai Station.'

Guess Momo was right. Tangerine shrinks a little. 'That'll be fine, but the Shinkansen won't wait long.'

'So just get off. The two of you can get off the train at Sendai, with my son and my suitcase. Several of my men are waiting on the platform. I also hired some of your fellow professionals.'

'Everyone at the station will be mighty surprised, sir. So many fine young men lined up on the platform.'

The melody signalling the arrival at the next station begins to play. It's a light and whimsical little tune. Tangerine smiles uncertainly again.

'If everything was going as it should have, this wouldn't be necessary, but sometimes this sort of thing is unavoidable. So I'll ask again. Is my son all right? And do you have the suitcase?'

'Ye-e-es, of course,' Tangerine replies.

'Then it'll all be over quickly. All you have to do is show my son and the suitcase and you can get back on.'

'Your son who's still breathing, sir, understood.'

After the automated station announcement, the conductor's voice sounds over the PA, informing the passengers that they'd be at Sendai momentarily.

'You stopped talking,' Minegishi says at the other end of the line. 'What happened?'

'The station announcement was too loud. We're pulling into Sendai.'

'You're in car number three, is that right? That's where my men are waiting. When the train gets to Sendai you get off, is that clear?'

'Oh, your son, right now he's in the toilet.' Tangerine speaks quickly without thinking, then winces. *What a limp excuse. You're smarter than that.*

'Once again, your instructions are to get off from car three and show the suitcase and my son to my men. That's all.'

'Actually, we had a disagreement with one of the conductors,' Tangerine says hastily, 'and we've moved to car nine. We won't make it to car three in time.'

'Then go to car six. It's right between nine and three. You can make that in time, right? I'll have my men wait outside six. Get off from car six. With my son.'

'Just out of sheer curiosity, sir,' Tangerine says, trying to make his voice casual, 'what happens if your men think there's something off about us? I don't imagine they'll just start shooting right away . . .?'

'Is everything okay with my son and the suitcase? If it is, then you have nothing to worry about.'

'But your men might misunderstand. If we get into an argument and things get sour there on the train platform, it'll be a big headache.'

'For who?'

Tangerine doesn't know how best to answer. He knows he can't exactly make a case for the innocent bystanders. 'There are so many passengers on the train, they might panic if there's gunfire.'

'There aren't that many people on board,' Minegishi says flatly.

'Actually, sir, it's basically full.' Tangerine lies without hesitation. He doesn't think there's any way Minegishi could now how many people are on the train.

'It's not full. I locked down most of the seats.'

'You locked . . .?'

'Once I knew which train you would be on with my son I bought all the available seats.'

'All of them?' Tangerine's voice jumps at the unexpected news. Then his normal scepticism creeps back in. *It isn't impossible, but why would he need to do that?*

'I wanted to remove as many variables as I could. Reduce my risk. Who knows what could happen on the Shinkansen. The fewer passengers there are the easier it is for you two to keep my son safe. Am I wrong?'

Dead wrong. As dead as your son, who got it right away. Tangerine fights down the urge to tell Minegishi. And among the few people on the train, several are professionals. Minegishi's buyout strategy didn't seem to do his son any good at all.

314

'How much does something like that cost?'

'Not too much. Each car seats a hundred, so that's less than a thousand tickets.'

Tangerine scowls. It isn't surprising that Minegishi's financial standards are on a different scale than his – most people who hire him and Lemon live on a different scale – but the way he's using his money here seems silly. What actual good did it do? And did he ever consider that the conductors might think it strange that all the seats are purchased but so few people are actually on the train?

A little girl's peals of laughter can be heard on the phone. Minegishi's daughter, most likely. The dissonance between the domestic scene he's picturing and the fatal events aboard the Shinkansen doesn't sit right with Tangerine. How can Minegishi be spending leisure time with his daughter while he knows his son and heir is out there in danger? The only explanation is that his values are completely different from the average person, that his psychological wiring is twisted.

'Regardless, you told me that the train is full of people, which is a lie. That train's not full. If I were you I'd quit it with the lies and exaggerations. I'll always catch you. And when I do that'll just make it worse for you. But hey, I want you to relax. As long as you don't cause any trouble in Sendai, everything will be just fine.'

The line goes dead.

The Shinkansen is starting to drop speed, leaning into a gentle curve.

No time to think. Tangerine passes through car nine and into eight.

'What's going on?' asks Nanao uncertainly, following behind, but Tangerine doesn't answer. He just stalks on, occasionally laying a hand on a headrest for support, careful to keep his balance against the shuddering of the slowing train.

A handful of passengers are taking bags off the overhead rack, evidently planning to get off at Sendai. As Tangerine approaches the far door a kid comes through it and steps towards him. *Out of my way*, Tangerine tries to slip past, but the kid addresses him. 'You're Mr Tangerine, right? Mr Lemon was looking for you.'

Oh, right. He had forgotten all about Lemon. But there's no time now. 'Where is he?'

'He said he had to take care of something and went towards the back of the train.'

Tangerine takes a proper look at the kid. Shiny hair with no parting, large eyes like a cat's, elegant nose. *Another rich kid.*

No time. Tangerine steps through the door into the gangway. He can feel that the conductor has engaged the brakes.

'Hey, what are you doing? Where are you going? What's your plan?' Nanao won't shut up.

A group of passengers stands in the gangway, waiting to get off. They shoot dubious looks at Tangerine and the other two as they come rushing in.

Tangerine takes one look at the luggage rack and grabs the first black suitcase he sees, a sturdy oversized piece, much bigger than the one that he and Lemon had.

'What are you doing with that?' Nanao wants to know.

Stepping around the people waiting, Tangerine enters car seven. He blows past the passengers filing up the aisle to exit the train, who all look at him with annoyance.

He enters the next gangway. There's a line of people ready to get off. This is where he's supposed to be, between cars seven and six. He stands at a slight remove from the line. Nanao comes up beside him. The kid is close behind.

'Listen up.' He turns to Nanao. 'We need to get off for a minute at Sendai.'

'Is that what Minegishi said?'

'His men are waiting at the station. I need to go out to the platform with his son and his suitcase. His men will check that I have those two things.'

'This,' Nanao points, 'is a different suitcase.'

'That's right. And you're not Minegishi's son.'

'What?'

'The only thing we can do is try to lie our way out of this. Both the suitcase and his son are fakes. You just keep quiet, you hear me, just stand there.'

Nanao is already just standing there, unable to process what Tangerine's telling him.

'Me?'

The Shinkansen slowing down tips them all forward, then backwards. Tangerine can't keep his footing with his legs alone and he holds on to the wall for support.

'You pretend you're Minegishi's son, got it?'

The train keeps dropping speed, pulling into Sendai Station. 'But – Nanao starts looking around nervously. 'What should I –'

'Just come with me.'

The kid pipes up. 'Wouldn't it be better if you just ignored your instructions? If you don't get off, those men won't be able to tell what's going on with you, right? And as long as they don't know what the situation is I don't think they'd make any moves. You just play dumb and stay on the train until it leaves.'

Is that something a kid would say? Tangerine doesn't like it. The idea makes sense, but he doesn't want to change his plan at this point. 'If we don't get off, those men will get on. A whole lot of them. We don't want that to happen.'

The door opens. The line of passengers starts to file out of the train. Tangerine says to Nanao, 'Let's go.'

NANAO

THE DEPARTURE ANNOUNCEMENT ECHOES THROUGH Sendai Station and people with luggage start to board the Shinkansen. Nanao registers their movements out of the corner of his eye as he stands next to Tangerine on the platform. In front of them are three men in suits. *Two of us, three of them,* a voice cries inside of him. A couple of metres away is a tall man with a shaved head, and beyond him there are two muscular dudes who look like fighters. They're all standing there looking at him and Tangerine.

'This is like a football penalty kick. A line of guys forming a wall.' Tangerine is completely calm. Or at least he looks that way. His words are measured and his breath even.

'You must be Tangerine,' says the middle suit. His eyebrows are plucked bald and his eyes are beady. 'Heard a lot about you and your partner. We got an urgent call from Mr Minegishi, said we had to come check you out.'

Despite what the suit is saying, his tone is polite.

Nanao looks up slightly and notices a conductor standing further back on the platform. The man is clearly looking their way questioningly, which makes sense to Nanao – it's not a typical gathering of men. Certainly not lovers parting ways, and it doesn't have the feel of seeing off friends. But the conductor somehow seems to sense that it's safest for him to keep his distance.

Fooling Minegishi's men with the suitcase should be fairly simple. Tangerine just has to insist that it's the right one and they'll probably believe him. *The problem is me,* thinks Nanao, lowering his face, staring at the ground in front of his shoes. Pretend you're Minegishi's son, Tangerine said, but Nanao has no idea how to do that. How could he?

'Do you mind opening the bag?'

'It won't open,' replies Tangerine. 'We don't know how to open it. Do you guys know what's inside? I should ask you to open it for me.'

The suit with no eyebrows says nothing, but reaches out to the suitcase. He crouches down for a closer look, and his hand goes to the handle. There's a combination lock. He examines it like a collector looking at a rare vase, but as far as Nanao can tell the man hasn't figured out that it's a fake.

'What are these initials?' He looks up at Tangerine.

On the bottom of the suitcase are two English letter stickers that read MM. They're hot pink and glossy. It looks like something a teenage girl would use.

'Probably M for Minegishi.' Tangerine's voice is steady.

'Why are there two Ms? Mr Minegishi's first name is Yoshio.'

'Like I said, M for Minegishi.'

'I'm talking about the second M.'

'That one's for Minegishi too. Haha, hey, the name Yoshio means nice man. That's got to be a joke, right? Anyway, I didn't put the stickers on there. Don't ask me what they mean. The Shinkansen's leaving soon. Can we get back on?'

There are no more people getting off the train. No one else getting on either. The only other people left on the platform are waiting for the next train.

The suit gets back up, then stands directly in front of Nanao. 'Did he always wear glasses?' Nanao almost jumps out of his skin. He wants to tear his glasses off. He resists the urge.

'I made him wear them,' answers Tangerine. 'I don't know how much you heard, but Little Minegishi here,' at which the suit's eyebrow-less face stiffens slightly, 'I mean Mr Minegishi's son,' Tangerine corrects himself, 'he was being held by some dangerous characters. That means he's a target. There could very well be someone on the Shinkansen trying to hit him. I figured he needed a disguise.'

'And glasses?'

'Sure, and other little things too. He looks different from usual, right?' Tangerine seems totally unruffled.

'I suppose so,' the suit replies mildly. But then he pulls out his phone. 'He sent me a picture of his son.' There's a face on the screen. The suit moves to hold it up to Nanao's face.

'Hey, come on, the train's leaving.' Tangerine gives an exasperated sigh.

'Doesn't really look like the photo.'

'Of course he doesn't. We fixed him up so that no one would be able to tell. Hair, glasses. Okay, we'll be going now. You can tell Mr Minegishi everything's fine.' Tangerine lays one hand on Nanao's shoulder and motions towards the train. Nanao nods. *I can't wait for this roleplay to be done.* He tries his best to give off a self-important air to keep his relief from showing.

Then no-eyebrows says an unfamiliar name. Nanao almost ignores it, until it dawns on him that it might be Minegishi's son's name, so he looks up at the man. It seems his hunch is right. 'Guess your dad's the only one who can open this, huh?'

Nanao makes a goofy face and nods. 'I've got no idea.' But then he feels like he should do something besides just stand there. Uneasiness steals back in. Without really thinking about it, he reaches for the suitcase and starts to flip the numbers on the combination lock. 'I mean it would be great if all you had to do was play with the numbers . . .' The dials click as he spins them. Somehow he feels like the demonstration makes his ignorance more believable. It's a classic case of someone acting awk-wardly when they want to seem casual.

He doesn't think there's any chance that his fumbling with the lock could produce the correct combination. *No one would get it right, and me least of all, with my luck.* But he's forgotten about Murphy's Law: trying random combinations won't unlock the lock, except when you don't want the lock unlocked.

The suitcase bursts open.

He had been fiddling roughly with the lock and the momentum of its release causes the lid of the suitcase to spring loose, spilling out an ava-lanche of women's underwear.

No-eyebrows freezes, as do the other suits, and the man with the shaved head and the two muscle dudes. The unexpected sight clearly does not compute.

But one thing they know for sure is that this suitcase full of underwear doesn't belong to Minegishi.

Even Tangerine looks flabbergasted. The calmest person there is Nanao. He's used to this kind of sudden stroke of misfortune. Slightly surprised, but mostly feeling something along the lines of *Again?* Or more like, *I should have known.* He kicks off the platform and leaps into the train, Tangerine swept along in his wake. Just as they enter the gang-way the door slides shut behind them and the Shinkansen starts to move.

Out the window, the suit with no eyebrows is bringing his phone up to his ear.

'Well then,' Nanao says, looking at Tangerine, who is exhaling mightily. 'What happens now?' The Shinkansen picks up steady speed, paying no mind to their agitated state.

'Why did you open the bag?' Tangerine eyes him severely. He might be thinking Nanao had some scheme in mind, but his face is hard to read, cold and cadaverous.

'It just seemed like it would be more convincing if I tried the lock.'

'You thought that was convincing?'

'If I couldn't get the combination then they'd believe me.'

'But you did get the combination.'

'Guess I'm just lucky.' Nanao laughs at his little joke. 'Well, I imagine now they think something's up. At the very least that the bag was a fake.'

'That's for sure. Our stock was falling by the time we left Omiya. Now it's plummeting.'

'But the train doesn't stop until Morioka, so we're safe for now,' Nanao points out. He's casting around for a silver lining, and even though he knows it's just an illusion, he clings to it.

'Lemon would say the same damn thing.' As soon as the words leave Tangerine's mouth he wonders out loud, 'Where is Lemon, anyway?' He looks left and right. 'Hey, you, you said Lemon went to the back of the train.' He's pointing at the schoolkid. *He's still here?* thinks Nanao. The kid has been listening to him and Tangerine, and witnessed what just happened on the platform at Sendai. He must know that something dangerous is going on, but he isn't running away, isn't reporting anything to anyone. He seems to just be hanging out around them. *Where are his parents?* He looks like a clean-cut, well-behaved student, but maybe he has some teen angst that makes him feel drawn to the irregular. Nanao tries to picture it. Or maybe the kid just wants to brag to his friends about the crazy stuff he saw go down on the Shinkansen.

'Yes,' the kid nods, 'your friend hurried off in that direction,' pointing towards car six, 'like there was something he forgot to do.'

'Maybe he got off at Sendai,' says Nanao as the thought occurs to him. 'Why would he do that?'

'I don't know, maybe he got fed up with all of this and bailed on the job?'

'He wouldn't do that,' Tangerine responds quietly. 'He wants to be a useful train.'

'The man I was with is missing too,' says the schoolkid, looking back and forth between Nanao and Tangerine. 'What is going on here?' He has the air of a class president or team captain gauging the mood of the group before delegating responsibilities. 'Oh, and.'

'What is it?'

'About what you were saying a minute ago, the next stop isn't Morioka.'

'*What?*' Nanao fairly shouts at the unexpected information.

'What's the next stop?'

'Ichinoseki. We'll be there in about twenty minutes. Then Mizusawa-Esashi then Shin-Hanamaki, and *then* Morioka.'

'I thought the Hayate goes straight from Sendai to Morioka.'

'Not all of them. This is one of the ones that doesn't.'

'I didn't know.' Tangerine seems to have been under the same impression as Nanao. Nanao's phone rings and he pulls it out of his pocket. Tangerine says immediately, 'Answer it. Probably your Maria.'

There's no reason not to take the call.

'I assume you didn't get off at Sendai,' comes Maria's accusation.

'How did you know?'

'More importantly, are you okay? I was worried that Tangerine and Lemon might have got you.'

'I'm with Tangerine right now. You want to talk to him?' Nanao sounds like he's making a self-deprecating joke.

Maria says nothing for a moment. She must be worried. 'They captured you?'

'No, no. We're helping each other out.' As he says it he looks over at Tangerine, who shrugs. 'I'm doing what you suggested and giving them the bag.'

'I only said to do that as a last resort.'

'And now's the time for last resorts.'

Maria goes quiet again. In the silence Tangerine gets a call on his own phone and steps away to take it. The schoolkid is left standing on his own, but he doesn't go back to his seat. He just stands there, watching the two men.

'What's the next station?'

'Actually, Maria, did you know that it's not Morioka after all? It's Ichinoseki.'

'Then that's where you should get off. Forget about the bag. Just get out of there. The train must be cursed. It's too dangerous! Get out and don't look back.'

Nanao smiles bitterly. 'The train is fine, it's me that's cursed.'

'Don't let your guard down around Tangerine and Lemon. They're dangerous too.'

'You don't need to tell me.'

Nanao ends the call. A few moments later, Tangerine comes back over. 'It was Minegishi.' His expression is unchanged but he gives off a heavy feeling.

'What did he say?' the schoolkid wants to know.

Tangerine gives the kid a sharp look of warning, then turns to Nanao. 'He told me to come to Morioka.'

'To Morioka.'

Apparently Minegishi was more solicitous than angry. He wanted to know why Tangerine showed his men the wrong bag.

'I was thinking, should I apologise, should I play dumb, should I talk back? I ended up saying, Your men were giving me a hard time, so I wanted to put them in their place.'

'Why would you say that?' It seems like an answer that would make Minegishi even more upset.

'I thought it would make it harder for him to figure out what's going on. If I've turned on him or if I'm just screwing around. The truth is we didn't turn on him. We just messed up.'

Yeah, and that mess-up cost Minegishi's son his life. Nanao feels his gut twist.

'If you have nothing to hide,' Minegishi had apparently said, 'then you'll come to Morioka. And if you get off early, I'll just take it to mean that you're running. And then you'll be sorry that you ran. I'll make you suffer so much you'll wish you had just come to Morioka.'

And Tangerine had answered, 'Of course we'll come to Morioka. Your son can't wait to see you.'

After relating the conversation to Nanao, Tangerine shrugs again. 'So now Minegishi is on his way to Morioka Station.'

'He's going himself?'

'Yeah, when he should be relaxing at his villa,' says Tangerine with annoyance. 'He got a call telling him that something weird was going on, that he might want to check it out for himself.'

'Someone told him that?'

'That guy back at Sendai Station. Best if you have a look yourself, he said.'

Nanao doesn't know how to respond at first. *Would Minegishi's subordinate really have made the boss come out?* 'Well,' he says after a moment, 'I wish you the best of luck. I'm getting off at Ichinoseki.'

Tangerine's gun appears, pointed at Nanao. It's a small piece, sleek, looks more like an odd-shaped digital camera than a firearm.

The schoolkid's eyes widen and he takes a step back.

'You're staying with me, Ladybird.'

'Sorry. I'm getting off. Off this job, off this train. Your bag is in the crew room and the woman who did Minegishi's son is in the multi-purpose room after the green car. You can explain everything to Minegishi.'

'No.' Tangerine's voice is iron-hard. 'You think you have a choice here? You think when I pull a gun on you that I'm bluffing?'

Nanao can neither nod nor shake his head.

'Um, aren't you going to look for Mr Lemon?' The kid sounds like the class president again, trying to wrap up the convoluted threads of a bizarre student council meeting. *Kids have it so easy,* thinks Nanao.

KIMURA

AS SHIGERU KIMURA PUTS THE telephone receiver down, his wife Akiko asks, 'Who was that on the phone?'

They live in an old residential community far to the north of Tokyo, up Route 4 all the way to Iwate. It was built by an eager developer back in the boom years. As time went on and the economy worsened, the young residents moved out to more urban areas, the population shrank, the plans for the unbuilt sections of town never got off the page, and the area became drab and nondescript. The colours on the buildings faded, giving the impression that the town was thrust suddenly from growth into old age. But for Shigeru and Akiko Kimura, an elderly-feeling town was just right, away from the noise and fads of the city. When they found a small stand-alone house here ten years back they bought it without thinking twice, and have lived here happily since.

'It was a call from someone on the Shinkansen,' he answers.

'Was it now?' Akiko says, laying a tray with rice cakes and spicy crackers on the table. 'Here we are. Take turns eating the spicy and sweet ones.

All that's missing is some fruit.' She sunnily reviews their snack. 'What did they want?'

'When I called Yuichi before he said he was being held. Help me, he said.'

'Yes, I remember. You said he was on the Shinkansen, playing some practical joke on you.'

'I did. But now I think it might not have been a joke.' Having trouble connecting the dots, Shigeru Kimura can only speak in vague terms. 'The schoolkid I talked to before just called again.'

'Did he say Yuichi was up to something?'

'What he said was strange.'

He shares with his wife what he heard. She cocks her head uncertainly, then picks up a cracker and pops it in her mouth. 'Not too spicy. Do you want to try calling Yuichi again?'

Shigeru works the digital telephone awkwardly, trying to find his way through the menu to call back the most recent incoming call. When he finally figures it out and pushes the button, the line goes straight to a message saying that the phone he's trying to reach has been turned off.

'I don't like this,' Akiko says, munching on another cracker.

'I'm worried about Wataru.' Shigeru feels something leaden in his stomach, expanding, dark and indistinct but mortally heavy. Since the boy on the phone didn't speak in specifics, he can't stop his imagination from casting about wildly.

'Is Wataru in danger?'

'I don't know.' He picks up the phone again to call the hospital. 'What the hell was Yuichi thinking, leaving Wataru and getting on a Shinkansen? Do you think he was coming up here to see us?'

'If he were, I think he'd have said so. Even if he was trying to surprise us, at the very least he'd check to make sure we were at home.'

'Maybe he got tired of looking after Wataru and ran off?'

'He's an alcoholic, and he's lazy, but he's not the sort to do that.'

Shigeru dials the hospital. No one picks up. The ringtone keeps beeping. Finally a staff member answers. It's a nurse he's met several times before, and her voice immediately softens when he gives his name. 'Is everything all right with Wataru?'

'I just looked in on him earlier and there were no changes, but I'm happy to go and have another look.' Shigeru waits a minute or two before she comes back to the phone. 'He looks pretty much the same, but if anything happens I'll be sure to contact you.'

He thanks her, then pauses for a moment. 'I was napping and had an upsetting dream about him. That there was a dangerous man sneaking into the hospital to get Wataru.' He sounds sheepish.

'My goodness.' The nurse doesn't seem to know how to respond. 'You must have been worried.'

'I'm sorry to bother you with it. I suppose old folks put too much stock in dreams.'

'Oh, no, I completely understand.'

She's obviously doing her best to be polite, which he appreciates. It's nicer than making him feel like he's a nuisance. He ends the call and hangs up.

'You're worried there might be some trouble?' Akiko knits her brows as she lifts her teacup to her lips and takes a sip.

'I think there might have already been. And my hunches are usually right.' He strokes his white stubble and thinks. 'Something's off.'

'What do you mean by something?'

'The person who called. Before he seemed like an ordinary schoolkid, but this time felt different. I could tell.' He sits up stretches his arms overhead. His frame creaks and his joints pop.

Shigeru thinks back to the call. It was a male voice, who said he was fourteen, and though he spoke clearly he didn't actually say very much. 'You know, you and your wife must be relaxing, I probably shouldn't have called,' he had apologised, as if he had done something wrong. 'Sorry, that's all I have to say. I'm hanging up now.' Then the line went dead, leaving Shigeru Kimura in the dark.

'Do you think that boy was up to something?' Akiko takes another cracker. 'These are sweeter than they are spicy, really.'

'You know that I'm usually right about this sort of thing.'

'But even if you are, what do you want to do about it? You couldn't get in touch with Yuichi? Then let's call the police.'

Shigeru hauls himself to his feet and heads to the linen closet in the adjacent tatami room.

There are rolled-up futons on the shelves.

'You're taking a nap? You always nap when you're worried.' Akiko sighs and munches another cracker. 'And most times you have a bad dream.'

But to Shigeru, his mind enshrouded by a dark mist, it seems like the nightmare has already started.

FRUIT

WHERE IS LEMON?

Tangerine moves down the aisle towards the rear of the train, alert for any signs of his partner. But there's nothing.

'I'm telling you, he probably got off at Sendai,' says Nanao from behind his glasses, following Tangerine into the gangway. 'Something urgent must have come up.'

Tangerine wheels round. 'And what could have been so urgent?' Nanao stops short.

His body is tense and he looks jumpy, but he's also put himself at the perfect distance to handle any sudden attacks. Tangerine is impressed. This guy may seem nervous and unreliable, but when it comes to their type of dangerous work it has to be said that he's a professional. And there behind him is the schoolkid. His hanging around is beyond annoying, but Tangerine can't be bothered to get rid of him.

'Like maybe there was someone he didn't like the look of and he followed them off the train,' Nanao hypothesises.

'. . . The same thing occurred to me.'

330

Lemon could very well have fixed on someone who came out of the toilet and followed them. Tangerine doesn't know who this suspicious character could have been, but Lemon works more from instinct than from reason, and could easily have made a snap decision to tail a suspect. It wasn't that hard to imagine. Tangerine had been on the platform with Nanao but he hadn't had a chance to look up and down the length of the train and might have missed seeing Lemon disembark, if it happened.

'But if he did do that I would expect him to get in touch,' Tangerine says, more to himself than to Nanao. 'That's what he's done before. He can be lazy and sloppy, but when there's a change of plans he always calls.'

Useful trains run on time, Lemon always says. When they need to change tracks they let someone know, if not beforehand then as soon as they can. It's a matter of principle for Lemon.

Tangerine takes out his phone and stares at it. No calls.

As he's looking at his own phone, the schoolkid gets a call. Tangerine doesn't hear any ringing or buzzing because of the rumbling of the train, but all of a sudden the kid is pressing his phone to his ear and stepping over to the area beside the door. Wanting to shake off this juvenile nuisance, Tangerine turns and moves on.

The automatic door to the next car opens and Tangerine enters, once again scanning the passengers' faces and bags. No one who looks like Lemon. No one who looks like they would have had anything to do with Lemon.

He steps into the next gangway, followed by Nanao. 'Like I said, he got off at Sendai.'

Tangerine stops again. 'Something tells me he didn't.' He turns back round to face Nanao once more. The reverberations of the train pounding the tracks are like a thundering heartbeat. Tangerine pictures them riding inside a giant steel artery.

'Hey, Ladybird.' A sudden thought. 'Did you talk to Lemon at all?'

'Talk to him? When do you mean?'

'Whenever.'

'Talk to him, sure, I guess we talked a little.'

'Did he say anything about my key? A key I'm looking for. Or maybe he had some other message for me.'

Nanao looks wary. 'A key? A key for what?'

'Never mind,' says Tangerine.

What if? he thinks. *What if Lemon's dead?* He finally allows the possibility to enter his mind. *Could be.* It wasn't impossible, and in fact on this particular Shinkansen trip it seems entirely likely. *Why didn't I consider that before?* Tangerine is surprised at how long it took him.

If Lemon was killed, then it had to have just happened, which means that the killer is most likely somewhere nearby. Tangerine can't say for certain that it wasn't Nanao, and if it was, he thinks maybe Lemon would have tried to leave some message or clue.

'He didn't say anything to you?'

'Nothing about a key, no.' Nanao doesn't look like he's trying to hide anything. Then Tangerine realises that when he left Lemon behind outside the toilet he himself had continued towards the front of the train, which is where he found Nanao. So Nanao had no chance to kill Lemon without Tangerine knowing. Once he puts the pieces together, that much is obvious. He smiles wryly.

'It's hard to imagine anyone taking him out.'

'He is certainly tough,' Nanao says earnestly. 'And one thing he did say to me was If I die I'll come back again.'

For a second Tangerine gauges whether that was a message from Lemon, but then he dismisses the possibility. Lemon is always saying that. Any time he meets someone new, he brags to them about being immortal, that he'll always come back. Sometimes he'll say something about coming back as Lemon Z, though Tangerine doesn't know what exactly that means.

'Yeah, well, Lemon and I don't give up easily. No matter what happens, we always come back when you least expect it.'

At that moment a conductor enters the gangway from the rear of the train. He's young-looking, but he walks with his head up and his shoulders back, emanating a sense of duty and reliability.

Nanao doesn't hesitate. 'Excuse me, about the suitcase I gave you earlier. It belongs to him,' and he points at Tangerine.

The conductor takes a quick look Tangerine's way. 'Ah, yes, I made an announcement about it earlier but no one came to collect it. It's still in the crew room. Would you mind coming to get it now?'

'Good idea,' Nanao says, turning to Tangerine. 'Let's go and get it, okay?'

Tangerine hesitates. He still hasn't searched the whole train for Lemon. But he doesn't want to let the suitcase get away again. Probably best to secure it while he has the chance.

'Mr Tangerine,' says a small voice, and he notices that the schoolkid is back. Must have chased them down after finishing his phone call. *Persistent little shit.* Tangerine is moving past the point of annoyance towards genuine dislike. The kid probably wants to meddle in adult affairs so he can feel grown up, but all he's doing is being a tremendous nuisance. Tangerine starts to think about what he can do to get rid of him, when the kid speaks up again. 'I found something weird.'

The conductor pays no special attention to the kid. 'Shall we go and get your suitcase?' With that he sets off towards the front, clearly expecting them to follow him.

They do, Nanao behind the conductor, then Tangerine, with the kid bringing up the rear.

When they pass through car seven and into the gangway between seven and eight, the kid tugs on the back of Tangerine's jacket. Urgent little tugs, like he's trying to get his attention. Tangerine turns round to find the kid eyeing the toilet door suggestively.

'Hey,' Tangerine says to Nanao. 'You go ahead and get the suitcase. I'll wait for him while he goes to the toilet.' He jerks his chin towards the kid.

The conductor doesn't seem to notice that anything is amiss, and maybe Nanao's put together what's going on, because he just nods, and the two disappear into the next car.

As soon as they're gone Tangerine steps up to the toilet door. 'This is where you found something weird?'

The kid makes a mild face. 'Yes, this thing right here.' He points to a bit of copper wire sticking out of the door.

Tangerine's eyes widen. It's Lemon's copper wire. No doubt about it. Same as the one he used to lock the toilet door from the outside when they hid Little Minegishi's body.

'It's weird, right? The toilet's locked and it says occupied, but it doesn't sound like there's anyone in there. Something funny's going on. I'm a little creeped out.' This schoolkid looks like he's frightened of the bathroom the way a little kid is afraid of the dark.

'Did Lemon leave this here?' Tangerine takes the end of the wire and yanks it upward.

The lock releases with a clack.

'Are you sure you want to go in?'

Tangerine ignores him and slides the door open. The scene that greets him is decidedly different from a typical train bathroom. Standard toilet, but also bodies spilled on the floor, limbs twisted and coiled like a nest of serpents. It's a horror show scene, a grotesque tangle of arms and legs.

Tangerine's world goes silent.

Two men piled at the base of the toilet bowl but the weave of flesh doesn't look human.

More like some new species of gargantuan insect. A puddle of blood on the floor sloshes around. It looks like piss.

'What *happened*?' Behind him, the kid's voice is shrill.

'Lemon.' Tangerine says the name softly.

Sound returns to his ears. The rattling of the Shinkansen penetrates to his very core. He pictures Lemon's face. Not the face in front of him, eyes closed beneath a bloody hole, but the man who was always chattering away by his side. The gleam in his eyes when he would say, childlike, that he wanted people to think he was a good train. Tangerine feels his chest split open and shatter into small pieces. A cold wind gusts into the hole in his heart. He realises he's never felt this before, which leaves him even more shaken.

A line from a book echoes in his mind. *We perished, each alone.*

We spent so much time together. But at the end, we're all alone.

THE PRINCE

PEERING INTO THE BATHROOM FROM behind Tangerine, the Prince retreats one step, then another. He makes sure he's pretending to be scared, all the while watching Tangerine's face. He doesn't fail to notice that the man goes momentarily pale and rigid, seemingly about to explode into shards of broken glass. *I didn't think you'd be so fragile.* The Prince almost says it aloud.

Tangerine enters the toilet and closes the door, leaving the Prince alone in the gangway. He's disappointed; he wants to see what Tangerine will do. This man who seems so cool and collected, would his control slip at the sight of Lemon's dead body, or would he struggle to keep his emotions in check? – the Prince wishes he could watch.

After a short while the door opens and Tangerine emerges. His expression is back to normal, which is a bit of a letdown to the Prince. 'The other one in there, that's the man you were with, right?' He jerks his thumb backwards with one hand and closes the toilet door behind him with the other. 'He's been shot in the chest, but not in the heart. What do you want to do?'

'What . . . do I want to do?'

'Lemon's dead, but your friend is still alive.'

The Prince can't quite comprehend what he's being told. *Kimura's alive?* He was certain that the man had been shot dead by Lemon. It's true that there didn't seem to be very much blood, but the thought of him surviving the shooting makes the Prince suddenly think that Kimura might never die. He has to check himself from complaining about the man's tenacity.

'Don't get me wrong, he's not exactly doing well,' Tangerine adds. 'He isn't dead, but he's barely breathing. So what do you want to do? Although it's not like he can get intensive care on the train, so there probably isn't much you could do for him. You could run crying to the conductor and get them to stop the train and call an ambulance.'

It only takes the Prince an instant to decide how to respond. He never had any intention of stopping the train and getting the authorities involved.

'He kidnapped me.'

The Prince explains how Kimura was taking him around against his will, about how he was so frightened. Of course it's all made up, but that's his story. He tells Tangerine that finding out Kimura's on the verge of death is scary and confusing but ultimately a relief. He tries to hint that he'd be happy if Kimura would just give up and die.

Tangerine doesn't seem all that interested. His eyes are stony and difficult to read. The Prince would expect an adult to say that they should call the police anyway, but Tangerine must have his own reasons for not wanting the train to stop, and he says nothing.

He also makes no move to leave the area in front of the bathroom. He just stares down at the Prince. 'There are two bodies in the toilet. Your friend isn't dead yet, though he will be soon. But Lemon's body is on top. Which means that your friend was shot and put there before Lemon died. I'd guess it was Lemon who shot your guy, and then after that Lemon was shot.'

'By whom?'

'There's a gun in there too. But only one.'

'Only one gun. So who shot him?'

'First Lemon shoots your friend, then before your friend fully dies he goes berserk and wrestles the gun away. Then he shoots Lemon. I don't know if that's actually what happened, but it's one possibility.'

It would be wonderful if that's what you think. Even as he's on his guard, the Prince feels like laughing out loud. This Tangerine is a smart one. He reasons things out. *I love dealing with smart people.* The more logically someone thinks, the harder it is for them to escape the chains of self-justification, and the easier it is for the Prince to move them in the direction he wants.

Tangerine leans over to inspect the protruding length of copper wire. 'But this right here, this doesn't sit right.'

'The copper wire – what's it for?'

'Lemon used it to lock the door from the outside. A little trick he does. Did it all the time.' Tangerine tugs at the end of the wire. Not emotionally, not with any sadness for his friend. It looks like he's just testing the feel and strength. 'I'm wondering who locked it after Lemon died. There had to have been someone else besides the other man in the bathroom.'

'You're like a detective.' The Prince isn't trying to poke at Tangerine, he genuinely means it. He pictures a scene he read in a book once, with a famous inspector who calmly and unemotionally explains the murder while pacing back and forth before the corpse.

'I'm not playing guessing games here. I'm just putting together the most probable scenario based on the facts I can see,' Tangerine says. 'I'd guess that Lemon shot your friend, put the body in the toilet, then locked it. That's when he used the wire.'

The Prince doesn't see where Tangerine is going and just nods uncertainly.

'But then after that someone else shot Lemon. Then that person put Lemon in the toilet too. Probably thought it would be safest to hide the two bodies together. Then whoever that was used the wire to lock the door again.'

'I don't know what –'

'Whoever it was probably saw Lemon use the copper wire. Then they did the same thing to lock the door again. Watched Lemon do it first and then copied him.'

'You think Mr Lemon taught them how?'

'No, he didn't teach them. Just that whoever did it saw Lemon use the wire to lock the door first.' Tangerine fingers the end of the wire. Then he takes a few steps further up the gangway. He bends over and examines the floor, leaning in close to search for any clues. He runs his fingers over some dings on the wall. Just like a policeman investigating a crime scene.

'By the way, you and Lemon talked, didn't you?' Suddenly Tangerine is right in front of him. He sounds like the question just popped into his head.

'What?'

'You talked to him a little, right?'

'When he was alive?'

'I'm not asking if you talked to him after he died. Did he tell you anything?'

'Wh-what would he have told me?'

Tangerine thinks for a moment. 'Something about a key.' He cocks his head and stares.

'A key?'

'I'm looking for a key. Lemon knew something about it. Did he say anything?'

Actually, the Prince almost says. He recalls the last words he heard out of Lemon's mouth, when the man was fighting desperately to stay awake and with his last ounce of energy gasped out, The key, it's in a coin locker in Morioka. Tell Tangerine, he had said. The Prince didn't know what he meant by a key, which is why it stuck in his head. Now he's thinking about the key, wondering if telling Tangerine about it might bring something interesting to light.

It's on the tip of his tongue. *He did mention a key, though I don't know what he meant –* the words are about to spill over.

But as he's opening his mouth an alarm goes off in his head. *It's a trap.*

He has no proof. Just a feeling telling him to pull out. 'No, he didn't say anything about that,' answers the Prince.

'Is that so?' Tangerine is quiet, but he doesn't sound especially disappointed.

The Prince watches Tangerine. *Should I have told him about the coin locker in Morioka after all? But not saying anything didn't do me any harm. The situation's the same as it was before. Or maybe I even gained a little ground.*

'But there's something I still don't get,' Tangerine says suddenly.

'What?'

'When your phone rang before, you walked away from us. That was on the gangway between cars five and six.'

'I think so, yes.'

'And your seat is in seven.'

He remembered that? Tangerine had only passed his seat once. *That was enough for him to remember?*

Tangerine's eyes bore into him.

The Prince tells himself to keep steady. He knows that the man is just trying to rattle him. 'You see,' he says timidly, 'I went back to my seat, and –'

'And?'

'And I had to go to the toilet, so I came this way.'

Good, the Prince nods to himself, *perfectly acceptable answer.*

'Is that right?' Tangerine nods as well. 'Tell me, have you ever seen this before?' He produces a small, crumpled sheet of colourful stickers and spreads it open. The Prince recognises the characters as being from *Thomas and Friends*.

'What's that?'

'I found it in Lemon's jacket pocket.'

'He sure liked *Thomas*.'

'Enough to drive me up the wall.'

'So what about it?' the Prince asks again, despite himself.

'Some stickers are missing.' He points to two empty white spaces.

The Prince remembers when Lemon was down and he pressed a sticker to the ground.

A picture of a green train that the Prince had then peeled off and thrown away.

'He didn't give any to you, did he?'

There's the sensation of invisible feelers extending from Tangerine's body, colourless and transparent plant tendrils, brushing the Prince's face searchingly. Stroking the surface to reveal what's hidden inside.

The Prince's mind is sprinting. He doesn't know how to answer, whether to feign ignorance or to make up something about the sticker that sounds plausible.

'He gave me one, but I was scared and I threw it in the trash.'

The Prince is thankful that he's still so young.

He knows that Tangerine could very well follow his instinct and become violent, try to interrogate him by force about Lemon's death. No doubt the man has done it many times before now.

But he's not doing it to the Prince. *And why not?* Because the Prince is still a child. That one fact makes Tangerine hold back. He thinks this person is too young and weak to hurt without solid proof, his better nature wants to find something more concrete before he starts meting out punishment. *Even though no one's better nature ever did them any good.*

Tangerine is smarter than Lemon, with more depth and substance. He has a more developed interior life, which gives him better powers of imagination. This leads to a greater capacity for empathy. Which in the end only makes him weaker. Tangerine will be easier to control than Lemon. *Which means I'll probably beat him.*

'Oh, you threw it out, did you? And what character was it?' Tangerine's face is serious.

'What?' The train bucks and the Prince loses his balance. He puts his hand on the wall to catch himself.

'The sticker you got. One of these missing ones. Which character was it? Do you remember the name?' The sheet of stickers in Tangerine's hand is flecked with blood.

The Prince shakes his head. 'I don't know the name.'

'Well, that's strange,' murmurs Tangerine. The Prince's stomach drops, like he was walking a tightrope and suddenly stepped out into cold, empty space.

'What's strange?'

'He always wanted everyone to learn all the names of Thomas's friends. Any time he gave anyone a sticker or a toy he made sure to say their names. One hundred per cent of the time. He never just gave anyone anything. If he gave you a sticker, then you heard the name. Even if you don't remember it, you heard it.'

The Prince weighs his next move. Something tells him not to respond. He concentrates on carefully pulling his foot back from the abyss, regaining his balance on the tightrope.

'I would guess,' Tangerine says, looking at the outlines of where the two stickers used to be, 'that he gave you this one over here,' and points to one space. 'The green one. Right?'

'Oh, that's right!' The sticker he threw away *was* in fact the green train.

'That's Percy. Cute little Percy. Lemon loved him.'

'I think that was the name.' The Prince doesn't fully commit, waiting to see what happens.

'Hmm.' Tangerine's face gives nothing away. 'And do you know what character was over here?' He points to the other empty space.

'No, I don't.' The Prince shakes his head again. 'He didn't give me that one.'

'I know who it was.'

'You know which one used to be there?'

'I know.' Tangerine swoops in and grabs the Prince by the lapel of his blazer. 'Because it's stuck to you right here.' He lets go just as suddenly.

The Prince stands rooted to the spot.

'Look. This is the Diesel. The mean old Diesel.' There on Tangerine's finger is a black train with a square face.

The Prince is taken by surprise at the unexpected appearance of the sticker, but he fights desperately not to let it show. He manages to say, 'You know a lot about *Thomas and Friends* too, Mr Tangerine.'

Tangerine's face fixes into a slight scowl. There's a hint of a smile in there too, whether he intended it or not. 'That's all he ever talked about. I'd hope I remember at least a thing or two.' Then he pulls a small paperback out of his rear pocket. 'I found this in his jacket too.' It has a subdued orange cover with nothing on it but the title and the author's name. Tangerine runs his fingers across it, then opens to the bookmark. 'He made it this far.' His voice is even. Then he mutters, 'Lemon never liked that one. And neither did I. He's a bad seed.'

'Um.'

'The Diesel is malicious and spiteful. Lemon always told me, never trust the Diesel. He lies and forgets people's names. And now I find the Diesel sticker on your jacket.'

'It must have just . . .' The Prince looks from side to side.

When Lemon grabbed the Prince, he must have stuck it on, his very last act. The Prince hadn't noticed at all.

This is not going well. The thought stabs at him. *But there's still hope.* Based on his past experiences, there's plenty of reason to think things could still go his way.

Tangerine still doesn't have his gun out. Maybe because he knows he could have it out and ready any time he wanted, or maybe he has some reason not to pull it out yet. Either way, he doesn't seem concerned about it.

Now the man starts talking, composed and serene. 'There's a passage in Dostoevsky, in *Crime and Punishment.*'

The Prince is disoriented by the sudden change of direction.

'It says, "Science now tells us, love yourself before all men, for everything in the world rests on self-interest." Basically, the most important thing is your own happiness. If you take care of that, it helps everyone else to be happy too. Now I've never spent much time thinking about other people's happiness or unhappiness, so I hear that passage and it rings true to me, but what do you think?'

The Prince responds with his own question, his favourite: 'Why is it wrong to kill people? If someone asked you that, what would you say?'

Tangerine doesn't look at all thrown. 'Well, here's what Dostoevsky would say. In *Demons*. "I find that crime is no longer insanity, but simply common sense, almost a duty; anyway, a gallant protest. How can we expect a cultured man not to commit a murder, if he is in need of money?" There's nothing unusual about transgression, he's saying. It's completely normal. Which is how I feel too.'

Tangerine is pulling fancy-sounding quotes from novels, but the Prince doesn't think they actually answer his question. And while he agrees with the part about crime being common sense, the suggestion that it's a gallant protest strikes him as narcissism, able to provide surface amusement at best. Once again, he's disappointed.

Just another answer based in emotion, even if it is more spirited than the usual answer.

Just more words. I want a more detached answer to why murder isn't allowed.

But at the same time he thinks back to the phone call he took just after passing Sendai Station, the man lurking around the hospital, waiting to move on Kimura's son. 'I'm inside,' said the man. 'I'm dressed like a nurse. I'm guessing you passed Sendai by now? I didn't hear from you and was wondering if I need to keep waiting.' He had sounded restless and eager to do the job.

'Don't do anything yet,' the Prince replied. 'Just remember the rules: if you call me and I don't pick up after ten rings, then you can go ahead.'

'Okay. Understood.' The man was breathless with excitement. Here was someone who loved no one but himself, who had no problem murdering a child for money. No doubt he'd been telling himself that it wasn't even murder, that he'd just fiddle with the medical instruments and destabilise the little boy's situation a bit. People are so devoted to self-justification.

'You're in school, right?' Tangerine asks him. 'How old are you?'

'Fourteen,' says the Prince.

'Perfect.'

'Perfect?'

'Are you familiar with article 41 of the criminal code?'

'Huh?'

'Article 41 says that people under fourteen don't get sentenced for crimes. Did you know that? But once you turn fourteen you can be punished like anyone else.'

'I didn't know that.' Although of course he knows that. The Prince knows all about that sort of thing. But that didn't stop him from doing what he does even when he turned fourteen. It's not like he was doing the things he did until now simply because he knew he couldn't be punished by law. The law is just something to keep in mind when he does the things he wants to do. His crimes exist in a different dimension from the petty details of the law.

'I'll share with you one more passage I like. This one's from *The Sailor Who Fell from Grace with the Sea.*'

'What does it say?'

'It's a quote about article 41 from a kid, about your age. He says, "It's the symbol of the dreams adults have for us, while at the same time being the symbol that those dreams will never be fulfilled. Because they're stupid enough to think that we can't do anything, they gave us a glimpse of a single patch of blue sky, one fragment of perfect freedom." I like it because of the faraway feel of the writing, but it also holds a clue to your question, about why it's wrong to kill people. Saying it's wrong to kill is an expression of an adult dream. Just a dream. A fantasy. Like Santa Claus. Something that doesn't exist in the real world, a picture of a beautiful blue sky that someone in great distress painted, after which they hid under the covers with their picture, looking at that instead of at the real world. That's how it is with most laws. They're just symbols, designed to make people feel better.'

The Prince still doesn't understand why Tangerine started quoting from novels out of nowhere. But he loses some respect for him for having to rely on someone else's words.

Then he notices the gun.

Two guns. Right in front of him.

One of them is pressed up against his chest. The other one is in Tangerine's open hand, held out to the Prince like a lifeline.

What is this?

'Listen to me. I'm more than just a little angry. Kids like you piss me off especially. But just shooting you when you're defenceless, that doesn't sit right with me. I don't pick on the weak. So I'll give you this gun. Then we'll each have one, and it'll be a question of who gets shot and who does the shooting.'

The Prince doesn't want to make a move. He can't yet tell what his opponent is planning. 'Hurry up and take it. I'll teach you how to use it.'

Watching Tangerine carefully, the Prince closes his fingers around the gun in the man's hand. Then he retreats two steps.

'Grab the slide here and pull it backwards. Hold on to the grip and lower that switch. That's the safety. Then all you have to do is point it at me and pull the trigger.' Tangerine's face is expressionless and his manner is calm. *Is he really even angry?*

The Prince is about to adjust his hold on the gun and perform the actions as instructed when it slips in his hand and drops to the floor. He feels a rush of panic, knows that Tangerine will seize this moment to attack. But the man just smiles faintly. 'Calm down. Pick it up and try again. I won't start until you're ready.'

It doesn't feel like he's lying. The Prince bends down to pick up the gun, but a thought flashes in his mind: *Does it mean something that my hand would slip at such a crucial moment?* For someone like him whose surplus of luck has always kept him safe, messing up like this feels unnatural. Which makes him realise: he was probably *supposed* to drop the gun. It was a necessary mess-up.

'I don't need the gun,' the Prince says, holding it out for Tangerine to take back.

A cloud passes over the man's face and his brows draw together.

'What's wrong? You think surrendering will save you?'

'No, that's not it.' The Prince is confident now. 'I think it was a trap.'

Tangerine is quiet.

I knew it. More than just feeling relieved, the Prince has a sense of accomplishment. *My luck still works.* He doesn't know the technical specifics, but he can sense there's something irregular about the gun. He can imagine that trying to shoot it would hurt him somehow.

'I'm impressed you knew. If you pull the trigger on that thing, it explodes. I don't think it would kill you, but it would injure you pretty badly.'

My luck is a force field. The Prince is no longer afraid of Tangerine. *At this point Tangerine might even be starting to fear me.*

At that moment the door behind Tangerine slides open and someone steps through.

'Help me,' shouts the Prince. 'He's gonna kill me!' Shouting as pitifully as he can.

'Help!'

Not even a second goes by. Tangerine's head swivels hard. It was facing directly to the front, and now it's facing directly to the side. He topples over, the gun falling with him.

The floor of the Shinkansen receives the body and bears it along, the juddering of the train like the ritual clamour of a funeral procession. Over the body stands Nanao.

NANAO

HE HAS NO SIGHS LEFT. Nanao stares down blankly at Tangerine's broken-necked corpse.

Why does this keep happening?

'He was about to kill me,' says the kid in a trembling voice.

The irritation Nanao feels towards the kid is as paralysed as the rest of his emotions. 'What was going on here?'

'These people were shooting each other.'

'These people?' He doesn't miss the plural. The boy points at the bathroom.

'If you pull that copper wire up it'll open.'

Nanao follows instructions and sure enough the door unlocks.

He looks inside and his eyes pop open. There's a body at the base of the toilet. Two bodies. They're just tossed in there, like junk, like discarded home appliances.

'Oh no, that is *it*, I have had *enough* of this!' Nanao whines in sheer frustration. 'Enough already!'

He knows that he can't just leave Tangerine's body there on the floor, so he moves it into the toilet, which was already fairly full. *Corpse storage only,* he thinks darkly.

Searching Tangerine reveals his mobile phone, which Nanao takes, and a folded piece of paper. He unfolds it: a giveaway entry ticket. *What's this all about?*

'Something's written on the back,' says the kid.

He flips it over. There's a picture of a train in ballpoint pen. Underneath it says Arthur.

'What is it?'

'A drawing of a train.' Nanao folds it back up and puts it in his own pocket.

He finishes arranging things in the bathroom and steps back out to the gangway.

'You saved me,' says the schoolkid, pulling his backpack over his shoulders.

Nanao thought he had seen something in the kid's hand that looked like a gun, but there's nothing now. *Just my imagination.* He closes the door and fumbles with the copper wire until he gets it locked.

He replays in his mind what had just happened.

After retrieving the suitcase from the crew room, he had come back to find Tangerine pointing a gun at the kid.

The look on the kid's face, the catch in his voice as he cried out, spurred Nanao into immediate action. Layered over this defenceless child pleading for help he saw the kidnapped boy he had long ago abandoned.

His mind emptied out and he moved automatically, stepping up behind Tangerine and wrenching his head sideways. Something primal in Nanao's body made him use deadly force, sensing that if he attacked Tangerine without finishing him off he'd be putting himself in danger.

'Why was he trying to shoot you?'

'I don't know. He found the bodies in the toilet and just started going crazy.'

So seeing his friend dead pushed him over the edge? It didn't seem impossible.

'I can't even tell who killed who.' Nanao manages to sigh again. He no longer cares about the details. He just wants to get off this ridiculous train. It feels like the Shinkansen is misfortune itself, hurtling along at two hundred and fifty kilometres an hour. The northbound Misfortune and Calamity, and Nanao is onboard.

He debates for a moment what to do with the gun that Tangerine dropped. Then he throws it in the trash.

'Oh –' The schoolkid makes a little noise.

'What?'

'I bet we'd feel safer if you held on to it.'

'Holding on to it will only lead to trouble, trust me.' Nanao thinks keeping his distance from anything dangerous is the wisest choice given his luck. He tosses out Tangerine's phone too. 'Best to just get rid of it.' He takes the suitcase by the handle. 'I'm done. I just want off.'

The kid's face stiffens and his eyes look moist. 'You're getting off the train?'

'I don't know what I'm doing.' Now that Tangerine and Lemon are gone, he can't guess what Minegishi will do. But it seems likely that Minegishi's wrath would have fallen on those two, not him. Nanao's job was to steal the bag and get off the Shinkansen. If he disembarks at the next station with the bag in hand, there should be no problem. He might not get a perfect score, but his grade would still be a low A. At least he thinks so. That's what he wants to think.

The announcement sounds for Ichinoseki, the next station stop. *Perfect timing.*

'Would – would you please stay with me until Morioka?' The schoolkid looks like he's about to burst into tears. 'I'm scared.'

Nanao wishes he could seal his ears shut. He has no interest whatsoever in any further entanglements. Nothing good could possibly come from him going all the way to Morioka. And he can think of more than a few bad things that might happen.

'Because – because –' The kid has something he can't quite seem to get out of his mouth. A nasty premonition settles on Nanao. The sense that some inconvenient truth is about to come pouring out of this kid that he won't be able to escape. The thought terrifies him. He even starts to bring his hands up to cover his ears. '– if I don't get to Morioka, there's a little boy who will be in danger.'

Nanao's hands stop millimetres from his ears. 'What are you talking about?'

'Like a hostage situation. The son of someone I know, he's only five or six, he's in the hospital. And if I don't get to Morioka, his life will be in danger.'

'His life? What exactly is going on?'

'I really don't know for sure.'

This is precisely the sort of thing Nanao didn't want to hear. He feels a bloom of concern that this schoolkid reaches Morioka safely, but at the same time he wants to get off the Shinkansen as soon as he possibly can.

'You'll be fine. I doubt anything else will happen between here and Morioka.' Nanao doesn't believe the words he's saying. They're like a half-hearted prayer that he doubts will have any effect on anything. 'Just go back to your seat and you'll be okay.'

'You promise nothing else will happen?'

'I mean, I can't say for absolute certain.'

'I don't know what will happen when I get to Morioka. I'm afraid.'

'I doubt there's anything I could –'

The door from car seven opens and a man steps through. Nanao stops mid-sentence.

Not wanting to seem suspicious, he freezes, which of course only makes him seem more suspicious.

'Oh, hello,' the man says.

Nanao turns to look. It's the exam-prep instructor. The man stands there looking unsubstantial, almost half transparent. Like you could pass your hand right through him. Like a ghost.

The instructor scratches his head sheepishly. 'I told my students I was travelling in the green car. I realised that if I don't go and see what it's like in there then I won't be able to convince them that I really had a green car seat, so I was on my way to check it out.' The man sounds genuine. He grins with embarrassment, having explained what he was doing there before Nanao could even ask.

'Sounds tough, being a teacher,' Nanao says with a half-smile.

'Is this a friend of yours?' asks the kid warily.

This kid must think that everyone on board the train is some kind of dangerous character, Nanao realises. *I doubt he ever expected to have a gun pulled on him or to discover dead bodies in a toilet. Kids should just stay in the playground.*

'Not exactly, we just ended up talking to each other a bit,' explains Nanao to the boy. 'He's an instructor at an exam-prep school.'

'My name's Suzuki,' says the man. He didn't need to introduce himself, but he did anyway, which Nanao takes as a sign of his forthrightness.

Then he gets an idea. 'Mr Suzuki, how far are you going on the train?'

'To Morioka. Why?'

Nanao hasn't thought it through. He just conveniently tells himself that there's a reason they encountered Suzuki here and now. 'Would you mind staying with this kid?'

'Sorry?'

'I need to get off at Ichinoseki. I was hoping you'd look after him.'

Suzuki seems thrown off by Nanao's sudden request, which makes sense, because it's more of a demand than a request. The kid looks just as upset. He stares at Nanao like he's being abandoned.

Finally Suzuki speaks. 'Is he lost?'

Nanao cocks his head. 'No, not lost. He's just scared of riding to Morioka by himself.'

'I need to stay with you –' The kid is clearly not happy with this change of plans. His face is a mixture of insubordination and anxiety.

'I need to take this,' Nanao says, lifting up the suitcase, 'and get off at the next station.'

'But –'

'I don't mind travelling with the young man, but it doesn't seem like that will settle his fears.' Suzuki looks flummoxed.

Nanao heaves a sigh.

The Shinkansen sheds speed as they approach Ichinoseki. Nanao watches the flowing landscape outside the window, then steals a glance at the schoolkid, who is also looking out the window. He notices in that moment that the kid is surprisingly calm. *That's not right. Isn't he a little too collected after a train ride full of guns and corpses? And what about me? I snapped Tangerine's neck right in front of him. And it wasn't an accident either, I meant to do it, and I did it like I knew exactly what I was doing. Shouldn't he be more afraid of me, or at least ask some questions about what's going on here? Why does he want to travel to Morioka with a killer?*

And then the answer comes to Nanao. *It's all been too much for him. He doesn't know how to process it so he's shut down.* It makes perfect sense, after the kid was nearly shot. *Poor little guy.*

KIMURA

< 1 | 2 | 3 | 4 | 5 | 6 | 7 | 8 | 9 | 10 >

SHIGERU KIMURA STOPS RUMMAGING AROUND in the closet and turns to his wife. 'Did you move it again?'

'Oh, weren't you going to take a nap?' Akiko nibbles a cracker. 'I thought you were getting out the futon.'

'Have you been listening to anything I said? It's not time for a nap!'

'But you don't even know what's going on,' chides Akiko, picking up the small chair from the living room and carrying it over to the closet. She shoos Shigeru out of the way and positions the chair, then climbs up on top of it. She stretches up and opens the storage cabinet above the closet.

'Oh, it's up there?'

'You never put things where they ought to go.' She pulls out a bundle wrapped in a *furoshiki*. 'This is what you're looking for, isn't it?'

Shigeru takes it and sets it on the floor.

'Is this really what you want to do?' Akiko clambers down from the chair with a pout. 'I can't shake this feeling.'

'What feeling is that?'

'More like a smell.' His face is grave. 'One I haven't smelled in a long time.'

'And what smell is that?' She glances at the kitchen, muttering that she hasn't cooked anything especially pungent.

'Bad intent. I could smell it through the phone. It stank.'

'Oh, that takes me back. You used to say that all the time, dear. I smell bad intent. It's like you're haunted by the spirit of bad intent.' Akiko folds her knees under her and sits up straight in front of the contents of the *furoshiki*.

'Do you know why I wanted to quit our old line of work?'

'Because Yuichi was born. That's what you said. You wanted to be around to watch your son grow up and thought we should change careers. And I was happy to hear it, because I had wanted a change for a long time.'

'That wasn't my only reason. Thirty years ago, I got fed up with all of it. Everyone around me stank.'

'Like the spirit of bad intent?'

'People who like to hurt others, who like to humiliate others, who above all else want to advance their own position. They reek of it.'

'You honestly sound ridiculous.'

'Everyone around me stank of bad intent, and I became disgusted. So I made a change. The supermarket's been hard work, but I've never once got a whiff there of bad intent.'

Then Shigeru Kimura's mouth forms a bitter smile at the thought that his son took up the same type of work that he himself had left behind. When he first heard the rumour from a friend, that his son was starting to help out on rough jobs, Shigeru was so worried that he even thought about tailing his son to keep an eye on him.

'Why are we talking about this again?'

'Because whoever just called had that old stench. Oh, did you check the Shinkansen times?'

When Yuichi had said on the phone earlier that he was on the Shinkansen, Shigeru thought something felt off, though he had nothing to go on but his instinct, and the ever-so-slightly rancid whiff that came off the other person he spoke to. After the call ended he had said to Akiko, 'Yuichi says he'll be arriving at Sendai in twenty minutes. Check and see if there's a northbound Shinkansen with that schedule.' Akiko complained mildly as she trundled over to the shelf beside the TV and started flipping through the timetable booklet.

Now she nods to him. 'Yes I did, and there is a train on that schedule. Arriving at Sendai at eleven o'clock sharp. Ichinoseki at eleven twenty-five, Mizusawa-Esashi eleven thirty-five. Did you know you don't have to search through all these pages any more, you can look all this up on the Internet one-two-three. Remember when we used to do jobs together, oh, I researched so many timetables and wrote down so many phone numbers, I used to have a notepad this thick, do you remember that?' She demonstrates the thickness with forefinger and thumb. 'We wouldn't need that nowadays, would we?'

Shigeru Kimura leans back against the wall and looks up at their old clock. Five after eleven. 'If we leave now we should be able to make Mizusawa-Esashi easily enough.'

'Are you really getting on the Shinkansen? You're serious?'

Kimura had gone out earlier to pass the community circular to the neighbours, so he is already dressed in his khaki slacks and deep-green jacket. All set, he says to himself, and then, 'Aren't you coming too?'

'Of course I'm not.'

'If I'm going, then you're going.'

'You really want me to go?'

'We always did this together back then.'

'That is true. There are more than a few times where you only made it out alive because I was there. I'm sure you remember. Though I'm not sure I remember you ever thanking me. Really, though, it's been thirty years . . . !' Akiko stands and rubs the muscles on her legs, grumbling about stiffness and aching knees.

'It's just like riding a bike. Your body knows what to do.'

'I think it's very much different from riding a bike. These are nerves you have to use to keep sharp. Our nerves are so far from being sharp, they're like fluffy cotton.'

Now Shigeru steps up onto the chair to the cabinet and pulls out two rolled-up garments, which he tosses on the floor.

'Oh, those waistcoats bring me back. Although I suppose people don't call them waistcoats any more, nowadays they say vests.' Akiko runs her hand over one of the vests. Then she hands the other to Shigeru. 'This one's yours. We could combine the two and call them vestcoats!'

Shigeru makes a long-suffering face as he pulls off his jacket and slips on the leather vest. Then he puts his jacket back on over it.

'What do you plan to do once we're on the Shinkansen?'

'I want to find out what's going on with Yuichi. He said he was going up to Morioka.'

'And you don't think it's all just some sort of prank?'

'That schoolkid, although I don't even know if he actually is a school-kid, but regardless – there's something I don't like about him.'

'Still, do you really think all this is necessary?' After pulling on her own vest, Akiko looks down at the tools of their trade, laid out atop the open *furoshiki*.

'My alarm bells are ringing. We need to be prepared. Luckily it's not a plane and you don't have to go through security to get on the Shinkansen. Hey, the hammer on this thing is messed up.'

'You don't want to use that revolver anyway. The shell casings fly every-where and you're always so eager to shoot, I'd rather you have a weapon with a safety.' Akiko takes one of the guns and loads a magazine into the handle. It slides into place with a heavy click. She immediately pulls back the slide. 'This one will do. Take this one.'

'I clean that one regularly.' Shigeru takes the gun from Akiko and slips it into one of the twin holsters built into his vest.

'The gun might be in good working condition, but it's been thirty years for you. Are you sure you'll be able to use it?'

'Who do you think you're talking to?'

'What about Wataru? I'm more worried about him.'

'He's in the hospital. I don't imagine anything too terrible could happen to him there. And I can't think of any reason why he'd be in any particular danger. Don't you think?'

'Maybe there's someone from back then who has a grudge against us and wants to take it out on him?'

Shigeru Kimura freezes in mid-motion, then turns to look at his wife. 'I hadn't thought of that.'

'Thirty years have gone by, and we've become senior citizens. Someone who was scared of us back then might think that now's their chance.'

'Then they thought wrong. You and I are just as dangerous as we were back then,' says Shigeru. 'Although these past few years we have been doting on Wataru.'

'True enough.' Akiko starts to check the other guns. Her hands seem to move of their own accord, practised movements, with the quiet thrill of handling a favourite toy from childhood. Akiko was always more careful with guns than he was, and she was a better shot too. She chooses a gun and inserts it into her holster, then buttons up her jacket.

Kimura steps over to the phone and finds the number from the most recent call, which he writes down on a notepad. Just in case, he also copies the number for the hospital. 'Do you remember Shigeru's number? The other Shigeru. He's the only person we know in Tokyo.'

'I wonder how Shigeru's doing. Shall we go, dear? If we don't leave now we might miss our train.'

THE PRINCE

THE HAYATE APPROACHES ICHINOSEKI STATION. The platform appears, then starts to slide by. As the train slows, Nanao adjusts his black-framed glasses and stands in front of the door. 'All right, Mr Suzuki, I'm leaving this kid in your hands as far as Morioka.'

'As long as you're all right with that,' responds the man who claims to be an exam-prep instructor. The Prince can't tell if it's addressed to him or to Nanao, but either way it's more or less meaningless, so he ignores it.

'Are you really leaving me?' he calls out to Nanao's back. Thoughts work at high speed. *Should I let him get off the train? Or should I try to stop him?* His whole plan in going to Morioka was just to check out this Minegishi. Since he had Kimura along for the ride, he thought he would try to use him to test Minegishi, but now Kimura's out of the picture, barely breathing if he's even still alive, playing floor mat for two dead fruits.

So maybe I should use Nanao instead. To do that, he needs to find out how to control Nanao. How to put Nanao's will on a collar and lead. The only thing is, he doesn't have the key to keep the collar locked. With Kimura, the key was his son's life, and the Prince was also able to make good use of Kimura's hatred for him. But he doesn't yet know Nanao's weak spot.

Given how deftly Nanao broke Tangerine's neck, it seems obvious enough that he's not a law-abiding individual, so it isn't hard to imagine that by digging a little the Prince could find some vulnerability to exploit.

Then should I do whatever I can to stop him from getting off? Probably not. That would just make him think I was up to something. I may just have to accept that he's getting off the train. The Prince continues his inner dialogue.

I think I'll just go to Morioka, have a look at Minegishi's compound and head back to Tokyo. I'll deal with Minegishi when I'm fully prepared, he decides. He may have lost Kimura, but he has plenty of other pawns. Best to come back when they're all lined up.

'Could I at least have your phone number?' he asks. It seems like he should hang on to a means of contacting Nanao. *Maybe he can become one of my pawns too.* 'I'm worried about what might happen. If I knew I could call you . . .'

Next to him, Suzuki makes a noise of agreement. 'That's a good idea. I'd like to be able to get in touch when we reach Morioka, to let you know everything is okay.'

Nanao looks flustered, but reflexively takes his phone out. 'We're at the station, I need to get off,' he says agitatedly.

Then the Shinkansen comes to a stop. It lurches forward, then settles back. The movement is more than the Prince expected, and he staggers once.

Nanao staggers much more. He crashes into the wall and drops his phone, which bounces on the floor then skids into the luggage area, right between two large suitcases, like a squirrel that fell from a tree and scurried down a hollow among the roots.

Nanao leaves behind his own suitcase and leaps towards the luggage area to retrieve his phone.

The Shinkansen's doors open.

'Come on, come on,' Nanao sputters, down on one knee and contorting his body to reach between the bags, grasping frantically. He can't reach, so he stands back up and hauls one of the large bags out, then ducks back down and finally scoops up his phone. He stands again, only to bash his head on the luggage rack.

The Prince just stares, amazed. *He is a total mess.*

Hands pressed to his head, Nanao gets to his feet and tucks back in the suitcase he had pulled out. Then he staggers absurdly towards the open door.

It slides shut in front of him, without the least shred of compassion.

Nanao's shoulders slump.

The Prince doesn't know what to say next.

The train eases forward, back into motion.

Hand still gripping the handle of his suitcase, Nanao doesn't look surprised, and not at all embarrassed. 'This sort of thing happens to me all the time. Pretty much standard at this point.'

'Well, what are we doing standing around here? Let's go take a seat,' suggests Suzuki.

After leaving Sendai, the already sparsely populated train is almost empty, so there's no need for them to go back to their original seats. They enter the next car, number eight, and sit down together in the vacant first row. 'I'm too scared to be alone,' the Prince says convincingly, and the two adults believe him. Nanao takes the seat by the window, the Prince sits in the middle, and Suzuki is by the aisle.

The conductor comes by so Suzuki explains they switched seats. The uniformed young man doesn't even ask to check their tickets, just grins and nods and walks on.

Nanao looks glum, and murmurs to himself, 'It's not so bad.'

'What's wrong?'

'Oh, just thinking that compared to my usual bad luck this wasn't such a big deal.'

There's a sad heroism in Nanao's tone, and he's clearly trying to convince himself of what he's saying. *Maybe his luck left him and came to me.* Unable to understand what it's like to be unlucky, the Prince can't find the right words to say.

'Since you're still here, you might as well stay with the boy until we get to Morioka,' Suzuki suggests genially. He sounds like he's encouraging a student who failed an exam, a tone particular to teachers that makes the Prince's skin crawl, but of course he doesn't let that show.

'Yes, please,' he chimes in. 'I'd love it if you could stay with me.'

'I'm going to go and have a look at the green car.' Suzuki gets up with an air of relief that the problem has been solved and he's no longer responsible. This instructor has no idea that there are dangerous men and dead bodies on the Shinkansen, hasn't seen any guns being waved around, which is why he can be so easy-going. *Ignorance is bliss, Mr Suzuki,* thinks the Prince as he watches the man retreat up the aisle.

He turns to Nanao, now that it's just the two of them. 'Thank you so much,' he says, trying to sound as relieved as he can. 'I feel so much better with you here.'

'That's kind of you to say,' Nanao replies with a chuckle. 'If I were you, I wouldn't want to be anywhere near me. All I ever have is bad luck.'

The Prince bites his lip to keep from laughing at the thought of Nanao's slapstick performance in the gangway. 'What do you do for a living, Mr Nanao?' Not that he doesn't have an idea. *Probably in the same line of work as Tangerine and Lemon, helping other people to commit their crimes. Another small thinker.*

'I live on the Shinkansen,' Nanao says, frowning. 'I can't get off at any station. I must be cursed. You saw what happened just now at Ichinoseki. Something like that always happens. I'll be on this train for the next ten years.' Then he seems to become aware of how stupid he sounds. 'Never mind.' After a second, he says, 'Can't you guess what I do? You saw it, before.'

'You not being able to get off the train?'

'No, I'm being serious now. Before then. I do jobs. Dirty work.'

'But you seem like such a good person, Mr Nanao.' He tries to transmit a message to the man: *I'm a defenceless child, you're the only one I can count on, I trust you.* The Prince's first step is to make Nanao feel the urge to protect him.

This man is so bereft of luck, has such low self-esteem, that it should be simple to gain influence over him and rob him of his free will.

'You're confused right now and you don't really know what's going on, but I can tell you for certain I am not a good person. I'm no hero. I kill people.'

You're the one who's confused, the Prince wants to say. *I know exactly what's going on.*

'But you saved me. I feel much safer with you than I do on my own.'

'Well, maybe.' Nanao speaks softly, and though he looks put out he's also blushing.

Once more the Prince has to fight to keep from laughing. *His sense of duty switched on so his thinking switched off. Automatic. Like a middle-aged man grinning at a compliment from a woman. Pathetic.*

He looks out the window. Rice paddies race by; in the distance the mountain ridges inch along.

In no time they're approaching Mizusawa-Esashi. The Prince wonders if Nanao will try to get off again, but he seems to have made up his mind to stay on until Morioka. Or maybe he just doesn't want to make a fool of himself in the gangway when he can't get off again. Whatever the case may be, Nanao doesn't show any reaction to the station announcement.

There's still a chance that Nanao will have a sudden change of heart and burst out of the seat for the exit. But the Shinkansen pulls into Mizusawa-Esashi Station, the doors open, then close, and the train pulls away. Nanao just leans back in his seat, sighs with resignation, and stares into space.

The Shinkansen continues northward.

After a few minutes a phone starts buzzing. The Prince checks his own phone, then addresses Nanao. 'Mr Nanao, is that your phone ringing?'

Nanao comes to with a start and fumbles in his pocket, then shakes his head. 'Not me.'

'Oh –' The Prince realises it's Kimura's phone. He takes it out of the front pocket of his backpack. 'It was that man's from before.'

'From before? Who, the one you were with?'

'His name was Mr Kimura. Hey, it looks like it's from a payphone.' He stares at the screen for a moment, thinking about what to do. There's no reason he can think of that anyone would be calling Kimura from a pay-phone. 'Should I answer it?'

Nanao just shakes his head. 'None of my decisions ever lead anywhere good. You need to decide for yourself. But if you do answer, you probably don't need to go into the gangway. There's barely anyone else in the car.'

The Prince nods and answers the phone. 'Yuichi, is that you?' asks the voice on the line. *Kimura's mother,* guesses the Prince. He feels a rush of elation. She must have heard about his earlier phone call from her hus-band and been beside herself with worry. No doubt she was imagining all the awful things that could have befallen her son and grandson, her anx-iety multiplying until she couldn't stand it any more and picked up the phone. There's no fear quite as delightful to him as that of a parent for their child. She must have been so racked with fear that it took her longer than he'd have expected to call.

'Oh, he's not here,' answers the Prince. Then he starts working out the best way to fan the flames of her anguish.

'And where are you right now?'

'I'm still on the Shinkansen. The Hayate.'

'I know that. I mean what number car?'

'Even if I told you, what good would that do?'

'We thought we'd come and see you. My husband and I.'

The Prince notices for the first time that Kimura's mother sounds unusually calm. Stable, like a mighty tree with roots dug deep.

The door behind him opens.

He turns, phone still pressed up against his ear, just as a man walks in.

Medium height and build, white hair and a deep-green-coloured jacket. Thick brows shade his narrow eyes, which are hard and piercing.

The Prince cranes his neck awkwardly to get a better look at the man standing over his shoulder. A smile spreads across the man's face. 'So you really are a schoolboy.'

NANAO

HE LOOKS LIKE A HAPPY retiree, ruddy-cheeked and easy-going, and
he steps up to the row in front of where Nanao and the kid sit. Then the
man stomps on the lever and roughly swivels the seats around.

Now the two rows of three-seaters are facing one another. The man sits
opposite them, a look of challenge on his face. It all happens too quickly
for Nanao to protest. Before he can process it, there they all are, like three
generations on a family trip.

The door behind them slides open again and a woman appears, also
past retirement age. 'Ah, here you are.' She sits down next to the man,
facing them, as if it's the most natural thing in the world. 'I found you
much more quickly than I thought I would, dear.' Then she looks over
Nanao and the schoolkid as if she's inspecting the merchandise.

Thrown off by the sudden arrival of this strange couple it takes Nanao
several moments before he manages to open his mouth. 'Um –'

'You know,' the woman cuts him off, 'it's my first time using the payphone in the Shinkansen, but I didn't see any phone wires. How do you
think it connects the call?'

'Who knows, maybe through the electric line on the track.'

'We should really get mobile phones. It would make things so much easier.'

'I'm just glad that Yuichi's phone can receive calls from the on-board payphone. I hear there are some service providers that don't let you.'

'Is that right?' The woman directs the question to Nanao. *How should I know?* he wonders.

'Excuse me, grandpa, grandma, but what are you . . .' The kid trails off. He looks nervous.

It's true they're an older couple, but they don't look at all diminished by age, certainly not enough to be called grandpa and grandma. *Maybe for a schoolkid there's nothing else it makes sense to call them,* Nanao muses dazedly, but then the man speaks up.

'You know exactly what you're doing, don't you?'

'Wha –' The kid sounds startled.

'You're treating us like useless old-timers on purpose. You didn't just randomly call us grandpa and grandma. Am I wrong?'

'Now, dear, don't frighten the boy,' the woman says lightly. 'This is why people have no patience for older folks.'

'This one's no cute little boy. He chooses his words very carefully. And he stinks.'

'I stink?' The kid makes a sulky face. 'That's not a nice thing to say, when we're just meeting for the first time. I didn't mean anything bad by calling you grandpa.'

'We may be meeting in person for the first time, but you know me. I'm Kimura. You called me just a little while ago.' The man grins. His voice is mild, but his eyes are piercing. 'What you said on the phone worried me, so we rushed over to catch the train at Mizusawa-Esashi.'

The kid opens his mouth in an *aah* of recognition, like he's putting the pieces together. 'You must be Mr Kimura's parents.'

'I guess you could say we're a little overprotective, to come rushing when our son is in a scrape. Where is Yuichi, anyway?'

Nanao puts the pieces together too. *Yuichi Kimura is the man this kid was with, the man on the floor in the toilet. But why would the kid have called Kimura's father?*

'You said it to me yourself, on the phone. Yuichi is in trouble, and my grandson Wataru is in danger too.'

'Oh, that was just —' The kid falls silent. His lips seem to be squirming.

'You said, You and your wife must be relaxing, I probably shouldn't have called. Remember?'

'That was just —' He looks at his lap. 'They made me say that. Mr Kimura threatened me. Him and another man.'

What other man? As Nanao sits listening, he takes in the kid's profile. Well-proportioned face, perfect nose, beautifully shaped head. It's like looking at an elegant piece of pottery. A memory wells up, of a rich classmate telling him that he should try to become a footballer or a criminal if he ever wanted to escape poverty. That classmate had the same type of pristine looks. *Guess the lucky ones even look the part.*

'He's just an ordinary schoolkid, who got wrapped up in a dangerous situation. You don't need to be so hard on him.' Nanao intervenes before he can stop himself.

'Just an ordinary schoolkid, huh?' The man looks at Nanao. His face is wrinkled and dry. But there's an undeniable dignity there, like a great tree standing firm even as its bark is peeling off, with a thick trunk that the fiercest of winds can't shake. 'I don't think he's just an ordinary schoolkid.'

As the words leave the man's mouth his hand darts into his jacket.

Nanao reacts, a purely automatic motion. He whips the gun out of the back of his belt, at the same instant the man draws his gun and aims it at the kid.

They're all sitting so close that both the kid and the man have guns inches from their faces. The whole scene feels surreal to Nanao. Usually when people have their seats facing like this it's so they can chat and play cards. Yet here they are with two guns drawn.

The man wags the gun at the kid's nose. 'If you tell us the truth you might still get out of this alive, my young friend.'

'Dear, if you don't take that out of his face he won't be able to tell you anything even if he wants to,' says the woman soothingly. She seems entirely relaxed.

'Come on, this is crazy.' Nanao doesn't like how quickly things have escalated. 'If you don't put your gun away, I'll shoot.'

The man looks at Nanao's gun as if he's noticing it for the first time. 'Give me a break. That thing's not even loaded.'

Nanao's mouth clamps shut. It's true, the magazine is in the trash. *But how did he know that?* It doesn't seem like something someone could tell with a mere glance. 'What are you talking about, of course it's loaded.'

'Okay, then give it a go. I'll shoot too.'

Nanao is embarrassed at being treated like an amateur, but now isn't the time to worry about ego. He slowly puts the empty gun back in his belt, keeping his eyes on the man.

'Do you even have tickets? The Shinkansen is all reserved seating, you know.' The kid's voice is level.

'Don't give me any of your crap. Anyway, all the tickets were sold out.'

'Sold out?' Nanao looks around the nearly empty car. 'But there's basically no one here.'

'I know, it's very strange. Maybe a group tour cancelled at the last minute. It doesn't matter. It's not like the conductor's going to kick us off. So. Where is Yuichi? What happened to him? And what's happening with Wataru?'

'I don't really know,' the kid says darkly. 'All I know is that if I don't make it to Morioka, something bad will happen to Wataru, there in the hospital.'

Nanao stares at the kid's profile again. Based on what he's hearing now, the little boy the kid said would be in danger if he didn't reach Morioka must be the couple's grandson. The connection between the couple and the schoolkid still isn't clear.

But there's something that he wants to know even more: *Who the hell are these two?* A closer look makes him think that the woman also has a weapon under her jacket. *Granny with a gun?* They both seem so in control of themselves that it's hard to imagine they're ordinary citizens. *No, they're professionals. I've never heard about professionals this old.*

Nanao doesn't know what he's fallen into, but it's more than obvious that the man thinks the kid is his enemy. *Doesn't make sense. Nothing on this whole trip has made any sense, and this least of all. A couple of retirees with guns, interrogating a school student.*

Just then a phone starts vibrating with an incoming call. It buzzes merrily, like it's poking fun at the four people sitting there.

They all sit there, holding their breath, listening. Everything else around them seems to go quiet.

Nanao feels for his phone over his trouser pocket, but his isn't the one buzzing.

Oh, says the kid, shifting his backpack onto his lap and opening the zip. 'That's my phone.'

'Don't move.' The man jabs at him with the muzzle of the gun. They're so close that it looks more like he's threatening the kid with a knife.

'But my phone –'

'Stay still and forget about it.'

Under their words Nanao can hear the buzzing. He counts, three times, four. 'You know I really should answer this.'

'What's wrong with him just answering the phone?' Nanao has no real reason for saying this. It's more like the feeling a parent has when they want to cover for their child who's broken a school rule.

'No way.' The man is unyielding. 'I don't like this one. He says he's just answering the phone, but he's up to something.'

'Really, dear, what could he possibly be up to?' The woman is as sunny as ever.

'I don't know exactly. But what I do know is that when you're up against a smart guy, you can't let them do anything they want to. Absolutely never. Doesn't matter how small a thing it is, they'll be up to something

369

that we can't see. One time I was facing down a guy who ran a ramen shop. I had my gun on him. And not because the ramen was bad. I was telling him to hand over something, some important package, I forget what it was. Suddenly the phone in the shop starts ringing. The ramen guy said if he didn't pick up someone might think something was wrong. I thought he had a point, so I played nice and let him answer. Don't say anything funny, I told him. He picks up and starts taking some orders, miso ramen, chashu ramen, like someone's calling for delivery. But what I didn't know was it was a code. Not five minutes later the reinforcements showed up, a bunch of bad characters. We had a shootout in that tiny little ramen shop. Of course I survived, but it was a real pain in the ass. Or there was another time when I was in some office somewhere leaning on the boss. The phone rang and I was nice enough to let him answer. The second he did, *bang!* So what does all this tell us?'

'That thirty years ago we didn't have mobile phones,' says the woman sarcastically.

She's obviously heard these stories countless times.

'No, it tells us that in situations like these it's never good when a call comes in.'

'Or at least it wasn't thirty years ago,' she chortles.

'It's true today too.'

Nanao looks towards the schoolkid. The backpack is now on the seat between them, open. The kid seems to be thinking about something, concentrating. Doubt creeps into Nanao's mind. The juvenile fear the kid had emanated when he was begging for help has evaporated. Now his calmness, so steady even with a gun on him, seems strange. Before, Nanao had chalked it up to shock, but the kid seems just fine now.

Then something catches Nanao's eye. In the open backpack he can see something peeking out that looks like the grip of a gun. *A gun? Why does a schoolkid have a gun? Did he put it in there?* No answers come to him. The only thing that's certain is that there's a gun in the backpack.

And, Nanao thinks, trying to look natural, *I can use that.*

Nanao's own gun isn't loaded. The man knows that. Which means he's under the impression that Nanao is unarmed. He wouldn't be expecting Nanao to pull a gun out of the backpack. The couple and the kid are both dangerous. Anything could happen, and if he isn't careful he could end up hurt, or worse. *If I get the gun, I can get control of the situation.*

He starts to focus, watching for his chance to snatch the gun. If he makes a mistake he'll be shot for certain.

The phone stops buzzing.

'Oh. Whoever was calling gave up.' The kid lowers his face.

'If it was important they'll call back,' the man snaps.

There's a small pulsing of air, a staccato exhalation through the nose. Nanao glances at the kid and then double-takes: his head is down, he's biting his lips, unable to contain his laughter.

THE PRINCE

HIS WHOLE BODY TREMBLES WITH the laugh he's trying to fight down, a laughter welling up from the deepest parts of him, which he can't completely hide. *This old man is the same as all the rest,* he gloats. *Acting so tough, making such a big deal of how much more experienced he is than me, like this is the easiest thing in the world for him, but in the end he's just another victim of overconfidence, too blind to see the pitfall even after he's stumbled in.*

The missed call was almost definitely the man at the hospital in Tokyo. He must have had a question, or maybe the reality of what he was doing started to set in and he got fidgety, or maybe he was just tired of waiting.

They had set it so that if the phone rang more than ten times and the Prince didn't answer, the man should go ahead with the job. And just now it had rung far more than ten times without the Prince answering.

He doesn't know for sure if the man will be bold enough to go through with it, but judging from his lucky life so far right about now the man will be on his way to Wataru Kimura's room with murderous intent. The Prince is used to people and animals behaving exactly as he wants them to.

This is your fault, he wants so badly to tell the man in front of him. *You thought threatening me with a gun would give you the advantage but all it did was cost your precious grandson his life.* He almost feels sorry for the old man, feels a giddy urge to console him. At the same time he's begun calculating how to make use of this development. If he does it right he can even control this old couple. First he'll share with them news of their tragedy then feast on the sight of the man blindsided by anguish and the woman blank with shock, and after that he'll play on their guilt, rob them of their powers of decision-making, place their hearts in chains. *I'll just do what I always do.*

But not yet. It's easy to picture what would happen if he told them their grandson was in grave danger: the man would go berserk and wave his gun around, probably call the hospital and entreat them to save the boy. This particular information needed to be kept hidden for a little while longer.

'Hey,' says the man. 'Talk. Or I'll shoot you before you ever get to Morioka.'

'Why?' blurts Nanao. 'Why are you so set on shooting him?'

'Really, I swear, I don't know what's going on!' The Prince rides on Nanao's momentum and returns to being a panicked schoolboy.

'Do you really think this child is lying, dear? It doesn't look that way to me.' The woman's face reminds him for a moment of his own departed grandmother. There's a breath of nostalgia, but no affection. More than anything he feels reassured she'll be easy to manipulate. Old people can't help but smile at children and treat them indulgently. It's not a question of human morality or duty, it's pure animal instinct. Creatures of the same species must protect the newer lives among them. They're designed that way. 'But where *is* Yuichi? Did he get off at Sendai? Is that why he can't come to the phone any more?'

'I'm telling you, this kid stinks.' The man leans back in his seat and thrusts his chin at the Prince. But he also puts the gun away in the vest under his jacket. He hasn't let down his guard, but he feels a bit less aggressive. 'Either way. Let's check on Wataru. I asked Shigeru to look in on him but the whole thing was so rushed I can't be sure if he's on top of it.'

'Shigeru *is* somewhat careless,' laughs the woman.

They sent someone to the hospital?

'Shall I go to the payphone and give him a call?'

This is bad, thinks the Prince. *I need to buy some time.*

Then Nanao asks, 'Is your grandson sick?' The Prince is grateful for Nanao's question.

Now they'll waste time talking. *Because I'm so lucky.*

'He fell off the roof of a department store. He's been in a coma in the hospital since.' The man's answer is blunt, maybe so that he won't let his emotion show.

The Prince brings his fingertips to his mouth. 'Oh no, really?' He makes a shocked face, like it's the first time he's hearing about it. 'From the roof? He must have been so scared!'

But inwardly he's grinning ear to ear. He remembers the uncomprehending terror on the little boy's face, that moment he shoved him out into space.

The man continues, his voice husky. 'Wataru being in a coma is like when the goddess Amaterasu hid her light away in the cave. The whole world is dark. We need all the other gods to dance and laugh and call Wataru back. Otherwise this awful darkness will never leave.'

The Prince strains to keep his laughter in. *You're the only ones in the dark. The rest of the world is just fine. It really doesn't matter if your grandson lives or dies.*

'What do the doctors say?' asks Nanao.

'They're doing everything they can, but there's not much you can do really. They say he could wake up any time, or he might never wake up.'

'You must be so worried,' says Nanao softly.

The man gives a warm smile. 'Whereas you, young man, you don't smell at all. I'm almost shocked, I don't get any bad intent off you. But from the way you pulled out that gun, I'd guess you're in the same line of work as us. So what gives? It's not that you feel fresh because you're new to this, since I wouldn't say that you are.'

'No, I've been doing this for a little while now.' Nanao smiles ironically.

'I just have terrible luck. So when I hear about the bad things happening to people it's easy for me to imagine how they feel.'

'Um, there's something I've been wondering for a while,' says the Prince, hoping to keep them talking, instead of making a phone call.

'And what's that?' The man gives him a look both dubious and irritated.

'I wonder if we know the answer to his question,' muses the woman.

'Why is it wrong to kill people?' Same question as always. The question that always shocks grown-ups, that they try to swat away with platitudes, that they can never answer.

'Oh —' Nanao makes a sudden noise. The Prince turns, thinking maybe he's about to try telling him why, but he sees that Nanao is looking towards the front of the train. '— here comes Mr Suzuki.'

Sure enough, Suzuki the exam-prep instructor is making his way down the aisle.

'Who's he?' The man draws his gun again and points it at Nanao.

'Just someone I met on board. We're not friends or anything, we just talked a few times. He's a civilian. He doesn't know that I have a gun. He's just a teacher at an exam-prep school. He was worried about the kid and was sitting with us,' Nanao explains quickly. 'That's why he's coming this way.'

'I wouldn't trust him,' says the man. 'You sure he's not a professional?' He squeezes the grip of the gun.

'If you think he is, then shoot him when he comes over here,' Nanao says firmly. 'But you'll be sorry you did. Mr Suzuki's a good, honest man.'

The woman leans out into the aisle and props her hand on the armrest so she can turn round to get a look. She turns back after only a moment. 'As far as I can tell he's just an ordinary man. He doesn't look like he's up to anything, and he obviously isn't armed. The only mischief he might have been up to was seeing what it felt like to sit in the green car, and now he's back.'

'You think so?' asks the man.

'You're exactly right, ma'am.' Nanao nods his head earnestly.

The man puts his hand inside his jacket pocket, still gripping the gun and aiming it at Nanao through the fabric. 'If anything feels off, I'll shoot.'

Then Suzuki steps up to them. 'Well, it certainly has got lively over here. And who are these people?'

The woman's eyes crinkle into a smile. 'We got on at the last station, and we just thought it would be so lonesome, just the two of us old folks in an empty train, and these two young men were kind enough to let us sit with them.' She spools off the made-up story, cool as a cucumber.

'Ah, I see,' nods Suzuki. 'Isn't this nice!'

'He said you're a schoolteacher?' The man's voice is low and his eyes are sharp. He doesn't blink once.

'At an exam-preparation school. I suppose you could call me a teacher.'

'Well, that's just what we need. Have a seat. Next to granny.' He motions Suzuki to the aisle seat, facing Nanao and the Prince. Suzuki follows along, and as soon as he's seated the man continues. 'This kid just asked a heavy question.' He already seems to have cleared Suzuki of any suspicion, though he may just be keeping an eye out for the right moment to start shooting.

'And what is that?' Suzuki widens his eyes inquisitively.

'He wants to know why it's wrong to kill people. You're a teacher, what do you have to say to that? Go on.'

Suzuki looks startled at being put on the spot. Then he turns to the Prince. 'That's what you want to know?' His brows knit with concern, or sadness.

The Prince stops himself from rolling his eyes. Almost everyone he asks gets that same expression. Or else their cheeks turn red from indignation. 'I'm just curious,' he answers.

Suzuki inhales deeply and lets it out over several seconds, as if to settle himself. He doesn't look worked up, just forlorn. 'I'm not quite sure how to answer that.'

'It's hard to answer, isn't it?'

'Well, it's more that I'm not sure what it is you really want to know.' Suzuki's face is taking on a more and more teacherly cast, which the Prince finds distasteful. 'First,' he says, 'I'll give you my personal opinion.'

Is there even such thing as an opinion that isn't personal?

'If you were going to kill someone, I would want to stop you from doing it. And the other way round, if someone was trying to kill you, I'd want to stop them too.'

'Why?'

'Because when someone is killed, or when someone attacks another person even without killing them, it's heartbreaking,' says Suzuki. 'It's a sad, hopeless thing. I'd rather it never happened.'

This Prince has absolutely no interest in hearing anything like this. 'I understand what you're trying to say, and I feel the same way,' he lies. 'But what I want to know isn't an ethical reason like that. If there was someone who didn't feel that way, wouldn't they be okay with murder? There's such a thing as war, and the death penalty, but none of the grown-ups think there's anything wrong with those.'

'True enough.' Suzuki nods, as if he had been expecting the Prince to say that. 'Like I said, that was my own personal feeling on the matter. But that's what matters most. I believe people should never kill other people, under any circumstances. Dying is the saddest thing there is. But that's not the kind of answer you're looking for. So,' he continues, his voice suddenly kind, 'there's something I'd like to ask you.'

'What's that?'

'What would you do if I peed on you right now?'

The Prince was not expecting anything so juvenile. 'What?'

'What would you do if I forced you to take off all your clothes?'

'Is that the sort of thing you're into?'

'No, no. But think about it. It's wrong to pee in the train car. It's wrong to force someone to strip. You shouldn't gossip. You shouldn't smoke. Don't get on the Shinkansen without buying a ticket. You need to pay money if you want to drink a carton of juice.'

'What are you talking about?'

'I'd like to beat you up right now. Would that be all right?'

'Are you serious?'

'What if I were?'

'I wouldn't want you to.'

'Why not?'

The Prince weighs his answer. *Should I tell him it's because I don't want him to, or that he should feel free to go ahead and beat me up?*

'Life is full of rules and prohibitions.' Suzuki shrugs. 'Rules about everything. If you were by yourself all the time, there wouldn't be any problem, but as soon as someone else enters the picture, all sorts of rules spring into existence. We're surrounded at all times by infinite rules with no clear basis. Sometimes it feels like we're barely allowed to do anything. So that's why I think it's strange that out of all the rules you ask about, you're most interested in why it's wrong to kill people. I hear it from other kids, too. You could be asking why it's wrong to punch people, why you can't just show up at anyone's house and sleep there, or why you're not allowed to build a campfire in the school playground. Or why it's wrong to insult people. There are plenty of rules that make far less sense than the prohibition on murder. That's why every time I hear someone your age ask why it's wrong to kill people, I get the sense that they're just taking it to the extreme, to make the adults feel uncomfortable. Sorry, that's just what it seems like.'

'But I really do want to know why.'

'Like I said, life is full of rules, endless rules. Now, there are plenty of rules that even if you break them you can still make up for it. Say I stole your wallet, I could just give it back, or if I spilled something on your clothes, even if they were completely ruined I could still buy you new clothes. It might put a strain on our relationship, but things can more or less go back to the way they were. When someone dies, though, you can never take that back.'

The Prince snorts, and is about to ask if that's because a human life is a beautiful thing, but before he can say it Suzuki continues. 'And I'm not saying this because there's anything particularly beautiful about human life. But think of it this way. What if you were to burn the only existing copy of a manga? Once it's gone, you can never get it back. I don't think human lives and manga have the same value, but as an objective comparison you could say they're similar for that reason. So when you ask why it's wrong to kill people, you might as well ask why it's wrong to burn a super-rare manga.'

'This is one talkative teacher,' laughs the old man.

Far from being excited, the more Suzuki talks the calmer he becomes, making the Prince feel like there's something slightly off about him.

'And now that I've said all of that, I'll give you my conclusion.' Suzuki sounds like he's telling his students that this will be on the test, and they should listen up if they want the answer.

'Yes?'

'If people were allowed to commit murder, the state couldn't function.'

'The state?' The Prince scowls at this, worried that the answer will degenerate into abstraction.

'If people knew that they might be killed by someone tomorrow, economic activity would grind to a halt. To begin with, there's no economy without stable rights of ownership. I'm sure you can agree with that. If there was no guarantee that the thing you bought would belong to you, then no one would have any use for money. Having money would cease to mean anything. And then we consider a person's life, which is the most important thing they possess. If we look at it that way, then for economic activity to function properly there would have to be protection for people's lives, or at least the pretence of protection. Which is why the state puts into place rules and prohibitions, one of which is the prohibition on murder. It's just one of the many important rules. With that in mind, it makes perfect sense why wars and the death penalty are allowed. Because they serve the needs of the state. The only things that are allowed are the things the state sanctions. Which has nothing to do with ethics.'

The Shinkansen pulls into Shin-Hanamaki Station.

It stays there beside the platform for a minute, as if it were catching its breath. Then it starts off again, and the landscape resumes its flow.

NANAO

NANAO LISTENS WITH GREAT INTEREST to what Suzuki is saying. There's something refreshing about seeing the exam-prep instructor holding forth to the schoolkid so dispassionately.

'And some countries, far away maybe, might say that it's fine to kill someone. I can't say for sure, but it could be that somewhere in the world there's a country or a community where murder is allowed. The prohibition on murder all comes down to state agenda. So if you were to go to a country like that, you'd be free to kill people, and people would be free to kill you.'

It isn't the first time Nanao's heard this sort of argument, but Suzuki's methodical way of laying out his thoughts makes it easy to listen. Nanao has killed, many more times than just once, and listening to a lengthy discourse about the reasoning behind the prohibition on murder isn't about to make him search his soul or change his ways, but he likes Suzuki's delivery, both gentle and resolute.

'If you're looking for reasons why murder isn't allowed that aren't ethical in nature, then the only possible explanations are legal. So looking for an explanation besides the law is sort of sneaky, like asking why we have to eat vegetables besides the fact that they're full of nutrients.' Suzuki exhales for a moment. 'But here I'd like to say again what I said first, that I just think it's wrong to kill people. For me, laws and state agenda have nothing to do with it. When someone disappears from this world, when their self vanishes, it's both terrifying and tragic.'

'When you say that, do you by any chance have someone particular in mind?' asks the old man.

'Yes, I was wondering the same thing,' says the woman.

'My wife died, though it was a long time ago now.' Suzuki looks away. This must be the reason why Nanao could never detect any light in his eyes. 'Actually, she was murdered.'

'Oh no.' The woman's eyes widen.

Nanao is just as surprised.

'What happened to whoever killed her?' the old man wants to know, evidently ready to step in and take revenge.

'He's dead. They're all dead, and that's that.' Suzuki still sounds calm. 'When I think about why it all happened, why my wife is gone, I still don't understand it. The whole thing feels like a dream. The light just wouldn't change, and by the time I started wondering when it would turn green, there I was, on the platform.'

'What does that mean?' The old man laughs gruffly. 'Some kind of hallucination?'

'I always thought that Tokyo Station was the end of the line, I never expected a train would keep going through without stopping . . .'

Suzuki's voice gets softer and softer, he keeps saying things that don't make sense, and there's a sudden desperate look in his eyes, like he's been sucked into a nightmare from long ago and can't find his way out. All at once he shakes his head and seems to come back to himself.

'Whenever I start thinking about my wife it's like I've fallen into a dark, cramped hole. Or I picture her wandering lost in a pitch-black desert. She's all alone, unable to cry out or hear me calling to her, blind and scared and wandering forever, and there's nothing I can do to save her. I can't find her. If I'm not careful I sometimes feel like I might even forget about her. There by herself in the dark, with nothing but a bottomless sadness.'

'You're losing me a little,' says the old man. 'But I can tell you're a good guy. It's decided, we're going to send Wataru to study with you.' He's only half joking. 'Let me have your card.'

Suzuki reaches into his suit jacket obligingly, then laughs. 'Oh, I left my things at my seat. All the sweets I bought!' Once more he seems like a carefree university student. 'I have to go and get them before we arrive at Morioka.' He stands. 'I'm visiting my wife's parents for the first time since she died. It's taken me a long time until I was ready to see them.'

'Is that right? Well then, you'd better go and pay your respects!' The man's voice is rough, but he also sounds pleased to hear about the reunion.

Suzuki departs towards the rear of the train. 'Well, are you satisfied?' The man looks at the kid. 'Was his answer good enough for you? If you ask me, whether to kill or not kill is up to everyone to decide for themselves, so I can't say I'm fully on board with what our teacher friend was saying. But he did have some good points. So what do you think?'

Something intense flashes in the kid's eyes. Nanao tries to identify what it might be, if the kid is angry or impressed, but before he can pin it down the kid's expression returns to normal, and the tension is gone, like air being let out of a balloon.

'No, I didn't think it was a very helpful answer. I was disappointed.' The tension may be gone, but his voice is definitely barbed.

'Oh, look, he's upset. Well, that's just fine with me. I'm getting tired of his snotty attitude, like he sees through everything.' The man's voice rings out loud and clear, and he has his gun back out. 'Hey, Mr School-boy. I'll tell you something.'

'What?'

'That question you asked. When I was your age, I used to ask the same thing.'

The woman next to him laughs through puckered lips, gently whistling.

'You think you're so clever, but everyone asks that when they're young and dumb, why is it wrong to kill people? to try and get a rise out of the adults. Kids ask, if we're all going to die anyway, what's the point of living? and they think they're so philosophical, like they're the only ones who have ever had that thought. It's like you're bragging to us about having the measles. We all got over it a long time ago.'

'I agree,' says the woman. 'I don't like children who brag about not crying at movies, because no one cries at movies when they're young. People don't start getting weepy over nothing until they're older. I never cried at the movies when I was young, no one does. If someone wants to brag about not crying, they should do it when they're old. Oh, I'm sorry, I didn't mean to start sermonising.' She makes a show of putting her fingers to her lips, then zipping them shut with a smile.

Her gesture reminds Nanao of the zip on the backpack, and his eyes drop down to find it still open. The gun's right there.

I really should take that. Wait for the right moment – He focuses.

But just then the Prince bows his head and says in a delicate voice, 'Grandma, grandpa, I'm sorry.'

THE PRINCE

HE FEELS ANGRY, AND THIS makes him even angrier. Suzuki wasn't talking down to the Prince, but his answer felt somehow like a parable, and it produced an unexpected recoil that was almost biological. Like seeing an insect with a swarm of legs, or a plant of a particularly garish hue.

And hearing the couple go on and on about how their years of experience make them so much wiser is irritating him to no end.

He takes a deep breath to cool his head and subdue his anger, and then he does it. 'I'm sorry. But I think it's too late for your grandson.'

It's finally time for the reveal. The man and the woman are both completely motionless. *As soon as I mention your grandson, you're ready to fall apart. And you thought you were so strong.*

'That call that came in earlier. I needed to answer it.'

'What are you talking about?' The man's face twists and darkens. Not because he's trying to look fierce, but because he's trying to fight down his agonised concern, the Prince knows.

'That's what I was told. Make sure you answer the phone, they said.

384

Otherwise the boy in the hospital dies. I needed to answer before it rang ten times.'

The man is silent. The only sound is the rattling of the Shinkansen.

'But you wouldn't let me answer.' The Prince makes his voice docile and his shoulders tremble ever so slightly. *I hope you're satisfied*, is what he would love to say. *You acted like you were so smart but you couldn't even protect your grandson. I beat you and I'm just a schoolkid.*

'Is this true?' The man is quiet. *Now he's starting to think this isn't just a game. He's sitting there, helpless, waiting to hear what I'll say.* The Prince feels a surge of physical pleasure, running right up his spine.

'It's true. If only I had answered . . .'

'Dear.' The woman looks shaken for the first time. Doubt has finally sprouted up from under her tough skin.

'What?'

'Let's try calling.' She starts to stand.

'Good idea,' says the Prince. It's a safe bet that by now the deed is done. 'Do you want to use my phone? Oh, but I'm not supposed to move,' he says snarkily, looking right at the man.

The man's face hardens. Before he was cautious of the Prince touching the phone, but now his body is screaming the opposite. Give me your phone, it wails. *This feels good,* thinks the Prince. *A good first step.* Next, to firm up his dominance in the power dynamic.

He's about to take his phone out of his backpack when he senses Nanao's eyes on him, on the bag. He knows why immediately.

The gun. Nanao wants the gun.

The Prince's heart does a little leap.

He got the gun in the backpack from Tangerine, and it's no ordinary gun. It's rigged to explode when someone pulls the trigger, injuring them in the process. An exploding booby-trap gun. And Nanao doesn't know that, which is why he wants to use it.

I should let him, thinks the Prince with glee.

He doesn't know exactly what will happen if the thing explodes. But he can guess that both Nanao and the man sitting right in front of him will be hurt by the blast. Even if it isn't fatal, it will certainly slow them down.

The scene will sink into chaos.

And when it does, the Prince will find a way to slip off. *That's exactly how it'll go.*

Of course he can't say for certain that he won't be harmed, but he thinks the chances are low. He should be fine as long as he jumps for the aisle the moment Nanao aims the gun. More than anything he has faith in his luck to pull him through. *Whenever anything like this happens, I always make it out safely.*

A pleasant melody starts to play on the speaker system, followed by an announcement: in five minutes, the train will be arriving at Morioka.

That's when it all happens, one thing after another.

First, at the other end of the car, a child calls out in an excited voice, 'Grandpa!' The little boy was only calling out to his own grandfather, but the old couple both start at the sound of the young voice. Because of the way their seats are facing they hear the child's voice coming from behind them. They seem to be hearing their own grandson calling out to them. Their attention is drawn backwards, and the woman leans out into the aisle to turn round and look.

That's when Nanao makes his move. He grasps the backpack with his left hand and darts his right hand inside.

The Prince has a thrill of ecstasy at his luck, that the little boy would distract the couple so Nanao could grab for the gun. *He'll grab it and aim it and pull the trigger and then they'll be done for.* The Prince shoots up out of his seat.

But there's no explosion.

Halfway into the aisle, he turns round. Nanao didn't pull out the gun.

Not only that, but he's just sitting there staring at the hand he withdrew from the bag, not moving a muscle, like his power was cut.

Only when the Prince looks at Nanao's arm does he grasp what's happened, and the sight startles him so much that he skips backwards.

The old man is frozen too, still holding his gun, eyes wide as plates. The woman's mouth hangs open.

Nanao's arm is bizarrely swollen, like the veins have inflated.

That's what it looked like at first. But that's not it.

There's a snake wrapped around his arm.

'What's a snake,' sputters the man with the gun, then he guffaws, 'what's a snake doing *here*?'

'My goodness,' the woman says, astonished.

Nanao shrieks, but his body is still paralysed.

'What is going on here?' The old man can't stop laughing.

'It's got you all wrapped up, young man. You really *are* unlucky!' The woman makes a courteous effort to suppress her laughter, but it's too much for her to contain and she begins clucking heartily.

'When did that thing get in there?' Nanao's voice and arm tremble in concert. 'It wasn't in there before! I knew it would show up again, but why right now?'

The Prince just stares. He can barely believe this is happening.

Nanao starts shaking his arm and squealing, 'It won't come off,' like a frantic little boy. 'Try splashing it with some water,' suggests the woman, and Nanao leaps past the Prince like a man on a mission, through the door and off into the gangway.

The woman is still laughing, and next to her the man grins. 'Outstanding,' he repeats several times. 'What is a snake doing on the Shinkansen? I don't believe it. You were right, that is one unlucky fellow.'

Confusion assails the Prince. *What is happening? Why would there be a snake here, now?* It was completely unforeseen. He feels a churn of rage, but also dread, fear that his good luck has been seized between the jaws of some shadowy beast of misfortune, that it's being ripped to pieces.

Then he hears a buoyant laughing, coming from the old man.

Thinking the man must be cracking up again about the whole snake episode, the Prince looks at him. He's peering upward, near the ceiling, teeth bared in a broad smile. Staring at a point over the Prince's head. 'There he is.'

The woman looks up in the same direction and adds her smile to his. 'Oh, yes, it's him!'

What are they talking about? The Prince follows their gaze, craning his neck up and round. He anticipates seeing someone entering the car, the exam-prep instructor, or Nanao, but there's no one. It's not clear where he should be looking. His eyes dart left and right. He turns back to them, but they're still staring in the same direction. The Prince turns round again.

That's when he notices the digital ticker on the wall over the door.

Text slides by: Shigeru to Shigeru. Wataru is safe. Intruder is dead.

MORNING GLORY

| 1 | 2 | 3 | 4 | 5 | 6 | 7 | 8 | 9 | 10 |

THE INSECT CLIMBS THE LONG dandelion stalk like a spiral staircase, front to back, back around to front, winding its way upward. It toils faithfully, like it has an important delivery to make, a payload of good fortune.

Hey, Morning Glory, are you listening to me? The voice of the go-between sounds from the phone. Where are you?

Beside a dandelion and a ladybird, answers Morning Glory. He's thinking about some children he encountered on one of his jobs, who loved to collect insect trading cards. They must all be teenagers by now. Time goes by so fast. He alone stays still, removed from the rushing flow, possibly because he's clinging on to a boulder in the current, but for whatever reason, he can't move forward. He's all alone.

A dandelion and a ladybird? Is that a code or something?

No code. I really am standing beside a dandelion and a ladybird. In front of the hospital you told me to come to. I can see the main entrance. Where are you? he asks.

Morning Glory has an unconscious urge, his hand reaches down to the dandelion and plucks off the yellow head with a satisfying pop.

I'm near the patient rooms. My friend asked me to go to one specific room, which I did, and I was just in time, because a man in a white coat came along.

You were supposed to be waiting for a man in a white coat?

No, the go-between answers. He just asked me to go to his grandson's hospital room and check up on the boy. Just as I was getting there, I spotted a man in a white coat coming. I hid under the bed. It wasn't easy, there were all those cords and plugs and wires tangled up down there, and you know, my body being the size it is, but I managed to hide in time. Then the man in the white coat came in and started pushing buttons on the life-support machine.

There's nothing out of the ordinary about a man in a white coat operating a medical device. What makes you suspect him?

I could see his shoes from under the bed. They were dirty. Stained with mud. Something didn't seem right about a medical professional wearing shoes like that.

You should quit your job as a go-between and do the Holmes thing.

So I jumped out and asked what he was doing.

You, jumped out from under the bed? With that body?

It's an expression. Okay, no, I wriggled and crawled and somehow made it out from under the bed.

He must have been surprised.

He was so surprised he ran away. Ran down the hall and jumped into the lift.

That is suspicious. And where are you now?

Morning Glory gets the feeling he's been asking that for some time.

I'm still waiting for the lift. They take forever in this hospital.

I see. Morning Glory looks back down at the ladybird. It's reached the top of the stalk.

Naturally it has no idea that until a minute ago there was a small yellow flower there. It waits for the right moment to take off into the air.

Tentomushi in Japanese, but in English it's called a ladybird, or a ladybug, and sometimes, rarely, ladybeetle. Somebody once told him that the lady in the name was the Virgin Mary. He can't remember who he heard it from. There's the memory of someone whispering it in his ear, and there's the memory of reading it in a picture book. There's also a memory of his teacher writing it on the board when he was young, and there's the memory of hearing it from one of his clients. All these recollections are equally vivid, which is to say, they're all equally hazy, and he has no way of knowing which is real. All of Morning Glory's memories are that way.

Bearing the seven sorrows of Mother Mary into the sky. That's why it's called the ladybird.

Morning Glory doesn't know what the seven sorrows are. But when he thinks about that tiny creature carefully loading the sadness of the world onto its spots, black surrounded by vivid red, then climbing to the very tip of a flower before taking off, he gets a warm feeling. The ladybeetle goes up as high as it can go, then it stops, as if preparing itself. After the space of a breath its red shell flicks open wide, its wings flutter, it flies. He wants to imagine that anyone who witnesses it feels their sadness lightened, even if only by a tiny amount, the size of those seven spots.

The exact opposite of my work, reflects Morning Glory. Every time I push someone, more shadows darken the world.

Hey, Morning Glory. The go-between continues talking. The man in the white coat should be leaving the building any minute. I need you to take care of him. I'm on my way down, but I don't think I'll make it in time.

You were asked to protect the boy in the hospital room. I don't think it matters if the attacker gets away.

No, says the go-between, my instructions were that if anybody tried to hurt the boy, I'm to show no mercy.

That seems pretty rough.

That's how those old-time professionals are. I mean, when they were in school there was still corporal punishment. But this friend of mine is the roughest of the rough.

So is this a formal job offer? Morning Glory wants to confirm. You want me to take out a man wearing a white coat? If so, that's not enough information. If you can't give me more details I can't do the job.

Watch for the man in the white coat.

That's too vague. Although I suppose it would be easy enough if a suspicious-looking man in a white coat comes running out of the hospital.

As soon as he says it Morning Glory laughs, a quiet soughing sound. Before his eyes a man appears, dashing from the hospital grounds. Bunched in his left arm is something white that looks very much like a hastily balled-up coat. Yes, that's exactly what it is.

He describes the man into the phone.

That's him, no doubt about it, the go-between pronounces.

I accept the job. Morning Glory hangs up.

The man with the white bundle looks left and right, flailing for direction. Then he scuttles across the street towards the traffic island. He brushes by Morning Glory, who notices the mud on the shoes as he passes.

Turning round, there's the man waiting for the light to change, pulling out a phone.

Morning Glory makes no noise as he slides up behind the man. He gauges his target's breathing. He watches the light. His hand opens, fingers wide, then closes once, opens again. His own breath slows, stops. Looks left at the oncoming traffic. Not heavy, but each vehicle running fast. Gauges the timing. Exhales, focuses on his fingertips, touches the back.

As he does, at the very same moment, the ladybeetle springs up into the air. The sorrows of that place lighten, even if only the barest bit, seven little black spots' worth.

The car's brakes reverberate with a screech. The phone falls from the man's hand to the ground.

KIMURA

IN THE BACK OF CAR eight, over the door, the message flows from right to left on the digital ticker, where there are normally news headlines and train announcements.

'What –' The schoolkid is twisted round looking at the screen. 'What does that mean?'

'Surprised?' Shigeru Kimura laughs.

Wataru is safe. The same sentence slides by five times, just to make the point.

'You surprised?' he asks again mockingly, as the relief spreads through his own breast.

'What happened?' The schoolkid is letting his emotions show clearly for the first time. He turns back to face Kimura, nostrils flaring and face turning red.

'Looks like Wataru is safe.'

'Was that on the news?' The kid can't grasp what's going on.

'You know, professionals used to really struggle with getting in contact. Back then there were no mobile phones.'

Akiko nods. 'Our friend Shigeru always loved the back and forth of communication.'

'Shigeru's a funny guy. He would choose jobs based on which new method of contact he wanted to try out. But it came in handy today.'

Before they left the house for Mizusawa-Esashi to catch the Shinkansen, he had called Shigeru. 'I want you to check in on my grandson,' he had said. 'Protect him. And if anyone looks suspicious, no mercy.' He was vague on the details, but there was no mistaking the urgency in his voice. 'If anything happens, call me at the payphone on the Shinkansen.' A rough plan to get in touch since he didn't have a mobile.

Shigeru immediately replied, 'I don't think the payphones on the Shinkansen take incoming calls any more. I'll get in touch with you another way,' he offered proudly.

'How?'

'Keep your eye on the digital tickers in the train carriages. If anything happens, I'll use those to get in touch.'

'You can do that?'

'I grew up a bit after you retired, Mr Kimura. As a go-between, I know a lot of people. And I happen to be on good terms with someone at the Shinkansen information broadcasting office.' Shigeru had sounded excited.

When the message vanishes for the last time, Kimura says, 'Give me your phone,' and seeing that the kid is in a daze he takes the opportunity to snatch the phone from his hand.

'What are you doing?' protests the boy, but Kimura cuts him off.

'Wait. If I make this call we'll find out what that news item means.' Of course, Kimura already knows what it means. Now he's just playing with the boy.

Kimura produces a scrap of paper from his jacket pocket and dials the number scrawled on it. Shigeru's number, which he copied down at home.

'Hello,' he hears his friend answer.

'It's me. Kimura.'

'Huh? Mr Kimura, did you get a mobile phone?'

'I'm on the Shinkansen. A suspicious little brat lent me his phone.' Kimura raises the gun to shoulder level, pointed at the schoolkid as always.

'Perfect timing. I just had a message sent to the digital screen on your train.'

'We saw it. Had a message sent by whom?'

'I told you, the man who runs the Shinkansen broadcast system.'

Kimura doesn't feel like he needs to spend time asking about the details.

'Um, Mr Kimura, I have some good news for you and some bad news,' says Shigeru.

Kimura frowns fondly. Thirty years back, whenever the pre-go-between Shigeru would go with the Kimuras on a job, he always talked about good news and bad news. 'Which one would you like first?'

'Start with the good news.'

'The man who targeted your grandson is down on the street, run over by a car, taken care of,' he says all in one breath.

'Did you do it?'

'No, not me. A professional did it. Someone with real skill, not like me.'

'You're right about that.' Kimura starts to let himself feel that Wataru is safe from harm.

The boulder he was carrying in his stomach is finally gone. 'What's the bad news?' he asks. The Shinkansen begins to drop speed and the sound of the tracks changes tone, the shaking starts to subside, like the train is slowly loosening its grip on the tracks that it has/had been holding so tightly. They'll be at Morioka Station soon.

The kid is watching Kimura with eyes wide open. He can't hear the whole conversation, so it would make sense for him to be feeling worried, but he's unexpectedly focused, straining to hear whatever he can from the voice on the other end of the phone. *Can't let my guard down around this one*, Kimura concedes.

'The bad news,' says Shigeru, speaking more carefully now. 'Mr Kimura, don't get mad at me, okay?'

'Spit it out.'

'When I was in your grandson's room, I had to hide under the bed. And then when I jumped out –'

'You jumped out from under the bed? Since when are you that frisky?'

'It's just an expression!' Shigeru says haplessly. 'But when I came out from under the bed I stumbled.'

'Did something happen to Wataru?' Kimura's voice instantly hardens.

'Yes, I'm so sorry.'

'What?' Kimura keeps himself from shouting. He guesses his friend might have knocked into one of the machines, maybe broken it.

'I stumbled, or maybe I should say flailed. Anyway, I woke him up, and he was sleeping so peacefully. But he opened his eyes and mumbled something and smacked his lips a couple of times. I know how much you're against waking people up when they're sleeping, Mr Kimura, I know you just hate it to death. But I didn't mean any harm by it.'

'Are you serious?'

'Sure, I'm serious. Why would I mean him any harm? I know how much you hate being woken up, and I've got the scars to prove it, so do you really think I'd go out of my way to wake up your grandson?'

'No, I mean are you serious that Wataru woke up?'

When Akiko hears her husband say that her whole face lights up. Opposite her, the schoolkid's face freezes over.

As the train approaches the final stop, a handful of passengers start making their way down the aisle, getting ready to disembark. Kimura worries for a moment that one of them might notice his gun, but they all walk right past and disappear into the gangway. There are barely enough to form a line for the door.

'It's true, your grandson really woke up. I apologise,' says Shigeru.

'No, I'm so very glad I asked for your help,' Kimura replies. When he called Shigeru, just about his only friend in Tokyo, he couldn't even say for certain if Wataru was actually in danger. But Shigeru truly saved the day. 'Sorry for springing that on you.'

'You've helped me many a time, Mr Kimura.'

'Yeah, but not for a long time. It's been quite a while since I retired.'

'It's true. Though your boy Yuichi also got into this line of work. I was surprised, when I first heard.'

'You knew about that?' *Like father like son*, Kimura muses ruefully, but at the same time he knows that it has to stop with Wataru. *Hopefully not like grandson too.*

'Actually, I saved Yuichi's skin a few times,' Shigeru says, sounding somewhat sheepish, not from any suggestion that Kimura is indebted to him, he's just reluctant to tell a parent about their child's bungles. 'Hey, there's something I was just discussing with a friend.'

'What's that?'

'That the strongest live the longest. You know what I mean. Whether it's the Rolling Stones or you, Mr Kimura. You're a survivor, which makes you the winner.'

'So you're saying the winner is the old man!' Kimura bellows good-naturedly, then ends the call.

The Shinkansen describes a gentle curve, showing its grace and power one last time before coming to the end of the line. There's an announcement about transfers.

Kimura hands the phone back to the schoolkid. 'Looks like the message on the ticker was right. Our grandson Wataru is safe.' Akiko leans towards him, asking if it's really true, jubilant.

The kid opens his mouth. 'Excuse me.'

'Save it. I'm not answering any of your questions,' Kimura declares flatly. 'We're at Morioka, anyhow. Listen to me now. There are plenty of things that I'm guessing you don't know. Who I was just talking to on the phone, how Wataru is safe. How he's awake. *You don't know.* I'm sure up to this point you've always looked down on adults, so certain that you had everything figured out. It's like your cheap little question, why is it wrong to kill people. You've convinced yourself you know everything. I mean, you *are* smart. And you've been laughing at everyone your whole life, all of us morons.'

'That's not true.' Even now, the kid is trying his helpless act.

'But there are things that you don't know, and you never will. I'm not going to tell you anything. You'll just stay in the dark.'

'Wait, please.'

'I've been alive for more than sixty years. So has she. You must think we're old and used up, that we have no future to look forward to.'

'No, I –'

'Well I will tell you one thing.' Kimura raises the gun to the kid's brow, presses it right between his eyes. 'It's not easy to make it sixty years without dying. You're what, fourteen, fifteen, you think you can make it another fifty years? Say whatever you want, but you won't know whether you can last that long until you get there. Could be an illness. Could be an accident. You think you're untouchable, a real lucky boy, but I'll tell you one thing you can't do.'

The kid's eyes flash. This time it's not the anticipation of victory, it's rage, a liquid fire in his eyes to match the anxiety on his pure, perfect face. His self-esteem must be wounded. 'Tell me what I can't do.'

'You can't live another fifty years. Sorry, but my wife and I will live longer than you will. You thought we were so stupid, but we've got more of a future than you do. Ironic, huh?'

'Are you really going to shoot me?'

'Don't mess with me. I'm a grown-up.'

'Dear, won't the number you called still be in his phone?' asks Akiko. 'You gave it back to him, but Shigeru's number is in there. Shouldn't we erase it?'

'Don't worry about it.'

'Oh, I shouldn't worry about it?'

'This one won't be using his phone any more.'

The schoolkid looks directly at him.

'Here's what's going to happen,' Kimura begins. 'I'm not going to kill you yet. I'll just shoot you so you can't go anywhere, then I'll carry you out. Do you know why?'

'No, I don't.'

'Because I want to give you a chance to reflect on what you've done.'

The kid's face brightens a shade. 'A chance . . . to reflect?'

'Don't misunderstand me. I'm sure you're great at pretending to be sorry. I bet you've made it this far by fooling all the adults with your sorry act. But I'm not so easily fooled. Out of everyone I've ever run across, you stink the worst. I bet you've done all sorts of terrible things. Am I right? So I'll give you a chance to reflect on them, but that doesn't mean I'm letting you off the hook.'

'But –'

Kimura talks right over him, level and matter-of-fact. 'You'll be a long time dying.'

'Really, dear, you're terrible,' Akiko says serenely.

'But, but your grandson, he's fine.' The kid is on the verge of tears.

Kimura erupts with laughter. 'I'm an old man, I can't see so well and I'm hard of hearing, I'm afraid your performance is lost on me. The fact is, you tried to hurt our grandson. That was a big mistake. There's no hope for you now. Like I said, I won't kill you all at once. Just a little at a time. And once you've thought long and hard and genuine about everything you've done . . .'

'What happens once he's done that?' enquires Akiko.

'I'll stop cutting him into tiny pieces and start taking off bigger chunks instead.'

The kid looks afraid, but he also seems to be trying to interpret what that means.

'Hey, this is not a figure of speech. I will actually cut you into pieces. And I don't want to deal with him screaming and crying, so I'll start by making it so that he can't scream, and I'll go from there.'

Akiko slaps him on the shoulder. 'We're not doing that again!' Then she turns and fixes the schoolkid with a smile. 'You know, I used to try to persuade my husband to go a little easier on people, but this time I won't try to stop him.'

'Why not?'

'Well,' Akiko says, 'you tried to hurt our grandson. Did you think we would let you die easy?'

At that the boy seems to give up on stratagems and ploys, feeling himself sink inexorably into the quagmire, and he fires one last desperate shot. 'Your son the alcoholic is in the bathroom, on the floor. He's *dead*. He cried like a baby until the end. Your whole family is weak, grandpa.'

Kimura feels a ripple of anxiety pass through him. Even though he knows that's exactly what this boy wants to happen, he can't stop it from growing. What keeps him steady are the words his wife speaks next, firm and with a note of laughter. 'Yuichi's a tough one. I'm sure he's alive. He'd be too worried about Wataru to give in, I'm positive.'

'You've got a point there,' Kimura nods. 'A giant shoe could stomp on him and he still wouldn't die.'

And with that the Shinkansen pulls into Morioka Station.

NANAO

NANAO CAREERS OVER TO THE sink and splashes the snake with water, but it only squeezes his arm tighter, making him even more frantic. *It's going to cut off the circulation, I'm going to lose my arm!* Panicking, he sets his arm on the lip of the sink and smashes his other fist down on it as hard as he can. It feels like he's squashing a hose. The snake goes limp and slides off. Nanao looks away from the sink to the area by the door, where a few passengers are preparing to exit at Morioka. He scoops up the dazed snake and winds it into a coil, carrying it in a way he hopes looks like he's carrying a small leather bag, hastily moving towards the trash bin on the wall where he discards it. He has a flash of fear that something else might jump out of the trash bin at him, but nothing does.

Unlucky. Although it didn't bite me, so maybe I'm lucky after all.

The Shinkansen continues to slow and a high-pitched keen reverberates. *Almost there. This absurd journey is finally over,* he thinks with a wash of relief. But then he has a vision of himself being unable to get off the train, and fear jolts him again.

Need to go back to car eight, get the suitcase. A handful of passengers waiting to disembark blocks the door. He really doesn't feel like pushing past them. Questions rise in his mind, what's happening with the couple and the kid, is the kid all right? But the episode with the snake has him so shaken up that he wants nothing more to do with what's going down in car eight. He's basically checked out. Then the shaking of the train ramps up one last time, taking his feet from under him. He tries to catch himself on the wall but misses and comes crashing down onto his knees. *That's it. I'm done.*

The brakes squeal. The train lurches wildly as it slides to a halt.

Beside the platform the train pauses, exhaling ponderously. Then the doors slide open with a puff of air. The atmosphere in the train seems to lighten and a sense of release floods in.

One by one the passengers step through the door to the platform. There aren't very many, but they each take their time, watching their footing as they step down.

A sudden bang splits the air.

Sharp, like a steel nail being driven into a wall, a split second of violent noise.

None of the passengers seem to notice. Maybe they think it's just the Shinkansen catching its breath, or a lock sliding into place on the wheels, or some other typical train sound that Nanao wouldn't be able to guess at, but they all seem to accept it as natural, the popping of joints in a tired machine.

Nanao knows it was a gun.

And probably in car eight.

In the two facing three-seaters.

Was the schoolkid shot?

He looks towards the back of the train, but there's no sign of Suzuki. He must have gone back to his seat for his things and re-entered the normal world, wondering why he had been hanging out with a strange man in glasses and a schoolkid.

Smart guy. No wonder he's a teacher.

Nanao looks at the door to car eight. It stays resolutely shut, a silent, immovable sentinel, barring entrance to the grisly scene unfolding inside.

He gets off the train at Morioka Station. *Even though I was supposed to get off at Ueno!* He almost shouts it aloud. It was supposed to be a five-minute train trip, but here he is, over two and a half hours later and five hundred kilometres to the north. And somehow he feels like he's got nowhere. Sucked into a journey he had no intention of taking, baffled and exhausted, his body leaden and his mind like gauze.

Men in suits are lined up along the platform. It's a strange sight. Groups of five stand in front of each train car, making a human wall. The disembarking passengers look at the men uncertainly, trying to figure out what's going on, but they all continue on to the escalators.

Five men stand in front of Nanao with the disciplined ease of soldiers. Soldiers in suits.

'You must be Nanao. Where's the suitcase? And what are you doing in Morioka?' is what Nanao fully expects them to ask. But they show no interest in him. It could be that they weren't told what he looks like, but whatever the reason, they make no move towards him.

Instead they surge into the train, all the men up and down the whole platform. The just-arrived Hayate will be sent off to the depot, or perhaps it will be cleaned before heading back to Tokyo, but the men have no qualms about interrupting the schedule as they search through the train, like they were ransacking someone's house.

They're like a horde of ants swarming a great earthworm, hollowing it out. They sweep through the innards, thorough and implacable.

It's only a matter of time before they discover the bodies in the toilet, and the Wolf's body where Nanao left it in the seat.

Nanao starts walking at a brisk pace, wanting to get away as fast as he can. There's a burly man standing at the front of the Hayate. Craggy dinosaur face and a body like a rugby player. *Minegishi, no doubt about it.* He's surrounded by men in black suits.

The army of ants burrowing into the Shinkansen are Minegishi's soldiers.

The conductor steps up to Minegishi. He must be protesting the disturbance in the train.

The conductor seems to have realised that this reptilian man is the ringleader behind all this chaos and is pleading with him to call it off.

Of course Minegishi doesn't do anything of the sort. He just waves the conductor off, impassive.

The conductor stands ramrod-straight and makes his case again. Nanao can't hear what he's saying but it's clear enough that it's not working, and the conductor passes by Minegishi towards the escalator.

Something jabs Nanao in the back, making him jump out of his skin. 'Gah,' he squeaks as he whips round, already reaching for his attacker's neck.

'Hey now, no rough stuff!' It's a woman in a black pinstriped suit, looking daggers at him. 'Maria.' Nanao exhales, bewildered. 'What are you – how – here –'

'Relax, it's really me. Not a ghost.'

'Aren't you in Tokyo?'

'When you didn't get off at Ueno I had a feeling we would be in this for the long haul. I knew for sure you'd run into trouble.'

'Which I did.'

'So I thought I should come to the rescue and I rushed up to Omiya and jumped on the train.' Maria looks over to where Minegishi is standing. 'That's Minegishi over there, isn't it? This is bad. We should get out of here. No good reason for us to be hanging around. What if he asks us about the bag? Too scary. Let's go.' She pulls Nanao by the arm.

'I think he's more worried about his son.'

'Something happened to his son?' But before Nanao can answer, Maria says, 'Forget it. I probably don't want to know.'

They continue towards the escalator. 'Where were you?' asks Nanao. He had been all through the Shinkansen and hadn't seen her. 'You got on, but you never came to the rescue even once.'

'Well . . .' Maria says, her voice trailing off for a moment. There's clearly something that's hard for her to say. 'I – I got on the Komachi.'

'Are you serious?'

'And there's no passage between the Komachi and the Hayate! I couldn't believe it! Why are they even linked up?'

'Even a preschooler knows that!'

'Well, there are some things preschoolers know that adults don't.'

'But how did you know I would stay on until Morioka?' He almost got off at Ichinoseki. 'What if I'd got off at Sendai?'

'That's what I imagined would happen, but . . .'

'But?'

'. . . but I fell asleep.'

Nanao's eyes bulge. 'You fell *asleep*? With everything that was going on?'

'I told you, I was up all night watching movies!'

'Why do you sound proud about that?'

'After we got off the phone I thought I would just close my eyes for a minute, and when I opened them again we were past Sendai. I called you, all worried, but you hadn't got off, of course. That's when I knew, with his luck he'll be on till the end of the line.'

'Everything I was dealing with, and you were sleeping.'

'You're the one who does the job, I'm the one who sleeps. Sleep is an important part of my work.'

'I thought you were tired because you were watching *Star Wars*.' Nanao pushes down his frustration and catches up to Maria, falling into step beside her.

'What about Tangerine and Lemon?'

'Dead. They're in a toilet on the train.'

Maria sighs. 'How many bodies are there on the train, anyway? What is it, the corpse train? How many?'

'Let's see.' Nanao is about to start counting them out, but decides he'd rather not. 'Five or six.'

'Or seven? Are you counting spots on a ladybird?'

'But they're not all because of me.'

'It's like you're carrying everyone else's bad luck around for them.'

'Is that why I'm so unlucky?'

'If it weren't the case, there's no way you'd be so unlucky. I think you're probably helping everyone else out.'

Unsure if Maria's words are praise or mockery, Nanao says nothing. As they're about to step onto the escalator a crash reverberates from behind. He can almost feel it. A tremor like a behemoth collapsing. The vibrations may not even be from sound, but from the gravity of what just happened. A voice cries out.

Nanao turns to see the black-suited men crouching on the platform trying to support someone. In that same spot where Minegishi was standing so solidly, he's now on the ground, toppled like a broken wooden doll.

'What –' Now Maria senses the disturbance too, and turns to look.

A crowd has formed.

'It's Minegishi,' murmurs Nanao.

'What happened?'

'Maybe he's anaemic and fell over.'

'We really don't wanna get involved with this. Let's get out of here.' She pokes him between the shoulder blades.

It's true, nothing good will come of them staying there. Nanao speeds up.

'There's something stuck in his back,' shouts a voice from behind. A clamour rises up around Minegishi, but by that time Nanao and Maria are already floating down the escalator. 'It's a needle,' shouts someone else.

Halfway down, Nanao turns to Maria standing behind him. 'Think it was the Hornet?'

Maria blinks rapidly. 'Hornet? Oh, not the insect. The poisoner.'

'I ran into her on the train. She was selling concessions. But I took her out.' Nanao's voice is low and distant. Then an image swims into his head, of the man in the double-breasted uniform confronting Minegishi. 'The conductor?'

'What about the conductor?'

'Wasn't there something about the Hornet maybe being two people?'

'Yeah, maybe a solo or maybe a duo.'

'I was sure it was just one person, but maybe there were two of them on the train after all. They must have been after both Minegishi and his kid.'

It might be that the woman pushing the snack trolley was responsible for the son and the conductor was taking care of the father at Morioka. *Who knows.*

They come to the bottom of the escalator and Nanao gets off first, Maria just behind him.

Now she steps up next to him. 'You know, Nanao, you might be on to something. The Hornet became famous by taking out Terahara,' she says, thinking out loud. 'Maybe they thought they could put another big feather in the cap with Minegishi.'

'Trying to recapture their former glory?'

'That's what everyone does when they're out of good ideas. They revisit their past successes.'

Apparently the authorities have been alerted to the disturbance on the train or Minegishi's collapse on the platform, because cops and railway staff and security go running past Nanao and Maria towards the escalator. They should be cordoning off the area, but maybe they don't know exactly what's going on yet.

I wonder if he knows, Nanao says to himself. *If that conductor is one of the Hornets, does he know that his partner is dead?* The question prods at him. Even though he was the one who killed her, Nanao feels a pang of sadness for the man. He has an image of a band with a missing member, waiting in vain for them to return.

'By the way, what happened to the suitcase? Didn't you have it?' Maria's voice brings him back.

Crap, he thinks, but then there's a swell of aggravation and anxiety. 'Who cares,' he says violently. 'Certainly not Minegishi.'

He feeds his ticket into the turnstile and steps through. But halfway in an alarm jangles and the little thigh-height gate swings shut.

A station attendant comes right over and inspects Nanao's ticket, then cocks his head quizzically. 'There's no problem with your ticket, I wonder why it isn't working. Give it a try at the last turnstile, down there.'

'It's fine, I'm used to this sort of thing,' Nanao says with a good-natured grimace. He takes his ticket and walks to the end of the row.

LADYBEETLE

| 1 | 2 | 3 | 4 | 5 | 6 | 7 | 8 | 9 | 10 |

AN ICY WIND BLOWS OUTSIDE, the temperature unusually low even for early December. *So much for the warm winter they've been talking about,* thinks Nanao glumly. The sky looks like it could lose its grip on the cords fastening it shut at any moment, open up and dump snow down everywhere.

He's at a large supermarket near Urushigahara Station, the kind that stocks everything from food and household items to stationary and toys. There's nothing in particular that he wants to buy, but he heads towards the registers with a box of mochi. Each of the open lanes has five or so people lined up. He tries to gauge which will be the fastest and settles on the second from the left.

His phone rings and he brings it up to his ear. 'Where are you?' asks Maria.

'In a supermarket,' Nanao answers, then gives the name and location.

'What are you doing all the way out there? There are plenty of super-markets near my place. I have whole bunch of stuff to tell you – hurry up and get here already.'

'I'll head your way as soon as I'm done here. But all the checkout lines are crowded.'

'I bet your line moves the slowest.'

Based on his past experience, Nanao would have to agree.

The customer at the front of his line finishes paying and moves on. The line shifts forward like it's on an automated track, taking Nanao along.

'So that schoolkid you were asking about,' says Maria.

'What did you find out?'

The events on the Shinkansen two months back shook up the whole country. News that multiple bodies had been found in the bathrooms and passenger seats naturally made people clamour for more information. But as the police investigation continued it became clear that none of the deceased were regular citizens: they were all shady characters in dubious circumstances, even down to the woman who was working the snack trolley. Most of the media adopted the vague language of the police and reported it as a feud within the criminal underworld. Basically shutting their eyes to any details not accounted for in the prescribed explanation. They must have felt they needed to settle the issue before people got scared about taking the train, which is to say, before there could be any damage to the national economy, so the accepted line became that this incident was an exceptional case, and that normal people didn't have to worry about anything like it happening to them. As for Minegishi, it was reported that a prominent resident of Iwate died suddenly at the train station due to difficulty breathing. The fact that it happened to be on the same platform as the death train was chalked up to pure coincidence, and no connection was drawn. Minegishi's bloody career and vast network of influence were never mentioned in the news.

Surprisingly, Kimura, the man who was with the schoolkid, was discovered in the toilet still alive. He was rushed to the hospital where his condition was stabilised. There was no further reporting on that story.

'What I found out was that there were signs of a gunshot found in car eight where you were sitting. But there was no blood.'

There's no information about what happened to the schoolkid and that older couple. From what Nanao saw, he has no doubt that the man would have shot, schoolkid or not. Then he likely would have carried the kid out, making it look like he was helping his sickly grandson.

'I looked into cases of fourteen-year-olds from Tokyo who've gone missing, but found out that there are a ton. What's this country coming to? Nothing but missing kids. Though I did hear about a small body that was found at the port in Sendai. The body couldn't be identified.'

'I wonder if it was that kid.'

'Could be, could be someone else. If you want me to I could probably get you pictures of all the kids that have gone missing.'

'Nah, don't worry about it.' Searching through those would be too depressing. 'What about the professional, Kimura?'

'Seems he's not walking yet, but he's doing a lot better than he was. His kid's with him all the time, quite the heart-warming scene.'

'No, I don't mean him. His father, and his mother too. They're in their sixties. The Kimuras.'

'Oh, them,' Maria says excitedly. 'The stories I heard about *them*. Legendary. You met some big fish, let me tell you.' She sounds like she's jealous of him having got to see a famous musician perform at the end of their career.

'They just looked to me like happy retirees.'

'Well, if the stories I heard are true, then your schoolkid might be dead but no one'll ever find the body.'

'What does that mean?'

'Those old-time professionals, when they get serious, they can be pretty extreme.'

'What do you mean by extreme, exactly?' And although Nanao asks the question, he cuts her off before she can answer, never mind, he says, he doesn't want to hear about anyone getting chopped into pieces or whatever she was about to say.

It turns out that there were multiple men with gunshot wounds found around car eight in the train at Morioka, all screaming in agony. Each one had been shot through both shoulders and both legs, immobilising them.

It could only have been the work of the Kimuras. They must have shot their way out of the train when it was crawling with Minegishi's men. It's hard for Nanao to picture the old couple in action, putting bullets in the same exact spot on numerous people as if stamping them with an official seal, but it had to have been them.

'And there's something else I've been thinking.'

'Tell me when I get there.'

'Just a preview.' Maria seems excited to share her theory with him. 'I think maybe our job didn't come from Minegishi, but from the Hornets.'

'What? But you were the one who said we were subcontracting for Minegishi.'

'True. But that was just a guess.'

'Really?'

'If the Hornets were going after Minegishi and his son, then Tangerine and Lemon would have been in the way. Having us steal the bag would have thrown those two off.'

'You think we were a diversion?' Nanao can't quite believe it.

'Exactly. They needed an opening to get the son with a poison needle. Which would be why they hired us to steal the bag.'

'If that's the case, then the person who contacted you with the bag's location after the train left Tokyo would have been either the snack trolley girl or the conductor, one of the two,' Nanao reasons. 'Both of them could move through the train and check on things without raising suspicion.'

'It could even be that they were the ones who contacted Minegishi along the way, to keep things on the train confusing. They might have been the ones who told him something isn't right, come to Morioka.'

'Why would they have –' But then it clicks. So that they could kill Minegishi too. Getting him to come to the station would make things easier for them.

They finish the conversation and Nanao hangs up. The line for the register has barely moved. He looks over his shoulder and sees that more people have filed into place behind him. Then he notices someone, there at the back of the line, and he almost calls out.

It's the exam-prep instructor, Suzuki. Dressed in a suit, looking healthy, a basket full of groceries in one hand. He notices Nanao and his eyes widen, but almost immediately he relaxes into a smile, pleased at the chance reunion. Though they barely know each other, it feels almost as if they're old friends.

Nanao nods, and Suzuki bobs his head in response. Then he gets a look like he's suddenly remembered something important and moves to a different line from Nanao.

The jangle of loose change rings out. Nanao turns back round and sees at the front of the line an old lady who has accidentally upended her purse. She stoops hurriedly to gather the fallen coins, the people behind her bending over to lend a hand. One coin skitters over to Nanao's feet where it spins in a neat circle. He tries to grab it but keeps missing.

Meanwhile the lines at the adjacent registers move right along. Nanao hears Suzuki laughing.

Near the exit to the supermarket, Nanao pulls the giveaway ticket out from his wallet. On the back is an illustration of a train in an amateur hand. Arthur, it says. It had been in Tangerine's pocket back on the Shinkansen. Nanao had taken it at the time, not quite sure why he was doing so, but then he forgot about it completely. Until the other day when he was doing laundry and found it. It reminded him of everything that happened on that terrible trip, and he was about to throw it out to rid himself of any remnants of the whole mess. But something stopped him, he couldn't say exactly what. He noted that the location of the supermarket was at a station he had never been to before, and he decided to visit it and see if the ticket had won him anything.

'I certainly didn't expect to run into you here.'

He turns towards the voice to find Suzuki standing nearby.

'You made the right move at the checkout. Any line I get in goes more slowly.'

Suzuki's eyes crinkle with laughter. 'I started way behind you. I would never have thought I'd finish checking out first. I still can't believe it.'

Suzuki had apparently been waiting for Nanao outside the supermarket, but then started wondering what was taking him so long and came back inside. That's when he saw Nanao waiting in line to enter the giveaway.

'There's only one line here, so I'm not worried,' Nanao says with a chuckle.

'You're going to enter the draw? You know, I wouldn't be surprised if you won,' says Suzuki. 'Your bad luck could all turn round right here.'

Nanao looks at the prize board. 'I'll feel a little let down if all of my bad luck until now was just so that I could win a travel voucher.'

Suzuki laughs again.

'Although it's true, I do kind of feel like I'll win. Making it out of that Shinkansen alive made me think that I was finally having some good luck. And I found this ticket on the train that day, so I'm hoping it'll be the start of a change of fortunes for me. I guess that's why I came all the way out here.'

'But your line at the register was still the slowest,' says Suzuki gently.

'True enough,' says Nanao with a frown. 'But I also bumped into you. Isn't that kind of lucky?'

'Maybe if I was a cute girl.' There's a hint of pity in Suzuki's voice.

The cashier waves Nanao forward to take his turn. He hands over the ticket with the train drawing. 'Just one play.' The cashier is an impressively plump middle-aged woman, nearly bursting out of her uniform. She kindly encourages him, best of luck, young man. Suzuki looks on with interest as Nanao grasps the handle on the lottery cage and starts spinning it. Through the handle he can feel the balls ricocheting around inside.

The cage spits out one ball, bright yellow.

Within a split second the hefty staffer rings a bell grandly. Surprised, Nanao looks over at Suzuki.

Congratulations, says another supermarket staff member as he brings over a cardboard box, open at the top, which he holds out and proclaims, 'Third prize!'

'Nice work,' Suzuki says, clapping Nanao on the shoulder, but when Nanao looks in the box his smile freezes. He's happy to have won, but he's not sure how he feels about the prize.

'What am I going to do with all this?'

The box is packed with fruit, two kinds, divided neatly in half. Fist-sized tangerines and bright yellow lemons.

The cashier is effusive with congratulations, oh what good luck, good for you, she's all smiles, so Nanao meekly accepts the box. *How am I going to carry this home? And what can I possibly do with all these lemons?* He keeps his questions to himself.

He takes a good look at the fruit. For the barest moment he feels a flash of pride emanating from the tangerines and lemons, almost like they're saying to him: *See, told you we'd be back.*

KOTARO ISAKA is a bestselling and multi-award-winning writer who is published around the world. He has won the Shincho Mystery Club Award, Mystery Writers of Japan Award, Japan Booksellers' Award and Yamamoto Shugoro Prize and twelve of his books have been adapted for film or TV.

SAM MALISSA holds a PhD in Japanese Literature from Yale University. He has translated fiction by Toshiki Okada, Shun Medoruma, and Hideo Furukawa, among others.